Essential Windows NT System Administration

Essential Windows NT System Administration

Æleen Frisch

O'REILLY®

Beijing · Cambridge · Farnham · Köln · Paris · Sebastopol · Taipei · Tokyo

Essential Windows NT System Administration
by Æleen Frisch

Copyright © 1998 O'Reilly & Associates, Inc. All rights reserved.
Printed in the United States of America.

Published by O'Reilly & Associates, Inc., 101 Morris Street, Sebastopol, CA 95472.

Editor: Mike Loukides

Production Editor: Mary Anne Weeks Mayo

Printing History:

> January 1998:   First Edition.

ISBN: 1-56592-274-3   [3/01]
[M]

Table of Contents

Preface

This book covers the fundamental and essential tasks of administering Windows NT Server and Workstation systems. The primary goal of this book is to make system administration of Windows NT systems straightforward. As such, the book tries to take a middle path between a general overview that is just too simple to be of much use to anyone but a complete novice, and a slog through all of the obscurities and eccentricities that only a fanatic could love. In other words, I won't leave you hanging when the first complication arrives, and I also won't make you wade through a lot of extraneous information in order to find what actually matters.

To put these same thoughts in another way, this book is designed to enable you to manage your Windows NT systems as productively as possible, and to make the task as pleasant and satisfying as it can be. Accordingly, this book covers all facets of Windows NT system administration: from the general concepts, underlying structure, and guiding assumptions that define the environment to the commands, procedures, strategies, and policies essential to success as a system administrator.

This sort of delicate balance also characterizes my attitude toward Windows NT itself: *I come neither to praise Windows NT nor to bury it.* When Windows NT works well, I'll be quick to say so, and when Windows NT presents challenges or problems, I'll tell you that too. For example, this book talks about the standard administrative tools Windows NT provides. However, it also goes on to discuss how to use them smarter and more efficiently, as well as when not to use them. Finally, it makes you aware of resources beyond those provided by Microsoft that are useful for filling in some of the things that Windows NT is missing.

Naturally, much of this information constitutes advice about system administration; I won't be shy about letting you know what my opinion is. But I'm much more interested in giving you the information you need to make informed decisions for your own situation than in providing a single, univocal view of the "right way" to administer a Windows NT system. It's more important that you know what the issues are concerning, say, assigning user rights, than that you adopt anyone's specific philosophy or scheme for doing so. When you are familiar with the problem and the potential approaches to it, you'll be in a position to decide for yourself what's right for your systems.

NOTE   Some readers may be familiar with another book I have written for O'Reilly & Associates, entitled *Essential System Administration*, which covers the administration of UNIX computer systems. While this book has a similar title, there is very little overlap between the two. In a few cases, brief sections of the earlier book have been rewritten for this book, and I have reused the odd sentence or paragraph or two from time to time, but all such borrowings constitute a small percentage of this book's total content. For me, this project has become an opportunity to review and rethink system administration in general, through the lens of Windows NT, and this book reflects the clarity and murkiness I found throughout the process.

Windows NT Versions Discussed

This book discusses Windows NT version 4.* The information discussed generally applies to both the server and workstation products, although differences between them are pointed out as appropriate.

I also talk about Windows NT running on computers based on both Intel and Digital Equipment Corporation Alpha processors; we'll refer to them as *Intel* and *Alpha* systems, respectively. Again, the differences between these environments will be discussed when relevant (although there are very few of them).

Audience

Several types of readers will benefit from this book:

- Full- or part-time Windows NT system administrators.

- Windows NT users who have acquired some system administration responsibilities or who simply want to learn to make the most productive and efficient use of their system and its resources.

---

* Much of the information in this book also applies to the previous version, Windows NT 3.51, although its user interface appears rather differently.

- UNIX system administrators and users who need to learn about Windows NT and integrate these systems into their current environments.

Since this book is designed for several different types of readers, you may encounter some sections discussing topics that you already know well. If so, just skip over them and go on to material that is new to you.

I assume you understand basic computer concepts and that you have some experience browsing and downloading files from the World Wide Web. I also assume you are reasonably familiar with the Windows NT user interface as well as with its user-level commands and procedures: working with menus and dialog boxes; accessing control panel applets; using the **Start** menu; changing the current directory; obtaining directory listings; creating, copying, renaming, deleting, and printing files; using the Windows NT command interpreter, including I/O redirection and pipes; setting environment variables; installing software packages; and so on. Finally, I assume you possess a very basic knowledge of scripts (traditionally called BAT files in the DOS/Windows world) and that Windows NT has already been installed on your systems (although we will discuss networking configuration in detail). If you need help with basic Windows NT installation, consult the Microsoft documentation included with the software.

This book is not intended for people who are already Windows NT gurus. Accordingly, it does not cover topics like device drivers and Windows NT internals.

Organization

I approach system administration from a task-oriented perspective, and so this book is organized around various facets of the system administrator's job, rather than around the features of the Windows NT operating system, the workings of the various hardware components in a typical computer system, or the system administration programs that Windows NT provides. All of these are the raw materials and tools of system administration, but an effective administrator has to know when and how to apply and deploy them.

NOTE   This book is the foundation volume for O'Reilly & Associates' Windows NT system administration series. As such, it provides fundamental information needed by anyone who takes care of Windows NT systems. At the same time, it consciously avoids trying to be all things to all people; the other books in the series treat individual topics in *complete* detail. Thus, you can expect this book to provide you with the essentials for major administrative tasks by discussing both the underlying high-level concepts and the details of the procedures needed to carry them out. It also tells you where to get additional information as your needs become more highly specialized.

This book has 12 chapters, three appendices, and a glossary:

Chapter 1, *Administering Windows NT Systems*, discusses the basics of Windows NT system administration, including an overview of the Windows NT environment. It introduces the most useful administrative tools and utilities and covers the Windows NT registry and the registry editor. It also includes a section of tips and tricks for using the Windows NT user interface most effectively.

Chapter 2, *Startup, Shutdown, and Server Configuration*, describes the normal system startup and shutdown processes. It also includes techniques for troubleshooting booting problems and for customizing the boot process and the Windows NT environment (including a discussion of the Server Manager).

Chapter 3, *User Accounts*, covers administering user accounts within a Windows NT domain. It discusses groups, user account controls, logon scripts and user profiles. It concludes with some advice for managing large numbers of user accounts.

Chapter 4, *Managing Processes*, describes monitoring and controlling processes within the Windows NT environment. It also considers the Windows NT Schedule Service for delayed and periodic command execution as well as some third-party batch command execution facilities.

Chapter 5, *Disks and Filesystems*, discusses the management of physical disks and the creation of partitions and filesystems. Later sections cover NT, fault tolerance, and disk-striping capabilities.

Chapter 6, *Files and Directories*, discusses file and directory ownership and protection under Windows NT. It includes an in-depth discussion of access control lists (ACLs) and the available tools for managing them.

Chapter 7, *Backups*, discusses the issues relating to backups on Windows NT systems and available options for performing them. It covers both the native Windows NT backup facility as well as some representative third-party backup software. It concludes by discussing methods for backing up the registry.

Chapter 8, *Network Configuration*, covers setting up and maintaining TCP/IP networks composed of or including Windows NT systems. It discusses server and workstation configuration (including DHCP), name service options (including DNS and WINS), routing options, and Remote Access Services. It also discusses managing primary and backup domain controllers.

Chapter 9, *Print Services*, describes setting up and administering print resources under Windows NT. It covers local printers, network printers, sharing printers across the network, combining multiple printers into a printer pool, and printing to and from non-Windows NT systems.

Chapter 10, *Security*, discusses the security issues inherent in the Windows NT environment as well as the facilities provided to address them. It includes consideration of system policies and user rights, trust relationships between Windows NT domains, and system auditing.

Chapter 11, *Performance Optimization*, presents an overview of system performance monitoring and tuning on Windows NT systems. It describes a general tuning procedure and considers several case studies from actual Windows NT systems. It concludes with a discussion of capacity planning.

Chapter 12, *Automating System Administration*, discusses using scripts to automate system administration tasks. Examples primarily use the freely available scripting language Perl. The chapter also covers the directory replication service.

Appendix A, *Quick Start for Experienced UNIX System Administrators*, provides a fast-paced overview of Windows NT system administration for experienced UNIX system administrators, arranged according to the UNIX view of the universe (including frequent cross references to the main text). It also contains information on sources for obtaining UNIX-style tools and facilities for Windows NT.

Appendix B, *Useful Windows NT Resources*, describes additional sources of information on Windows NT and its system administration, including books, periodicals, web sites, and freely available and commercial software packages.

Appendix C, *Windows NT Scripting Language Summary*, contains an overview of the Windows NT command language constructs, including examples.

The *Glossary* provides concise definitions of the many acronyms and technical terms relevant to Windows NT.

Conventions Used in This Book

Bold
> is used for command names, options, and keywords, including literal commands within normal text, for command script names, for menu selections and button, tab, and other item labels, and for the names of user rights.

Italic
> is used to designate filenames, file and directory paths, and for user account names and group names in normal text. It is also used to emphasize new terms and concepts when they are introduced, and to represent variables in regular text. Finally, italic type is used to highlight comments in sample computer output.

`Constant Width`
> is used in examples to show the contents of files or the output from commands.

Constant Bold

> is used in examples to show commands or other text that would be typed literally by the user.

Constant Italic

> is used in examples and command syntax definitions to show variables for which a context-specific substitution should be made. The variable *filename,* for example, would be replaced by an actual filename.

. . .

> stands for text within computer output that has been omitted for clarity or to save space.

ALT-X

> This notation indicates the use of the ALT key as a modifier key. It means to hold down the ALT key while hitting the "X" key.

CTRL-X

> This notation indicates the use of control characters. It means to hold down the CONTROL key while hitting the "X" key.

CTRL-ALT-X

> This notation means to hold down both the CONTROL and ALT keys while hitting the "X" key.

A►B►C

> This notation indicates a series of items to be selected in turn to reach a desired destination. The components **A**, **B**, and **C** may be menu items, buttons, or tabs.

copy Boot.Ini A:

> In the examples in this book, I have generally used lowercase characters for Windows NT commands and mixed case letters for standard filenames (both in the interest of readability). Except as noted, neither of them are case sensitive, however, and can be entered in whatever case combination you prefer.

C:\>

> When illustrating Windows NT commands, I use this prompt string.

he/she

> This book is meant to be straightforward and to the point. There are times when using a third person pronoun is just the best way to say something, e.g., "this setting forces the user to change his password the next time he logs in." Personally, I don't like always using "he" in such situations, and I abhor "he or she" and "s/he," so I use "he" some of the time and "she" some of the time, alternating semirandomly. However, when the text refers to one of the example users who appear from time to time throughout the book, I use the appropriate pronoun.

Figure convention

A blurry line within a window indicates that part of the window's contents have been omitted. It thus functions as a graphical ellipsis. See the figure below for an illustration of this concept.

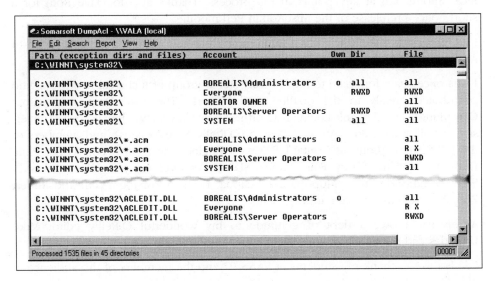

Comments and Questions

Please address comments and questions concerning this book to the publisher:

O'Reilly & Associates, Inc.
101 Morris Street
Sebastopol, CA 95472
(800) 998-9938 (in the United States or Canada)
(707) 829-0515 (international/local)
(707) 829-0104 (fax)

There is a web page for this book, which lists errata, examples, and any additional information. You can access this page at:

http://www.oreilly.com/catalog/esawinnt/

To comment or ask technical questions about this book, send email to:

bookquestions@oreilly.com

For more information about books, conferences, software, Resource Centers, and the O'Reilly Network, see the O'Reilly web site at:

http://www.oreilly.com

Acknowledgments

Many people were of great help as I wrote this book. John Montgomery, Joe Ochterski, Gary Trucks, Jody Leber, Dave Roth, and Michael Frisch provided technical information at key points in the process. Thanks also to Dave Roth for a short-notice prerelease of the MiscAdmin Perl module.

I am especially grateful to Digital Equipment Corporation for the generous loan of Alpha systems and to Son VoBa, Bill Desimone, and Angela Loh for arranging it.

I was once again fortunate to have a truly stellar group of technical reviewers who contributed greatly to the quality of this work. They are Dave Roth (Roth Consulting), David Blank-Edelman (Northeastern University), Jon Forrest (University of California, Berkeley), Eric Pearce (O'Reilly & Associates), and members of the NT Systems group at Digital's DECwest Engineering facility: Son VoBa, Phuc Dinh, Davis Feng, Carey Fujii, James "JD" Hicks, Wei Lu, Jeff Selzer, Eduardo Serrano, Ed Shoemaker, Mupopa Tshibuabua, High Vidos, Joe Yuen, and Robert Zhu. All errors that remain are my own.

As always, I owe a debt of gratitude to my wonderful O'Reilly editor Mike Loukides and my excellent copyeditor Laura Lasala.

I'd also like to thank my students at SANS 97 and the members of the audience at the 1997 O'Reilly Perl Conference for letting me try some of this material out on them.

Thanks also to my perennially long-suffering editors at *SunExpert* magazine, who had to put up with the habitual lateness in my *NTegration* column, caused by this project. Thanks also to Wendy Janocha and the fulfillment group at Gaussian for patiently waiting for their new database system.

The production group at O'Reilly & Associates put the finishing touches on this book. Mary Anne Weeks Mayo was the project manager and production editor and quality was assured by Jane Ellin, Clairemarie Fisher O'Leary, and Sheryl Avruch. Wendy Griffin wrote the index. Colleen Miceli copyedited the book, and Madeleine Newell helped with production. Mike Sierra contributed his FrameMaker tool-tweaking prowess. Robert Romano prepared the crisp illustrations you see in the book. The book's interior was designed by Nancy Priest, Edie Freedman designed the front cover, and Kathleen Wilson designed the back cover.

No one finishes a task of this size without a lot of support and encouragement from their friends and family. Accordingly, I'd like to thank Mike, Laura, Alice, Gary, and Mo for being there for me throughout this project and putting up with my inaccessibility.

Finally, I want to fondly remember my cat Sarah, who died during the final stages of this work, by dedicating this to her.

ÆF, 27 October 1997, Northford, Connecticut

1

Administering Windows NT Systems

About System Administration

Like all truly satisfying pursuits, system administration requires both breadth and depth of expertise. I'll invoke a popular metaphor and say that successful system administration involves more than wearing a lot of different hats; you also need to know which one to wear to perform a particular task or solve a particular problem and, equally important, what else you will need to get the job done right. Whatever challenges and frustrations the tremendous variety inherent in system administration may bring, it also keeps the workday interesting.

First-rate system administrators bring three kinds of strengths to their job:

Technical expertise

This includes both a knowledge of the tools and procedures required to keep the system and network operating efficiently and a detailed-enough understanding of how the system's various components work to address the problems that will arise.

While Windows NT is frequently marketed as an operating system that requires little or no system administration, this is an ideal honored more in the breach than in reality. Well designed system administration tools can go a long way toward making Windows NT systems management easy and painless under normal circumstances—and some of the Windows NT tools come reasonably close to this goal—but realistically, you can expect the unexpected to occur all too frequently.

The bottom line is that someone has to know how things really work: it should be you.

Problem solving skills

System administrators are distinguished from ordinary users, power users, and operators in that they know what to do when things go wrong. While all these classes of users are comfortable using the system under normal circumstances, only system administrators have to know what to do when things are anything but normal. This doesn't mean you have to know the solution instantly for every problem you encounter. Sometimes you will, but more often what you bring to the situation is a strategy for figuring out what has gone wrong and the tools for fixing it once you have done so.

Ordinary users of Windows NT systems and their associated networks are like ordinary automobile drivers; they know how to start and operate the car, how to add gasoline and when to take it in for periodic preventive maintenance. Power users also know how to change their own oil and spark plugs, when to add water to the radiator, and what to do if the battery dies or a tire goes flat. Operators are like automotive technicians who can carry out a variety of standard procedures—changing the oil and lubricating the engine, checking and replacing the brake pads, and the like—as well as diagnosing and repairing simple problems (e.g., the car won't start because the alternator has failed and needs to be replaced). System administrators are like master mechanics—the only ones who can perform complex operations and diagnose and repair major problems; they can trace the car's tendency to die in cold weather to a carburetor that needs to be rebuilt, and they can go on to rebuild it themselves. They are capable of doing so because they understand how the car's engine works at a deep enough level to track down the specific points of trouble when a problem arises.

If the automotive metaphor doesn't resonate with you, consider this one. Ordinary users are like cooks who can use a bread machine to make a loaf of fresh bread. Power users can use the machine to make several different varieties of bread, and they know how to use the machine to prepare dough for later baking in a normal oven. Operators can also make exotic kinds of bread, including ones requiring significant variations to the standard method of using the machine, and they can adapt recipes to it using the instructions provided with the appliance as a guide. System administrators are like the people who design the procedures for using the bread machine. Because they know what baking bread involves in detail, not only can they create recipes that work well in the bread machine, but they can devise procedures for adapting arbitrary bread recipes for use in the machine, and they can formulate troubleshooting strategies for use when the machine's final product doesn't turn out perfectly.

People skills

Successful system administrators are continually aware that computers are used by people and organizations and that managing them cannot be extricated from this social context. System administration often involves a tension between authority and responsibility on the one hand and service and cooperation on the other. The extremes seem easier to maintain than any middle ground; fascistic dictators who rule "their network" with an iron hand, unhindered by the needs of users, find their opposite in the harried system managers who jump from one user request to the next, in continual interrupt mode.

The trick is to find a balance between being accessible to users and their needs, and sometimes even their mere wants, while maintaining your authority and sticking to the policies put into place for the overall system welfare. The goal is to provide an environment where users can get what they need to do done, in as easy and efficient a manner as possible, given the constraints of security, other users' needs, the inherent capabilities of the system, and the realities and constraints of the human community in which all of them are located.

To put it more concretely, the key to successful, productive system administration is knowing when to address a shortage of disk space on a file server with a command that deletes the 500+ MB of scratch files created in several random directories by one of the system's users and when to walk over to her desk and talk with her face-to-face. The first approach displays technical finesse as well as administrative brute force, and both are certainly appropriate—even vital—at times. At other times, a simpler, less aggressive approach will work better to resolve your system's disk shortage problems as well as the user's confusion. It's also important to remember that there are some problems no Windows NT command can address.

This book provides the information you need in all three of these areas. Even if you're not a full-time system administrator, you'll find that developing these three areas will also serve you well in whatever your primary area of endeavor may be.

The System Administrator's Job

Sometimes it seems that there are as many system administrator job descriptions as there are people doing the job. Although things aren't really quite that random, I find it most helpful to describe system administration in terms of broad, general areas of responsibility:

- Installing and configuring computer systems and networks, updating them as necessary, and keeping them running properly on a day-to-day basis.

- Managing users and user accounts, including both the computer-related aspects of creating and maintaining user accounts and systems, and responding to user requests, questions, and problems.

- Taking care of the peripheral devices attached to the various computer systems (e.g., printers, tape drives, uninterruptible power supplies) as well as adding or removing them as needed.

- Overseeing regular system backups, which can range from performing backups yourself to designing and implementing a backup plan to be carried out by others under your supervision.

- Ensuring that the systems and networks for which you are responsible are secure and that valuable or sensitive data is protected from undesired access.

- Monitoring system and network activity in order to quickly detect any problems related to system security, performance, or general functioning that may arise, and then responding appropriately to anything you may find.

Exactly what each of these areas entails is something that varies a great deal among computer installations, as does the relative amount of emphasis placed on the various areas of responsibility, and of course both change over time. This book covers each of them in detail in an effort to prepare you for whatever you may face, now and in the future.

About Windows NT

> *O brave new world that has such people in it!*
> *'Tis new to thee.*
>
> —Miranda and Prospero
> *The Tempest* V.i.183-84

Windows NT is a 32-bit, microkernel-based, preemptive multitasking operating system providing privileged and unprivileged execution modes and compatibility with some legacy programs designed for DOS/Windows 3.1 systems and, to a lesser extent, OS/2 systems and POSIX-compliant systems.

What does this all mean and why should you care? Let's look at each bit of the preceding description individually:

- A 32-bit operating system, meaning that physical memory is addressed using 32-bit addresses, resulting in a maximum physical address space of 4 GB (2 to 3 GB of which is available to application programs). Most modern operating systems use a 32- or 64-bit design.[*]

---

[*] Microsoft has promised 64-bit memory access support for Digital Equipment Corp. Alpha processor-based systems in a future beta release of Windows NT.

- Built around a *microkernel*: the program that serves as the central core of the operating system is designed to be as small and efficient as possible. Only the most fundamental and important operating system functions are handled by this small kernel program; most operating system services are implemented by semi-independent secondary subsystems, all controlled by the microkernel. Many modern operating systems are based on a microkernel architecture.

- *Preemptive multitasking* means that the operating system* is responsible for deciding which process† gets to run at any given time and when one process must pause in order to let a different one run. Modern operating systems all use preemptive multitasking. (Indeed, I would argue that this is one of the defining features of any computing environment that can accurately be called an operating system.)

  The opposite of preemptive multitasking is a scheduling method known as *cooperative multitasking* (the scheme used by both Windows and MacOS). This scheme gives a running process complete control of the system until it voluntarily gives up control. It is designed for an environment like that of a traditional PC with a single user, where switching between tasks occurs as the user desires. Such an approach seldom works well when a computer system is required to perform multiple tasks simultaneously.

- Multiple execution modes: Windows NT provides two different modes under which processes may execute: *user mode* and *kernel mode*. Kernel mode execution is a privileged mode that allows complete access to every system resource and all of memory and is limited to the operating system itself. In contrast, processes executing in user mode (unprivileged mode) can obtain access to system resources only by making requests to the operating system. Thus, the portions of system memory used by the operating system are protected and can only be accessed by processes running in kernel mode.

  All other processes needing to access any portion of protected memory may do so only via services provided by the operating system; they can never access protected memory directly. The operating system also has the ability to grant or refuse access as appropriate for system integrity, which means that it is very difficult for an application program to corrupt system memory and thereby cause a system failure.

  Some mechanism for restricting application access to system memory (and the memory used by other processes) is a key component of all modern operating systems. Users familiar with traditional personal computer environments

---

* This portion of the operating system is traditionally known as the *scheduler*.

† Under Windows NT, the fundamental executable/scheduleable entity is actually a thread, not a process. However, we won't worry about this distinction until we consider system performance in Chapter 11.

such as DOS, Windows 3.1, Windows 95, and Macintosh System 7 and System 8 will realize at once that protected memory is a significant enhancement to the way things work on those systems.

- Compatibility with some legacy DOS, Windows 3.1, OS/2, and POSIX programs: Windows NT provides subsystems for running many 16-bit DOS and Windows programs and OS/2 programs. The operating system also complies with the POSIX 1 standard, which includes the POSIX application program interface, so POSIX programs can be ported more easily to Windows NT.

While these Windows NT features are important and beneficial, they are not as new and groundbreaking as its marketing tends to imply. In reality, they are essential parts of any viable, high performance operating system designed to address current computing requirements.

The NT acronym is officially translated as "New Technology,"* but what is really new about Windows NT is its bringing of real operating system functionality combined with a familiar look-and-feel (user interface) into the traditional personal computer world. It is also helpful to remember that Windows NT is a very young operating system, still developing and evolving, so we shouldn't be surprised when it experiences a few growing pains (and inflicts a few others on its users).

The Windows NT Architecture

Figure 1-1 illustrates the structure of the Windows NT operating system. It is separated into two sections: the upper section containing components that run in user mode and the lower section containing those that run in kernel mode. The heart of the Windows NT operating system consists of the modules running in kernel mode. Although you'll see it referred to by several names, including the "Executive Services" and the "NT Executive," in more common usage, it is simply the operating system kernel.

Most interactions with the computer hardware take place via the Hardware Abstraction Layer (HAL), although some device drivers also directly access the hardware. Isolating hardware access into a separate module allows most of the

---

* There are other legends about the origin of the name "Windows NT." My favorite takes note of the fact that Microsoft CEO Bill Gates hired David N. Cutler away from Digital Equipment Corp. in 1988 to design a new operating system. Cutler had managed the development of the RSX-11 and VAX/VMS operating systems for Digital. If you increment each of the letters in the string "VMS," you get "WNT." Compare this to the apocryphal legend of the origin of the computer's name in the film *2001: A Space Odyssey*: HAL can be formed by decrementing each of the letters in the string "IBM." Windows NT does have many design features in common with VMS, including multiple execution modes, similarity in some filesystem data structures, access control lists, the user rights (privileges) facility, and compatibility subsystems for running applications from the company's previous operating system.

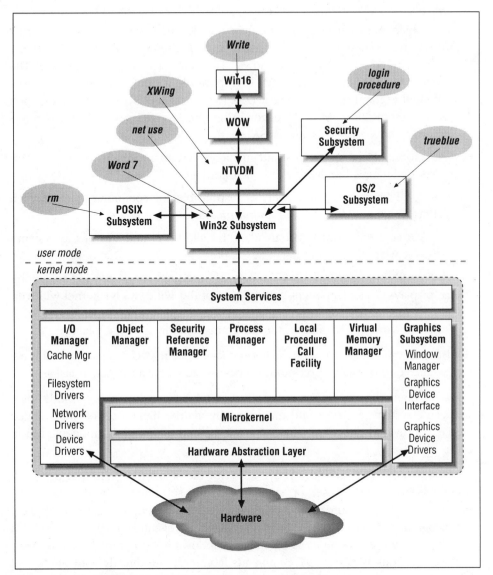

Figure 1-1. Idealized Windows NT operating system architecture

Windows NT operating system to remain independent of any particular computer architecture, thereby simplifying its ability to support multiple computer platforms and multiprocessor systems (at least in theory).

The core of the Windows NT kernel is the microkernel, which oversees the workings of all of the other modules, and handles communications between them and the HAL. The other components of the kernel each have a single specific area of responsibility:

- The I/O Manager controls most input and output on the system.

- The Object Manager creates, modifies, and deletes system *objects:* data structures corresponding to a specific instance of a resource (for example, a file, a process, or a port). Under Windows NT, most such items are objects. The Security Reference Manager (SRM) is responsible for enforcing system security settings by granting or denying access to objects and system resources upon request from the Object Manager. This process relies on data structures known as *security access tokens* (SATs).

- The Process Manager creates and manages system processes. However, process scheduling is handled by the microkernel.

- The Local Procedure Call Facility is responsible for communication between distinct processes (*interprocess communication*).

- The Virtual Memory Manager handles the allocation and use of the system's memory. We'll discuss it in detail in Chapter 11.

- The Graphics Subsystem provides services required for interfacing to graphical displays. This component became part of the Windows NT kernel with version 4 (previously, it was part of the Win32 subsystem). Note that current "official" Windows NT architecture diagrams don't include it explicitly.

All of these components provide *system services:* system-level operations and functions available to ordinary (user mode) processes to carry out common tasks.

The components in the upper part of Figure 1-1 all execute in user mode; they can access system resources and memory only via the limited set of unprivileged interfaces provided as system services. Some operating system components run in user mode.

The Win32 Subsystem provides processes with the standard application programming interface (API): a set of standard library subroutines used to perform operations, access resources, and otherwise request system services. All application programs (depicted as ovals in the diagram) eventually interact with this operating system component. 32-bit native Windows NT programs, such as Word 7 and the various Windows NT commands, communicate directly with the Win32 Subsystem.

Compatibility with programs designed for other environments comes via a series of secondary API subsystems. For example, supported POSIX commands communicate with the POSIX subsystem, which in turn interfaces to the Win32 subsystem; supported OS/2 commands are similarly handled by the OS/2 Subsystem.[*]

---

[*] At least, this is the official position taken by the Microsoft documentation. In some cases, such subsystems make calls to the kernel directly.

DOS and Windows 16-bit applications are handled by a series of nested subsystems (culminating as always with the Win32 Subsystem). The NT Virtual DOS Machine (NTVDM) provides a DOS-compatible environment for DOS programs. 16-bit Windows applications, such as the Write word processing utility provided with Windows 3.1, communicate first with a subsystem designed to handle such applications' 16-bit system calls; these calls are converted to the 32-bit calls used by Windows NT in a subsystem called Windows on Win32 (WOW). These applications also require a NTVDM environment because they also depend on DOS services.

The Windows NT login procedure uses a separate security subsystem in an analogous manner in order to authenticate users at login time.

Implications of the Windows NT design

The "client-server" design philosophy pervades the entire Windows NT environment, from the operating system itself to the simplest tool that it provides; you will need to be aware of it as you learn about administering Windows NT systems. These are its most important implications:

- Windows NT embodies quite a different view of a multiuser operating system than system administrators coming from non-Windows environments will be used to. Under Windows NT, distinct computer systems are almost always viewed as single user systems. Only one user may be logged in to any given system at a time; only a single user can use a given system's CPU resources interactively (we look at ways to address this deficiency in Chapter 4). Many administrative tools are similarly designed with single system assumptions deeply embedded within them.

  In the Windows NT environment, it is the *network* that is the true multiuser system. The network is the mechanism through which Windows NT intends multiple users to share all computer resources.

- The modular design of the Windows NT operating system carries through to the administrative and user facilities that it provides. They tend to be compartmentalized into a large number of tools with limited scopes of action. This approach works well when the underlying system components function independently of the rest of the system, but it can be inconvenient and counterintuitive when related items are arbitrarily separated into separate tools or separate components within tools. It also can result in inconsistencies in the ways that the various tools operate.

- The design model also implicitly deemphasizes the role of system administration. Once installation and initial configuration is complete, ordinary applications and the operating system are expected to function according to the design's predefined procedures. This works well as long as the situation conforms to what the designer has assumed will be normal conditions. As we know, however, reality takes delight in not corresponding to our expectations. In such cases, one would like the ability to modify the way the operating system works in order to address this discrepancy. Unfortunately, because all the alternatives have not been anticipated in advance by the designers, the hooks for modifying many aspects of Windows NT functioning aren't accessible to system administrators (and often not even to systems programmers).

- Finally, Windows NT reflects its Windows heritage in giving priority to the graphical user interface (GUI). This means that the primary system administrative tools are all GUI-based. While there are some command-line utilities that perform the same functions, many administrative tools have no command line equivalent. This makes automating system management tasks much more complex.

Windows NT Variations

Windows NT is packaged and sold in two main formats: a server version and a workstation version.* The two products are designed for systems with different functions within a network. *Workstations* are designed to be used primarily by a single user, although they can optionally share their resources with other systems. *Servers* are designed to provide resources and services to a collection of systems (workstations and possibly other servers) linked together by a local area network; they can provide computing resources and facilities (e.g., database services), disk space, access to printers, networking-related services (e.g., hostname resolution), and the like.

Windows NT groups computers into collections known as *domains*, each overseen by a special server system—the *primary domain controller* (PDC)—possibly assisted by one or more *backup domain controllers* (also servers).† These servers are responsible for user authentication and other related activities. We consider Windows NT domains and domain controllers in more detail in Chapter 3 and Chapter 8.

The same kernel is used for both versions of the Windows NT product; it is configured somewhat differently for the two environments. The most important differences are the following:

- The maximum number of processors in a multiprocessor system supported is two for the workstation version and 32 for the server version.

---

* At press time, Microsoft has recently introduced the Enterprise Edition of Windows NT Server which includes built-in clustering support and facilities for running distributed applications.

† Windows NT systems may also be part of workgroups, but domains are the native Windows NT facility for organizing groups of computers.

- The workstation version is limited to 10 simultaneous client connections for many system services (file sharing, printing, some Internet and web-related services).

- The server version includes some additional software: several administrative tools for managing domains, the Internet Information Server, various networking name service facilities, and others.

- Some of the subsystems in the server version provide advanced features not available in the workstation version: for example, fault-tolerant filesystems and remote booting capabilities for diskless workstations.

- Some parameters related to system performance are set differently in the two products (we'll consider them in Chapter 11).

- The workstation version costs substantially less than the server version (currently about $700 less for a 10-client license).

For more detailed information about the differences between the Windows NT server and workstation products, consult the works on this topic listed in Appendix B.

Service packs and hot fixes

Major releases of Windows NT products are distributed on CD-ROM. Minor releases between major versions are called *service packs.* They are updates that must be applied to the basic operating system. Within a major release, service packs are numbered sequentially. Successive service packs are cumulative and include all of the changes from the earlier ones for the same major release.

WARNING   You probably don't want to be the first on your block to install a new service pack as soon as it becomes available. I prefer to wait a bit and monitor the Windows NT-related newsgroups in order to allow any problems with it to be identified and solved (in other words, I let other people troubleshoot it for me). Even when you do decide to install a service pack, it is prudent to do so on a test system first, rather than on a critical production system (people who venture beyond the rim of known space should not be surprised if they encounter shadows).

Service packs may be downloaded* from the Microsoft FTP site from the directory *ftp://ftp.microsoft.com/bussys/winnt/winnt-public/fixes/*country/*nt40*; *country* is the

---

* Service packs may also be ordered on CD-ROM from Microsoft. The North American version of the latest service pack can be ordered by telephoning (800) 370-8758, faxing (716) 873-0906, or writing to Microsoft NT Service Pack 3, P.O. Box 1095, Buffalo, NY 14240-1095.

appropriate subdirectory corresponding to the various language-specific versions of the product (use *usa* as the *country* for the United States). The actual files to download are located in a subdirectory of *nt40,* whose name varies but is generally intuitive. For example, the files for Service Pack 3 for the U.S. version are located in the subdirectory *ussp3,* which in turn contains the subdirectories *alpha* and *i386* that hold the actual service pack files for the corresponding architecture. Thus, the required file for the Intel platform for Service Pack 3 is *.../fixes/usa/nt40/ ussp3/i386/nt4sp3_i.exe.*

Once the download operation has completed, run the executable, from either the command line or the **Start** menu, or by double-clicking on its icon. This unpacks it to a new subdirectory of *C:\Temp* (assuming that *C:* is the system disk) and automatically starts the program **Update**. Run the executable from the command line with the **/X** option to unpack it without installing it; you can then run **Update** manually when desired. Once the service pack is installed, the system must be rebooted.

It's prudent to allow the installation process to create an uninstall directory; that way, you can back out the service pack's changes to the system if problems appear.

NOTE   Service packs must be reapplied if you add new hardware to the system, install new software (such as a new service or network protocol), or restore a backup created before updating the system.

You can determine the current operating system version via the **Version** tab in the Windows NT Diagnostics administrative tool (it can be accessed from the **Start** menu via the path **Programs►Administrative Tools (Common)►Windows NT Diagnostics**). It is illustrated in Figure 1-2.

Microsoft also supplies *hot fixes* to correct specific problems that are corrected between service packs; hot fixes are usually minor patches to the operating system. In general, you should only install hot fixes that address problems your system is actually experiencing; this caution is necessary because full regression testing is not always completed before a hot fix is released.

Hot fixes may also be downloaded from the Microsoft FTP site. For example, hot fixes to Service Pack 3 are located in subdirectories *ftp.microsoft.com/bussys/ winnt/winnt-public/fixes/country/nt40/hotfixes-postSP3.* The *ReadMe.Txt* file located in each directory explains the purpose of the hot fix and the procedure for obtaining and installing it. Most hot fixes are delivered as self-installing executables, which you can activate by double-clicking on their icon (or running them from the command line). They may also be unpacked without installing by

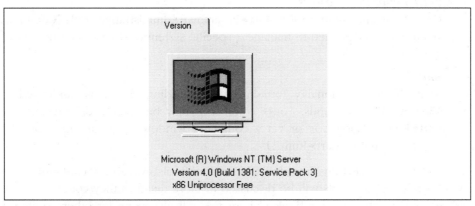

Figure 1-2. Windows NT version information

invoking them with the **/x** option. You can then run the **HotFix** utility included in the archive to install them at a later time.

Older versions of the **HotFix** utility may also be invoked with its **/Full** option (abbreviate to **/F**), to list the hot fixes that have been installed on a Windows NT system. It also lists the hot fixes installed on a remote system if you include a system name in the command, as in this example that produces a detailed listing of the hot fixes installed on the server *vala*:

```
C:\> hotfix \\vala /F
```

Use the **/?** option to **HotFix** to determine if it supports this option.

Administrative Tools

Windows NT provides four classes of administrative tools:

Control panel applets
> These utilities are accessed via the **Start➤Settings➤Control Panel** menu path or from the *Control Panel* folder under *My Computer* (some may also be reached in other ways). They are generally designed to display and modify system configuration settings. These programs typically use tabs to divide the settings they control into several groups.

Administrative wizards
> On server systems, these programs provide automated, step-by-step proce-dures for performing common administrative tasks such as adding new users and setting permissions on files and directories. They are accessed via the **Start➤Programs➤Administrative Tools (Common)➤Administrative Wizards** menu path or the **wizmgr** command.

Graphical administrative tools

> These tools are found on the **Start►Programs►Administrative Tools (Common)** menu. Each is designed to manage a specific system or domain component or subsystem.

Command-line tools

> Some of the functionality found in the preceding classes is duplicated in Windows NT commands. These commands may be entered directly into the **Start►Run...** dialog box or via a command window (you can open one by specifying **cmd** to **Start►Run...**).

The following subsections introduce the various tools available for administering Windows NT. These tools will be discussed in more detail as they come up in the subsequent chapters of this book (where we will also consider other additional useful programs and utilities beyond those provided with standard Windows NT).

Most tools must be run from an account with *Administrator* privileges. We discuss the *Administrator* account in detail in Chapter 3.

Control Panel Applets

Control panel applets allow you to view and modify the configuration of the local system. These are the most important control panel applets from a system administration perspective:

Date/Time

> View or set the system date, time, and time zone.

Licensing

> Manage licenses on the local system. On a server, it also allows you to change the Windows NT licensing mode (from per-server to per-seat).

Network

> Add, configure, and remove network adapters, protocols, services, and computer identification and the relationships among them.

Ports

> View and modify the settings for serial ports and add new ports.

Printers

> A shortcut to the *Printers* folder, from which you can add, remove, and manage printers and print queues, manipulate print jobs, and configure the printing subsystem.

Regional Settings

> Specify how dates, times, numbers, and currency are displayed and sorted.

SCSI Adapters
   Add and remove SCSI adapters and display the properties of SCSI devices.

Server
   Monitor the system's client usage and shared resources.

Services
   Configure and manipulate server processes (including their automatic startup
   at boot-time).

System
   Display various system characteristics and settings and specify some startup,
   shutdown, user environment, and performance-related system parameters.

Tape Devices
   Manage the system's tape drives.

UPS
   Manage system interaction with an uninterruptible power supply.

In addition, while the **Accessibility Options**, **Display**, **Keyboard**, **Mouse**, **Multi-
media**, and **Sounds** applets are primarily useful for configuring and customizing
the associated subsystems for your personal use, they occasionally have administrative uses as well.

Administrative Wizards

The administrative wizards are included on Windows NT server systems. These
automated procedures for common administrative tasks can generally be used on
either the local computer or on a remote computer (one of the first questions you
are asked is the system or domain context under which you want to perform the
action). They proceed as a series of dialog boxes requesting the information
required to complete the desired action.

There are eight administrative wizards, whose names are generally self-explana-
tory: **Add User Accounts**, **Group Management**, **Managing File and Folder Access**,
Add Printer, **Add/Remove Programs**, **Install New Modem**, **Network Client Administration** (allows you to set up the system as a server for subsequent network
installations of Windows NT), and **License Compliance** (checks a domain for unli-
censed products).

Standard Graphical Administrative Utilities

Table 1-1 summarizes the GUI-based system administration tools provided by
Windows NT. Each entry lists the name of the utility (which appears on the
Start►Programs►Administrative Tools (Common) menu in most cases), the
command executable name (by which it may be accessed from the **Run** menu),

and a brief description of its purpose. The "type" column in the table indicates whether each tool is provided by default on server systems (code letter **S**) and workstation systems (code letter **W**); the code letters **CT** indicate a server program that may be installed on a Windows NT workstation as part of a collection of client tools (discussed in a moment).

Table 1-1. Windows NT Administrative Tools

Tool	Command	Type	Purpose
Backup	ntbackup	S, W	Backup and restore files.
DHCP Manager	dhcpadmn	S, CT	Control the TCP/IP Dynamic Host Configuration Protocol service.
Disk Administrator	windisk	S, W	Manage disks and disk partitions.
DNS Manager	dnsadmin	S, CT	Control the TCP/IP Domain Name Service.
Event Viewer	eventvwr	S, W	Monitor hardware, security, and application-related system status messages and errors.
License Manager	llsmgr	S	Manage software licensing for one or more domains.
Network Client Administrator	ncadmin	S	Prepare system to provide network-based installation services and administration tools.
Network Monitor	netmon	S	Monitor and record network activity.
Performance Monitor	perfmon	S, W	Monitor, analyze, and record system usage data relevant to performance optimization.
Registry Editor	regedt32	S, W	View and modify settings in the system registry.
Remote Access Administrator	rasadmin	S, CT, W	Manage Remote Access Services (dial-up networking).
Remote Boot Manager	rplmgr	S, CT	Configure remote booting services.
Server Manager	srvmgr	S, CT	Manage shared resources and services; promote/demote domain controllers.
System Policy Editor	poledit	S, CT	Create and modify system policies, specifying allowed user actions and system access.
Task Manager	taskmgr	S, W	View and manipulate processes.
User Manager	musrmgr	W	Create and modify local (system-specific) user accounts.
User Manager for Domains	usrmgr	S, CT	Create and modify domain user accounts.
Windows NT Diagnostics	winmsd	S, W	View system characteristics and current settings.
WINS Manager	winsadmn	S, CT	Manage the Windows Internet Naming Service facility.

Most of these tools can be used to configure either the local system or a specific remote system (the latter is usually specified via an option named **Select Computer** or **Select Server** or something similar on the application's left-most menu). The Windows NT Server distribution CD contains versions of many of the server tools that may be installed on Windows NT Workstation and Windows 95 systems to enable you to perform system administration tasks on servers remotely.

These programs are installed on a workstation system by executing the **Setup.Bat** command in the *\Clients\Srvtools\WinNT* directory on the Windows NT Server distribution CD at the target workstation. The tools will be copied into the *C:\WinNT\System32* directory on the workstation. If you want the items to appear in the **Administrative Tools (Common)** menu, create shortcuts for each of the executables in the *C:\WinNT\System32\Profiles\All Users\Start Menu\Programs\Administrative Tools (Common)* directory (the quickest way is to drag their icons from the *System32* subdirectory to the destination directory; you can rename the shortcuts to their canonical names if you want).

On Windows 95 systems, the procedure is only slightly more involved:

- Insert the Windows NT Server distribution CD into the CD-ROM drive.

- Select **Start➤Settings➤Control Panel➤Add/Remove Programs➤Windows Setup➤ Have Disk**.

- Enter the path *X:\Clients\Srvtools\Win95* (where *X:* is the appropriate letter for the CD-ROM drive) into the resulting dialog box.

- Select the Windows NT Server Tools components and select the **Install** button.

This procedure installs the administrative tools into the *\Srvtools* directory on the disk containing the Windows 95 directory.

Other Sources of Administrative Tools

There are three other important sources of administrative tools for Windows NT:

- The Windows NT Resource Kits, sold by Microsoft and consisting of extra documentation and (unsupported) software. There are both workstation and server versions of the Resource Kit. They are available in the computer sections of most larger bookstores, at many retail software stores, and from mail-order hardware and software suppliers. The kits sell for about $55 and $150 for the workstation and server versions, respectively.

  The Resource Kits contain many important administrative programs, and you should consider them a required part of any Windows NT installation. It's unfortunate that there is additional cost associated with them, since their contents really ought to be part of the normal Windows NT products.

- Freely available software, available for downloading from the Web.

- Commercial software: trial or demonstration versions are often available on the Web.

The contents of the Resource Kits and the locations of major software repositories are both given in Appendix B.

Introducing the Windows NT Registry

The Windows NT *registry* is a central database of configuration settings.[*] It serves to replace the scores of initialization (*.Ini*) files found on Windows systems. Although Windows 95 contains a similar facility, the Windows NT registry uses a different format and is much more complex.

The registry is stored in a series of binary files usually located in the directory *C:\WinNT\System32\Config*. Logically, the registry is a collection of named *keys* and their *values*. Registry keys form the structure of the registry, and are organized hierarchically; locations within the registry are referred to using a syntax analogous to subdirectory pathnames. Values are terminal nodes in the registry tree containing actual system settings (known as *data*). Put most simply, keys are like directories and values are like files, with data corresponding to file contents.[†] A subtree of keys and values stored together in a single file is known as a *hive*.

The registry is composed of series of five tree-structured groups of keys, each headed by a *root key*:[‡]

- HKEY_CLASSES_ROOT: definitions of known system file types and OLE classes

- HKEY_USERS: configuration data for the default and defined user accounts

- HKEY_LOCAL_MACHINE: local system configuration data

- HKEY_CURRENT_USER: a pointer into the HKEY_USERS tree for the currently logged in user

- HKEY_CURRENT_CONFIG: a pointer into the HKEY_LOCAL_MACHINE\System\CurrentControlSet subtree for the current system configuration

You will typically access keys only within the HKEY_USERS and HKEY_LOCAL_ MACHINE trees.

---

[*] Readers familiar with AIX will note that the registry performs a function analogous to AIX's Object Data Manager database.

[†] Well, this is almost true. Occasionally, keys have values named "<No Name>" (which have data types and data as usual). In these cases, the value is referred to simply by the key name.

[‡] Hives need not correspond to root keys. A subtree headed by a root key may be stored as one or more hives. This list also ignores the HKEY_DYN_DATA pseudokey (accessible by programs).

Registry key values have one of 11 data types. Here are those you're likely to encounter:

- REG_BINARY: binary data

- REG_DWORD: integer data (often displayed in hexadecimal notation)

- REG_SZ: character string values

- REG_MULTI_SZ: a list of character strings (appearing one per line in the Registry Editor)

- REG_EXPAND_SZ: a character string value containing expandable parameters (variables replaced by their actual values when the key is used)

The other defined data types are:

- REG_DWORD_BIG_ENDIAN: also holds a 32-bit integer, high byte first

- REG_FULL_RESOURCE_DESCRIPTOR, REG_RESOURCE_LIST, and REG_RESOURCE_REQUIREMENTS_LIST: complex data types for hardware configuration and system resource data (such keys are not editable)

- REG_LINK: a pointer (quasi-symbolic link) to another location within the registry

- REG_NONE: used for untyped data

Using the Registry Editor

Ideally, you shouldn't have to worry about the system registry or modify the values of any of its settings. However, as of the current version of Windows NT, this ideal is far from achievable; there are many system features that are accessible in no other way. While it is a bad idea to make random, experimental, or gratuitous changes to the registry, from time to time you will need to modify registry entries for a variety of reasons: to change the way the system functions, to correct a problem, to add or modify keys or values to enable additional system features.

Windows NT provides a utility known as the Registry Editor for accessing and modifying the registry: **regedt32.*** By default, neither an icon for this tool nor an entry in the **Administrative Tools (Common)** menu is present, but you can always create them. The Registry Editor is a powerful tool that requires care when used. Microsoft's standard message about it (see the following Warning) is worth paying attention to.

---

* The Windows 95 utility, **RegEdit**, is also included. It has a more powerful searching facility than the Windows NT utility.

WARNING   "Using Registry Editor incorrectly can cause serious, systemwide
              problems that may require you to reinstall Windows NT to correct
              them. Microsoft cannot guarantee that any problems resulting from
              the use of Registry Editor can be solved. Use this tool at your own
              risk." [Microsoft Corp.]

Prudent use of the Registry Editor involves several activities:

* Back up the registry files before you begin (this process is discussed in
  Chapter 7).

* Be sure that you have a bootable, saved configuration that you can fall back
  on if necessary (discussed in Chapter 2).

* Plan your actions before you undertake them and test them afterward.

* Use the Registry Editor with care. Keep in mind that changes to the registry
  are immediate and that there is no undo command. Use the utility in read-only
  mode (**Options➤Read Only Mode**) when you just want to examine registry
  entries.

* Keep records of the changes you have made.

Figure 1-3 illustrates the process for changing an existing registry value: you select
the window for the desired root key in the Registry Editor and then navigate to the
desired key by selecting successive items in the left side of the browsing window.
The values and associated data stored at the current location appear in the right
side of the window; values and data are separated by colons.

To modify a value, double-click on its entry in the right side of the browsing
window. A dialog box appears containing the current setting, which you can
modify as necessary (note that the value's data type is indicated in the dialog box's
titlebar). For example, the illustration changes the HKEY_USERS\
DEFAULT\Desktop\ScreenSaveTimeOut value from 60 to 10 (seconds in this case).
Once you click **OK** to close the dialog box, the change is made immediately. Use
the **Cancel** button to abandon any changes.

The Registry Editor may also be used to add new keys and values to the registry
via these two options on its **Edit** menu:

Edit➤Add Key
    Adds to the structure of the registry only, by creating a new subkey of the
    current key. The Registry Editor prompts you for the name of the new key.

---

* If your window is missing one of these sections, select **View➤Tree and Data**.

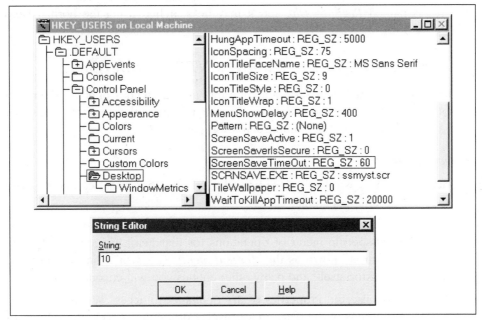

Figure 1-3. Using the Windows NT Registry Editor

Edit►Add Value

Adds a value (a terminal leaf) to the current key in the registry. The Registry Editor prompts you for the value name, its data type, and the desired data setting.

Registry keys have owners and access permissions just like files and directories do. We'll consider them in Chapter 10.

The Registry Editor is an easy way to change the value of a particular registry setting (or to add a new one). Sometimes, though, you will want to find a registry component whose name you don't know. The Resource Kit provides the **scanreg** utility for searching registry key names, value names, and value data for strings; it is a command line utility with the following syntax:

```
scanreg -s string scope-options [other-options]
```

One or more options specifying the items to be searched must be included: **-k** says to scan key names, **-v** searches value names, and **-d** scans the data. For example, the following command searches all key and value names for the string "cd":

```
C:\ > scanreg -s cd -kv
Key   : "\Software\Microsoft\Multimedia\Audio\WaveFormats"
Value : "CD Quality"
End of search: 1 matching string(s) found.
```

The Resource Kit includes a help file that documents registry keys and values. The file is named *RegEntry.Hlp*, and it may be searched using the normal Help facility methods.

Tips and Tricks for the Windows NT User Interface

We'll end our discussion of system administration tools with a brief consideration of some power tips for the Windows NT user interface, the sorts of things that take a while to figure out or stumble across on your own.

Know your desktop

- SHIFT-click in a window's close box (the X in its upper right corner) to close the window and its parents.

- Right-clicking—clicking with the right mouse button—on most items brings up a context-specific menu of operations for that item, including its **Properties**; this menu is known as the *shortcut menu*. This works on files, desktop icons, the desktop itself, and many other entities you will encounter.

  For example, use the **Properties** of *My Computer* to access system properties and the **Properties** of the desktop for display properties. Access the **Properties** of the taskbar to set its properties and to change the **Start** menu for all users; other items on the taskbar's right-click menu manipulate all open windows.

- ALT-double-clicking with the left mouse button immediately opens an item's **Properties**. Pressing ALT-ENTER when the item is selected does the same thing.

- Use CTRL-TAB to move between the various tabs in a multipanel dialog box; CTRL-SHIFT-TAB cycles among them in reverse order.

- Use the icons in the tray in the lower-right corner of the taskbar to access many control panels and other tools. For example, hold the mouse over the time in the tray to get the date. Right click on it to set the date and time.

- CTRL-ESC brings up the **Start** menu.

- Use the **Start▶Run...** menu path to access directories and files quickly by entering the desired location in its dialog box. Entering a directory name displays that directory. Entering a filename opens it in the appropriate application program or runs the file itself, if it is executable.

- Customize the **Start** menu by dragging and dropping things on it, using the **Start▶Settings** menu item, or by adding the desired items to the *Programs* folder (or one of its subfolders) in *C:\WinNT\Profiles\All Users\Start Menu* or *C:\WinNT\Profiles*\username*Start Menu* (to modify the systemwide or a single user's **Start** menu, respectively).

- Select an item, then SHIFT-right-click on it to get a context menu, including an **Open with** option, which allows you to specify the application program with which to open it. For example, select a file, then SHIFT-right-click on it and enter **E W O** RETURN to open a file with *Wordpad*.

- You can start the **Find Files or Folders** facility (located on the **Start** menu) by pressing the F3 key from the desktop (if you are in an application, click on the desktop and then press F3 to open it).

- On keyboards that include the new Windows key (adjacent to each ALT key), there are additional keyboard shortcuts available, including:

  — WIN-R opens the **Run** dialog box.

  — WIN-F immediately opens the **Find Files or Folders** facility.

  — WIN-M minimizes all currently open windows, and WIN-SHIFT-M undoes a WIN-M operation.

  — WIN-Break opens the **System Properties** dialog box.

  In general, WIN-x selects the desktop items whose names begin with the specified letter, when that key combination is not already defined. Once an item is selected, pressing ENTER opens it, and ALT-ENTER opens its **Properties**.

Browsing

- You can specify whether or not a new window is opened every time you change folders when browsing via the **View➤Options➤Folder** path from any browse window.

- Holding down the CTRL key when you double-click on a folder to open it reverses whatever setting is in effect for the current operation.

- SHIFT-double-clicking when browsing opens folders in Explorer view instead of the normal browsing view.

- The backspace key moves up one directory level when browsing.

- Hold down the CTRL key to select multiple, nonadjacent items within a browsing window.

- SHIFT-DELETE bypasses the recycle bin for the currently selected files. You can also make this the default behavior by right-clicking on the Recycle Bin and modifying its **Properties**.

- Customize browse windows' **File➤Send To** menu (**Send To** is repeated on the shortcut menu) by adding items to the folders named *SendTo*, located in *C:\WinNT\Profiles\Default User* or *C:\WinNT\Profiles*username. Right-drag items to a folder to add them to the **Send To** menu for subsequently created users or the specified current user. Be aware that program executables will need to be in the user's path in order to be accessible. On a workstation, simply modify the *SendTo* folder in *C:\WinNT.*

Working with files and directories

- Hold down the CTRL key while dragging an item to force a copy operation.

- Right-drag an item to its new location to get a menu of options: **Create Shortcut, Move, Copy, Cancel**.

- View a folder's **Properties** to view total number and size of files in a subtree.

- Open *My Computer* and click on a disk to see its total capacity and remaining free space (displayed at bottom of window).

- View a disk's **Properties** to display its current used and free space.

- If you change the value of the registry key HKEY_CLASSES_ROOT\.bat from "batfile" to "txtfile," double-clicking on a *.BAT* file edits it rather than run it. Similarly, changing the value for the key for HKEY_CLASSES_ROOT\.cmd from "cmdfile" to "txtfile" does the same thing for command files (*.CMD* is the conventional extension for Windows NT script files).

Using and customizing the command window

- Open a command window by running the **cmd** command in the **Start➤Run…** dialog box.

- Use the Tab key for *filename completion* within command windows. When entering a command, if you type the first couple of letters of a file or directory name and then press the Tab key, Windows NT fills in the remainder of the name for you automatically (try it!)*. If more than one name matches the characters entered so far, then the first matching item is used. In this case, use the arrow keys to cycle through the list of matching items.

- Right-click its upper-left corner when the window is open, and select **Properties** to change its default size, appearance, and functioning:

  — The **Layout** panel sets the default window size and buffer size (number of remembered previous lines).

  — The **Options** panel sets command history length, allows you to select insert mode as the default command editing mode, and enables quick edit mode to cut and paste text within command windows. In this mode, you highlight the desired text with the left mouse button and click the

---

* If it doesn't work, it's easy to enable it: the character used for filename completion is controlled by the CompletionChar value of the HKEY_CURRENT_USER\Software\Microsoft\Command Processor registry key. The Tab key corresponds a setting of 0x9. You can specify a different key by setting it to the ASCII character number for the desired key (in hex). Changes to this setting apply to subsequently created command windows

right mouse button to copy it to the buffer. You can subsequently paste the saved text at the current cursor location by right-clicking. You can also use the **Edit** submenu on the shortcut menu for these operations.

— Other panels let you select the fonts and colors used in command windows.

— Select **Save properties for future windows with same title** upon exiting the **Properties** dialog box to make your selections the new command window defaults. They're in effect whenever you open a command window with the **cmd** command.

The Windows NT Filesystem

Windows NT uses a substantially more compact filesystem[*] tree for its system files than many other operating systems. It includes the following directories at the top level of the system disk (usually *C:*):

Program Files
> Subdirectories hold some Windows NT executables. Application programs often install files under this directory by default.

Temp
> Scratch directory used for temporary files.

WinNT
> Top-level directory for the Windows NT system files. The built-in environment variable *%SystemRoot%* points to the drive and directory at the top of the Windows NT file tree; its usual value is thus *C:\\WinNT*.[†]

These are the most important subdirectories of *%SystemRoot%*:

Profiles
> User profiles subdirectories (user profiles specify the user's Windows NT environment).

System32
> Windows NT command executables, dynamic link library files (DLLs), and some configuration files.

---

[*] Here, we use the term *filesystem* to refer to the aggregate of all of the disk partitions—the entities that get assigned drive letters—and the entire directory trees that they hold, in other words, everything under *C:*, *D:*, and so on for every partition on the system. This same term is also used to refer to a formatted disk partition, as in "the Disk Administrator is used to create a filesystem on the new partition" or "The NTFS filesystem type has many advantages over the FAT filesystem." Which use of the term "filesystem" is meant will always be clear from the context.

[†] I haven't worried about this distinction in previous sections. However, we will use the canonical terminology from this point on.

System32\Config

> Registry files, event logs, and user accounts database.

System32\Drivers

> Device drivers.

System32\Spool

> Print spooling subsystem files.

System32\Repl

> Directory replication service (a facility for automatically synchronizing the file-systems of several computer systems) top-level directory.

Fonts

> TrueType and other font files.

Repair

> Files required for creating an emergency repair disk.

Help

> Windows NT help files.

System

> Windows 95 files are located here (and in *%SystemRoot%* itself) if it is also installed on the computer. This directory is also used by some legacy 16-bit applications.

Windows NT Network File Naming Conventions

Windows NT uses a notation for specifying the location of network files and directories known as the *uniform naming convention* (UNC).* Within a Windows NT domain, the full pathname for a file may be given as:

```
\\host\share_name\[directory\...\directory]\file.ext
```

Host is the name of the system where the file resides, and *share_name* is the name by which a specific directory location on that host is made available as a network resource. These two items are followed by a path to the file from that point. You will see this notation, and subsets of it, throughout the rest of this book.

Never Forget That It's a PC

When I started as a system administrator, no one I knew ever dared to open up one of the computers and start messing with things inside (although many of us would have liked to). New peripheral devices were attached to the outside of the

---

* Sometimes referred to as the *universal naming convention.*

computer, and all hardware maintenance was handled by the computer vendor's field service technicians.

Managing Windows NT systems is nothing like this.* Working with the computer hardware is a large part of the job, and getting familiar with the inside of the chassis is an essential part of becoming a proficient system administrator. People coming from other PC-based environments will be aware of this already. However, some UNIX system administrators and people coming from environments dominated by mainframes will have a bit of adjusting to do.

While many Windows NT system administrators are capable of building computers from their basic components (motherboard, disk drives, power supply, and so on), it is not necessary to go this far if you don't want to. In practical terms, what you need to be able to do is to add new components—most often, new devices and their required controllers—to the system unit of a Windows NT computer and reconfigure existing components as required for compatibility with the new items. We'll discuss the specifics of adding various peripherals and their controllers at many points later in the book. For now, we will consider the hardware characteristics of generic PC devices of which you need to be aware.

Devices use several parameters for communicating with the computer's CPU:

Interrupt request numbers (IRQs)
> A series of standard signals used by devices to request attention from the CPU. In general, only one device should be assigned to each IRQ.

I/O port addresses
> Sections of system memory used by devices. I/O address ranges must be uniquely assigned and must not overlap.

DMA channels
> Allow devices to communicate directly with memory without using the CPU. Each DMA channel should be assigned to one device. Some devices consume two or more DMA channels (e.g., sound cards).

System memory addresses
> These correspond to sections of system memory above the canonical DOS 640-KB limit and are used occasionally by devices requiring more system memory. System memory address ranges must be uniquely assigned and must not overlap.

Windows NT has no "Plug-n-Play" capability at present, so most devices must be configured manually. IRQ conflicts are the most common problem you will

---

* Except perhaps on high-end Alpha servers.

encounter, followed by I/O address conflicts. Table 1-2 lists common IRQ assignments.

Table 1-2. Common IRQ Assignments

IRQ	Common Use
0	System timer
1	Keyboard
2	Cascade: switch over to 2nd IRQ controller
3	COM2, COM4 (2nd and 4th serial ports)
4	COM1, COM3 (1st and 3rd serial ports)
5	LPT2 (2nd parallel port)
6	Floppy disk controller
7	LPT1 (1st parallel port)
8	Real-time clock
9	Redirected IRQ2
12	PS/2 mouse port
13	Math coprocessor error signal
14	IDE hard disk controller

Thus, IRQs 10, 11, and 15 are generally available for you to assign to new devices. It is also possible to reassign the IRQs for serial and parallel ports the system is not using, provided that you disable the port in the system's (power-on) hardware setup program first. If your system contains only SCSI disks (including the CD-ROM drive), then IRQ 14 is also available.

Network cards often use IRQ 10 or IRQ 3. SCSI adapters often use IRQ 11.

NOTE   It's a good idea to keep records of the hardware settings for impor-
              tant computer systems.

The Windows NT Diagnostics (**winmsd**) administrative tool's **Resources** panel can be used to determine most settings in use on the current system. Use the buttons at the bottom of the panel to select the setting type to examine. Figure 1-4 shows a typical IRQ listing. Not all standard system IRQs are included in the listing, but the display is still useful for determining the assignments of devices that have been added to the system. This system has a network card using IRQ 3 and a SCSI controller using IRQ 10.

On Intel systems, I often find it helpful to test and configure new devices by booting the computer with a DOS diskette prior to attempting to install them

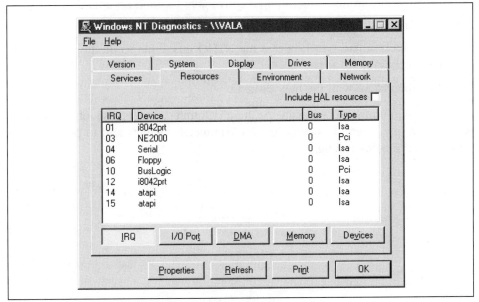

Figure 1-4. System IRQ setting display in the Windows NT diagnostics tool

under Windows NT. The diagnostic and configuration programs provided with many devices by their manufacturers generally run only in the DOS environment. I've also learned the hard way to make sure that a new device actually works before telling Windows NT about it. You can probably guess how: I spent what seemed like hours trying to debug the Windows NT settings for a device that turned out to be just plain broken; nonfunctioning new devices are many times more common in the PC world than they are for larger computer systems.

Other tabs in the diagnostics utility display additional useful information about the system. For example, the **System** tab lists the processor type and BIOS revision dates, the **Memory** tab displays the amount of physical memory on the system and statistics about current memory usage, and the **Drives** tab lists system and network disk resources.

Use the utility's **Print** button to print out some or all of this system configuration information or to save it to a text file (you will be prompted for the desired destination).

Windows NT also provides a hardware detection facility known as NTHQ (for NT Hardware Query). NTHQ is included on the Windows NT distribution CD in the directory *\Support\HQTool*. In order to use this facility, complete the following steps:

- Copy the files in that directory to a convenient location on a hard disk.

- Insert a blank floppy disk into the diskette drive.

- Run **MakeDisk.Bat**, which copies the NTHQ image file to the floppy disk, creating a bootable diskette.

- Boot the system with the new diskette.

Once NTHQ comes up, you can use it to determine the settings of all hardware devices on the system, to determine any parameter conflicts and to perform some limited functionality testing.

2

Startup, Shutdown, and Server Configuration

Keeping the system running is the most visible aspect of system administration, since you are the one users call when the system crashes. Shutting down and bringing up Windows NT systems are actually very simple processes, but the many issues and choices you face as you perform them merit careful consideration nonetheless. In the same vein, it is important to have a conceptual understanding of the startup process in order to recognize problems and intervene when something goes awry.

WARNING   All systems need to use the built-in shutdown procedures. DOS is the only operating system (and I'm using that term loosely) where suddenly turning off the power on even an idle system is guaranteed to be safe; every other operating system environment, from Windows 3.1 and System 7 to Windows NT, UNIX, OpenVMS, and MVS, needs to be shut down in an orderly way, and neglecting to do so under any of them runs the risk of file corruption and data loss.

In this chapter, we begin by examining the Windows NT boot process and then consider ways to customize and secure it. Next, we consider common problems that arise during the boot process and ways to diagnose and address them. We then turn our attention to configuring and managing system services and their associated server processes, and finally conclude the chapter by looking at system shutdown procedures.

Booting a Windows NT System

We'll start by considering a generic Windows NT boot process and then go on to discuss the specifics of the Intel and Alpha environments.

The boot process begins after electrical power is initially applied to the system, after the system experiences a hardware reset, and after shutting down via a shutdown and restart command. On Windows NT systems, it generally proceeds as follows:

- Automatic hardware testing comes first, regardless of the operating system that will ultimately be loaded. This activity is handled by the computer hardware itself. The Power-On Self Test (POST) program is stored in ROM on the CPU board (motherboard). It begins with a superficial check of the system's memory and then queries the status of standard system components, such as the keyboard, mouse, disk drives, and so on. Some peripheral adapters (e.g., SCSI cards) also perform self-initialization as part of this process.

  During this phase, you may also optionally invoke the computer's built-in hardware setup program, which allows you to display and configure many low-level device settings.

- Loading the operating system happens in two distinct phases: the hardware starts a simple boot loader program, and this program in turn determines the location of the operating system and then loads and executes it.

  There are several steps to starting up Windows NT:

  — Selecting the specific operating system to run from the boot menu (labeled **Please select the operating system to start**).

  — Specifying a predefined hardware configuration. The opportunity for doing so is indicated by the message: **Press spacebar NOW to invoke Hardware Profile/Last Known Good menu** and by the presence of the hardware configuration selection menu on systems with more than one defined configuration.

  — Verifying the system's hardware configuration and detecting any new hardware (a somewhat lengthy and tedious process on Intel systems). This step is readily identified by its characteristic blue screen display.

  — Loading and starting the Windows NT kernel. This program is named **NTOSKrnl.Exe** and is located in the *%SystemRoot%\System32* directory.

- The boot process finishes as the operating system initializes itself and its data structures and then starts the login service and other system services. Once everything is ready, the system will be accessible to local and network users.

Be aware that the login banner appears somewhat before the boot process has finished, while some subsystems are still initializing.

The Boot Process on Intel Systems

On Intel systems, loading the operating system is actually a three-phase process:

- The first program to be loaded (by the hardware) is the master boot program stored in the first sector on the first hard disk, which holds *Master Boot Record* (MBR) as well as the disk's partition table. This disk location is inaccessible except to the few utilities designed specifically to access it (the best known of these are the DOS **fdisk** utility and the Windows NT Disk Administrator).

- The master boot program identifies the system partition (usually the first active primary partition on the first hard disk) and loads the boot program it finds there. This second boot program is named **NTLDR** and is located in the root (top-level) directory of the system partition (usually *C:*). **NTLDR** uses these additional files in the same directory to carry out some of its tasks:

Boot.Ini
   This file defines the various selections on the Windows NT boot menu that **NTLDR** presents to the system administrator.

NTDetect.Com
   NTLDR runs this program after a hardware configuration has been selected, either manually by the system administrator or by defaulting to the last successfully booted ("Last Known Good") configuration. **NTDetect.Com** performs the hardware check, which occurs next.

- When all hardware verification completes successfully, **NTLDR** loads and initiates the Windows NT kernel.

The Boot.Ini file

The *Boot.Ini* file defines the Windows NT booting options available, and it is used to construct the corresponding menu that appears at boot-time. Here is a simple example:

```
[boot loader]
timeout=5                        Display menu for five seconds, then boot the default OS.
default=multi(0)disk(0)rdisk(0)partition(1)\WINNT

[operating systems]              These are the various menu selections.
multi(0)disk(0)rdisk(0)partition(1)\WINNT="Windows NT Server 4"
multi(0)disk(0)rdisk(0)partition(1)\WINNT="Windows NT [VGA mode]"
     /basevideo /sos
multi(0)disk(0)rdisk(0)partition(1)\WINDOWS="Windows 95"
```

Each entry is a single line within the file.

Following its initial header line, the first section of this file contains settings related to the default boot process for this system: the number of seconds until the default is selected automatically and the disk location of the default operating system. The second section of the file defines the various options that appear on the boot menu.

The operating system locations in this file are specified in a notation known as an *ARC path*, consisting of the I/O bus, disk, disk partition, and directory location. For IDE disks,* this notation takes the form:

```
multi(m)disk(0)rdisk(n)partition(p)\directory
```

where *m* is the number of the IDE channel (the first channel is 0), *n* is the disk number on that IDE channel (beginning with 0), *p* is the partition number within the disk (beginning at 1), and *directory* is the top-level directory of the operating system. For example, the first two entries in the preceding *Boot.Ini* file both select the Windows NT operating system installed in partition 1 on the first disk on the first IDE channel located in the *WINNT* directory. In each entry, the ARC path is followed by an equals sign and then a character string enclosed in double quotation marks; the latter is used as the label for the entry in the boot menu.

The second entry, labeled "Windows NT [VGA Mode]," illustrates the use of boot options. This entry includes the **/sos** and **/basevideo** options as its second field. **/sos** causes Windows NT to display the name of each device driver as it is loaded, producing a more verbose boot-time display, and **/basevideo** specifies that the operating system should load using standard VGA video mode (useful when you are having problems with a new video driver or monitor settings). There are several other available options designed for running the operating system in debug mode.†

The third entry in the sample file specifies the Windows 95 operating system installed under *Windows* on the same disk partition. The following simpler entry format is equivalent:

```
C:\ = "Windows 95"
```

For SCSI disks, the ARC path notation varies a bit:

```
scsi(m)disk(n)rdisk(0)partition(p)\directory
```

---

* Popular disk types are discussed in Chapter 5.

† Windows NT systems programmers may find the **/kernel** and **/hal** options helpful, as they allow you to specify an alternate filename for the kernel executable and the HAL dynamic link library.

where *m* is the number of the SCSI bus (beginning with 0), *n* is the SCSI ID of the desired disk, and *p* and *directory* are the partition number and directory location as before.* For example, the following *Boot.Ini* entry specifies the Windows NT operating system located in \ *WINNT* in the second partition on the disk with SCSI ID 3:

```
scsi(0)disk(3)rdisk(0)partition(2)\WINNT="Latest Beta Version"
```

A second SCSI adapter in the system would use scsi(1) as its first component. For multibus adapters, however, which provide multiple SCSI buses via a single add-in board, the first bus is always scsi(0) and the second SCSI bus is indicated by adding 32 to the value given to the disk component (in this case, *n* becomes the SCSI ID+32).

Using the *Boot.Ini* file to boot from partitions where Windows NT is not installed is not supported.† Thus, it cannot be used to add partitions for other operating systems to the Windows NT boot menu, not even vanilla Windows 95. Thus, the following type of entry is illegal when Windows NT is not installed in the specified partition:

```
multi(0)disk(0)rdisk(0)partition(2)\WINDOWS="Windows 95"    Illegal!
```

The *Boot.Ini* is an ordinary text file. Before you can edit it, however, you will need to change its system and read-only status:

```
C:\> attrib -R -S C:\boot.ini
Edit the file ...
C:\> attrib +R +S C:\boot.ini
```

It's perfectly safe to add new options to the file to create new selections on the boot menu, but be very cautious about deleting current ones that work.

The default boot menu selection and the length of the timeout period may also be set using the **Startup/Shutdown** tab of the **System** control panel applet (also reachable via *My Computer's* **Properties**). The timeout period for selecting a hardware configuration can be similarly specified using its **Hardware Profiles** panels where you can define and modify hardware profiles and specify the default configuration.

---

* The value of the rdisk component is zero as long as the SCSI device does not use multiple logical units; otherwise, it takes the appropriate LUN.

† Although it sometimes works anyway; for example, Linux can be booted from an entry like this one provided that *lilo* is installed into the corresponding partition's boot sector:

```
multi(0)disk(0)rdisk(0)partition(2)="Linux"
```

The Boot Process on Alpha Systems

On Alpha systems, the **AlphaBIOS** program performs the hardware testing and the boot program loading functions, which are handled by the master boot program on Intel systems. Once it has completed its work, it loads the **OSLoader.Exe** program, which in turns loads and starts the Windows NT kernel. On current systems, the default location for **OSLoader.Exe** is *D:\os\winnt40* (the *D:* drive is a 6-MB FAT filesystem comprising the second partition on the system disk; we discuss the standard layout of the system disk on Alpha systems again in Chapter 5). This program loads **NTOSKRNL.Exe** from its usual location in *%System-Root%\System32*.

The same sort of boot menu is presented to the system administrator as on Intel systems. However, it is the **AlphaBIOS** facility that presents it, and that is used to customize it. The program may be accessed by pressing the F2 key during or immediately after the hardware testing phase of the system boot process. This produces a textual menu corresponding to a variety of system setup activities.

Whether or not a timeout period is used with the boot menu, as well as the length of the timeout period, are controlled from the **AlphaBIOS** program's **CMOS Setup** selection, via these fields:

Auto Start

> Set to **Enabled** to specify that the default boot option should be invoked automatically when the timeout period expires; the **Disabled** value for this setting means that the system should wait indefinitely for a user selection.

Auto Start Count

> Specifies the length of the timeout period in seconds.

You can modify either value by tabbing to the corresponding field on the screen and then using the arrow keys to change the current value. Press F10 to save your modifications and return to the **AlphaBIOS** main menu, or press ESC to return immediately to the main menu, discarding any changes.

You may add and modify the items on the boot menu via the **Utilities▶OS Selection Setup...** menu path. Figure 2-1 shows the resulting dialog box.

The fields in the enclosed box in this dialog box define boot menu selections. The **Boot Name** field is the text that appears for this item on the boot menu (shown at the top of the dialog box). The two fields labeled **Boot File** specify the disk partition and directory location of the operating system loader program, and the two fields labeled **OS Path** similarly specify the disk partition and directory location corresponding to *%SystemRoot%*; the figure illustrates the normal default values.

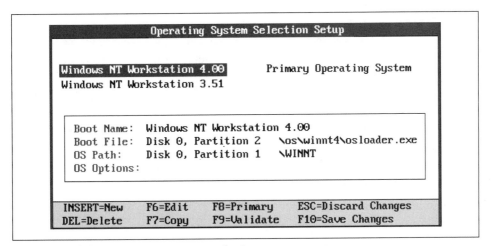

Figure 2-1. AlphaBIOS operating system selection setup screen

The field labeled **OS Options** can be used to specify options to the Windows NT operating system. Two useful options are **/sos**, which causes Windows NT to display the name of each device driver as it is loaded, producing a more verbose boot-time display, and **/basevideo**, which specifies that the operating system should load using standard VGA video mode (useful when you are having problems with a new video driver). There are several other available options designed for running the operating system in debug mode.

The display at the bottom of the dialog box indicates the function keys used to add and modify boot menu entries. For example, the F8 key sets the currently selected item as the menu's default selection. Be very cautious about changing working entries; it is a better practice to create a new entry including the desired modifications. When you finish examining and modifying the boot menu, use F10 to save changes and exit and ESC to cancel changes and exit.

The default boot menu selection and the length of the timeout period may also be set via the **Startup/Shutdown** tab of the **System** control panel applet (also reachable via *My Computer*'s **Properties**). The timeout period for selecting a hardware configuration can be similarly specified via its **Hardware Profiles** panel, where you can define and modify hardware profiles and specify the default configuration.

Securing the Boot Process

The boot process is a major Achilles heel with respect to system security on personal computers. For example, on Intel-based computers, by default anyone who has physical access to the computer and a bootable diskette (for example, DOS or Linux) can easily gain complete access to the system.

Current systems provide mechanisms for addressing this traditional vulnerability, usually via the built-in hardware setup program. We'll consider the features provided on Alpha systems as our example here; the ones available on Intel-based computers are similar but vary from manufacturer to manufacturer.

Hardware setup programs can provide several features for securing the boot process:

- Assigning a password that must be entered before the system will boot

- Specifying the order of boot devices, allowing you to set the hard disk as the primary boot device instead of the floppy drive, and in some cases to disable booting from the floppy drive altogether

- Assigning a password to protect access to the setup program itself or disabling automatic access to it at system initialization time

For example, the **AlphaBIOS** setup program on Alpha systems allows you to protect the setup program and the boot process with a password. To set the password, enter the setup program (F2 key), select **CMOS Setup** from the main menu, and then press the F6 key to enter the **Advanced CMOS Setup** area. Use the **Alpha-BIOS Password Option** field to select the type of password and to set its value. The **Enable Setup Password** allows you to protect the **AlphaBIOS** program itself with a password, and the **Enable Start-up Password** option allows you to specify a password that will be required to boot the system or to run the **AlphaBIOS** setup program. If you select this latter option, which is my recommendation, then the same password will be used for both types of access. These two options are mutually exclusive: selecting one of them undoes the effect of the other. Finally, you can use the field's **Disabled** option to remove password protection from a system.

Physical floppy drive locking devices provide another way of protecting the system against unauthorized access. These devices are quite inexpensive, generally costing only a few dollars. The best ones use a key locking mechanism.

Multi-OS Configuration Options

Both Alpha and Intel computers can be configured with multiple different operating systems: for example, Windows NT and some version of UNIX. Independent operating systems like these are installed into separate disk partitions or on separate disks (the latter is preferable since it minimizes the risk of the operating systems inadvertently interfering with one another).

On Intel systems, there are a variety of methods for specifying which operating system to boot:

- Set the partition containing the operating system you want to boot next as the active partition. You can accomplish this by booting from a DOS diskette and then using the **fdisk** utility (be sure to copy it to the diskette), or from within Windows NT using the Disk Administrator facility (**Partition➤Mark Active**). This method works well when you do not change operating systems very often. Some commercial operating system selection utilities function in the same manner.

- Select an operating system at boot-time. Several commercial utilities enable you to do so. They generally use one of two schemes to accomplish it. The first requires a separate partition on the system disk to store information about the installed operating systems and which one is currently the default. This partition becomes the one marked as active, and a program located there loads the desired operating system from the appropriate partition.

  The second, which is preferable because it doesn't gratuitously consume a disk partition, replaces the standard master boot loader with a more sophisticated program capable of recognizing and selecting among multiple installed operating systems. V Communication's excellent System Commander product is the best known of this type. The Linux **lilo** facility also functions in this way, and **lilo** has no problems booting Windows NT; set it up in **lilo**'s configuration file in the normal manner for a DOS-type operating system.

WARNING   Installing multiple operating systems introduces security concerns because they can make it easier for unauthorized users to gain access to the system.

Common Booting Problems and Remedies

When the system won't boot, the most important question to ask is, "What changed?" Since systems don't just suddenly stop working without cause, tracking down boot problems inevitably means figuring out what is different now than when the system was working. The first thing to examine when the system won't boot is any changes that you or anyone else have recently made to the system. An incorrect system configuration is by far the most common cause of boot failures, and hardware failures comprise the majority of the remainder.

When the system won't boot, try again to boot it with a minimal, vanilla boot process. There are several such methods available:

- Boot using the Last Known Good configuration. The system automatically saves the system configuration whenever a user successfully logs in.* You can use the saved configuration by pressing the space bar when the message for the Last Known Good menu appears and then entering **L** at the hardware configuration screen.

- Boot using a saved hardware profile: specifying a saved hardware profile rather than the current configuration at boot-time may allow you to back out recent changes that are causing problems. I generally update my saved hardware profile whenever I successfully add new hardware to the system, naming it something like: *Just In Case 6/13/97.*

- Perform the early stages of the Windows NT boot process from diskette, bypassing any suspect files on disk.

- Boot from the Windows NT setup diskettes and examine and possibly repair the system using an emergency repair disk (discussed later in this chapter).

We consider the specifics of performing the final two options later in this chapter.

Obviously, the key to diagnosing and eventually correcting a booting problem is to locate the specific point of failure. Often, the point at which the error occurs indicates what component is causing the trouble. In addition, any item that you've recently changed—settings you've modified, hardware you've added or reconfigured, and so on—is also a likely suspect. We'll consider several specific types of failures individually.

System configuration errors

This type of problem usually occurs in the *Boot.Ini* file or in the system registry. If you suspect that the former is the problem, the first thing to try is booting with a different entry from the boot menu that you know will work. If you succeed in gaining access to the system, you can correct or back out recent changes.

If you cannot find a working entry in the *Boot.Ini* file, then try booting from diskette (as described later in this section). As a last resort, perform the system repair procedure to restore a good version of the file.

Registry-related problems should be approached in a similar manner. The Last Known Good system configuration uses a saved version of the registry rather than the current one. If this gives you access to the system, you can again roll back the changes you have made or restore backup copies of the registry files. If this approach fails, however, you will have to perform a system repair using the emergency rescue disk, which restores the registry information saved on that diskette.

---

* This means that the configuration is not updated if the system is merely rebooted.

The system will almost always boot from that, but it will probably need a fair amount of reconfiguration afterward.

Problems resulting from new hardware

New hardware can interfere with the boot process in a variety of ways: it can introduce a setting conflict with an existing device, a required device driver can fail to load, the device itself can be bad, and so on.

The first thing to try is booting with the Last Known Good configuration to get the system to a workable state where you can examine device settings. The NT Hardware Query (NTHQ) utility can also be helpful in sorting out device conflicts (it is discussed in Chapter 1). Be aware that the device settings you enter during Windows NT device installations are merely informing the operating system of the characteristics of the device; they do not alter the device in any way, even if it is software-configurable. For this reason, it is better to configure the device explicitly before installing it.

A device driver can fail to load for a new device, usually because it is an unsupported or incompatible version. You can check the latest Hardware Compatibility List on Microsoft's web site to verify that a device is supported (see Appendix B for the address). If the device is supported but the driver fails to load, see if there is an updated device driver available from the manufacturer (drivers are almost always available for downloading from the hardware vendor's web site).

A failure in the new device itself can sometimes interfere with the boot process. If at all possible, test the device before installing it under Windows NT (there is more bad new hardware than there ought to be). For example, network adapters typically come with a utility disk that tests the device and configures its settings. Run the diagnostics before trying to connect to the network under Windows NT.

As a last resort, remove the new hardware and see if the system returns to its previous working state. Other system problems can result from or occur simultaneously with the addition of new hardware: you can inadvertently detach a connection when installing the new device, turning the power back on after adding the device can cause another marginal component to fail, and the like. If the system still won't boot after you've pulled the new hardware, you'll have to look elsewhere for the cause.

Occasionally, adding a bad device can break the system so badly that the system hardware is unable to even start the boot process, and the system just beeps when power goes on. In such cases, immediately turn the power off and check the new device as well as other system components.

Missing or corrupted system files

The system will be unable to boot if the kernel or other files essential to the boot process are missing or have become corrupted. This type of failure occurs very rarely, and when it does, the cause is virtually always human error.

If the problem file is one of the preliminary booting programs, you can boot from diskette and then restore the damaged file from backup. However, if the problem is with the kernel itself or another essential system file (for example, a critical device driver), you must repair the system with the emergency repair disk.

MBR-related problems

There are two sorts of low-level disk problems that can cause boot failures:

* The system's primary boot program can become corrupted or infected by a virus (the latter occurs only on Intel systems at this point).

* The disk partition table can become corrupted (although the partitions themselves are fine). Human error using a low-level disk utility is the cause of this sort of failure in most cases.

If there is a problem with the master boot program, it must be restored before the system will be accessible. On Intel systems, the undocumented **/MBR** option to DOS's **fdisk** command restores the standard program to the master boot record (MBR). On Alpha systems, the **AlphaBIOS** firmware would have to be repaired.

On Intel systems, the **DiskSave** utility included in the Resource Kit can be used to save MBR and system disk partition tables to floppy disk. Copy the program to a bootable DOS diskette, and then reboot the system into DOS. **DiskSave** presents the following menu:

```
F2  - Backup the Master Boot Record      Save master boot program.
F3  - Restore Master Boot Record
F4  - Backup the Boot Sector             Save disk partition table.
F5  - Restore Boot Sector
F6  - Disable FT on the Boot Drive       Disable mirroring on system disk.
ESC - Exit the program
```

When you save the MBR or the boot sector, **DiskSave** asks for a filename in which to store the data. Should it ever become necessary, these saved copies can be restored to disk using this same menu.

Other hardware failures

Failures in other key system components can also cause the system to fail to boot: the monitor dies, the system power supply fails, the motherboard gets fried. In these cases, a DOS boot from diskette will fail as well. The solution to the problem will then be obvious: get the hardware fixed.

Booting Windows NT from Diskette (Intel Systems)

While Windows NT can't be fully booted from diskette (since the kernel is far too large), the steps in the booting process prior to setting the hardware configuration can be performed from diskette; the kernel will still load from disk. You can create such a diskette as follows:

- Insert a diskette into the floppy disk drive. Format the diskette (one way is to select **Format** from its right-click menu), making sure that the operation is a full format, not a quick format. It's a good idea to reformat used diskettes whether you think they need it or not to ensure the integrity of the diskette's filesystem.

- Copy the *Boot.Ini, NTLDR,* and *NTDetect.Com* files from the system root directory to the floppy (include *BootSect.DOS* as well if the system is dual-booting). I usually modify the label of one of the selections in *Boot.Ini* so I can quickly recognize a diskette-based boot option.

When system is booted with this diskette, the secondary boot loader and the hardware detection programs run via the copies on the diskette, which are known to be good. The diskette can thus be used to distinguish between problems with these files and other sources of boot failures (e.g., a corrupt kernel file).

Creating and Using Emergency Repair Disks

The **rdisk** command can be used at any time to make an *emergency repair disk* (ERD): a diskette containing compressed versions of the system registry files and a few other files. You want to create an ERD for each of your key systems. Figure 2-2 shows the utility's primary dialog box.

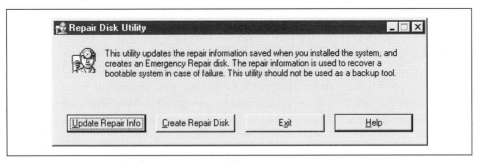

Figure 2-2. Creating an emergency repair disk

Use the **Update Repair Info** option if the system configuration has changed since the last time, or if you are not sure whether it has or not. After the repair information is updated on disk, you have the opportunity to create the emergency repair diskette. Use the **Create Repair Disk** option to make a new ERD without modifying the current repair information.

In order to use an emergency repair disk on Intel systems, you also need the Windows NT setup diskettes and the distribution CD. On Alpha systems, you need only the distribution CD, since the setup program is incorporated into the hardware AlphaBIOS setup program. You can create a set of setup diskettes by running the command **winnt32 /ox**. This executable is located in the distribution CD's *I386* top-level directory.*

Repairing a system with an emergency repair disk is a straightforward, if tedious, process. First, boot the computer from the Windows NT Setup Disk 1, inserting the second setup disk when prompted. When the setup menu appears, select **R** to invoke the system emergency repair procedure. It displays the following menu:

```
[X] Inspect registry files          Check registry files for corruption.
[X] Inspect startup environment      Check for necessary boot components.
[X] Verify Windows NT system files   Verify all Windows NT files.
[X] Inspect boot sector              Check the disk's boot sector.
Continue (perform selected tasks)    Select this item to begin repairs.
```

Each item in the menu indicates a part of the Windows NT environment that the repair process can examine. By default, all of them are scheduled for examination. You may focus on the most likely problem areas by removing the check mark from items to be skipped.

Selecting the **Continue** option begins the repair process. As it proceeds, you need to insert the third setup disk and the ERD when requested. The process first checks the integrity of the disk and then goes on to verify the Windows NT components you have indicated. Once the registry check is complete, the repair process displays a list of possibly corrupt files; if any files are included in the list, you may choose to restore them from the ERD.

Subsequent parts of the repair process compare the current system state to that defined by the original Windows NT installation media. If differences are found, the original files are restored from the Windows NT distribution CD. You are asked to confirm each file replacement (although you may enter a response of **A** to any such prompt to automatically answer yes to all subsequent prompts). Note that this process merely compares system files to their original versions. Thus, if

---

* There is a small glitch that you'll need to address if you've installed Service Pack 2 or later. One file on Setup Disk 2 needs to be updated in this case. To do so, use the **diskcopy** command to create a copy of Setup Disk 2, and then replace the file *Setupdd.Sys* in its root directory with the version included in the service pack distribution. Note that you must obtain this file from the unpacked archive itself; it is not installed anywhere else on the system as part of the service pack installation. See article Q168015 in the Microsoft Knowledge Base for further information (consult Appendix B for details).

you choose to verify the Windows NT system files and you have installed any service packs, you can expect tens to hundreds of differences to be found.

WARNING   Installing Service Pack 3 significantly complicates these emergency repair procedures (in fact, one is tempted to say it breaks them). Microsoft's recommended repair procedures for these systems is to first repair the system with an ERD created after installing Service Pack 3, next uninstall the service pack, then create another ERD from the resulting system, and finally repair the system again using that new disk. See article Q146887 in the Microsoft Knowledge Base for all of the ugly details.

When the system repair process fails to produce a working system, there are two options left to you:

- Upgrade Windows NT over the existing installation by booting from the setup disks and then selecting the upgrade option from the resulting menu. You will have a fair amount of system reconfiguration to do afterward, but other files in the same disk partition should remain intact.

- Reinstall Windows NT from scratch and restore the system filesystem from backup. This option is necessary when disk corruption is widespread and when the system disk itself fails and must be replaced. In the first case, you will need to first address the disk problems with a disk repair utility (see Chapter 5).

The Event Viewer

The Event Viewer administrative tool can be useful for troubleshooting hardware problems and for identifying areas that might become problems in the future. You should examine the event log regularly on key systems. The facility tracks and displays three classes of system messages: system-related (generated by the system's hardware and subsystems), security-related, and application-specific. You may select the type of message to view with the first three options on the utility's **Log** menu. We consider system events in this section.

Figure 2-3 illustrates the Event Viewer's event listing. By default, all events in the current event log are displayed in reverse chronological order. Use **View>Filter Events** to limit the display to those of interest.

System events generally fall into three categories: informational (typically status messages from various systems), warnings (indicating a nonfatal problem with some system component), and errors (failures in a system component or subsystem).

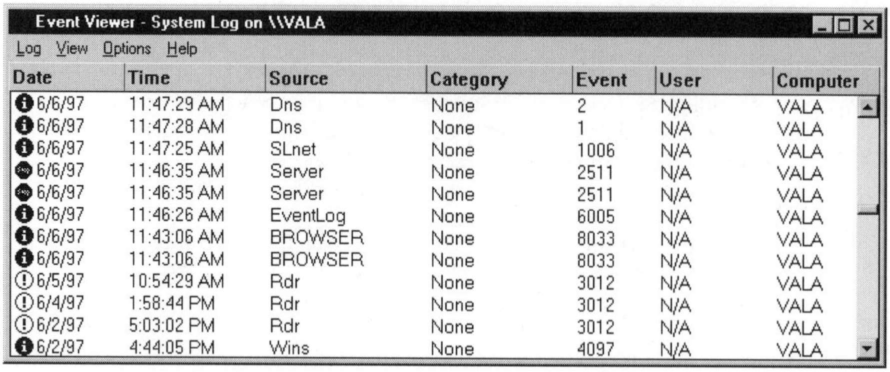

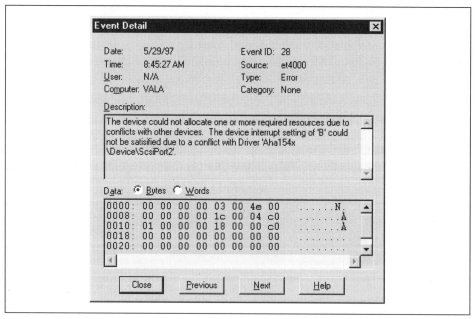

Figure 2-3. System message list in the Event Viewer

Double-clicking on an event produces detailed information about it. Figure 2-4 illustrates a detailed view of a hardware error event. This event corresponds to an IRQ conflict; both the network adapter and the SCSI adapter are attempting to use IRQ 11 (given in hexadecimal in the event description).

Figure 2-4. Event detail view

You can also use the Event Viewer to examine the event log on another system by using the **Log➤Select Computer**... menu path.

System errors for a single system are easy enough to monitor using the Event Viewer. However, if you want to monitor the logs on more than a few systems, you need to find ways to automate the process. We discuss this topic in detail in Chapter 12.

Setting the Characteristics of the Event Log File

The system event raw data is stored in a series of log files—one per event class—located in the directory *%SystemRoot%\System32\Config*; these files have the extension *.EVT.* The Event Viewer's **Log** menu has several items for managing these log files:

- Archive log files with **File➤Save As**.

- Use **Log➤Clear All Events** to empty the log file for the kind of events currently being viewed (i.e., system, security, or application). You will have the option of archiving the current data before it is deleted.

- Specify the size and other characteristics of the log files with **Log➤Log Settings**. Figure 2-5 shows the resulting dialog box.

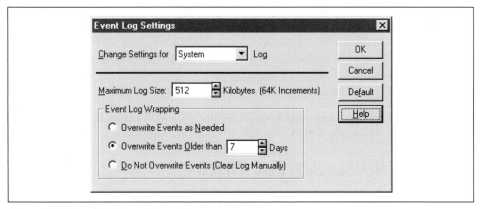

Figure 2-5. Specifying Event Log settings

The **Event Log Wrapping** area specifies what should be done if the event log file reaches its maximum size. **Overwrite Events as Needed** ensures that all new events are recorded. In this mode, the event log acts as a circular buffer: when the list reaches the end of the file, recording continues at the beginning. **Overwrite Events Older than** *n* **Days** allows you to specify the minimum age of events that are overwritten; in this mode, when the log file is at its maximum size and all qualifying events have been overwritten, event recording will cease. The final option, **Do Not Overwrite Events**, stops event recording when the log file becomes full.

If you choose either of the final two options, it's important to archive and clear the event log regularly to avoid missing important system messages.

Determining the Time of the Last System Boot

The Event Viewer would be a logical place to find out when the system was last booted. However, this event is not, in fact, always recorded, although the time when the event log service was last started will give some indication of the most recent boot-time.

You can easily determine when the system was booted using the **net statistics** command:

```
C:\> net statistics server
Server Statistics for \\VALA

Statistics since 6/17/97 2:52 PM
...
```

The second nonblank line of output gives the time of the last boot as the beginning of the period covered by the rest of the command's output.

The freely available **SysInfo** utility, written by Mika Malo, can also be used to determine how long the system has been up:

```
C:\> sysinfo

    OS: Windows NT version 4.0 build 1381
   Cpu: 1 x pentium
  User: Administrator
System: VALA
Uptime: 0 Day(s) 22 Hour(s) 54 Minute(s) 32 Second(s)
```

Managing Server Facilities

Windows NT systems are designed to provide resources and services to users and computers on the network. Such systems function as servers of various types, regardless of which Windows NT product (Server or Workstation) they are running. Windows NT systems run a collection of system processes that provide these services. These server processes are generally initiated at system startup. Windows NT provides the **Services** control panel for managing and configuring the services provided by the local system. The Server Manager administrative tool (provided on server systems) administers services on both local and remote computers; there are also several Windows NT commands that provide the same functionality.

After starting the Server Manager utility (via the **Start➤Programs➤Administrative Tools (Common)➤Server Manager** menu path or the **srvmgr** command), you select the computer whose services you want to manage from the list in its main windows and then choose **Computer➤Services**.... Opening the **Services** control panel performs the same operation automatically for the local system.

Stopping and Starting Services

Once the **Services** dialog box is open, its **Start**, **Stop**, **Pause**, and **Continue** buttons may be used to initiate, terminate, temporarily pause, and resume the selected service, respectively. The following **net** commands perform the same task:

- The **net start** and **net stop** commands start and stop the service specified as their argument.

- The **net pause** and **net continue** pause and resume the specified server process.

You can obtain a list of currently running services by executing **net start** without an argument. However, the **SCList** utility included in the Resource Kit performs the same job in a superior manner. Without any options, the command lists all installed services along with their current state. Including the **/S** or **/R** option limits the list to services that are stopped or running (respectively). You can also include a system name to list the services on a remote system. For example, the following command lists the services installed on the system in the local domain named *pele*:

```
C:\> sclist /R pele
-----------------------------------
- Service list for pele
-----------------------------------
running        Alerter              Alerter
running        AutoExNT             AutoExNT
running        Browser              Computer Browser
...
```

When specifying a service to any of these commands, you may use either the short or full version of the service name given in **sclist**'s output. Enclose any name containing embedded spaces in double quotation marks.

The **NetSvc** utility in the Resource Kit can query and manipulate individual services on remote hosts. It has the following syntax:

netsvc *service* *computer* /*subcommand*

where *service* is the name of the desired service, *computer* is the name of the system whose service you want to affect (it may be the local host), and *subcommand* specifies the operation you want to perform. The most useful defined subcommands are **/start**, **/stop**, **/pause**, **/continue**, and **/query** (to determine service's current status). They are equivalent to the corresponding **net** commands.

Configuring Services

You can specify various aspects of how a service executes using the **Startup...** button in the **Services** dialog box; Figure 2-6 shows the resulting dialog box.

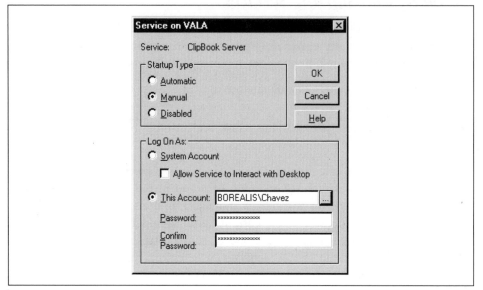

Figure 2-6. Configuring a service

The **Startup Type** field specifies whether the service is started automatically at boot-time, must be started manually by the system administrator, or is disabled entirely (and thus may not be started by any means).

By default, services are executed using the *System* account, which has unlimited privileges and access to system resources. The **Log On As** area allows you to specify an alternate user account to be used for running the service. For example, Figure 2-6 indicates that the specified service be run from the *Chavez* user account rather than as *System*. In general, services should be run with the least privilege necessary for them to function correctly. Some services must be run as *System*, but others are more securely run via a special user account created and configured expressly for that purpose. We return to this topic in Chapter 10.

Each individual service is also enabled or disabled within each defined *hardware profile*: a predefined set of system configuration and service startup settings that may be selected at boot-time. The **Service** dialog box's **HW Profiles...** button allows you to specify this setting for the currently selected service. Figure 2-7 illustrates this facility; it indicates that the AutoExNT service is enabled in the Original Configuration hardware profile (which is the default) and is disabled in the other saved hardware profile.

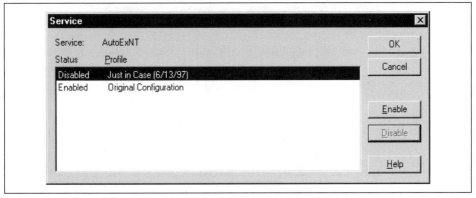

Figure 2-7. Enabling and disabling services by hardware profile

This service characteristic may define a hardware profile that contains only the bare minimum functionality required to access the local system. System administrators familiar with the UNIX environment can use it to configure a hardware profile that is more or less analogous to single user mode (see Appendix A for more information).

NOTE   You can use the hardware profiles facility to create a boot configuration similar to UNIX's single user mode by disabling all but a few essential services.

Redirecting System Alerts

The Server Manager facility may also be used to configure the desired recipients for system alert messages (by default, they are sent to administrators on the local system). These messages rely on the Alerter and Messenger services on the local system and the Messenger system on any remote system to which you want to direct them.

In the Server Manager, select the computer whose alert destination you want to configure and then use the **Computer▸Properties** menu path (double-clicking on the server name is equivalent). Select the **Alerts** button on the **Server** dialog box to reach the **Alerts** dialog box (Figure 2-8); the same button in the **Server** control panel applet also allows you to configure alert destinations for the local system.

You specify the desired user account name or computer name (which corresponds to the alerts destination on that system) by entering the name in the **New**

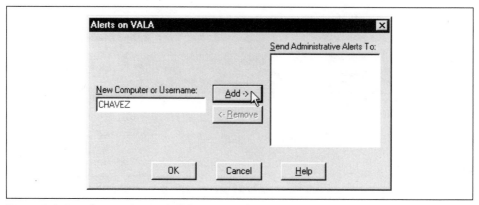

Figure 2-8. Specifying a destination for system alert messages

Computer or Username field and then clicking the **Add** button. The dialog box may also be used to remove items from the current list.

You must restart the Alerter and Server services for the changes to take effect:

```
C:\> net stop alerter & net stop server
...
C:\> net start server & net start alerter
```

Creating a System Initialization Script (Reviving AutoExec.Bat)

By default, Windows NT doesn't use system installation scripts at boot-time the way that many other operating systems do. However, the Resource Kit includes a service that allows you to specify a system startup script. Installing this facility involves these steps:

- Move the files *AutoExNT.Exe* and *ServMess.DLL* from wherever you've installed the Resource Kit files to *%SystemRoot%\System32*.

- Add the AutoExNT service using the **InstExNT** utility included in the Resource Kit:

  ```
  C:\> instexnt install [/interactive]
  ```

  Include the **/interactive** option if you want to enable the initialization script process to appear in the system process list and be accessible from the desktop.

- Create a Windows NT script file containing the desired commands and save it in text format as *%SystemRoot%\System32\AutoExNT.Bat*. Set the file ownership and protection as appropriate. The user account from which you plan to use the service should own it, and only this user and administrators should have anything but read access to the file (and possibly not even read access; these topics are discussed in detail in Chapter 10). As always, run this service with the minimum required privileges, creating a new user account for it if appropriate.

- Start the AutoExNT service via the **net start autoexnt** command or the **Services** control panel applet. Note that the service will fail to start if you forget to create the *AutoExNT.Bat* file first.

- Perform any additional desired configuration for the service via the usual mechanisms in the **Services** control panel.

Here is a simple *AutoExNT.Bat* script:

```
echo "Running AutoExNT.Bat" >> C:\Admin_Bin\Boot.Log
date /T >> C:\Admin_Bin\Boot.Log
time /T >> C:\Admin_Bin\Boot.Log

C:\WinNT\net.exe start lpdsvc >> C:\Admin_Bin\Boot.Log

if exist C:\NTTools\NAVNT\N32ScanW ^
   C:\NTTools\NAVNT\N32ScanW E:\

C:\Admin_Bin\Perl\Perl.Exe disk_sum.pl

echo "Clearing the scratch directory" >> C:\Admin_Bin\Boot.Log
if not exist E:\G98\Scratch mkdir E:\G98\Scratch
erase /Q /F E:\G98\Scratch\*.*
```

The beginning of the script notes the date and time of the boot in a log file. The next three commands start the service that handles incoming print jobs from UNIX systems, perform a virus scan, and run a Perl script that summarizes and records current disk usage statistics for this system. The next section of the script ensures that a scratch directory, *E:\G98\Scratch* (used by an application program), exists and is empty. The **if** command creates the directory if it does not exist, and the following **erase** command removes all files within that directory.

This sample file illustrates several of the important principles to keep in mind whenever you create system scripts:

- Use full pathnames for all nonbuilt-in commands.

- Make the script as conservative as possible. Check to make sure that a service the script needs has already been started or that a file it needs is present, since you can't be sure at exactly what point in the boot process the script will run. In addition, be aware that initialization scripts often end up being run in other contexts and at other times than those for which their writers originally designed them.

- Handle all of the cases that might arise from any given action, not just the ones that you expect to result. This often includes handling invalid arguments to the script and providing a usage message.

- Provide lots of informational and error messages for the administrators who will see the results of the script.

WARNING   The *AutoExNT.Bat* file runs near the end of the boot process. Note, however, that the operating system allows user access to the system while this script is running. In other words, there is no guarantee that the commands in the file will be completed before users gain access to the system.

Resources for Custom Services

The Resource Kit contains three facilities designed to install and remove system services:

- The Service Creation Wizard (**SrvInstW**) may be used to install and remove services on the local system and on remote hosts. The **InstSrv** command also provides this functionality from the command line. Both of these commands can install executables already prepared to run as services.* For example, the following command installs the specified executable as a service named Ticker:

  `C:\> instsrv Ticker D:\Exp_StkTk\StkTkr.Exe`

  Further service configuration may be done using the **Services** control panel applet. The service may similarly be removed with the command **instsrv Ticker remove**.

- The **SrvAny** program is designed to enable arbitrary applications to be installed as services. In this scheme, the **SrvAny** program must first be installed and configured as a service itself, and then some keys are added to the registry indicating the application controlled by that instance of **SrvAny**. See the documentation included with the facility for details. Be aware that it may take a significant amount of effort to configure some applications as a service.

- The **DelSrv** utility may be used to delete installed services. It takes the short service name given by the **SCList** command as its argument. Use this command with care.

---

* For example, applications must handle the WM_ENDSESSION or CTRL_LOGOFF_EVENT signals from the operating system.

System Shutdown

A system shutdown can be initiated in several ways:

- By selecting the **Shut Down...** command on the **Start** menu

- By pressing the CTRL-ALT-DELETE key combination and then selecting the **Shut Down...** button

- Via the **shutdown** command or the **shutgui** utility included in the Resource Kit

I find the **shutdown** command to be both the fastest and the most configurable method for shutting down a production system. It has the following syntax:

```
shutdown /L | \\computer [message] [options]
```

The command's first argument is either /L (for a local shutdown) or a computer name (to shut down a remote system). The optional *message* is displayed in the dialog box announcing the upcoming shutdown. The other available options are:

/R　Reboot immediately after shutting down.

/A　Abort a pending shutdown (overrides all other options).

/T:n

Wait n seconds before shutting down (the default is 20).

/Y　Preanswer all prompts with yes (e.g., confirmation prompts to save changes in current applications).

/C　Kill all running applications without saving changes first.

For example, the following command shuts down and reboots the local system in 30 seconds without any further prompting:

```
C:\> shutdown /L /t:30 /y /r "Brief reboot to install new software."
```

The **shutgui** utility provides a graphical interface to the same functionality.

A system shutdown begins by terminating any currently running applications and goes on to stop the various system services. Network connections are also closed.

The final step is to flush all remaining disk buffers; this phase can be identified by the **Please wait while the system writes unsaved data to the disk** message. This operation is necessary because Windows NT tends to postpone disk write operations as long as possible. If you turn the system power off while this activity is still in progress, data loss can easily result. Similarly, if the system loses power, unflushed disk buffers can again cause data loss. In Chapter 5 we discuss the **NTSync** utility, which can force such data to be written to disk.

3

User Accounts

Managing user accounts is one of a system administrator's most frequent tasks. User accounts are the means by which individual users identify themselves to computer systems and gain access to their resources. They are also a central part of the Windows NT mechanism for protecting resources from unauthorized access. Thus, user accounts function a lot like the photo ID badges required by many facilities to distinguish employees and guests from outsiders.

From the system's point of view, a user account doesn't necessarily correspond to an actual person. A user account is simply an entity that can own files and execute programs. For example, some user accounts exist for the sole purpose of owning the collections of files and executing the processes required by a specific application or subsystem. In most cases, however, a user account represents a particular individual who can log in, create and modify files, run programs, and otherwise make use of the system.

User accounts have a variety of attributes associated with them, in addition to the username: membership in one or more groups, a password and password modification rules, valid login hours and workstation locations, dial-up access permissions, a user environment (potentially including the desktop configuration, a script run at login time, and a home directory), and a set of system privileges known as *user rights*. After considering some preliminary user account concepts, we'll look at each of these items in turn.

User Account Basics

On Windows NT systems, user accounts are identified by the associated username, which labels the account and often is some part of the full name of the user who uses that account. Usernames can be up to 20 characters long and can contain lowercase letters, uppercase letters, numerals, and most ordinary symbols; the illegal symbols are:

```
" \ / [ ] < > | : ; + ? , *
```

Periods and spaces are fine as long as at least one other character appears somewhere in the username. Thus, *King Richard 3!* is a valid username (if not a convenient one to type).

NOTE   If cross-platform compatibility is an issue, it's a good idea to select usernames that comply with the requirements of the relevant operating systems. Thus, *King Richard 3!* would be a poor choice for a user needing to access UNIX systems from his Windows NT account.

Usernames are case-aware, but not case-sensitive. This means that Windows NT will store a username in the case combination in which it is entered, but that it may be entered in any capitalization scheme at login time and in commands. Usernames must be unique.

On Windows NT systems, there are three kinds of user accounts, which the documentation and tools refer to as "global accounts," "local accounts," and "user accounts" (yes, the terminology could be clearer). The differences among them become clear once you understand that there are two distinct user account contexts: the domain and an isolated individual system.

A Windows NT domain is a collection of networked computers whose common resources and security are overseen by a server designated as the *primary domain controller* (PDC). This system may be assisted by one or more *backup domain controllers*, and the other systems in the domain are Windows NT workstations and standalone servers.

In this context, there are two types of user accounts. *Global accounts* are the normal type of user account that users within a domain receive. Such accounts are recognized by and are valid on all of the systems within the domain. They may also have access within other domains that trust their home domain (*trust* is defined more explicitly in Chapter 10).

The other sort of user account defined for a domain is a *local account*. It also has access to systems and resources within the domain, but not to anything beyond it that is normally granted to the domain's users. These accounts are designed for users from other untrusted domains who need access to specific resources within the domain. However, such accounts may not be used to log in interactively within the domain, and they can never gain access to systems in other domains via the trust mechanism (discussed in Chapter 10). In other words, the account is only recognized within its home domain.

Within the User Manager administrative tools, different icons are used for these two types of accounts. Global domain accounts are represented by a bust of a person wearing a teal shirt, and local domain accounts use an icon of this person next to a computer monitor. Accounts local to a particular system use the same icon as global domain accounts within the User Manager.

Individual systems that are not primary or backup domain controllers can also have additional user accounts that are truly local: valid only on that particular system and not for any sort of domain access. Such accounts are not even recognized within any domain context: when logging into the domain, when accessing shared files or resources within the domain, when setting file permissions and user rights, and so on.

The **Domain** field on the login dialog box specifies the domain context for the current login process. If a domain is selected, the specified username must correspond to a global account in that domain (local domain accounts can't be used for interactive logins). If the **Domain** field is set to the hostname of the local computer, the account is interpreted as a local account on that system (and domain accounts won't be recognized).

Windows NT *groups* are collections of users who may be granted identical access to files and other resources as a unit. There are three types of groups:

- *Global groups,* which are recognized by and may be granted access to computers and resources throughout the current domain and within any other domains that trust it. Global groups can only contain global domain user accounts as their members; placing a local user within a global group would defeat the purpose of local accounts. The User Manager icon for a global group is two people next to a globe.

- *Local groups* (at the domain level), which are recognized by and may be granted access to resources only within their home domain. Like local users, these groups are never recognized by other domains. User accounts from the local domain and from any trusted domain may be members of a local group. A global group from the local domain also may be a member of a local group, but not vice versa. The User Manager icon for a local group is two people next to a computer monitor.

- Systems that are not domain controllers can also define groups that are truly local to that system and not recognized within the domain context. Similarly, when a user is logged into a system locally, domain-wide groups are not defined or recognized.

We'll consider all of these possible permutations again when we discuss trust in Chapter 10.

User account settings are stored in the Security Accounts Manager (SAM) database. The data is stored in binary form and cannot be edited directly. The associated files are stored in the directory *%SystemRoot%\System32\Config*.

Windows NT provides several facilities for managing user accounts: the **Add User Accounts** wizard, the User Manager administrative tools, and several commands. As we examine the various characteristics of user accounts, we will use the graphical interface provided by the User Manager for convenience of illustration. This is not meant to imply that it is always the best thing to use to create or modify user accounts. In this chapter's final section, we consider the tools that are most suitable for managing large numbers of user accounts.

Standard Windows NT User Accounts and Groups

Windows NT provides several standard user accounts on every system:

Administrator
> This privileged account is designed for performing system administration tasks. It can obtain access to all files and directories and to every system facility.* Since it is so powerful, it should be used with great care and only when necessary.
>
> Additional administrator-level accounts can be created as needed by copying *Administrator*. If many people have administrative access, it's a good idea to create separate administrative accounts for each of them, allowing their actions to be distinguishable. All administrative accounts should have passwords assigned to them.

Guest
> An account designed for limited-time or occasional users. This account is disabled by default in Windows NT 4.0; I strongly recommend disabling it in earlier versions as well, as it is a notorious security hole. For all but the most

---

* Items may be temporarily protected against the *Administrator* account, but *Administrator* can always change their permissions to gain access.

open sites, having a single, essentially anonymous, guest account is not a good idea. It is generally better to create a site-specific guest account (less conspicuously named) or individual accounts for guest users, which are disabled or deleted once their work is complete.

If you decide to use guest accounts of any sort, be sure that each one is assigned a password. You will probably also want to disable the user's ability to change the password (discussed later in this chapter).

System

A pseudo-account used for running many server processes and for assigning file access permissions. This account cannot be used by any user for logging in, resource access, or other system activities.

Various system facilities and application programs also create standard user accounts when they are installed. For example, the Internet Information Server facility creates an account named *IUSR_host*, where *host* is the name of the computer. Similarly, the SQL Server application creates two accounts (on my system, they are named *SQLAcct* and *SQLExecutiveCmdExec*).

Windows NT also provides several standard groups. The following global groups are created by default within each domain:

Domain Admins

Containing the domain's *Administrator* account by default. Members of this group have administrative privileges within the domain. Only accounts for system administrators should be added to this group.

Domain Users

Containing all global user accounts in the domain.

Domain Guests

Containing the domain *Guest* account.

The following local groups are also created:

Administrators

Containing the *Administrator* account and the *Domain Admins* global group. Once again, members should be added to this group with care, as it has full administrative privileges.

Account Operators, Backup Operators, Print Operators, and *Server Operators*

Groups that are less privileged than *Administrators* but more privileged than ordinary users. Each is designed to perform a specific administrative support task, and the account has access into that system area only. By default, all of these groups are empty.

Replicator

> A group used by the Directory Replicator Service (this facility is discussed in Chapter 10).

Users

> A group designed to hold ordinary users. By default, the *Domain Users* global group is a member of this group. User accounts are not added to this group by default, however, so whether to use it or not is up to the system administrator.

Guests

> A group designed for guest accounts for the local domain. It includes the *Domain Guests* global group and the *IUSR_host* account if present.

Windows NT workstations also have a local group called *Power Users,* which is designed to hold user accounts for those users who need to or are allowed to share resources with other users on the network.

There are also several implied groups used for specifying file and resource access but which are not actual groups to which you can add members. These are the *Interactive, Network,* and *Everyone* groups, corresponding to logged-in users, users accessing a file or resource via the network, and everyone not explicitly mentioned elsewhere in the file or resource permission settings, respectively. We'll see them again when we discuss access control lists in Chapter 5.

NOTE   Service Pack 3 adds the built-in group *Authenticated Users* (which originated in a Hot Fix to Service Pack 2). This group corresponds to all users who have been authenticated by the system by presenting a valid username and password. It is designed to replace *Everyone* in security settings. See Chapter 10 for more details.

Creating and Modifying Accounts with the User Manager

There are two versions of the User Manager administrative tool: the User Manager for Domains (the command is **usrmgr**), which accesses domain accounts and groups, and the User Manager (**musrmgr**), which is used to manipulate local accounts and groups on workstations and stand-alone servers. The two versions use the same interface.

There are two ways to add a new user account with these graphical tools: by selecting the **User➤Add** menu path and by copying an existing account (select the account and then use **User➤Copy…**). The latter feature is especially useful when you have set up one or more template accounts: disabled accounts designed strictly as starting points for new user accounts.

You can modify an existing user account by double clicking on its name in the list of users that appears in the tool's main window.

Once you have taken any of these actions, you will be presented with the top-level user account dialog box, titled **User Properties** (Figure 3-1), from which you can specify any user account setting. We'll consider them in detail in the next section.

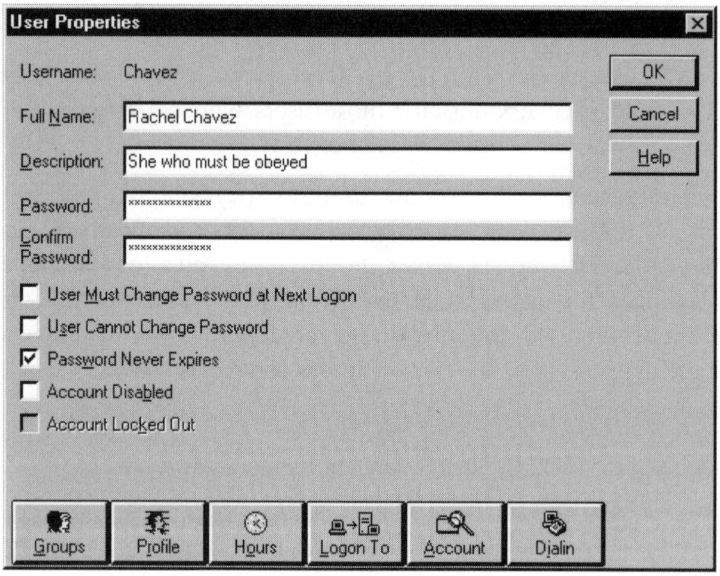

Figure 3-1. The User Properties dialog box

User Account Attributes

The **User Properties** dialog box contains fields for the user's full name, an optional description of the user account, and the account's password and account-specific password change settings. All other account attributes are reached via one of the buttons along the bottom of the dialog box:

Groups
    Specify group memberships for the account

Profile
    Specify various aspects of the account's startup environment

Hours
> Specify allowed hours of access to the system or domain

Logon To
> Specify allowed systems for interactive logins*

Account
> Specify the account type and expiration date

Dialin
> Specify settings for the Remote Access Service

Passwords and Password Policies

Passwords are the means by which users prove that they really are who they claim to be when they log in; more technically, passwords are the user account authentication method used by virtually all computer operating systems. A password is a case-sensitive character string that may contain letters, numerals, and symbols. Control characters, Alt-modified characters, and function keys are not allowed in Windows NT passwords. Although the password fields seem to accept Windows key-modified characters within a password, this modifier is ignored, and the characters are treated as if the Win key had not been depressed. The maximum password length is 14 characters.

NOTE   Passwords longer than eight characters can cause problems with
              some FTP client programs.

The passwords stored with the user accounts database are encoded using irreversible cryptographic techniques.† At login authentication, the *clear* (as entered) password and coded password are used to encrypt a block of data, and the results are compared. If they match, then the user entered the correct password.

Selecting Secure Passwords

Simply having a password is only the first step in making a user account secure. If the password is easy to find out or guess, it will provide little real protection. In

---

* The Windows NT user interface and documentation use the term "logon" to refer to the process of presenting one's credentials in order to gain access to a computer system. I use the term "login" for this process (which reveals my VMS and UNIX roots). Both of them mean the same thing.

† For this reason, they are often referred to as *encrypted passwords*, but this terminology is not technically accurate.

this section, we'll look at characteristics of good and bad passwords. The consider-ations discussed here apply both to choosing passwords for administrative accounts (which the system administrator chooses), and to user passwords. In the latter case, your input usually takes the form of educating users about good and bad choices.

The purpose of passwords is to prevent unauthorized people from accessing user accounts and the system in general. The basic selection principle is the following: *Passwords should be easy to remember, but hard to figure out, guess, or crack.*

The first part of the principle argues against assigned nonsense passwords, since they are hard for most people to remember. The second part of the principle means that passwords should be hard to guess, even if someone is willing to go to a fair amount of effort—and there are plenty of people who will if your system or site has something that they want. This means that the following items should be avoided as passwords or even as components of passwords:

*   Any part of your name or the name of any member of your extended family (including significant others and pets) and circle of friends. Your maternal grandmother's maiden name is a lot easier to find out than you might think.

*   Numbers significant to you or someone close to you: social security numbers, car license plate, phone number, birth dates, etc.

*   The name of something that is or was important to you, like your favorite food, recording artist, movie, TV character, place, sports team, hobby, etc. Similarly, if your thesis was on benzene, don't pick benzene as a password. The same goes for people, places, things you hate.

*   Any name, numbers, people, places, or other items associated with your com-pany or institution or its products.

I could list more such items, but this should illustrate the basic idea.

Passwords should also be as immune as possible to attack by password-cracking programs, which means that these items should not be selected as passwords:

*   English words spelled correctly (because lists of them are so readily available in online dictionaries). Given the wide and easy accessibility of online English dictionaries, this restriction is a good idea even at non-English-speaking sites. If two or more languages are in common use at your site, or in the area in which it's located, words in all of them should be avoided. Words in other sorts of published lists should also be avoided (for example, Klingon words).

*   Truncated words spelled correctly: "conseque" is just as bad as "conse-quence." Such strings are just as vulnerable to dictionary-based attacks as are the entire word, and most existing password-cracking programs specifically look for them.

- The names of famous people, places, things, fictional characters, movies, TV shows, songs, slogans, and the like.
- Published password examples.

Avoiding passwords like the items in the first list makes it harder for someone to figure out your password. Avoiding the items in the second list makes it harder for someone to successfully break into an account using a brute force trial and error method, like a computer program.

If it seems farfetched to you that someone would go to the trouble of finding out a lot about you just to break into your computer account, keep in mind that hackers roaming around on the Internet looking for a system to break into represent only one kind of security threat. In many, many cases, the bad guys target specific sites or systems, and getting on the system via any account is their first step. The account that opens the door need not necessarily have any obvious connection to the ultimate goal.

Simple modifications of any of these bad passwords, such as adding a single additional character, spelling it backward, or permuting the letters, are still bad passwords and ought to be avoided. For example, avoid not only "john" but also "nhoj" and "ohnj" and "john2." It doesn't take a password-guessing program very long to try all combinations of adding one character, reversing, and permuting.

Although they are risky themselves, items from the second list can serve as the base for creating a better password (I don't recommend using any personal items in passwords at all). Passwords that use two or more of the following modifications to ordinary words are much more likely to be good choices:

- Embedding one or more extra characters, especially symbols.
- Misspelling it by replacing one or more characters with a different one or swapping the places of two or more characters.
- Using unusual capitalization. All lowercase is not unusual; capitalization or inverse capitalization by word is not unusual (e.g., "StarTrek," "sTARtREK"); always capitalizing vowels is not unusual.
- Concatenating two or more words or parts of words to form something that is not another word.
- Embedding one word in the middle of another word ("kitdogten" embeds "dog" within "kitten").
- Interleaving two or more words: for example, "cdaotg" interleaves "dog" and "cat." With a little practice, some people can do this easily in their heads; others can't. If you need any significant delay between characters as you type in such a password, don't use them.

Table 3-1 illustrates some of these recommendations, using "StarTrek" as a base (although I'd recommend avoiding anything having to do with Star Trek in passwords altogether).

Table 3-1. Creating Good Passwords from Bad Ones

Bad	Better	Better Still
StarTrek *predictable capitalization*	sTartRek *unusual capitalization*	sTarkErT *unusual capitalization and reversal*
startrak *misspelling*	starTrak *misspelling and unusual capitalization*	$tarTra# *misspelling, symbols and unusual capitalization*
StarDrek *slang*	jetrekdi *embedding*	jetr@kdi *embedding and symbols*
trekstar *word swapping*	sttraerk *interleaving*	sttr@erK *interleaving, unusual capitalization, and symbols*

Of course, these would all be poor choices now. When selecting passwords and advising users about how to do so, keep in mind the overall goal that passwords be hard to guess, for humans and programs, but easy to remember and fast to type.

When choosing successive passwords—and especially administrative passwords—try to avoid falling into a recognizable pattern. For example, if you always capitalize all the vowels, and someone knows this, you effectively lose the value of the unusual capitalization. Similarly, successive passwords are often chosen in the same way; don't always choose names of planets for your passwords. Having two or three recognizable patterns is nearly as bad as sticking to one pattern all the time. It is especially important to break such patterns when someone with long-time access to an administrative account—and hence well aware of past patterns in passwords—leaves the system or loses his administrative access.

A current fad in password selection is to form a password from the initial letters of each word in a memorable phrase, often a song lyric. Such passwords are easy to remember despite being nonsense strings. Transforming the resulting string results in an even better password. Two examples are given in Table 3-2.

Table 3-2. Forming Passwords from Memorable Phrases[a]

Phrase	Password	Better Password
"Now it's a disco, but not for Lola"	niadbnfl	Ni1db!4L
"I can well recall the first time I ever went to sea"	icwrtftiewts	@cWrt1t@eW2c

[a] The lines are from the songs *Copacabana*, by Barry Manilow, and *Old Admirals*, by Al Stewart. Naturally, you wouldn't want to use either of these passwords now.

As the second password illustrates in Table 3-2, you don't have to limit yourself to eight characters under Windows NT. Keep in mind that longer passwords are harder to crack.

The **User Properties** dialog box also contains several check boxes controlling when a user can and must change her password:

User Must Change Password at Next Logon
When checked, this setting will force the user to change her password the next time she logs in.

User Cannot Change Password
If checked, the user is not allowed to change her password.

Password Never Expires
If checked, the system or domain password expiration settings do not apply to this account.

Account Disabled
If checked, the account is disabled and may not be used for any sort of system access.

Account Locked Out
This field is checked when an account is locked (disabled) by the system because the number of login failures exceeded the maximum for the system or domain. The system administrator can unlock the account by clearing this check box. However, the box can't be checked manually (use the **Account Disabled** field to accomplish this).

The System/Domain Password Policy

You can set a few restrictions on passwords for all user accounts via the User Manager's **Policies▶Account** menu path. The corresponding dialog box is illustrated in Figure 3-2.

The various areas of this dialog box each specify one characteristic for valid passwords and password use:

Maximum Password Age
Specifies how long users may keep any password before they are forced to change it. The default is 42 days. Whether or not to use this feature depends on the level of security required by your site and how responsible your users are. For example, an isolated site of software developers probably doesn't need to have passwords expire. At the other extreme, a university network connected to the Internet should definitely use the password expiration feature. When using this feature, I generally specify a value of six months,

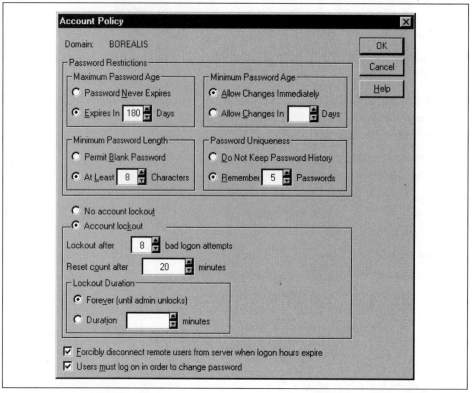

Figure 3-2. Password policies

although a shorter period may make more sense in some cases (for example, the length of a quarter or semester).

Minimum Password Age

Determines how long after a user changes his password he can change it again, in other words, how long he must keep any new password that he selects. The idea behind mechanisms like this one is to keep a user from simply changing his password and then changing it right back after a forced change from a password expiration. The default is to allow immediate changes. When I use password expiration periods, I set this to at least two days.

Minimum Password Length

The minimum number of characters in a valid password. The default setting allows blank passwords (0 characters). The minimum prudent value for this setting is 8 which I tend to use for compatibility with other operating systems. A higher value of 12 or more provides nontrivial improvement in password security, provided that good passwords are chosen. The maximum value is 14.

Password Uniqueness

Specifies how frequently old passwords can be reused. If the **Remember __ Passwords** field is filled in, the system will store this many coded passwords for each user account, and users will not be allowed to select any of them as a new password. The default value is 0 (disabling the feature), and the maximum value is 24. This setting is also designed to discourage users from attempting to evade required password changes by oscillating between a small number of passwords. I usually set this field to 10.

The settings in the **Account lockout** area determine various parameters controlling automatic account locking:

- The **Lockout after __ bad logon attempts** field indicates how many failed login attempts must accumulate before the account is locked. This number needs to be higher than you might initially guess, because failed login attempts can occur as part of normal network access to the system. For example, if a user attempts to use a system resource on a system where his password is different than on his current system (the system where he is logged in), then two or more failed logins will be generated automatically as Windows NT presents his current, invalid password to the remote server. Figure 3-3 shows the security events generated by such an action. In this case, two of the three failures (indicated by the lock icon) occurred before the dialog box appeared; only the third corresponds to a genuine typing error.

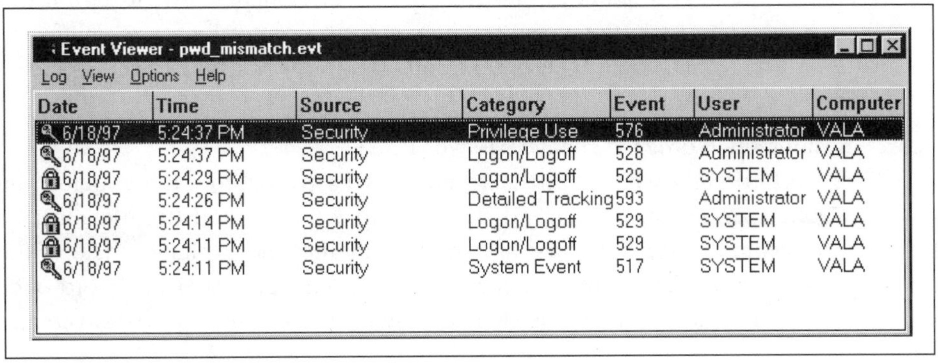

Date	Time	Source	Category	Event	User	Computer
6/18/97	5:24:37 PM	Security	Privilege Use	576	Administrator	VALA
6/18/97	5:24:37 PM	Security	Logon/Logoff	528	Administrator	VALA
6/18/97	5:24:29 PM	Security	Logon/Logoff	529	SYSTEM	VALA
6/18/97	5:24:26 PM	Security	Detailed Tracking	593	Administrator	VALA
6/18/97	5:24:14 PM	Security	Logon/Logoff	529	SYSTEM	VALA
6/18/97	5:24:11 PM	Security	Logon/Logoff	529	SYSTEM	VALA
6/18/97	5:24:11 PM	Security	System Event	517	SYSTEM	VALA

Event Viewer - pwd_mismatch.evt
Log View Options Help

Figure 3-3. Events generated by a password mismatch

Such invalid logins are generated before the user is ever presented with a dialog box requesting a valid username and password. You will need to take this into account in selecting the value for this setting.

- After the amount of time specified in the **Reset count after** field has elapsed from the most recent login failure, the count is reset to 0. The failure count is also reset after a successful login.

The interaction between these two fields specifies how the system reacts to a string of failed logins (such as someone trying to guess a password). For example, if the account lockout parameters are set to 5 attempts and 30 minutes, then someone can guess four bad passwords without locking the account, but then he has to wait 30 minutes before trying four more.

I generally use automatic account locking with values of 8 to 10 attempts and several hours. With these settings, I can be reasonably sure that the account will not be locked inadvertently through normal use and that a potential intruder will have to wait much longer than she is likely to before trying again.

- The **Lockout duration** field specifies how long the account remains locked if the automatic locking mechanism is triggered. The default is 30 minutes. When I use account locking, I generally set this field to **Forever** since I want to be sure that I speak to the user if the account becomes locked.

Automatic account lockout is disabled by default. When it is enabled, by default accounts are locked after five failed login attempts, the reset period is 30 minutes, and locked accounts are unlocked automatically after 30 minutes.

The two remaining fields in the dialog box:

Forcibly disconnect remote users from server when logon hours expire
> If checked, users are disconnected from all applicable resources when their accounts' valid login hours expire (they are set elsewhere, as we'll see). If this field is not checked (the default), then current connections are unaffected when a user's valid login time period ends, but he won't be allowed to create any new connections.

Users must log on in order to change password
> This field controls what happens when a user's password expires before he has gotten around to changing it. If this field is unchecked (the default), he simply has to change it the first time he logs in after the expiration date. If the field is checked, then only an administrator can change a user password once it has expired, and the user is denied system access until the password has been changed.

Additional password controls

Many computer systems include facilities where the system administrator can specify additional characteristics of valid passwords; these *triviality checks* are designed to increase the likelihood that users select secure passwords. Windows NT includes an optional facility of this sort, included starting in Service Pack 2. It consists of a DLL for "strong" password filtering, which requires passwords to fulfill the following requirements:

- Must be at least six characters in length

- May not contain the username or the user's full name as any part of them

- Must contain three of these four character types: lowercase letters, uppercase letters, numerals, and symbols

To enable this feature, copy the *PassFilt.DLL* file to the *%SystemRoot%\System32* directory. Then add the value PASSFILT to the registry key HKEY_LOCAL_MACHINE\System\CurrentControlSet\Control\Lsa\Notification Packages. Note that this is a multivalued key (REG_MULTI_SZ). Take care not to remove any existing entries (e.g., FPNWCLNT) when you add the new entry (on its own line) to the end of the list.

This facility also accepts a custom version of *PassFilt.DLL*; see the article Q161990 in the Knowledge Base for details on creating one.

The Resource Kit also contains the **PassProp** utility, which can enable or disable password triviality testing once this library is installed.

When to Change Passwords

We'll conclude our consideration of passwords by looking at circumstances that require password changes. For example, make sure that there are no unprotected user accounts. This includes both accounts without passwords and active accounts for users who have left that are still protected by their original passwords. When a user leaves, always disable her account or change the password if it must remain active for some reason.

Passwords must be changed under any of these (and similar) conditions:

- Whenever someone other than its owner learns it, the password needs to be changed.

- When a system administrator leaves, all administrator passwords that she knew must be changed. Whether to force users to change their passwords at this time is a matter of discretion, but keep in mind that the system administrator had full access to the user accounts database. Thus, when a system administrator is fired or quits, every password on the system should be changed, since she had access to the file that has the encoded passwords and could potentially crack them at her leisure.

  We will see a utility for forcing users to change their passwords in Chapter 12.

- If you have even a suspicion that the user accounts database files have been copied by an unauthorized person, the prudent action is, again, to change every password.

Assigning Group Memberships

Groups are a mechanism that enables collections of users to share files and other system resources. As such, they provide one of the cornerstones of system security. We discuss using groups effectively as part of an overall system security plan in detail in Chapter 10.

Each user must be a member of at least one group. Users can optionally be members of multiple groups. On Windows NT systems, all of a user's group memberships are always active and consulted for resource access. One of the groups of which a user is a member is designated as his *primary group*. In practice, however, which group is chosen is of little importance, since this mechanism is currently used only by the POSIX and Macintosh services subsystems.

There are several ways of assigning group memberships to a user account:

- Use the **Groups** button on the **User Properties** dialog box and then use the **Group Memberships** dialog box to change the account's group memberships as desired.

- Double-click on a group in the User Manager's lower window and then add users to the group (or remove users from it) via the **Group Properties** dialog box.

- The **net group** and **net localgroup** commands may be used to manipulate Windows NT groups from the command line. They are discussed in the this chapter's final section.

Adding a new group is very similar to adding a new user account. You can create one from scratch (via items on the User Manager's **User** menu), or you can copy and then modify an existing group. Defining a group consists of assigning it a name and providing a brief description of the group. Members can be immediately added to a new group.

User Account Access Controls

Windows NT provides some simple facilities for specifying when and where a user is allowed to log in. The **User Properties** dialog box's **Hours**, **Logon To**, and **Account** buttons provide one means of access to these settings.

Figure 3-4 illustrates the **Logon Hours** dialog box reached via the **Hours** button. It may be used to set specific time periods each day when a user's access to the system is allowed and forbidden. Access is granted for periods covered by a solid bar and denied for periods corresponding to blank white boxes. In this example, user *Chavez* is allowed access on weekdays except from 2:00 A.M. to 5:00 A.M.

On Saturdays, she is allowed access only between 6:00 A.M. and 6:00 P.M., and she is not allowed any access at all on Sundays.

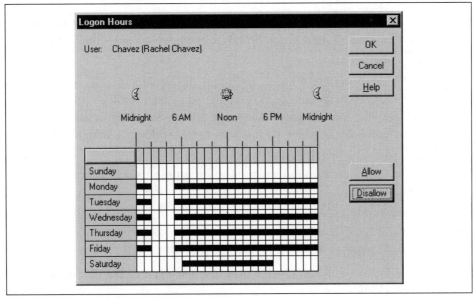

Figure 3-4. Specifying allowed login times

For domain user accounts, the **Logon To** button brings up a dialog box where you may specify up to eight systems at which the user is allowed to log in. If you decide to use this feature, be aware that the listed systems will be the only ones from which the user can gain access to the domain. What do you do if you want to give her access to more than eight systems? Unfortunately, at the moment the answer to this question is: *don't want that.* The current choices are limited to universal workstation access and subsets of eight or fewer workstations, and there is no way to allow access to all workstations except a specified set.

The **Log on locally** user right is another means for controlling whether or not a user can log in interactively to a system (user rights are discussed in detail in Chapter 10). On Windows NT workstations, this right is given to all user accounts by default, while on domain controller server systems, it is limited to administrators.

The **Account** button on the **User Properties** dialog for domain accounts allows you to specify whether a user account is local or global and to set an expiration date for the account. If set, the account is automatically disabled when the expiration date arrives. By default, user accounts don't expire.

Customizing the User Account Environment

Windows NT offers a variety of mechanisms for customizing the work environment associated with a user account. In this section, we consider three of them:

User profiles
> A stored set of system settings, including the desktop layout, system menu configuration and customization, and the like. User profiles provide a user with a familiar, personalized Windows NT environment regardless of the particular computer at which he happens to be working at any given time.

Home directories
> A specific filesystem location assigned to each user, usually intended to be his primary file storage site.

Login scripts
> A command file run automatically each time the user logs in, allowing you to ensure that specific operations are always performed at that time.

All three items can be assigned to a user account via the **Profile** button on the **User Properties** dialog box.

User Profiles

The **User Profile Path** field in the **User Environment Profile** dialog box (Figure 3-5) specifies the location of the user's user profile file. The path in that location should be fully qualified. It may refer to a directory on the local system or to a shared directory on a server (as is the case in the figure). If you want the same profile to be used on different computers, then the latter form is preferred.

A user profile includes the following components of the user environment:

- Items on the desktop and the desktop layout
- The configuration of the taskbar and the **Start** menu
- Control panel settings
- The contents of the **Programs➤Accessories** menu and settings associated with these utilities
- Settings for defined network printers
- Some application settings
- Help bookmarks

A user profile is created automatically if one doesn't exist the first time the user changes any of these items from their defaults; this profile is a copy of the *Default*

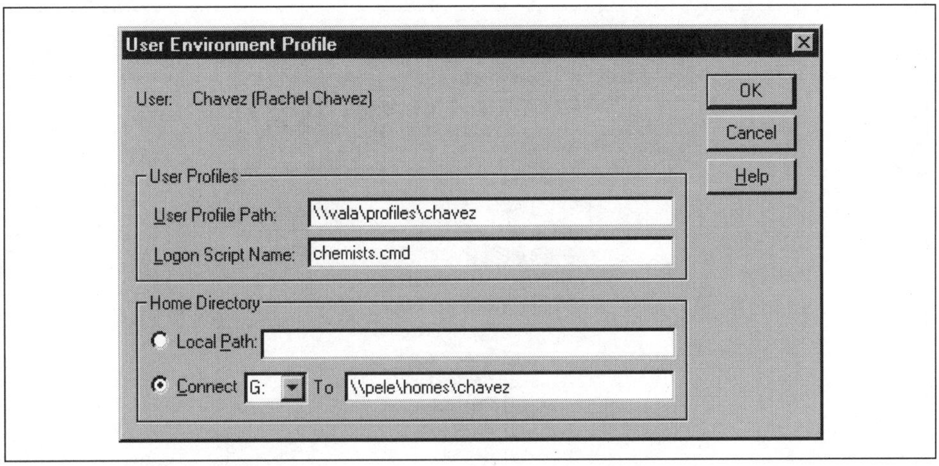

Figure 3-5. Specifying the user account environment

User profile. You can modify this default user profile to provide a customized default initial user environment if desired.

There are three types of user profiles. *Local* user profiles are specific to a single computer system and are not available elsewhere. *Roaming* user profiles are stored in a network-accessible directory and are used on every computer the user logs into, unless the directory is unavailable for some reason. *Mandatory* user profiles are required, read-only, roaming user profiles. They are also stored in a directory accessible via the network. If this directory is currently unavailable when a user tries to log in, then she will not be allowed to log in to the domain (although any local account she may have on the computer will still be available).

Under Windows NT version 4, a user profile consists of a subdirectory tree storing all of its components (in earlier versions, the user profile was stored as a single file). Its structure is displayed in Figure 3-6, which shows an explorer view of user *Chavez*'s user profile.

The top-level user profile directory also contains a file named *NTUser.Dat,* which stores registry settings associated with the user profile.

Generally, roaming and mandatory user profiles are copied from the server when the user logs in (the exception occurs when the locally cached copy of a roaming user profile is more recent than the version on the server). Changes to local user profiles are saved on the local computer when he logs off again, and changes to a roaming user profile are saved both in the locally cached copy and on the server (if accessible).

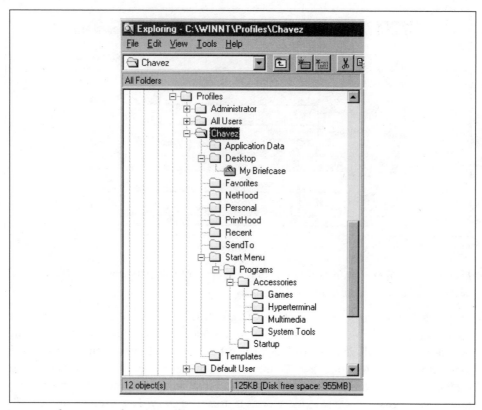

Figure 3-6. Contents of a user profile

We'll now focus our attention on roaming and mandatory user profiles for domain user accounts. These profiles are typically stored in the *%SystemRoot%\Profiles* directory on the primary domain controller.

Creating a roaming user profile

The procedure for creating a roaming user profile is quite straightforward:

- Make sure that the *%SystemRoot%\Profiles* directory is shared (shares are discussed in Chapter 5) and set the appropriate permissions on the directory (see Chapters 6 and 10).

- Copy an existing user profile using the **User Profile** tab on the **System** control panel applet; select the user profile to copy from the list of available profiles, and then click on the **Copy To...** button. Enter the path to the top-level directory for the target user profile in the **Copy profile to** field. For example, if you are creating a profile for user *Goren*, then enter *C:\WinNT\Profiles\Goren* into this field. The specified subdirectory is created if it doesn't already exist.

It's often useful to create several template accounts to serve as starting user profiles for various classes of users. These profiles can be set up once and copied quickly when a new user account is created. If you decide to use this strategy, be sure to disable any such accounts.

- Associate a user account or a group with the new profile using the **Permitted to use** area's **Change** button. You may select any group or user account from the list of names in the resulting **Choose User** dialog box. By default, the list contains only the names of groups. Use the **Show Users** button to display the names of all user accounts in the list (the user list will follow the group list after you click this button). Once you have selected a user account or group name, use the **Add** button to copy it to the **Add Name** field.

    Of course, the quickest way to use this dialog box is to type the name of the desired user account or group directly into the **Add Name** field.

- Specify the appropriate directory path to the user profile for the corresponding user account in the User Manager (**User➤Properties…➤Profile**). This step can be a little tricky. Be sure that you specify the profile path via its network shared path, not its local path (i.e., as *\\vala\profiles\Chavez* and not as *C:\WinNT\Profiles\Chavez*, for example). Keep in mind that the profile path is interpreted *locally* on every computer that the user logs into, so you must use a fully qualified network-accessible path to refer to the same location in every computer context. If you specify a local path, that path is used on *each* computer at which the user logs in.

- Log in as that user and modify the profile as necessary.

When creating roaming user profiles, be aware of any hardware differences among the various workstations at which the user is likely to log in. The most common difference is in the display type. If you need to create a roaming user profile to use on computers with different types of displays, set the display type in the user profile to one that they all support (i.e., the lowest common denominator), usually VGA or SVGA mode.

Making a profile mandatory

When roaming user profiles are used, users still have the ability to select between the roaming user profile and the local user profile via the **System** control panel applet (**User Profiles➤Change Type**). The profile type they select in the **Change Type** dialog box will be used the next time they log in.

Mandatory user profiles provide a way of preventing users from overriding the configuration you have set up. Mandatory profiles are downloaded from the server when the user logs in (although a cached local copy is used if available). If a user's mandatory profile is not available when he wants to log in, he is refused access to the domain. Any changes a user makes to a mandatory user profile are discarded when he logs out.

Before you implement mandatory user profiles, be certain that they provide the best mechanism for the effect you are trying to accomplish. The Windows NT user profile mechanism is designed to enable you to provide users with a consistent and convenient user environment; it is not really intended as a means for setting up or enforcing a security policy, although it can be used to accomplish this to a limited extent. In general, if you are considering mandatory user profiles to limit users' activities, then you probably want to use the system policy facility instead (discussed in Chapter 10), which is specifically designed for this purpose.

Use the following procedure to convert a roaming user profile to a mandatory user profile:

- Rename the *NTUser.Dat* file in the corresponding top-level profile subdirectory to *NTUser.Man*.

- Add the *.Man* extension to the name of the user's folder under *%SystemRoot%\Profiles* (yielding *username.Man*).*

- Change the user account's profile path in the User Manager.

Mandatory user profiles may also be assigned to a group of users to provide an identical user environment to all of the group's members. To create and assign a mandatory user profile to a group, use the following procedure:

- Create a new user profile as described in the preceding subsection, and associate the desired group with it using the **System** control panel (**User Profiles➤Copy To...➤Change...**).

- Convert the profile to a mandatory user profile.

- Select the desired group via the User Manager's **User➤Select Users...** menu path.

- Modify the user accounts within the specified group via **User➤Properties...➤Profile**, entering the corresponding user profile subdirectory into the **User Profile Path** field of the **User Environment Profile** dialog box.

Designating a Home Directory

The User Manager's **User Environment Profile** dialog box (**User➤Properties...➤Profile**) contains a field specifying the user's home directory. If defined, this directory becomes the default for many file open and save operations and for

---

* Mandatory profile folders updated from NT 3.51 use the **.PDM** extension instead.

some applications without a predefined default directory. Command windows also use the user account home directory as their initial current directory.

There are two options for specifying the home directory location:

- Use the **Local Path** field to specify a fully qualified path on the local computer to the desired directory. You will need to create the directory manually, but it need not exist when you specify it to the User Manager.

- Use the **Connect** fields to specify a directory anywhere on the network and to assign a drive letter to it. It is common practice to assign the same drive letter to the home directory for every user. Be sure that you select a letter that is high enough not to conflict with any physical or mapped drive on any system (*Z:* is often chosen to avoid such problems). Home directory drive letters can also be assigned in the user's login script (as we'll see below).

When you assign a home directory to a user account, the directory is created automatically with the correct ownership.

You can remove a home directory definition from a user account by selecting the **Local Path** option and entering a blank path.

Login Scripts

The third aspect of the user environment that may be specified via the **User Environment Profile** dialog box is the user's login script. A login script is an executable file that runs automatically whenever the user logs in. Login scripts are often Windows NT command scripts or scripts written in another scripting language, but any executable file may be used.

NOTE   Login scripts don't modify the environment for subsequent user processes, so they shouldn't be used to set the values of environment variables. Use the Windows NT environment variable facility for this purpose (discussed in Chapter 4).

Login scripts are stored in the *%SystemRoot%\System32\REPL\Import\Scripts* directory; this location is chosen for use with Directory Replication service (discussed in Chapter 12), and any path that you enter for a user account's login script location is interpreted relative to this location. The same login script may be assigned to as many users as is appropriate.

Here is a simple login script written in the Windows NT command language for user *Chavez*:

```
echo off
net use H: \\vala\ananke\homes\chavez
```

```
net use I: \\demeter\chem
net use lpt2: \\demeter\matisse
C:\bin\kix32.exe motd.scr
```

After disabling command echoing, the script defines the *H:* and *I:* drive letters
(see Chapter 5) and defines a network printer. The script's final line uses the
messagebox facility from the Kix95 scripting language (included in the Resource
Kit) to display a window with a message.

The following built-in environment variables are useful in user login scripts:

%username%
> Contains the user account name.

%homedrive%
> Corresponds to the drive letter where the user's home directory is located.

%homepath%
> Corresponds to the full directory path to the user's home directory on the
> appropriate disk drive.

%processor_architecture%
> Specifies the current computer type, **x86** or **ALPHA**, allowing you to create a
> login script that works properly on either type of computer.

Remember that applications to be started at login time can also be placed in the
Start Menu\Programs\Startup folder within the user profile.

Other User Account Attributes

We'll consider these other user account attributes in later chapters of this book:

- Settings for the Remote Access Service (RAS) (dial-up access) in Chapter 8.

- User rights and system policies in Chapter 10.

Renaming User Accounts and Groups

Both user accounts and groups may be renamed within the User Manager utility
using its **User➤Rename** menu path. Since both users and groups are stored internally as a numeric ID, their names serve merely as a user-friendly label for the
actual system data structure to which it corresponds.

When you change the name of a user account or a group, all internal system references to it are changed automatically as well. For example, file ownership and
access permissions now reflect the new name. However, the actual account
settings and the names of files are not changed. Thus, if you rename user account
Chavez to *Verdugo*, the user profile path still points to *%SystemRoot%\Profiles*

Chavez until you explicitly change it, and you will also have to rename the corresponding directory on disk.

Removing User Accounts

The User Manager's **User▸Delete** menu path may be used to delete user accounts and groups. You should be certain that this is what you want to do before proceeding, however (disabling a user account, instead, is always an option).

To fulfill certain security requirements (see Chapter 10), the numeric internal user and group account IDs are never reused. When a user account (or group) is deleted, the corresponding number is retired by the operating system. If a new user account of the same name is later created, it is given a new ID number, and it has absolutely no relationship to the previous account. Since the internal ID numbers are different, the two accounts are simply ones that happen to share a common value for one of their settings, namely the account name. The same holds true for deleted and re-created groups.

This means that user account and group deletions are irreversible. For this reason, it is often better to disable a user account rather than to delete. That way, any file ownerships, file permissions (access control list entries), and other system configuration information that refer to the user account will still function, but no one will be able to use the account for computer or domain access. Similarly, it is almost always better to remove all members of a group rather than to delete the group entirely, unless you are completely sure you will never need to revive it.

Customizing the Login Process

Windows NT provides several ways of customizing the login process that the user sees. Many of them involve setting the various values of the HKEY_LOCAL_MACHINE\Software\Microsoft\Windows NT\CurrentVersion\Winlogon   registry key. Here are its most important values:

DontDisplayLastUserName
> Controls whether or not the name of the last user to log in successfully is prefilled in the username field in the login dialog box on the local system. This feature is convenient, but can pose security problems for some sites. The values 0 and 1 (text strings) enable and disable the displayed username, respectively. The default value is 0.

ShutdownWithoutLogon
> Determines whether a **Shut Down...** button is included in the login dialog box. If so, any person with physical access to the system will be able to shut it down without logging in first. Most sites consider this an unacceptable secu-

rity risk, so the default for this setting, as of Windows NT version 4, is 0. Changing this setting to 1 adds the button to the dialog box.

The **RegKey** utility included in the Resource Kit provides a convenient interface for some of the two values. It is illustrated in Figure 3-7.

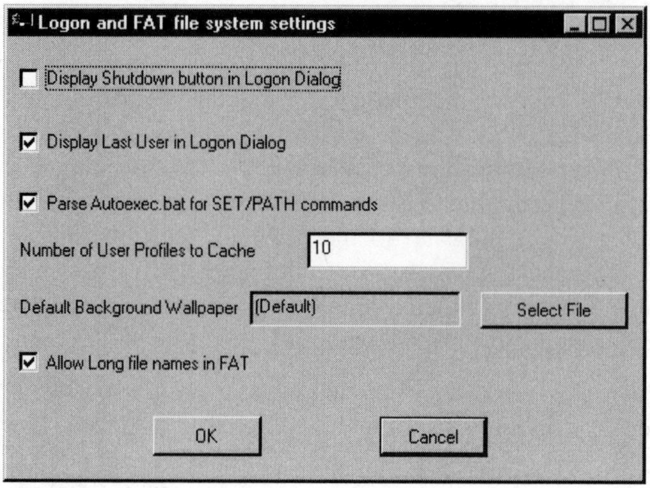

Figure 3-7. The RegKey utility

LegalNoticeCaption and LegalNoticeText

> These two values allow you to construct a customized message that is displayed before the login dialog box when a user enters CTRL-ALT-DEL to begin the login process; they specify the message box's title and contents, respectively. This facility can generate any message on the local computer, including ones to fulfill legal requirements against potential intruders.

RunLogonScriptSync

> Specifies whether the login script must complete executing before the user is given access to the system (0 means no and 1 means yes). The default value is 0.

All these items may also be set with the System Policy Editor (discussed in Chapter 10).

You can change the image that appears on the computer screen when no one is logged in by substituting your own bitmap format file for the standard ones in *%SystemRoot%*: *WinNT256.Bmp* and *WinNT.Bmp* on workstations and *Lanma-256.Bmp* and *LanmanNT.Bmp* on servers. The files with "256" in their name are 256-color bitmaps. Be sure that you substitute true bitmap files of the same (or lower) color depth for the standard files, or no image will appear. Large bitmap images also don't always work; substitute another file of approximately the same size as those Windows NT provides. As always, it's a good idea to rename or save a copy of the original files before installing your new versions.

You can also change the screen saver that runs when no user is logged in and its behavior by modifying the following values of the HKEY_USERS\Default\Control Panel\Desktop key:

SCRNSAVE.EXE
> Specifies the name of the screen saver executable file in *%SystemRoot%*. The default file for Windows NT version 4 is *logon.scr.*

ScreenSaveTimeOut
> Specifies the number of seconds before the screen saver is activated. The default is 900 seconds.

ScreenSaveActive
> Specifies whether a screen saver is used between user logins. The default value of 1 (as of Windows NT 4.0) enables a screen saver.

The NT Default User Registry Editor (NTDURE), a freely available utility written by Michael G. Martin, provides another convenient interface to many of these registry settings. Its dialog box is illustrated in Figure 3-8.

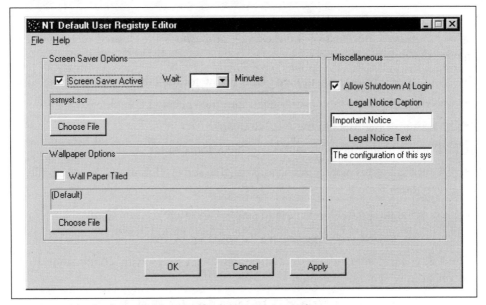

Figure 3-8. The freely available NT Default User Registry Editor

Bypassing the Login Process

Windows NT provides an optional automatic login mechanism where a user is automatically logged in when the system boots. This feature is disabled by default, and it should only be enabled for isolated systems that are in 100% physically secure locations.

This feature is controlled by the AutoAdminLogon value of the HKEY_LOCAL_ MA-CHINE\Software\Microsoft\Windows NT\CurrentVersion\Winlogin registry key. The value does not exist by default. You must create it (its type is REG_SZ) and assign it a setting of 1 to enable this feature. When enabled, the facility uses the settings in the DefaultDomainName, DefaultUserName, and DefaultPassword values of the same key for the automatic login attempt (you must create them if they do not already exist).

The System Policy Editor may also be used to edit these registry values (see Chapter 10).

Sending a Message to a User

The **net send** command can send a message to one or more logged-in users. It has the following syntax:

```
net send who message
```

where *message* is the text of the message, and *who* is the desired recipient of the message. The latter may be:

*   A username or messaging name (see below for the latter).

*   A computer name (any user logged into the specified computer).

*   An asterisk (all users in the local domain).

*   /Domain:*name* (all users in the specified domain).

*   /Users: all users with connections to the server (for example, open files or directories).

For example, the following command sends a message to user *Chavez:*

```
C:\> net send chavez "The meeting is moved up to 2pm"
```

The following command sends a message to all users with connections to the server from which it is executed:

```
C:\> net send /users "Vala will be taken down for PM at 9:30."
```

The **net name** command can define additional names that function as message recipients. By default, the computer name and the username are defined as message recipients whenever a user is logged in (unless they have already been redefined).

The **net name** command without any arguments displays all currently defined messaging names:

```
C:\> net name
Name
------------------------------------
VALA
CHAVEZ
```

In this example, the names *vala* and *Chavez* correspond to the computer name and username, respectively.

When used to define or redefine names, **net name** has the following syntax:

```
net name name /add | /delete
```

For example, the following command defines the new name *WebCzar*, making the current user the recipient of messages sent to that name:

```
C:\> net name webczar /add
```

Substituting **/delete** for **/add** removes the definition of *WebCzar.*

If you execute a command like this one:

```
C:\> net name chavez /add
```

and you are not user *Chavez*, and she is not currently logged in elsewhere, you redefine the name *Chavez*, redirecting any messages sent to it to yourself instead. If user *Chavez* should log in after this has taken place, then she will not have any messaging name but that of her local computer associated with her login session.

Defined names do not persist across login sessions; add the appropriate **net name** command to a login script to simulate permanent name definitions.

Managing Many Users

There are several strategies for automating the creation and maintenance of large numbers of user accounts.

One way is to edit multiple user accounts simultaneously in the User Manager Administrative Tool:

- Select the desired users in the User Manager, either individually or by Windows NT group (via **User▸Select Users…**).

- Select **User▸Properties** to open the main user account modification window and then navigate as necessary to the desired dialog box.

- Make the necessary changes to the accounts in the usual manner, using the **%username%** construct as the final path component (it serves as a reference to each account's username). Figure 3-9 illustrates the use of **%username%** in the **User Profile Path** and **Home Directory** fields.

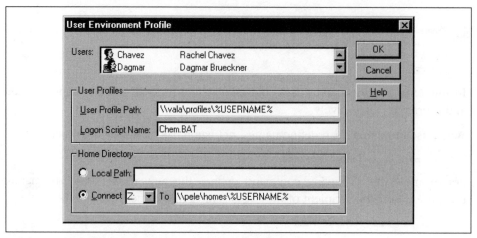

Figure 3-9. Changing multiple user accounts simultaneously

- Exit from the dialog boxes to apply the new settings to the group of accounts. You receive a warning message if the settings in some of the accounts are not currently identical.

Beyond a certain point, however, the User Manager becomes unmanageable due to its increasing memory requirements and decreasing performance. When your patience is exhausted, it's time to find other, more efficient ways of accomplishing its tasks. There are three main ways to do so:

- Use the **Add User** wizard to add new user accounts without having to access the whole set of them each time. This facility provides some relief for the very limited tasks that it can perform.

- Use the command-line tools to manipulate user accounts and groups.

- Create scripts to perform these processes with minimal administrator input and intervention.

The third approach uses the command-line tools as the means of automating these tasks, and it is to them that we now turn our attention.

Commands for Manipulating Users and Groups

Windows NT provides several commands for displaying information about and creating and modifying user accounts. The primary command is **net user**. Given a username as its argument, this command displays information about the specified user account:

```
C:\> net user chavez
User name                    Chavez
Full Name                    Rachel Chavez
Comment
User's comment
Country code                 000 (System Default)
Account active               Yes
Account expires              Never

Password last set            6/17/97 2:22 PM
Password expires             Never
Password changeable          6/17/97 2:22 PM
Password required            Yes
User may change password     Yes

Workstations allowed         All
Logon script                 Chem.BAT
User profile                 C:\WINNT\Profiles\Chavez
Home directory               \\pele\homes\Chavez
Last logon                   6/24/97 2:14 PM

Logon hours allowed          All

Local Group Memberships
Global Group memberships     *Domain Users        *Phys
```

The **net user** command can also add and modify user accounts, with the following syntax:

net user *user* [*password*] [**/add**] *options*

where *user* is the username of the account to be added (include **/add**) or modified, *password* is the password for the user account (use an asterisk for this argument to be prompted for a password), and *options* are one or more options specifying various account settings. The available options are summarized in Table 3-3.

Table 3-3. The net user Command Options

Option	Effect	Examples
/add **/delete**	Adds or deletes the specified user account (the default is to modify an existing account).	/add
/domain	Operates on a domain account rather than a local account (not needed on domain controllers).	/domain
/active:*yesno*	Enables or disables the account.	/active:no *(disable account)*

Table 3-3. The net user Command Options (continued)

Option	Effect	Examples
/comment:*text*	Provides a description of the account.	`/comment:"DB Admin"`
/countrycode:*n*	Specifies the country code for the account (0 means to use the default country).	`/countrycode:002`
/expires:*when*	Sets the account expiration to the specified date (use the keyword **never** to disable account expiration).	`/expires:1/1/99` `/expires:never`
/fullname:*name*	Specifies the user's full name.	`/fullname:"Rachel Chavez"`
/homedir:*path*	Sets the user's home directory.	`/homedir:C: \Homes\Chavez`
/passwordchg:*yesno*	Indicates whether or not the user can change her password (the default is **yes**).	`/passwordchg:no`
/passwordreq:*yesno*	Indicates whether or not the account is required to have a password (the default is **yes**).	`/passwordreq:yes`
/profilepath:*path*	Specifies the location of the account's user profile.	`/profilepath:C:\WinNT\ Profiles\Chavez`
/scriptpath:*path*	Specifies the location of the account's login script (relative to the default script location).	`/scriptpath:Chem.Bat`

/times:*when*	Indicates times the user is allowed to be logged in. By default, the user can log in at any time, which is specified by the keyword **all**. Otherwise, *when* is a series of valid day and time entries: one or more days and day ranges are followed by one or more times and time ranges (all of these are comma-separated). Multiple entries are separated by semi-colons.	`/times:m-f,6am-6pm`
		`/times:m,w,f,6-18; t,th,7-20`
		`/times:m-f,0-3,6-24; sa,6-18`
		`/times:m-f,0-24;sa-su, 9-17`
		`/times:all`

/workstations:*where*	Specifies computers where the user is allowed to log in. By default, the user can log in to any computer, which may be specified by an asterisk (*). Otherwise, *where* is a comma-separated list of up to eight computer names.	`/workstations:*` `/workstations:demeter, leda,lilith,pele`

For example, the following command adds the user account *Pavlova* for Olga Pavlova, supplying values for her profile path and login script, setting an account expiration date of January 1, 1999, and requesting a prompt for entering her initial password:

```
C:\> net user pavlova * /add /domain /fullname:"Olga Pavlova" ^
     /expires:1/1/99 /profilepath:\\vala\profiles\Pavlova  ^
     /scriptpath:Chem.Bat
Type a password for the user:          Password is not echoed.
Retype the password to confirm:
The command completed successfully.
```

The command form **net user** *user* /delete may be used to remove a user account, although disabling the account is probably preferable (append /domain if you execute the command from somewhere other than a domain controller).

You can add users to and remove users from groups with the **net group** and **net localgroup** commands. Without any arguments, these commands list the names of all global and local groups on the local system or domain (both support a / domain option to operate on the domain from nondomain controller systems). If you specify a group name as either command's argument, the members of the specified group are listed:

```
C:\>net group chem
Group name      Chem
Comment         Chemistry Users

Members

-------------------------------------------------------------
Alvin                   Dagmar                  Pavlova
...
```

The /add and /delete options add or remove a group, and add or remove one or more members to or from the group. For example, the following commands create the global group named *Bio*, add users *Chavez* and *Pavlova* as members, and remove user *Alvin* from the domain local group *Baseball*:

```
C:\> net group Bio /add /comment:"Biology users"
C:\> net group Bio chavez pavlova /add
C:\> net localgroup Baseball alvin /delete /domain
```

The Resource Kit includes commands that list group members in a more useful format: one name per line. The **global** command lists the members of a specified global group, and the **local** command lists the members of a specified local group. Both take the group name and the domain name (or a server name) as their arguments. For example, the following command lists the members of the *Chem* group in the Windows NT domain Borealis:

```
C:\> global chem borealis
Alvin
```

```
Dagmar
Pavlova
...
```

The Resource Kit's **showgrps** command lists the groups that a specified user belongs to:

```
C:\> showgrps chavez
User: [BOREALIS\chavez], is a member of:

    BOREALIS\Domain Users
    \Everyone
    BOREALIS\Phys
    BOREALIS\Bio
```

The username may be optionally preceded by a domain name and backslash to list the group memberships of a user from another domain.

The **usrstat** command in the Resource Kit may be used to list all user accounts in a specified domain, along with their last login times:

```
C:\> usrstat borealis
Users at \\VALA
    Administrator -     Sys Admin - logon: Tue Jun 24 14:18:32 1997
          Chavez -  Rachel Chavez - logon: Tue Jun 24 14:14:59 1997
          Frisch -    Mike Frisch - logon: Tue Jun 24 07:02:49 1997
           Guest -  Guest Account - logon:                  Never
  King Richard 3! -  Coeur de Lion - logon:                  Never
           Sally -   Sally Quince - logon: Wed Jun 11 12:21:20 1997
    ...
```

The **net accounts** command may be used to specify some global password policy settings. Without any arguments, **net accounts** displays the current values for the password policy settings:

```
C:\> net accounts
Force user logoff how long after time expires?:   Never
Minimum password age (days):                         20
Maximum password age (days):                        120
Minimum password length:                              8
Length of password history maintained:               10
Lockout threshold:                                    8
Lockout duration (minutes):                         120
Lockout observation window (minutes):                30
    ...
```

The command uses the following syntax to modify one or more of these settings:

```
net accounts /domain [/maxpwage:days] [/minpwage:days] ^
    [/minpwlen:n] [/uniquepw:m] [/forcelogoff:mins]
```

where *n* is the minimum password length, and *m* is the number of previous passwords remembered by the system. The argument to the **/forcelogoff** option may either be a number of minutes or the keyword **no**, which disables the corresponding feature. Eliminate the **/domain** option to affect the password policy on the local system.

For example, the following command sets the maximum password age to three months and the minimum password length to 10 characters for the domain:

```
C:\> net accounts /domain /maxpwage:90 /minpwlen:10
```

The command form **net accounts sync** forces an immediate update of the user accounts database on backup domain controllers.

Automating Account Creation and Modification

Unfortunately, Windows NT provides little help for dealing with large numbers of users. The Resource Kit includes the **AddUsers** command to add multiple users in bulk from a prepared text file. This command allows you to specify the account name, full name, password, home directory drive mapping (if applicable), home directory path, user profile path, and login script path for each new user account. You can also create global and local groups and add members to them.

Here is a sample of the input file that **AddUsers** requires:

```
[User]
Will,David Will,xxx,,Z:,\\pele\homes\Will,\\vala\profiles\Will,Chem.Bat
...
[Global]
BioChem,Biochemistry users,Will,Dagmar
...
[Local]
...
```

The three sections of the file hold user account specifications, global group definitions, and local group definitions. Within each entry, fields are separated by commas. The user entries provide the account settings mentioned at the start of the section (in the same order). The group entries hold the group name, group description, and users to be assigned to the group as members. Note that groups must not already exist.

The file is processed by the **AddUsers** command, as in this example, which adds the users and groups in the file *new.txt*:

```
C:\> addusers /c new.txt
```

See the command documentation for full details on using this facility.

Clearly, a tool that is more flexible and complete than **AddUsers** is needed to manage large numbers of user accounts. We examine a Perl script that fulfills these functions in detail in Chapter 12. For now, I'm simply introducing it.

This script, which we've named **amu** (for add and modify users), has the following characteristics:

- Performs the same operation (with the obvious variations for username) for many, many user accounts via a single invocation

- Manages user account settings and group memberships in the same utility

- Automatically applies any default values preset by the system administrator

- Figures out whether an account is being added or modified

- Creates the user home directories, login scripts, and user profiles automatically, if they don't already exist

- Records its actions in a log file

- Takes its input from the command line, from a text file, or by prompting the system administrator

The **amu** command is best introduced by example. The following command adds the users *Davis, Greene,* and *Forche* as members of the *Chem* and *Bio* groups, applying the preset default values for all unspecified account settings:

```
C:\> perl amu.pl Davis Greene Forche -g Chem,Bio
```

This command creates the user accounts, assigns initial passwords, applies a variety of standard account settings to them, and creates and assigns their home directories, user profiles, and login scripts.

The following command adds the users *Davis, Greene,* and *Forche* as members of the *Chem* and *Bio* groups, prompting the system administrator for each user's full name:

```
C:\> perl amu.pl Davis Greene Forche -g Chem,Bio -p fn
Full name for Davis: Edgar Davis
Full name for Greene: Joel Greene
...
```

The following command adds user *Chavez* to the *Chem* group and sets the expiration date for her account to December 31, 1999:

```
C:\> perl amu.pl Chavez -g +Chem -x 12/31/99
```

The following command adds or modifies the users whose information is given in the file *fix.txt*:

```
C:\> perl amu.pl -f fix.txt
```

See Chapter 12 for a discussion of this Perl script.

4

Managing Processes

Processes are the means by which users get work done on a computer system, and managing processes can make up a substantial part of a system administrator's day-to-day workload. In more technical terms, a Windows NT process is a system object that has a virtual address space, a chunk of executable code, various system resources, and one or more *threads* associated with it. Threads are the fundamental executable entities on a Windows NT system; the program counter, stacks, register values, execution priority, and other attributes typically possessed by a running program belong to the thread. A process running on a single processor system will generally have one thread associated with it, and a process running in parallel on multiple heads of a multiprocessor system will often use one thread per CPU. Except in the latter context, processes and threads need not be distinguished for most system administrative tasks.

Windows NT processes have the following attributes:

- A numeric process ID (PID)

- An access token specifying data related to file permissions and system privileges

- A base priority class indicating its general level of importance with respect to other processes within the system, its affinity to execute relative to other processes

- An allowed processor set indicating which processors it may use on a multiprocessor system

- Quotas for system resources such as memory and execution time

- Its execution time so far

- A set of I/O counters and memory counters

- Defined exception and debug ports

- An exit status

Similarly, threads have a related set of attributes, of which these are the most important:

- The PID of the process that owns it

- A numeric base priority specifying its importance relative to other threads, its affinity to execute relative to other threads

- A dynamic priority that is recomputed frequently, taking into account factors such as how recently the thread has executed

- Its execution time so far

- An allowed processor set for the thread (which is some subset of the process's allowed processor set)

- An exit status

In this chapter, we will discuss the mechanics of creating and manipulating processes. We will defer consideration of the Windows NT scheduling process— how the operating system decides which thread to run at any given time—until Chapter 11.

How Commands Run: Search Paths

Like most operating systems, Windows NT uses *search paths* to locate the executable file for users' commands. A search path is simply an ordered list of directories in which to look for commands, and a faulty (incomplete) search path is the most common cause for "name not recognized"-type error messages.

Search paths are stored in the PATH environment variable. Here is a typical PATH:

```
C:\> path
C:\WINNT\SYSTEM32;C:\WINNT;C:\NTRESKIT;C:\NTRESKIT\Perl;
C:\MSSQL\BINN;D:\ADMIN\BIN
```

The various directories in the PATH are separated by semicolons. The search path is used whenever a command name is entered without an explicit directory location (for example, in the **Start►Run** dialog box or in a command window); it is also used by some applications to locate libraries and other support files that they need to run. Locations within a search path may be specified using the appropriate drive and directory or in UNC format (e.g., *pele**homes**Chavez**Bin*).

When Windows NT attempts to locate a command or file, it first determines whether it is one of the commands built in to the command interpreter (e.g., **dir** and **copy**). If not, it looks in the current directory for an executable file of that name.* If none is found, the various search path directories are searched in order. Thus, the order of the directories in the search path is important: when more than one version of a command exists on the system, the one that is found first will be used. Ensuring that system directories always precede locally created directories in search paths protects against a malicious user substituting his own version of a standard command for the real one. For similar reasons, all directories in the search path for any user account with administrative privileges must not allow write access to ordinary users.

Windows NT maintains two search paths: a system search path used by every user and an individual search path specific to each user account on the system. A user's actual search path consists of the concatenation of the two (system path first).

The **Environment** tab of the **System** control panel applet provides one method for viewing and modifying the system and current user path (illustrated in Figure 4-1). Any user may examine the search paths there and modify her user search path, but only an administrator may modify the system search path. The system search path appears as the PATH variable in the **System Variables** list within this dialog box, and any user-specific search path appears in the **User Variables** list. The two fields at the bottom of the dialog box are used to enter and modify environment variables and their values. For example, the illustration shows the dialog box as it appears when the system path is being modified.

The Resource Kit provides the **PathMan** utility, offering a command line method for modifying search paths. It has the following syntax:

> **pathman** *opt path* [*opt path* ...]

where *path* is a set of colon-separated directory locations, and *opt* is one of the following options:

/au Add path to the end of the user's search path.

/as Add path to the end of the system search path.

/ru Remove components in the path from the user's search path (if present).

/rs Remove components in the path from the system search path (if present).

For example, the following command adds *vala**Bin* and *pele**Bin* to the system search path, adds *E:**DBTest* to the current user's search path and removes *C:**Bin* from the system search path:

> `C:\> pathman /as \\vala\Bin;\\pele\Bin /au E:\DBTest /rs C:\Bin`

---

* Executable files are indicated by their extensions as defined in the PATHEXT environment variable (discussed later).

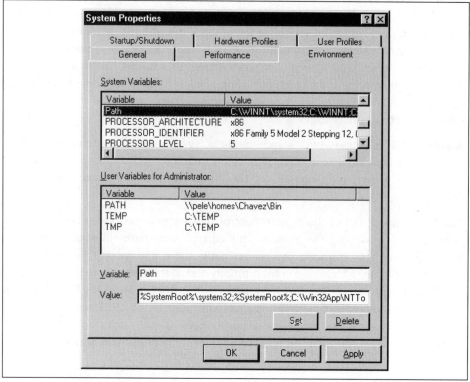

Figure 4-1. Modifying search paths

PathMan adds new components only if they aren't already present within the search path.

Updated search paths modified via either of these methods are stored immediately, but they do not apply to the current user environment (for example, to any current command windows). However, any new processes that you initiate will use the modified search path. Search paths may also be modified via the standard DOS mechanism (i.e., **PATH=...**), but such changes apply only to the command window in which that command is executed, and they do not persist.

The role of AutoExec.Bat

By default, any PATH definitions in an *AutoExec.Bat** file in the root directory of the system disk are also added to the search path created for a user when he logs

---

* Except for extracting the path and possibly other environment variables, this file is not used by Windows NT. Don't confuse it with the *AutoExec.NT* and *Config.NT* files located in *%SystemRoot%\System32* (used by the NTVDM subsystem when DOS applications are run), or with the user account login scripts discussed in Chapter 3.

in (to maintain backward compatibility with earlier Windos operating systems). The ParseAutoexec value of the HKEY_CURRENT_USER\Software\Microsoft\ Windows NT\CurrentVersion\Winlogin registry key controls whether or not *Auto-Exec.Bat* is examined when the search path is constructed. If you set this value to 0, then the *AutoExec.Bat* file will not be used. The System Policy Editor and the Resource Kit's **RegKey** utility (discussed in Chapter 2) can also modify this value.

The PATHEXT Environment Variable

The PATHEXT environment variable specifies a series of default file extensions to be applied to command names that include no explicit extension, as the operating system searches for the corresponding command executable. Its value is a semi-colon-separated list of extensions, which are applied in turn as each component of the search path is examined in order to locate the command. Its default value is *.Com;.Exe;.Bat;.Cmd.*

Foreground and Background Processes

When you open an application program or enter a command in a Windows NT command window, the operating system creates a process to execute the desired program. Such processes initiated directly from a login session are conventionally known as *interactive* processes, because they generally interact with the user via the computer keyboard and mouse. Interactive processes may run in the *fore-ground,* retaining control of the login session (e.g., keyboard and mouse) until the process completes or the user explicitly pauses or terminates it, or they may run in the *background,* executing independently of the login session that created them (and any further user input). Finally *batch* processes are background processes run automatically from a batch queue by the operating system and are not associated with any login session.

This conventional differentiation between process types is easiest to understand in the context of a command window. If you run the **Erase** command, you initiate an interactive, foreground process. This command may prompt you for confirmation before deleting the specified files, and it retains control of the command window until it completes or you terminate it manually. You can also run the **Erase** command as a background process, which executes independently of the command window, allowing you to enter additional commands while it runs. Finally, you can submit the same command to the Schedule Service for future execution (discussed later in this chapter), and the operating system runs it at the designated time whether or not you happen to be logged in.

The Windows NT environment complicates these traditional distinctions in several ways. First of all, an interactive foreground process generally controls only the window in which it executes, not the whole login session; several such processes can coexist simultaneously, and the user can switch between them as desired. (This is true for any windowing user environment.)

More importantly, Windows NT allows background processes to interact with the current login session in many cases. For example, jobs initiated by the Schedule Service or by a batch queuing system may run in an interactive mode. Similarly, system server processes, usually the quintessential background processes (since they are started automatically at boot-time without any user action), may also be configured to allow interaction with the desktop.

Displaying Information About Processes

Windows NT and the Resource Kit provide several different tools for examining and manipulating processes. We begin with the graphical Task Manager and then will consider some command-line tools.

Using the Task Manager

There are several ways to access the Task Manager tool:

- Use the CTRL-SHIFT-ESC key combination (the fastest way).
- Press CTRL-ALT-DELETE and select the **Task Manager** button.
- Right-click on the taskbar and select the corresponding menu item.
- Enter the **TaskMgr** command into the **Run** dialog box or a command window.

The Task Manager has three tabs: the **Applications** panel lists current application programs, the **Processes** panel lists all running processes on the system, and the **Performance** panel displays some simple statistics related to current system performance. Statistics about current overall system use appear at the bottom of the Task Manager window.

The **Applications** tab is illustrated in Figure 4-2. This user is currently running five applications. The buttons at the bottom of the panel can manipulate the processes associated with these applications. The **End Task** button terminates the selected application, and the **Switch To** button transfers control to the selected application. The **New Task** button functions like the **Run** dialog box (**Start➤Run**), and you may use it to start a new application.

The **Processes** tab of the Task Manager is probably the most important to a system administrator. It displays a continuously updated list of all processes running on the system, along with various statistics about them. Its default configuration is illustrated in Figure 4-3.

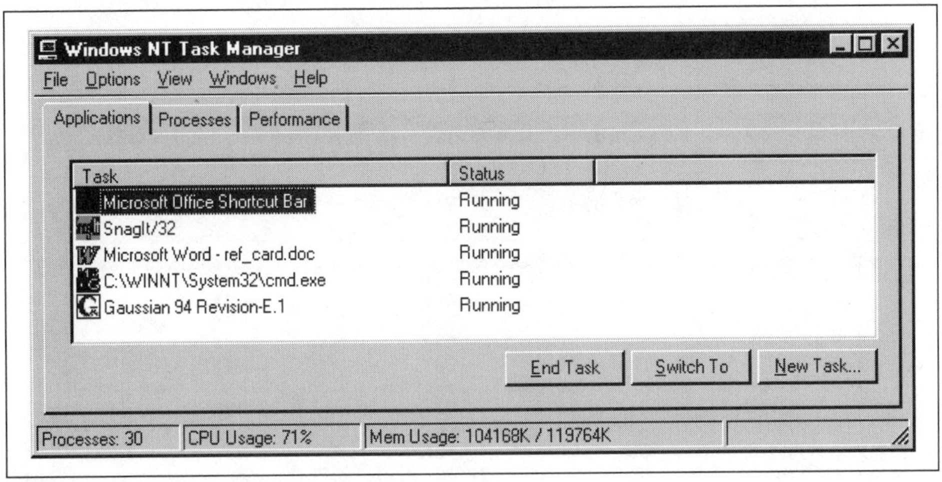

Figure 4-2. The Task Manager's Applications tab

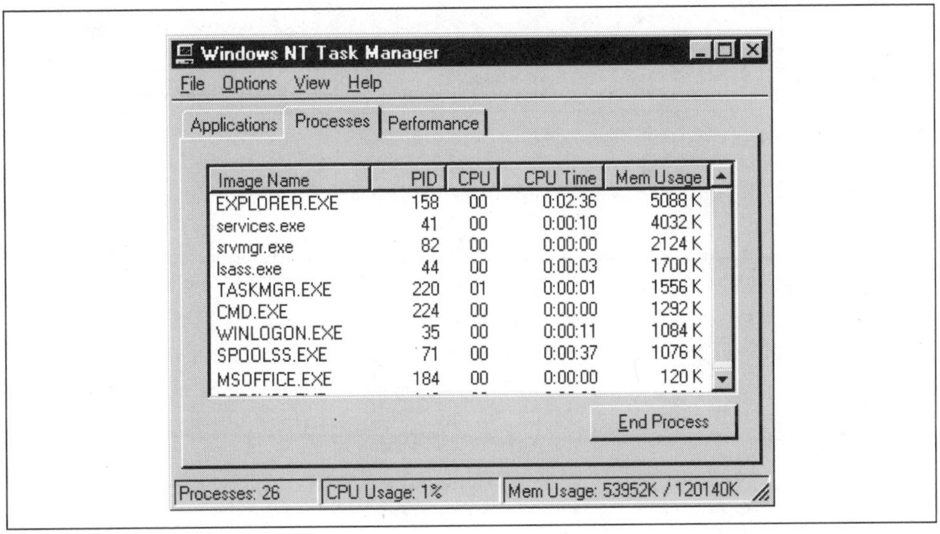

Figure 4-3. The Task Manager's Processes tab

By default, processes are listed in order of increasing process ID. You may sort the process list in some other way by clicking on the desired column label. Clicking the same button a second time reverses the sort order. Thus, clicking on the **Image Name** column lists processes by name in alphabetical order, and clicking on it a second time lists them in inverse alphabetical order (Z to A).

Use the **View▶Select Columns** menu path to customize the columns appearing in the display. Figure 4-4 shows a customized version of this tab. Changes that you make to the display are saved when you end the Task Manager session, and they become the defaults for future sessions. There are many different process statistics available for display; the most useful are summarized in Table 4-1.

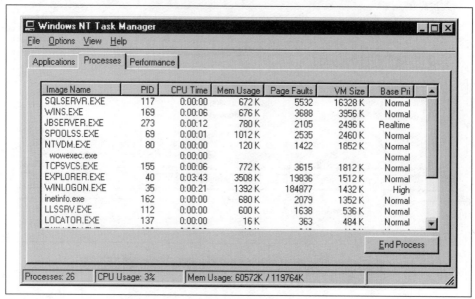

Figure 4-4. Customized Task Manager Processes tab

Table 4-1. Useful Columns for the Task Manager Processes Tab

Column (Heading)	Displayed Data
Image Name (Image Name)	Executable image corresponding to the process
Process ID (PID)	Process ID
Short Term CPU Usage (CPU)	Percentage of total system CPU capacity consumed by the process during the most recent update period
Total CPU Time (CPU Time)	Total CPU time (in seconds) used by the process throughout its lifetime
Memory Usage (Mem Usage)	Amount of memory (in KB) used by the process (also known as its *current working set*)
Page Faults (Page Faults)	Total number of page faults generated by the process throughout its lifetime (a page fault occurs whenever data that the process needs must be transferred from disk to physical memory)
Virtual Memory Size (VM Size)	Amount of space used by the process in the paging file (in KB)
Base Priority Class (Base Pri)	The priority class for the process: **Low**, **Normal**, **High**, and **Realtime** (see Chapter 11)
Handle Count (Handles)	Total number of objects in use by the process (system resources of all types)

Table 4-1. Useful Columns for the Task Manager Processes Tab (continued)

Column (Heading)	Displayed Data
Paged Pool	Amount of user memory (which can be paged to disk) used by the process (in KB)
Nonpaged Pool (NP Pool)	Amount of system memory (nonpagable) used by the process (in KB)
Thread Count (Threads)	Number of threads corresponding to the process (most useful for multiprocessor systems)

The **Processes** tab may also be used to manipulate processes as well as view information about them. You can use the **End Process** button at the bottom of the panel to terminate the selected process. However, it is best to stop and start system server processes with the **Services** control panel applet or the **net start/stop** commands.

You can change the priority class of a process by right-clicking on it and then using the **Set Priority** item on the resulting menu. Process priorities are discussed in detail in Chapter 11.

The default update speed for the display is once per second. You can modify this using the **View►Update Speed** menu path. The values in its menu have the following meanings: **High** updates the display every 0.5 seconds, **Normal** selects an update rate of once per second, **Low** corresponds to an update rate of once every four seconds, and **Paused** means that the display is updated only upon request (via the F5 key). Selecting a slower update rate results in better overall system response while the Task Manager is running.

Resource Kit Tools for Managing Processes

The Resource Kit includes several utilities for viewing information about and manipulating processes. The **TList** ("task list") command displays a quick list of current processes. Include its **/T** option to produce a tree-structured listing showing process relationships:

```
C:\> tlist /t
System Process (0)
System (2)
  smss.exe (21)
    csrss.exe (26)
    WINLOGON.EXE (35)
      SERVICES.EXE (41)
        SPOOLSS.EXE (71)
        SQLSERVR.EXE (103)
  ...
EXPLORER.EXE (40) Program Manager
  MSOFFICE.EXE (249) Microsoft Office Shortcut Bar
    snagit32.exe (242) SnagIt/32
```

```
CMD.EXE (251) C:\WINNT\System32\cmd.exe - tlist /t
  TLIST.EXE (87)
```

System processes appear first. Indented processes are children of those above them in the tree. For example, the SQL Server process was started by the system services main process (SERVICES.EXE). Similarly, the process for the SnagIt screen capture utility was initiated by the Microsoft Office Shortcut Bar process, which was in turn started by the Windows NT window manager, EXPLORER.EXE. Within each entry, the process image is followed by the PID in parentheses and by any description that the application provides.

Specifying a PID as the parameter to **TList** requests details about the specified process. The resulting display lists statistics about the process, including the executable that is running, the process's current and peak memory use, and a list of the shared libraries (DLLs) that it is using:

```
C:\> tlist 251
  251 CMD.EXE            C:\WINNT\System32\cmd.exe - tlist 251
    CWD:     C:\NTRESKIT\
    CmdLine: "C:\WINNT\System32\cmd.exe"
    VirtualSize:    17008 KB    PeakVirtualSize:    17072 KB
    WorkingSetSize: 1292 KB     PeakWorkingSetSize: 1296 KB
    NumberOfThreads: 1
      278 Win32StartAddr:0x01378960 LastErr:0x0000007a State:Waiting
      4.0.1381.4  shp  0x01360000  cmd.exe
      4.0.1381.4  shp  0x77f60000  ntdll.dll
      4.0.1381.4  shp  0x77e70000  USER32.dll
      4.0.1381.4  shp  0x77f00000  KERNEL32.dll
      4.0.1381.4  shp  0x77ed0000  GDI32.dll
      4.0.1381.4  shp  0x77dc0000  ADVAPI32.dll
      4.0.1381.4  shp  0x77e10000  RPCRT4.dll
      4.0.1381.4  shp  0x77c40000  SHELL32.dll
      4.70.1147.1 shp  0x77bf0000  COMCTL32.dll
      4.0.1381.4  shp  0x77720000  MPR.dll
```

In this example, which corresponds to a command window, the process is currently using about 17 MB of virtual memory (which is very near its peak size), although its working set indicates that it could run with as little as about 1.3MB. The final section of the output displays the DLL list for a command window.

Alternatively, **TList** accepts a string as its argument and displays detailed information about all processes whose task name matches the string. The string can be a complete command name or a wildcard expression[*] that matches a complete command name. Here are some examples:

tlist cmd   *Display information about all CMD.EXE processes.*
tlist *cm*   *Display information about all processes whose names contain "CM."*

---

[*] The documentation for **TList** says that the string may be a regular expression, but the command does not seem to understand arbitrary regular expressions.

> **tlist cm**   *Display information for processes named CM (usually produces no output).*

Note that **/T** cannot be combined with either type of argument to **TList**.

The **PStat** command gives a more detailed listing of current system processes and their statistics. Here is an example of the first portion of its output:

```
Pstat version 0.3:  memory: 64948 kb  uptime: 1  2:12:04.912
                     Total real memory        Time since last boot (days  hh:mm:ss)


PageFile: \??\C:\pagefile.sys       Paging file usage statistics.
    Current Size: 65536 kb  Total Used: 19944 kb   Peak Used 54504 kb


Overall system memory use statistics
Memory:64948K Avail:27260K TotalWs:35180K InRam Kernel:3284K P:8168K
Commit:62544K/43364K Limit:119764K Peak:106168K Pool N:2836K P:9796K


 Table of processes.*
 User Time  Kernel Time   Ws  Faults  Commit Pri Hnd Thd Pid Name
                       14664   91774                          File Cache
0:00:00.000 1:51:16.086   16       1       0   0   0   1   0 Idle Process
0:00:00.000 0:03:16.282   44    2086      36   8 536  29   2 System
...
0:00:00.771 0:00:00.660 2260    6240   16328   8 141  17 117 SQLSERVR.EXE
0:00:01.261 0:00:03.595  608    4056     820   8  37   2 249 MSOFFICE.EXE
0:00:05.117 0:00:09.423  280    6638     820   8  28   1 242 snagit32.exe
...
```

The most important columns of the process table are the following:

User Time
    CPU time accumulated so far by the process running its executable image.

Kernel Time
    CPU time consumed by the operating system performing tasks on behalf of the process. The total process CPU time is the sum of user and kernel times.

Ws Working set size: the current amount of physical memory being used by the process (KB).

Faults
    Total number of page faults since process initiation.

Pri Numerical base priority.

Pid Process ID.

Name
    The executable image the process is running.

The remainder of the output from **PStat** consists of detailed information about each process that is of interest mainly to systems programmers.

---

* This part of the output is similar to that of the UNIX **ps** command.

The **PMon** command provides a continuously updated process list display that is similar to that produced by **PStat**. Use the ESCAPE key to exit from **PMon**.

The **PUList** command provides yet another quick process list. When used without arguments, the list includes the executable name, PID, and owner for each current process on the local system. **PUList** may also be given a system name as its argument in order to produce a list of processes running on a remote Windows NT system; for example, **PUList \\pele** lists the processes running on host *pele*. In the latter mode, usernames are not included in the output.

Finally, the **PViewer** and **PView** provide a very detailed and incredibly detailed display window for a single process (respectively). We'll consider these utilities in Chapter 11.

Terminating a Process

We've already discussed how to terminate a process via the Task Manager. Other graphical tools that display process information (such as **PViewer** and **PView**) also provide mechanisms for terminating the process (usually, it's a button). The Resource Kit also includes two commands for this same purpose, **Kill** and **RKill**.

The **Kill** command accepts a process ID as its argument. For example, the following command kills process 152:

```
C:\> kill 152
```

Kill also accepts a string as its argument in the same way as **TList**. Thus, the first of these two commands terminates all open command window processes (except the one from which it is executed), and the second command terminates all processes with the characters "CM" in their names:

```
C:\> kill cmd
C:\> kill *cm*
```

As you'd expect, **kill cm** won't kill anything on most systems.

The **Kill** command's **/F** option may be used to force termination of a process that survives the normal termination signal.

The **RKill** command can list and terminate processes on a remote system. The Remote Kill service must be running on the remote host (it may be installed with the Resource Kit's **Service Install** wizard—the command is **SrvInstW**), specifying the file *RKillSrv.Exe* (in the Resource Kit directory, usually *C:\NTResKit*), as the executable for the service. It must be run via the *System* account and started automatically. After installing it, start the service manually (with **net start "Remote Kill Service"**, for example).

Once the Remote Kill Service is installed and running, the **RKill** command works
for that system. The command has the following syntax:

> **rkill /view **_server_   *List processes on remote server.*
> **rkill /kill **_server PID_   *Kill a remote process.*

Here are some examples:

```
C:\> rkill /view \\pele
The operation completed successfully.

System Process 0
  System 2
    smss.exe 25
      csrss.exe 33
      winlogon.exe 39
        services.exe 45
          SPOOLSS.EXE 71
          llssrv.exe 79
          rpcss.exe 99
          inetinfo.exe 121
          RKILLSRV.EXE 172
        lsass.exe 48
        nddeagnt.exe 109
        ssflwbox.scr 44
explorer.exe 149
  cmd.exe 74

C:\> rkill /kill \\pele 74
```

The first command lists the processes running on host *pele*, and the second
command terminates the command window process (PID 74).

The Schedule Service

The Schedule Service is a Windows NT facility that allows you to schedule
programs for delayed future execution and repeated periodic execution.[*] You can
use it to perform backup operations automatically, to clean up editor backup files
every night, to extract events from and summarize the event logs once a week, or
to perform any number of other tasks. The Schedule Service performs administrative functions silently, without any explicit action.

When the service is running, the **At** command provides one way of administering
the Schedule Service. Without any arguments, it lists pending jobs on the current
or specified system:

---

[*] Thus, the Windows NT Schedule Service provides similar features to the UNIX **at** and **cron** facilities (although it shares a name only with the former).

```
C:\> at
Status ID  Day             Time      Command Line
------------------------------------------------------------------
         0  Each Su         2:00 AM   C:\adminbin\findhogs.bat
         1  Each 1          2:15 AM   C:\adminbin\cleanup.bat
         4  Tomorrow        7:00 PM   E:\chem\carbon.bat
         5  Each M T W Th F 1:00 AM   C:\adminbin\sumevent.bat
         6  Today           3:22 PM   perl.exe \\pele\test.pl

C:\> at \\pele
Status ID  Day             Time      Command Line
------------------------------------------------------------------
         0  Each Su         2:00 AM   C:\adminbin\findhogs.bat
         2  Tomorrow        8:00 AM   E:\chem\carbon.bat
```

The first **At** command lists the pending jobs on the local system, and the second lists those on host *pele*.

When it is used to schedule a future or periodic job, the **At** command has the following syntax:

> **at** [*host*] *time* [*when*] *command*

where *host* is the name of the computer on which the task is to be scheduled and *command*, along with any arguments to it, is the desired command to be executed. (Fully qualified pathnames are preferred for security reasons.)

The *time* argument specifies the time of day the command should be started. The following are all valid formats for 4:00 P.M.: **4pm**, **4:00pm**, **16:00**. The forms "4" and "16" alone are not valid and will produce an error message. The *time* argument is required when adding a new task to the Schedule Service.

The time may be optionally followed by one of the following switches, which further specify when the command is to be executed:

/next:*date(s)*

Specifies that the command is to be run once at the indicated time on each listed date. The comma-separated list of dates may include days of the week and dates of the month: for example, **Monday,15** specifies next Monday and the next 15th day of the month (i.e., this month or next). If the *date* is omitted, it defaults to the current day of the month (generally meaning next month on the same date).

/every:*date(s)*

Specifies that the command is to be run each time the specified days of the week and dates of the month occur. Once again, if the *date* is omitted, it defaults to the current day of the month.

Note that individual items in date lists do not interact. Thus, **Friday,13** means Friday *and* the 13th of the month and is not limited to Friday the 13th.

By default, Schedule Service jobs run in the background. The **/Interactive** option may be added after the time parameter to allow desktop input while the job runs.

The **At** command may also be used to remove current Schedule Service tasks, using the following syntax:

at [*host*] *ID* **/delete**   *Delete a specified job.*
at [*host*] **/delete** [**/yes**] *Delete all current tasks (with optional preconfirmation).*

For example, the following command deletes job 15 on the local system and all jobs on host *pele* (without further prompting):

```
C:\> at 15 /delete & at \\pele /delete /yes
```

Pending jobs may not be changed, but must be deleted and then resubmitted.

The **WinAT** facility included in the Resource Kit provides a graphical interface to the schedule system. It allows you to modify current jobs by performing the deletion and resubmission for you, but be aware that the job ID will change. This utility may be used to view the local Schedule Service (the default) or the service on a remote system (use the **File➤New** menu path).

The Resource Kit also includes the **Soon** utility, which forms an appropriate **At** command based on a specified delay interval in seconds. It has the following syntax:

soon [*host*] [*secs*] [**/interactive**] *command*

The default delay period is 5 seconds for the local system and 15 seconds for a remote system. For example, the following command starts the *vala\ adminbin\cleanup.bat* script on *pele* in 1 minute:

```
C:\> soon \\pele 60 \\vala\adminbin\cleanup.bat
```

Use **Soon**'s **/D** option to change its default delay period. For example, this command sets the default delay period to 30 seconds on the local system and 2 minutes on remote systems:

```
C:\> soon /D /L:30 /R:120

Current Settings:     InteractiveAlways = OFF
                     LocalDelay (seconds) = 30
                    RemoteDelay (seconds) = 120
```

Access to the Schedule Service

Access to the Schedule Service is limited to administrators by default. This is a reasonable setting since all jobs executing from the Schedule Service run as the same user as the service itself (usually *System*).

You can extend access to it to the *System Operators* group by adding the SubmitControl value to the HKEY_LOCAL_MACHINE\System\CurrentControlSet\ Control\Lsa registry key. This value should have a data type of REG_DWORD and be set to 1.

Tools for Creating a Compute Server

As we've noted before, Windows NT is not a traditional multiuser operating system. On a given computer system, only one user may be logged in interactively at a time. Some types of applications (such as database systems) have been designed with a client/server architecture in which the bulk of the computing is performed on the server computer system by a single process, thereby eliminating the need for any users to connect directly to the server. However, not all applications are amenable to such a strategy.

This disregard of multiuser system access may once have made sense in the traditional microcomputer environment when the processor in an individual system was not capable of supporting more than a single user. However, it's a significant drawback when Windows NT runs on high-end systems with their substantial computing resources.

The Windows NT Schedule Service also provides a limited mechanism for sharing a system's CPU resources among multiple users, but it is a long way from being a secure, general purpose batch facility. In this section, we look at some commercial packages that provide facilities of this sort for Windows NT systems.

There are a variety of ways that you might want to share a powerful computer system among a group of users. For example, such a system might be used to run one or more resource-intensive applications in a controlled way, limiting the number of jobs that can be running at any one time and the amount of system resources that any one of them may consume. At the other extreme, a powerful server computer might be deployed to handle routine, not particularly CPU-taxing tasks for a large number of users (for example, electronic mail and word processing). We'll consider these two different strategies separately.

The Camellia Batch Job Server

The Batch Job Server (BJS) package from Camellia Software adds an excellent batch queuing system to Windows NT. It allows the administrator to create one or more batch queues on a server; users may submit jobs to a queue from their own workstation (provided they are allowed access to the batch system), and the batch server automatically runs the jobs in sequence. The system administrator can specify the number of jobs that can be run at the same time from each queue as well as resource limits for each job. He can also manipulate any active or waiting job, canceling it, temporarily restraining it within the queue, changing its place on the list of waiting jobs, and so on.

The BJS package consists of two parts: a server process that runs on the Windows NT system, which will be the compute server and a client program that users run on their own system to submit jobs to the batch system.

The package also includes an administrative tool that can configure and manage the system either locally or remotely. We will consider these two major functions separately. The first step for performing either management or configuration is selecting the desired server system to administer via the tool's **Server➤Connect...** menu path.

Once the server has been designated, the batch system running on it can be configured by selecting **Server➤Administer...**. Configuration and systemwide maintenance is performed from the resulting **Server Administration** dialog box, illustrated in Figure 4-5.

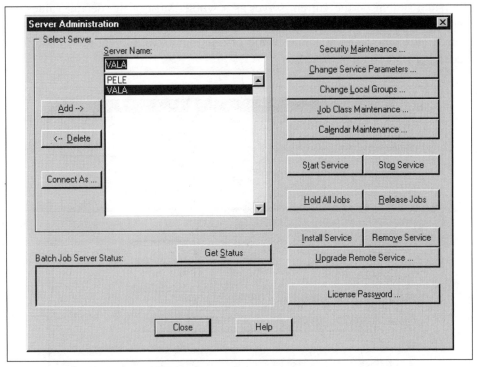

Figure 4-5. The BJS Server Administration tool

For a new BJS installation, the dialog box's **Install Service** button is used to install the server as a system service. Once it is installed, you can configure the service in the normal way via the **Services** control panel applet, including designating a user account under which the service will run. (The short name of the BJS service is **jbserver**.)

The **Server Administration** dialog box's **Get Status** displays the current status of the BJS server in the output area below it, illustrated in Figure 4-6.

Figure 4-6. Displaying BJS server status

The BJS package allows you to specify operating parameters for the server via the dialog box's **Change Server Parameters...** button, which results in the dialog box in Figure 4-7. This dialog box allows you to specify usage and resource limits for the batch system on the current server as a whole. Most of the default values are reasonable. However, I set the time period before completed jobs are removed from their queue to its minimum value of one minute to prevent the queue from becoming cluttered with old jobs.

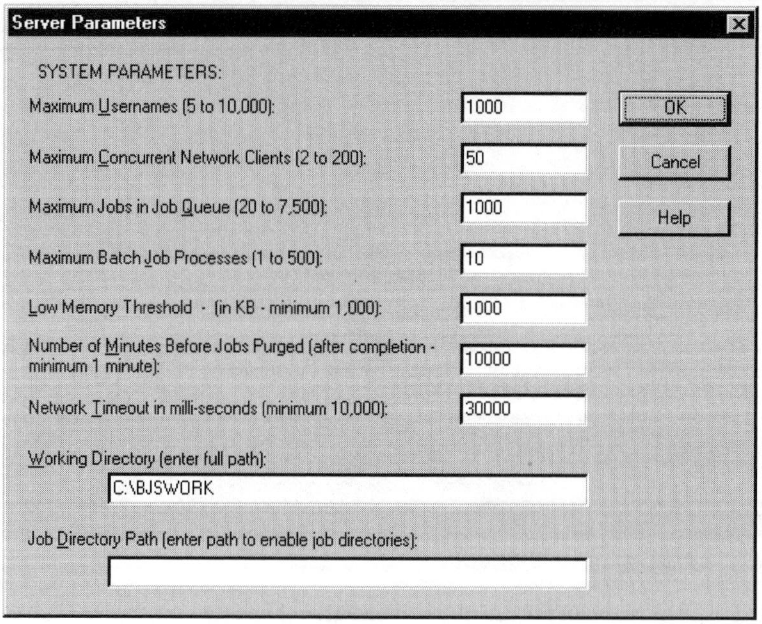

Figure 4-7. BJS server parameters

Individual queues—which the BJS package calls *job classes*—are created and configured via the **Server Administration** dialog box's **Job Class Maintenance...** button. The resulting dialog box allows you to specify the name and description of each queue. By default, the package provides a single job class, appropriately named Default. Pressing the **View/Edit Configuration Options...** button brings up still another dialog box containing the configuration settings for the queue (illustrated in Figure 4-8).

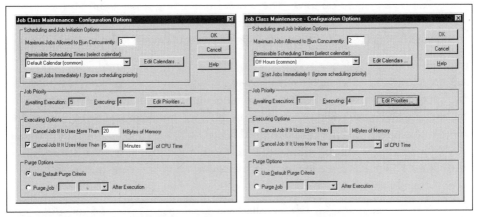

Figure 4-8. Configuring BJS batch queues

These are the most important queue settings:

Maximum Jobs Allowed to Run Concurrently

Specifies how many jobs from this job class may be running at any given time.

Permissible Scheduling Times

Selects a calendar for the queue (calendars indicate permissible and forbidden times for job execution).

Job Priority

The **Awaiting Execution** priority specifies the importance of jobs from this job class with respect to all other pending jobs. This priority level is used when the systemwide job maximum is reached. The **Executing** priority specifies the Windows NT priority class for the resulting process (it may currently be set to Normal or High).

Cancel Job If It Uses More Than ___ MBytes of Memory

Sets an upper limit on the amount of memory used by the job. If a job exceeds this amount, it is automatically canceled.

Cancel Job If It Uses More Than ___ of CPU Time

Sets a limit on the total amount of CPU time the job may consume as it executes.

Figure 4-8 illustrates two different job classes. The left dialog box corresponds to a queue named *Short*, which can execute up to three simultaneous jobs. This job class limits system resource use to 20 MB of memory and 5 minutes of CPU time. Pending jobs from this queue have normal pending and execution priorities.

The right dialog box in the figure corresponds to a job class named *Long*, from which only two jobs may run at the same time. It uses an alternate calendar to specify allowed times for its jobs to run (calendars are defined via the dialog box's **Edit Calendar...** button). The queue's pending jobs wait at the lowest possible priority level, but jobs from this job class execute at Normal priority. The queue imposes no resource limits on jobs that execute from it, however.

Together with the overall server parameters, properly designed and configured queues allow you to control overall system usage and to ensure that the system does not become overwhelmed by too many simultaneous jobs. For example, on this system, the systemwide maximum number of batch processes is set to 4 to prevent the system from being overused. Thus, when two *Long* jobs are running, only two *Short* jobs will be allowed (even though the job class limit is three jobs). In Chapter 11 we consider techniques for determining the best queue setup for a given system workload.

Access to the batch system is controlled via local groups. By default, three new groups are created when the BJS package is installed (although you can change the group associated with each function at any time via the **Change Local Groups...** button on the **Server Administration** dialog box). From a system access standpoint, the most important group is *Batch Users*, whose members are allowed to submit batch jobs. In addition, users must authenticate themselves with their passwords the first time they use the BJS system.

Users submit jobs using the administrative or client utility's **Job➤Maintain/Submit Jobs...** menu path. Doing so is a two-step process: first, the job is defined, and then it is submitted to the system. Jobs are defined using the **Job Database Maintenance** dialog box, illustrated in Figure 4-9. The fields below the list of defined jobs (which is empty in the illustration) are used to specify the job's name, script file and its arguments, and username under which the job will execute (ordinary users may execute jobs only as themselves). The job class is specified using the **Edit/View Scheduling and Execution Criteria** button.

Once a job is defined, the **Submit Now!** button submits it to the server for eventual execution.

The system administrator can manage queues and the jobs within them using the **Active Job Summary** list, which appears when you connect to a BJS server as illustrated in Figure 4-10. The various items on the **Job** menu can examine and manipulate individual jobs. Jobs can be canceled (if running) and removed from the system (although they remained defined within the job database), temporarily

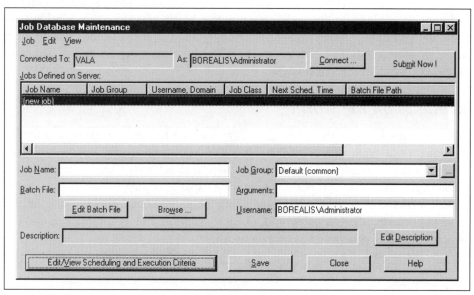

Figure 4-9. Defining a BJS batch job

held (prevented from starting) and later released, and have their pending and execution priorities modified. The status log for any running job may also be viewed by double clicking on its entry in the list.

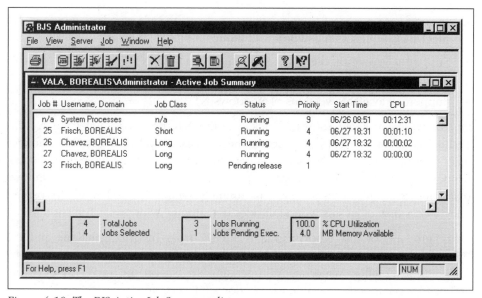

Figure 4-10. The BJS Active Job Summary list

The BJS package includes other features, which we do not have space to explore, including capabilities for periodic execution of batch jobs (like the Windows NT Schedule Service), facilities for summarizing system usage over time, and an alternate job submission mechanism via a designated directory to which the user simply copies the desired job script.

Windows on the World

Batch systems like the BJS package are well-suited to running many unattended programs on a single server system. However, sometimes using a server to run a large number of relatively small user tasks makes sense. For example, even medium-size Windows NT systems would be capable of supporting many simultaneous sessions of typical word processing or spreadsheet applications. In this model, however, the server would need to support full graphical sessions on remote computer systems across the network.

Ideally, a solution for this type of server use would have the following characteristics:

- Add functionality via a normal Windows NT server process that can be configured and secured in the usual ways.

- Provide multiple, independent connections to the server from a single remote host (rather than just a single window containing a virtual Windows NT desktop).

- Include access control to its facilities, implemented via standard Windows NT mechanisms such as passwords and groups.

- Support a variety of client systems: other Windows NT systems, Windows 95 systems, and UNIX.

- Support all available versions of Windows NT.

Of this type's available software packages, the NTerprise package from Exodus Technologies comes closest to meeting these goals. It adds a service to a nondomain controller Windows NT server system that can provide multiple independent windows on a Windows NT server from any computer supporting X Windows (including other Windows NT systems running X emulator software). Its biggest drawback is that, as of this writing, it does not support Windows NT version 4.0.

Other products of this type include NTRIGUE from Insignia Solutions and the WinFrame family from Citrix Systems. Both products currently operate by providing a modified Windows NT operating system on the server in question, and neither is currently available for Windows NT version 4.0.

Microsoft has announced it is licensing technology from Citrix aimed primarily at supporting so-called Windows terminals: low-cost, diskless workstations, whose disk and major computing resources will be provided by a Windows NT server system. This project, code-named "Hydra," may eventually provide a partial solution to the Windows NT multiuser support dilemma, but it is not clear how generally applicable its facilities will be.

5

In this chapter:
- *Adding Hard Disks*
- *Managing Disk Partitions*
- *Filesystems*
- *Network Filesystem Access*

Disks and Filesystems

Managing the filesystem—the aggregate of disk resources available to system and domain users—is one of the system administrator's most important tasks. You are responsible for ensuring that users have access to the files and data they need and that these files remain intact, uncorrupted, and secure. In a Windows NT environment, administering the filesystem includes:

- Making files and directories available to local and domain users

- Monitoring and managing the (usually) finite disk resources

- Protecting against file corruption, hardware failures, and user errors by establishing a well-planned backup schedule

- Ensuring data confidentiality by limiting file and system access

- Checking for and correcting filesystem corruption

- Connecting and configuring new storage devices when needed

For the Windows NT system administrator, all of these traditional tasks can be complicated by the fact that Windows NT filesystems are typically spread across multiple server systems in a local network. We'll consider all of them in this chapter and the next two, beginning with physical disks and ending with individual files and directories.

Making a physical disk available to users involves a series of steps:

- Installing and configuring the hardware (potentially including both the device and its controller).

- Performing low-level formatting of the disk. This step is usually performed by the manufacturer and is thus seldom necessary. On those rare occasions when it is, you perform it with a utility provided by the disk's manufacturer.

- Partitioning the disk, dividing it into one or more logically independent pieces.

- Creating filesystems on each partition, a process called *formatting* in the Windows world.

- Adding files and directories to the new filesystems.

- Specifying access permissions for these files and directories.

- Enabling network access (*sharing*) for some or all of the filesystem.

Once the filesystem resources are available to the network, only the normal maintenance tasks like backups and monitoring filesystem usage remain.

Adding Hard Disks

On Intel systems, there are two types of hard disks in common use: IDE disks and SCSI disks; Alpha systems come equipped with SCSI disks. The names IDE and SCSI actually refer to the interface used by the computer hardware to communicate with the disk, rather than the disk itself.* Specifications for various IDE and SCSI adapters (disk controllers) vary quite a bit, but high-end SCSI subsystems are many times faster than the best IDE-based ones (we'll consider disk I/O performance in Chapter 11).

Before you can add a new disk to a Windows NT system, you must configure the drive to work properly in the target system. If you are also adding an adapter card, it too must be configured. In the latter case, the primary concern is that the IRQ and other settings for the new disk controller must not conflict with those already in use elsewhere in the system.

IDE controllers can support up to two devices. In a typical IDE-based computer, one or more IDE controllers are included on the motherboard. There is also a variety of controller cards suitable for serving as a second IDE adapter. IDE disks are installed internally within the CPU cabinet.

When you add a second disk drive to an IDE controller, you usually need to perform some minor reconfiguration for both the existing and new disks. One disk must be designated as the master device and the other as the slave device; generally, the existing disk becomes the master and the new disk is the slave. The master/slave setting for a disk is specified by means of a jumper on the disk drive itself, almost always located on the same face of the disk as the bus and power connector sockets. Consult the documentation for the disk you are using to determine the jumper location and proper setting, as well as the procedures for

---

* Virtually all IDE devices these days are actually EIDE (Enhanced IDE), but we won't worry about this distinction here since it does not affect the procedures we'll be discussing. Purists will also note that the correct designation for this standard is ATA.

physically installing it into the computer. (Note that the master/slave setting is not an operational definition, and the two disks are treated equally by Windows NT).

WARNING   Filesystems on SCSI disks aren't guaranteed to survive a change of controller type (although they usually will); the standard doesn't specify that they must be interoperable. Thus, if you move a SCSI disk containing data from one Windows NT system to another using a different kind of SCSI controller, there's a chance you won't be able to access the existing data on the disk and will have to reformat it. Similarly, if you need to change the SCSI adapter in a computer, it's safest to replace it with another of the same model.

SCSI disks may be internal or external. These disks are designated by a number ranging from 0 to 6, known as the SCSI ID (SCSI ID 7 is used by the controller itself). Normal SCSI adapters can thus support up to seven devices, each of which must be assigned a unique SCSI ID. SCSI IDs are generally set by jumpers on internal devices and by a thumbwheel or push button counter on external devices. When you change the ID setting of a SCSI disk, the device must be power cycled before the change takes effect.

NOTE   On rare occasions, the ID display setting on an external SCSI disk won't match what is actually being set. When this happens, the counter is either attached incorrectly (backward) or faulty (the SCSI ID doesn't change even though the counter does). When you are initially configuring a device, check the controller's power-on message to determine whether all devices are being recognized and the actual SCSI ID assignments are being used.

There are a variety of connectors that you will encounter on SCSI devices:

- 25-pin DB-25 connectors resemble those on serial cables. They have 25 rounded pins positioned in two rows about $\frac{1}{8}$-inch apart. For example, these connectors are used on external SCSI Zip drives.

- 50-pin Centronics connectors were once the most common sort of SCSI connector. The pins on the connector are attached to the top and bottom of a narrow flat plastic bar about 2 inches long, and the connector is secured to the device by wire clips on each end.

- 50-pin micro connectors (also known as mini-micro connectors or SCSI II connectors) are distinguished by their flat, closely spaced pins, also placed in two rows. This connector is much narrower than the others: about one inch wide.

- 68-pin connectors (also known as SCSI III connectors) are a version of micro connectors designed for wide SCSI devices.

You can purchase cables in any combination of these connectors, as well as adapters to convert between them. An excellent mail order source for SCSI accessories is CTG (contact information is listed in Appendix B).

The various SCSI devices on a system are connected in a daisy chain (serially in a single line). The first and last devices in the chain must be terminated for proper operation. For example, when the SCSI chain is entirely external, the final device has a terminator attached and the SCSI adapter itself usually provides termination for the beginning of the chain (check its documentation to determine whether or not this feature must be enabled). Similarly, when the chain is composed of both internal and external devices, the first device on the internal portion of the SCSI bus will have termination enabled (for example, a jumper on an internal disk), and the final external device will again have a terminator attached.

Termination consists of regulating the voltages across the various lines comprising the SCSI bus. There are several different types of SCSI terminators:

- *Passive* terminators are constructed from resistors. They attempt to ensure that the line voltages in the SCSI chain remain within their proper operating ranges. This type of termination is the least expensive, but tends to work well only when there are just one or two devices in the SCSI chain and activity on the bus is minimal.

- *Active* terminators use voltage regulators and resistors to force the line voltages to their proper ranges. While passive terminators simply reduce the incoming signal to the proper level (thus remaining susceptible to all power fluctuations within it), active terminators use a voltage regulator to ensure a steady standard for use in producing the target voltages. Active terminators are only slightly more expensive than passive terminators, and they are always more reliable. The SCSI II standard calls for active termination for all SCSI chains.

- *Forced perfect termination* (FPT) uses a more complex and accurate voltage regulation scheme to force line voltages to their correct values. In this scheme, the voltage standard is taken from the output of two regulated voltages, and diodes are used to eliminate fluctuations within it. This results in increased stability over active termination. Forced perfect termination will generally eliminate any flakiness in a SCSI chain, and you should consider it any time your chain consists of more than three devices even though it is two to three times more expensive than active termination.

- Some hybrid terminators are also available. In such devices, key lines are controlled via forced perfect termination, and the remaining lines are regulated with active termination. Such devices tend to be almost as expensive as FPT terminators and so are seldom preferable to them.

You should also be aware of the distinction between normal and *differential* SCSI devices. In the latter type, there are two physical wires for each signal within the bus, and such devices use the voltage difference between the two wires as the signal value. This design reduces noise on the bus and allows for longer cable lengths. Special cables and terminators are needed for such SCSI devices (as well as adapter support).

On Alpha systems, one of the Advanced CMOS settings maintained by the Alpha-BIOS program controls whether SCSI termination is enabled or not on the SCSI adapter (select **CMOS Setup...** from the AlphaBIOS main menu and then press F6). If you have external devices connected to the SCSI, this item should be set to **External**.

Managing Disk Partitions

On PC systems, physical disks may be divided into no more than four distinct parts known as *partitions*. Traditionally, PC disk partitions are of two types: *primary* partitions, originally designed as the system partition, and *extended* partitions. Some DOS versions will recognize only a single primary partition per physical disk. The important distinction for the system administrator between these partition types on Windows NT systems is that extended partitions may be further subdivided into units known as *logical drives* and thereby provide a means for dividing a physical disk into more than four pieces. On Windows NT systems, a disk may contain up to four primary partitions, possibly including one extended partition.

Windows NT drive letters are assigned to disk partitions rather than to disks. Even an unpartitioned disk still contains one partition (consisting of the entire disk). By default, drive letters are assigned first to the primary partition on each disk and then to the extended partitions and logical drives. The Windows NT Disk Administrator tool may also be used to assign or change drive letter designations.

Figure 5-1 illustrates disk partitions and drive letter assignments. The first disk on this system has three partitions. The second of them is an extended partition divided into two logical drives (the volumes *Isis* and *Indira*). The second disk in the system has two partitions. Thus, between the two disks, there are six different disk partitions, each accessed via a distinct drive letter.

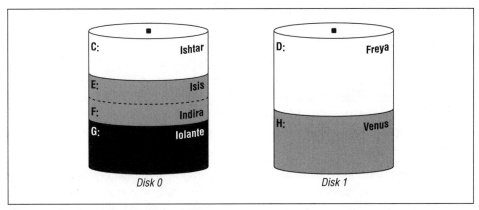

Figure 5-1. Disk partitions and drive letters

Using the Disk Administrator

Disk partitions may be managed via the Disk Administrator utility, pictured in Figure 5-2. This tool provides a graphical representation of the system's disks and their partitions.

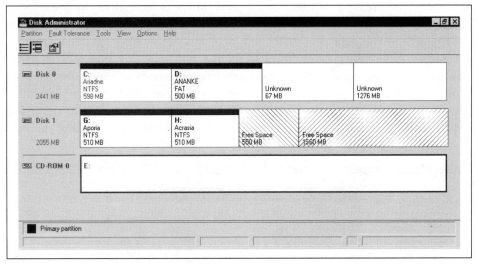

Figure 5-2. The Disk Administrator utility

Existing partitions are designated by drive letter and volume name (if applicable). For example, disk 0 in Figure 5-2 has two partitions named *Ariadne* and *Ananke*, as well as two others (which happen to be used by the Linux operating system).

Disk 1 also has two partitions, designated by drive letters, and extended partitions, as well as quite of bit of free space that has not been allocated to any partition. The third disk in the example display is a CD-ROM drive.

To create a new partition, select an area of free space and then choose **Create**... or **Create Extended**... from the **Partition** menu (depending on the sort of partition that you want to create). When you create a second (or greater) primary partition on a disk, the Disk Administrator displays a warning reminding you that DOS may not be able to access it. Unless you plan to use the disk with vanilla DOS as well, you can safely ignore this message.

If you created a primary partition, the new partition immediately appears in the display, and it is assigned the next available drive letter. If you create an extended partition, the new partition is still marked as free space until you create a logical drive within it. However, its background pattern changes from stripes running upper right to lower left to stripes running from upper left to lower right. For example, in Figure 5-2, Disk 1's 550-MB chunk (on the left) is an extended partition, and its 1560-MB chunk (on the right) is actual free space (the difference is subtle and easy to miss). To create a logical drive, select the extended partition and then choose **Partition▶Create**... from the menu.

Whenever you create a partition or a logical drive—or indeed any disk entity—in the Disk Administrator, you will be presented with a dialog box like that pictured in Figure 5-3. The title and field text will vary depending on what you are creating, but the dialog box always looks and functions the same. For example, the illustration shows the box's appearance when creating a primary partition. However, if you were creating a logical drive, then the words "primary partition" would be replaced by "logical drive" throughout the dialog box. Use the dialog box's size field within it to specify the size of the entity you are creating, choosing a value within the allowed range specified in the dialog box.

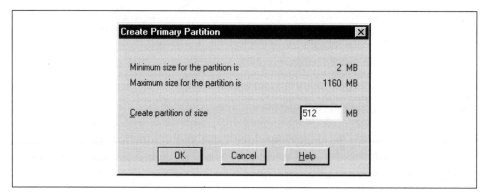

Figure 5-3. Specifying a partition's size

A selected partition may be deleted using the **Partition►Delete** menu path. Obviously, such a step should be taken with care, as all data within the selected partition will be lost once it is deleted.

If you have made changes to the system disk configuration that you decide you'd rather not implement after all, you still have an opportunity to abort them and revert to the disk configuration as it existed at the start of the Disk Administrator session. When you exit from the program, you are asked to confirm changes that you have made via the dialog box illustrated in Figure 5-4. If you select the **No** button, the changes you have made are discarded.

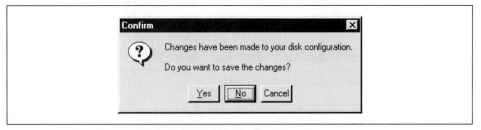

Figure 5-4. Disk Administrator confirmation prompt

The **Partition** menu's **Configuration...►Save** and **Configuration...►Restore** options may be used to save and restore a disk configuration to diskette. It's a good idea to back up the configuration in this way for complex disk partition setups. Such saved configurations may also be applied to different computer systems.

On the other hand, if you want the changes you have made in the Disk Administrator to take effect immediately, select the **Partition►Commit Changes Now...** menu path. This feature is useful, for example, when you have created a new partition and want to format it (discussed in the next section).

Disk Partitioning with the AlphaBIOS Program

On Alpha systems, the AlphaBIOS setup program may also be used to create and delete disk partitions (select **Hard Disk Setup...** from the main menu). The disk manipulation dialog box is displayed in Figure 5-5.

You create a new partition by selecting an area of unused space and then pressing the INSERT key. You are then prompted for the partition size (see Figure 5-6). You can similarly delete an existing partition by selecting it and pressing the F6 key.

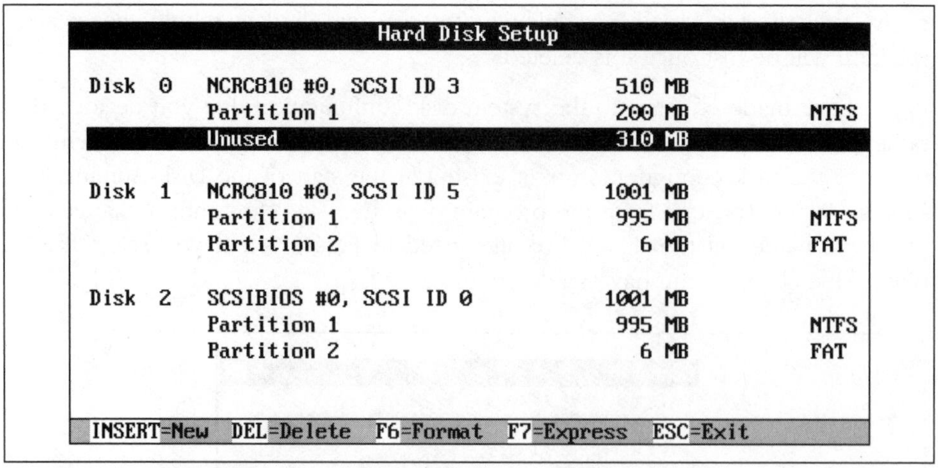

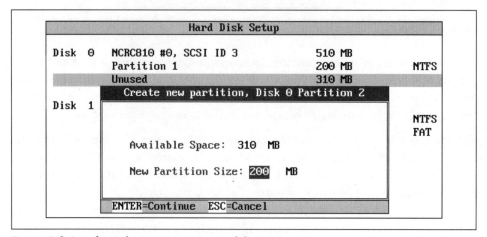

Figure 5-5. The AlphaBIOS hard disk setup facility

Figure 5-6. Specifying the partition size via AlphaBIOS

Partition Wizardry with PartitionMagic (Intel Systems)

The Disk Administrator utility works well for routine partition management tasks (as well as for administering Windows NT's advanced filesystem features, as we shall see). However, it is limited to these routine tasks.

PartitionMagic (from PowerQuest Corp.) is a far more powerful and flexible disk administration utility.* In addition to the normal partition operations, it is capable of performing the following tasks:

---

* As with all software, be sure to get the latest version of the software and the patches to it. Some versions of PartitionMagic require a patch to fix a bug in resizing NTFS filesystems.

- Resizing existing partitions (larger or smaller), provided that the disk configuration supports the desired size. Decreasing a partition's size requires some free space within it (to enable files to be relocated), while increasing a partition's size requires unallocated free space directly beyond the existing partition on the disk.

- Moving a partition to a new location on the same physical disk (again provided that the disk configuration allows it).

- Copying an existing partition (including all its data), either to the same disk or to a different disk.

- Changing the partition type of a partition.

- Hiding a partition (marking it as inaccessible without otherwise altering it).

Because it works by directly accessing a disk's partition tables, PartitionMagic doesn't run under Windows NT (since it requires that all device access take place via operating system services). In order to use it on a Windows NT system, you'll need to boot from a DOS diskette (or a Windows 95) partition first. After doing so, you can run the graphical version from a copy stored on the hard disk or you can run the text-based version (**PQMagicT.Exe**) directly from the product CD.

The ShowDisk Utility

The **ShowDisk** utility included in the Resource Kit may be used to display the complete disk layout characteristics of all disks on the local system. Here is a sample of its output:

```
C:\> showdisk
Opening \SYSTEM\DISK successful

Disk Registry Information Size........ 1268
Operating System Version............. 3
Checksum............................. 0x0
Dirty Shutdown?...................... 1
...
Disk Info Offset..................... 0x2c
Disk Info Size....................... 876
FT Info Offset....................... 0x398
FT Info Size......................... 348
FT Stripe Width...................... 0
FT Pool Size......................... 3
...

General Disk Information:
Number of Disks...................... 5
<reserved>........................... 0

  Disk #0:
    Number Of Partitions.......... 2
```

```
        <reserved>.................... 0x0
        Signature..................... 0x3d0622e7

        Partition #1:
            FT Type............... Not a Fault Tolerance Partition
            FT State.............. Healthy
            Starting Offset....... 0x7e00
            Length................ 627540480
            FtLength.............. 0
            <reserved 1>.......... 0x0
            <reserved 2>.......... 0x0
            Drive Letter.......... C
            Assign Drive Letter?.. Yes
            Logical Number........ 1
            Ft Group.............. Not an FT Partition
            Modified?............. Yes
            ...
        Partition #2:
            FT Type............... Not a Fault Tolerance Partition
            FT State.............. Healthy
            Starting Offset....... 0x25680000
            Length................ 524353536
            FtLength.............. 0
            <reserved 1>.......... 0x0
            <reserved 2>.......... 0x0
            Drive Letter.......... D
            Assign Drive Letter?.. Yes
            Logical Number........ 2
            Ft Group.............. Not an FT Partition
            Modified?............. Yes
            ...
```

The output from this command continues for the other disks on the system.

Filesystems

A disk partition remains inaccessible to users until a filesystem is created on it. The process of initializing a filesystem and setting up the data structures that it will use for keeping track of the files and directories within it is known as *formatting.*[*] We begin with a consideration of the various types of filesystems found on Windows NT systems before we turn to the mechanism of formatting partitions.

Filesystem Types

Windows NT supports the following types of filesystems:

---

[*] Sometimes known as *soft* formatting, in contrast to the lower-level (*hard*) formatting, which is performed at the disk level.

FAT

> The filesystem type supported by DOS and Windows 3.1/95 systems (FAT stands for file allocation table). Note that Windows NT does not currently support the 32-bit version of this filesystem type available under Windows 95 (FAT-32).

NTFS

> The native Windows NT filesystem type (we'll consider its characteristics in a moment).

HPFS

> The native OS/2 filesystem type. Support for HPFS filesystems was withdrawn in Windows NT 4.0, but you can reenable it with the following steps:

> — Copy the *Pinball.Sys* file from the *%SystemRoot%/System32/Drivers* subdirectory of a Windows NT 3.5 or 3.51 system or distribution CD to the same location on the target system.

> — Add a key named Pinball to the HKEY_LOCAL_MACHINE\System\CurrentControlSet\Services registry location.

> — Add the following values to the new registry key:

Value	Data Type	Data Setting
ErrorControl	REG_DWORD	1
Group	REG_SZ	Boot file system
Start	REG_DWORD	1
Type	REG_DWORD	2

> Given the lack of official support for HPFS, however, it is probably a good idea to convert such filesystems to NTFS as soon as possible.

CD-ROM filesystems

> Windows NT provides transparent support for reading CDs in the standard ISO9660 format.

The NTFS filesystem type

NTFS is a new filesystem type created for Windows NT that incorporates the normal features of other modern filesystems. These are its most important characteristics:

Journaling

> NTFS filesystems use techniques borrowed from real-time transaction processing to ensure file system structure integrity at all times. Before any change is made to the filesystem structure, it is first recorded in a designated log file (a circular buffer that is reused as necessary). During a system boot,

the filesystem structure is automatically made current with its log. This guarantees that even after a sudden power loss, the filesystem will return to some consistent state when the system reboots (although not necessarily to the exact state it was in when the power failure occurred).

This doesn't completely prevent data loss, however. Only changes to the structure of the filesystem are logged (for example, what file is using a particular disk cluster), the changes to its contents are not (what is actually stored in that cluster).

Enhanced file security

The NTFS file system supports *discretionary access control* (DAC), which allows permitted and forbidden access to be specified in considerable detail.

Lazy-write scheme

Disk write operations are actually performed to a cache in memory rather than directly to disk. The cache is periodically flushed to disk in the background. This scheme is designed to optimize overall system I/O performance. It can also result in file changes being lost in the event of a power failure.[*]

The freely available **NTSync** utility (written by Mark Russinovich) may be used to manually force all disk buffers to be written out at any time:

```
C:\> ntsync

NTSync 1.2 - Disk Flusher
Copyright (C) 1997 Mark Russinovich
http://www.ntinternals.com

Flushing: C D G H I J K L          Drive letters display as each one is synched.
```

The utility's **/R** option may be used to include removable media (e.g., Zip drives) in the operation. The utility must be run from an Administrator account.

Mirrored master file table and boot sector

In addition to the primary ones located at the beginning of the disk, the NTFS filesystem stores a second copy of all of its structural and boot-related data files in the middle of the disk.

The NTFS filesystem is unambiguously preferable to the FAT filesystem, and I recommend using it for all filesystems on Windows NT systems.[†] The only exception occurs when you need to share a disk partition between Windows NT and

---

[*] FAT filesystems on Windows NT systems also use a lazy-write strategy (in contrast to the DOS careful write scheme).

[†] Well, almost all. On Alpha systems, a small FAT (6 MB) filesystem is required to hold the boot programs. This restriction does not apply to Intel systems with Windows NT 4.0. Also, some older laptops won't hibernate to an NTFS partition and so may need a FAT partition for this purpose.

another operating system (DOS, Windows, Linux, or other UNIX) on the same computer (at different times, obviously), and the partition must be writeable by all of them. We look at tools for reading NTFS partitions from other operating systems later in this chapter.

In an NTFS filesystem, all files (and directories, which are really just a type of file) exist as records in the *master file table* (MFT). The NTFS filesystem itself uses the inaccessible system files listed in Table 5-1 to store its metadata (information about the filesystem structure). These files are stored in the first 16 records of the MFT.

Table 5-1. MFT Metadata Files

File	Contents
$Mft	Master file table contents
$MftMirr	Location of the copy of the metadata files elsewhere on disk
$LogFile	Transaction log
$Volume	Volume information, including its name and NTFS version
$AttrDef	Attribute definition table
$.	Root directory for the filesystem
$Bitmap	Cluster bitmap file indicating the status (used or free) for each cluster in the filesystem
$Boot	Boot file
$BadClus	List of bad clusters
$Quota	Reserved for future use for disk quotas
$Upcase	Unicode lowercase to uppercase conversion table (for translating filenames)

Within an NTFS filesystem, a file is a collection of attributes stored in an MFT record (and possibly elsewhere on disk), including the following:

- Basic file information, such as the file's DOS attributes, creation, modification and access times, and the number of hard links to it.

- The filename: Windows NT filenames can be up to 255 characters in length and may contain any letters, numbers, or symbols (Unicode characters) except the following: ? " \ / * : < > and | (spaces are fine). File extensions are recognized, but a period is still just another character in the filename.

  More than one filename attribute is usually present. One holds the long filename, another the short (eight-plus-three) DOS-style filename, and still others hold alternate filenames for files to which there are multiple hard links (discussed later in this chapter).

- Security attribute: the Windows NT access permissions.

- Data attribute: the data stored in the file.

- Additional indexing data for directories.

For all but the smallest files, the data attribute is too large to fit into the MFT record. In this case, that attribute indicates the disk location of the actual data. The security attribute can also be large enough to require storage beyond that available in the MFT record.

Sometimes, the MFT record data itself grows larger than a single record, and additional MFT records must be used. In this case, an attribute list is created for the record holding a list of the attributes for the file, along with their MFT record locations.

See Helen Custer's *Inside the Windows NT File System* (Microsoft Press) for more information about the NTFS filesystem design

Managing Filesystems

Filesystems may be created on disk partitions using the Disk Administrator tool or from the command line.* The Disk Administrator's **Tools➤Format** menu path may be used to format the selected disk partition. (If this menu item is disabled, then select **Partition➤Commit Changes Now** to write the modifications to the disk configuration to the device.) The resulting dialog box is illustrated in Figure 5-7.

You can use this dialog box to specify the filesystem type (via the **File System** menu), the volume label for the new filesystem, and whether or not file compression is enabled by default (discussed later in this section).

You can also use the **Format** command to create or recreate a filesystem from the command line. When applied to disk partitions, it has the following syntax:

```
format [/fs:ntfs] [/V:label] [/C] [/A:n] x:
```

where *x* is the drive letter of the partition you want to format, and *label* specifies the volume label for the new filesystem. Include the /C option if you want to enable automatic file compression for the filesystem. The /FS option specifies the type of filesystem to be created; its argument must be either **NTFS** or **FAT** (the default is the current type for an existing filesystem and FAT for a new partition).

For example, the following command creates an NTFS filesystem on drive *H:* with automatic file compression enabled, labeling the filesystem as *Rika*:

```
C:\> format /C /FS:NTFS /V:Rika H:
```

The **Format** command's /A option specifies the *allocation unit size* for the filesystem. This parameter specifies the cluster size for the filesystem, the unit in

---

* On Alpha systems, the Disk Setup facility of the AlphaBIOS program can also format disk partitions.

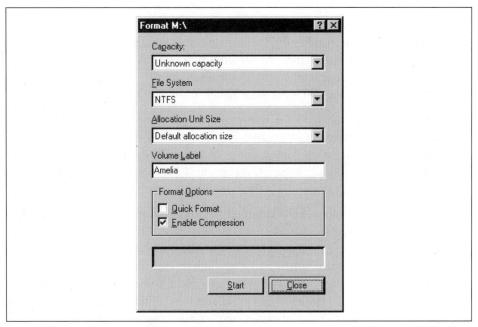

Figure 5-7. Formatting a partition with the Disk Administrator

which disk space is allocated. It usually defaults to 4 KB.* Its valid range is any power of 2 from 512 bytes to 64 KB. However, file compression cannot be performed on filesystems using a cluster size of more than 4 KB.

For most purposes, the default value works well and should be left alone. You might want to use a smaller size if you anticipate that the filesystem will be used for very many very small files (smaller than the default allocation unit size). In this case, a smaller size reduces the amount of internal wasted space. At the other extreme, if the filesystem will be used exclusively by an application that performs very large I/O operations (say, hundreds of kilobytes at a minimum), then a larger cluster size sometimes improves its I/O performance, as well as its allocation efficiency.

If you think the disk use on your system might benefit from a different cluster size, it's a good idea to create a sample filesystem and test it under the sort of usage you expect before committing to a nondefault value.

---

* For filesystems over 2 GB in size. The other defaults are 512 bytes for filesystems of 512 MB or less, 1 KB for filesystems from 513 MB to 1 GB, and 2 KB for filesystems between 1 and 2 GB.

Built-in file compression

Optional automatic file compression is available for NTFS filesystems. File compression occurs transparently to the user, and no special steps are needed when accessing compressed files. In file-browsing windows, compressed files can be displayed in an alternate color by turning on the corresponding browser option (accessible via **View▸Options...▸View**).

Compression can be specified for individual files, for directories and for the filesystem as a whole when it is created (which enables compression on its root directory). The compression setting for a directory is inherited by all files and subdirectories subsequently created within it. Files are compressed in place, remaining in the same location with the same name as before the operation.

Even if automatic compression is disabled for a filesystem, you can still enable it for a particular file or directory using the **General** tab of the item's **Properties**. For a directory, checking the **Compress** box in the **Attributes** area at the bottom of the panel (illustrated in Figure 5-8) marks that directory as compressed and immediately compresses all files within it; you also have the option of marking and compressing any subdirectories within it at the same time. For an individual file, checking the same box (now labeled **Compressed**) compresses the file. As you'd expect, clearing the check box for a compressed item reexpands it; for a directory, this also uncompresses all of the files within it.

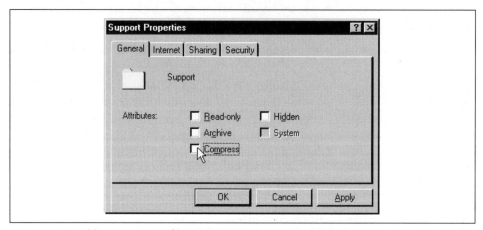

Figure 5-8. Enabling automatic file compression

The **Compact** command can perform these same operations from the command line. The command has the following syntax:

```
compact [/C | /U] [options] [file(s)]
```

If present, the first option specifies whether the specified items are to be compressed (/C) or uncompressed (/U). By default, the command displays the current compression state of the specified items (which defaults to the files in the current directory). Other useful options are: /S to recurse all subdirectories under any specified directory; /I to continue processing even after an error is encountered; and /Q to produce terse command output. For example, the following **Compact** command displays the status of the one file and two subdirectories in the current directories.

```
C:\> compact

Listing C:\Support\
New files added to this directory will be compressed.

    Sizes: uncompressed    compressed (both in bytes)
        0 :          0 = 1.0 to 1    BOOKS
        0 :          0 = 1.0 to 1 C I386
     1168 :        512 = 2.3 to 1 C README.TXT

Of 3 files within 1 directories
2 are compressed and 1 are not compressed.
1,168 total bytes of data are stored in 512 bytes.
The compression ratio is 2.3 to 1.
```

The *Books* subdirectory is not compressed, and the *I386* subdirectory and the file *ReadMe.Txt* both are compressed (indicated by the "C" to the left of the filename). New items added to the current directory will also be compressed by default. The final section of the output gives overall statistics for the group of files.

The first command of the following two commands compresses all of the files in the *Books* subdirectory and any subdirectories it may have, marking all of them as compressed directories. In contrast, the second command simply marks the *I386* subdirectory for automatic compression without affecting any of its current files or subdirectories. In both cases, terse command output is specified:

```
C:\> compact /C /S /Q  Books\*
C:\> compact /C /Q I386
```

If you want to mark each subdirectory within an entire directory tree for compression without affecting any of the current files, the command form is something like this:

```
C:\> compact /C /S C:\Support C:\Support\*.
```

This command marks all of the subdirectories in the *C:\Support* tree as compressed, but does not disturb any of the files themselves (provided that all regular files have nonnull file extensions).

The Resource Kit includes the **Compress** command for manual file compression and expansion; its counterpart is the standard Windows NT **Expand** command.

They create compressed or uncompressed versions of a set of specified files in a separate directory location. For example, the following command creates a compressed version of each file in *C:\NewDist* in *C:\Xfer*.

```
C:\> compress C:\NewDist\*.* C:\Xfer
```

The following command also compresses those files in *C:\NewDist* for which the compressed version (if any) in the target directory is older than the source file:

```
C:\> compress /D C:\NewDist\*.* C:\Xfer
```

The **Expand** command performs the reverse operation using the same syntax (although **/D** is not supported). Both commands also have a **/R** option, which renames the created files using the standard naming convention, which replaces the final character of the file extension for the compressed version with an under-score: for example, **Test.Exe** becomes **Test.Ex_**.

NOTE   The Resource Kit also includes the **ExpndW32** command, a graphi-
              cal utility for expanding files manually from the Windows NT distri-
              bution CD (or other Windows distribution media).

Mounting and checking filesystems

Mounting is the process by which a filesystem is made available to the system. For many operating systems, this task must be performed explicitly by the system administrator, either by manually mounting the desired filesystems or by config-uring the system to automatically mount them at boot-time. On Windows NT systems, all local filesystems are always mounted automatically when the system boots, and there is no standard mechanism for making an existing filesystem temporarily inaccessible to the system except by marking the corresponding disk partition as hidden with a low-level disk partitioning utility such as PartitionMagic.

There is a public-domain utility named **unmount** (written by Christoph H. Hoch-staetter) that can unmount Windows NT filesystems, provided that there are no open files and no other references to them at the time. It is designed primarily for use with removable media, such as that used with Zip, Jaz, and EZ drives. For example, this command unmounts the filesystem referred to by drive letter *G:*

```
C:\> unmount G:
```

The command fails if there are any references to the filesystem. It will not unmount partitions on disks containing multiple active partitions. The package also provides a **mnt** command for mounting unmounted filesystems.

Even with the best design, filesystems can still become corrupt from time to time. The most common cause of these problems are power failures. In such circumstances, the **ChkDsk** utility is used to check the filesystem's consistency, reports any problems it finds, and optionally repairs them. Only under rare circumstances will these repairs cause even minor data loss. **ChkDsk** is run automatically at boot-time on filesystems if they were not dismounted cleanly (for example, in the case of a system crash or a power failure). **ChkDsk** compares such items as the volume bitmap against the disk portions assigned to files in the filesystem, locating and optionally correcting any inconsistencies between the two sets of data.

NOTE **ChkDsk**'s scope is limited to repairing the *structure* of the filesystem and its component metadata. The utility can do nothing for corrupted *data* within structurally intact files.

A system administrator rarely needs to run this utility manually for NTFS filesystems, when flaky system behavior leads you to suspect there may be filesystem corruption (for example, a shared directory suddenly and consistently refuses to make itself available to network users). FAT filesystems in traditional Windows environments are notoriously prone to corruption. While they seem to be more reliable under Windows NT, I still run **ChkDsk** on each of them once a week (whether they need it or not).

The command form **ChkDsk /F** locates and repairs (/F) any problems with the filesystem specified by drive letter as its argument. If the filesystem is currently in use, however, repairs can't take place, and you have the option of scheduling the operation for the next system boot:

```
C:\> chkdsk /f k:
The type of the file system is NTFS.
Chkdsk cannot run because the volume is in use by another
process. Would you like to schedule this volume to be
checked the next time the system restarts? (Y/N) Y
```

Converting FAT filesystems

Existing FAT filesystems may be converted to NTFS filesystems with the **Convert** utility (but not vice versa). For example, the following command will convert the filesystem designated by the *K:* drive letter to an NTFS filesystem:

```
C:\> convert /fs:ntfs K:
```

The conversion process is nondestructive and preserves all existing files within the specified filesystem.

Viewing information about filesystems

There are several methods for obtaining summary information about the disk space usage within a filesystem:

- If you open **My Computer** and select a filesystem (click once on it), its total capacity and free space is displayed in the information bar at the bottom of the window.

- The **General** tab of the **Properties** dialog box for a filesystem displays its total capacity and current used and free space (Figure 5-9).

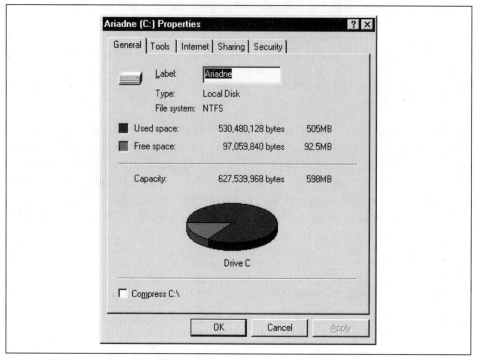

Figure 5-9. Viewing filesystem disk space usage

- Joachim Marder has written a freely available utility named **TreeSize**, which summarizes disk usage on a directory-by-directory basis (it provides function-ality similar to the UNIX **du** command).* Once the utility is running, you spec-ify the filesystem or directory in which you are interested via its **File➤Select Directory** menu path. An example of its output is given in Figure 5-10, which breaks down the disk usage in the system partition on *vala* by subdirectory; I have expanded the display for the *MSOffice* subdirectory to get a more detailed view of it. The free space within the filesystem and the total number of files it contains are displayed in the information bar at the bottom of the window.

---

* The **DirUse** utility in the Resource Kit provides similar functionality from the command line.

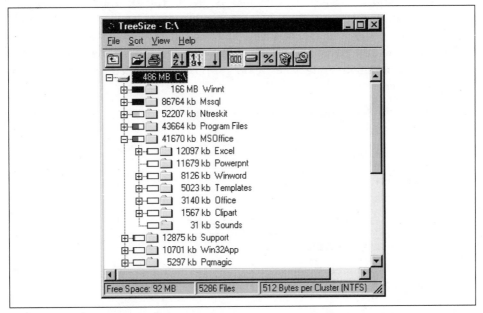

Figure 5-10. The TreeSize utility

- In Chapter 12 we construct a command-line utility for summarizing the status of all local filesystems. For now, we'll just look at its output:

```
C:\> perl df.pl
```

Label	Drive	Total MB	Used MB	Free MB	FS Type
Ariadne	C	598	550	48	Normal
ANANKE	D	500	459	41	Normal
Aporia	G	1021	0	1021	Stripe Set
Acrasia	H	510	0	510	Mirror
Aveya	I	686	7	679	RAID 5
Amelia	J	1162	156	1006	Volume Set
Amanda	K	300	286	14	Volume Set
Anitra	L	439	162	277	Normal

As the header lines indicate, all disk sizes are expressed in megabytes.

Displaying information about open files

Mark Russinovich has written a freely available utility named **NTHandle**, which displays information about current references to open files, including the processes that are using them. It has the following general syntax:

```
nthandle [/A] [/P proc] [string]
```

By default, information on all open files is given. The **/P** option can limit the display to those belonging to a specific process; its argument is a string that matches the process name (usually the executable name—see the **pulist** command). The optional *string* argument may be used to limit the display to files matching the specified string. The **/A** option provides detailed information about each file handle.

For example, the following command lists information about all open files whose names contain "figure":

```
C:\> nthandle figure
NTHandle V1.0
Copyright (C) 1997 Mark Russinovich
http://www.ntinternals.com


EXCEL.EXE          pid: ff    D:\Work\Figures.txt
CMD.EXE            pid: 113   D:\Work\Figures.txt
more.com           pid: 126   D:\Work\Figures.txt
```

The following command displays information about the open files in use by processes with names containing "excel":

```
C:\> nthandle /p excel
NTHandle V1.0
Copyright (C) 1997 Mark Russinovich
http://www.ntinternals.com
------------------------------------------------------------------
EXCEL.EXE pid: ff
      4: Section        C:\MSOffice\Excel\EXCEL.EXE
    140: File           C:\MSOffice\Excel\Examples
    144: File           D:\Work\Figures.txt
    150: File           C:\TEMP\~DF9FA6.tmp
    15c: File           C:\MSOffice\Excel\Examples\SAMPLES.XLS
    164: File           C:\TEMP\20.tmp
    178: File           C:\TEMP\~DF131C.tmp
    188: Section        C:\MSOffice\Excel\XL5EN32.OLB
    18c: Section        C:\WINNT\system32\VBAEN32.OLB
    190: File           C:\WINNT\system32\VBAEN32.OLB
    198: File           C:\WINNT\system32\stdole32.tlb
    19c: Section        C:\WINNT\system32\stdole32.tlb
    1a8: File           C:\MSOffice\Excel\XL5EN32.OLB
```

The following command displays information about open files whose names contain "figure" in use by processes whose names contain "excel":

```
C:\> nthandle /p excel figure
NTHandle V1.0
Copyright (C) 1997 Mark Russinovich
http://www.ntinternals.com


EXCEL.EXE          pid: ff   D:\Work\Figures.txt
```

Accessing NTFS Filesystems from Other Operating Systems

While files and directories within NTFS filesystems can be made available to computers running other operating systems in a variety of ways (as we shall see), they cannot be read directly by normal DOS, Windows, or UNIX commands. NTFS filesystems are officially invisible to DOS, Windows, and other operating systems, so moving a disk containing an NTFS filesystem to such a system (or booting another operating system on the same computer) would result by default in one or more inaccessible partitions. However, there are freely available utilities that can be used to read the contents of NTFS filesystems for both the DOS/Windows and Linux environments.

The NTFSDOS package written by Mark Russinovich and Bryce Cogswell provides transparent read support for NTFS volumes for DOS and Windows systems. Its executable may be run from the command line for ad hoc use or from within the *AutoExec.Bat* file for regular use. By default, the **NTFSDOS** command searches for NTFS filesystems and assigns them the next available drive letters. You can specify drive letters with its /L option (its argument is a concatenated list of drive letters with no internal spaces). Including the /N option reduces its memory use when you know that the filesystems you want to access are uncompressed. Once it's started, the NTFSDOS program remains in memory until the system is rebooted.

The NTFSDOS package has a number of limitations with respect to the sorts of filesystems it can successfully access: the cluster size must be 4 KB or less, disk striping (discussed later in this chapter) is not supported, the partition must be less than 2 GB in size and reside entirely below the disk's 2-GB boundary, files created without short filenames are invisible to pre-7.0 versions of DOS, and some SCSI disks need a DOS driver as well as NTFSDOS in order for their filesystems to be accessible.

NTFS filesystems may also be read directly by Linux systems with the *ntfs* package written by Martin von Loewis. The package includes an optional kernel module and several utilities:

ntdump
   Dump raw data from an NTFS partition

ntgrep
   Search raw data in an NTFS partition

ntdir
   List the contents of a directory in an NTFS filesystem

ntcat

> Display the contents of a file in an NTFS filesystem

The package's documentation discourages its use with the Windows NT partition used to boot the operating system.

Facilities for writing to NTFS filesystems are currently in develoment for both environments.

Advanced Filesystem Features

So far, we've considered only filesystems that occupy a single disk partition. However, Windows NT offers a number of advanced filesystem facilities that allow you to combine multiple physical disk partitions into a single filesystem:

- Filesystem volumes (as defined with a unique drive letter) can occupy more than one disk partition. Existing filesystems may be extended to provide additional disk space within them, and new filesystems spanning multiple disk partitions may be created via Windows NT *volume sets.*

- Striped filesystems may be created for higher I/O performance. *Disk striping* is used to increase I/O performance by splitting I/O transfers across the component physical devices, performing them in parallel. Such filesystems are able to achieve significant speedups over the performance of a single disk (although the improvement is not always "nearly linear," as is sometimes claimed). Disk striping is especially effective for single process transfer rates to a very large file.

- *Fault-tolerant* filesystems based upon the RAID principles are available for increased data protection from disk failures. RAID stands for Redundant Array of Independent Disks, and such devices are designed for increased data integrity and availability via redundant copies of the data. Fault-tolerant filesystems are available only on Windows NT servers.

All these advanced filesystems appear to users and applications as normal filesystems and require no special handling once they are created. This is possible because these advanced features are either supported directly by the NTFS driver (for volume sets) or implemented via the Fault Tolerant driver, which is positioned between the low-level disk driver and the normal NTFS driver.

Figure 5-11 illustrates the appearance of the various available filesystems within the Disk Administrator. In this configuration, there are four ordinary filesystems: *Ariadne* (*C:*), an NTFS filesystem, and *Ananke* (*D:*), a FAT filesystem, both located in primary disk partitions, and *Amanda* (*K:*) and *Anitra* (*L:*), both NTFS filesystems, which share the extended partition on disk 1. Drive *E:* is the system's CD-ROM drive, and drive letter *F:* is used by a mapped network disk. *Aporia* (*G:*) is a striped filesystem, and *Acrasia* (*H:*) and *Aveya* (*I:*) are two types of fault-tolerant filesystems. *Amelia* (*J:*) is a filesystem spanning two physical disk partitions, forming a volume set. Finally, disk 3 contains an area of unpartitioned free space.

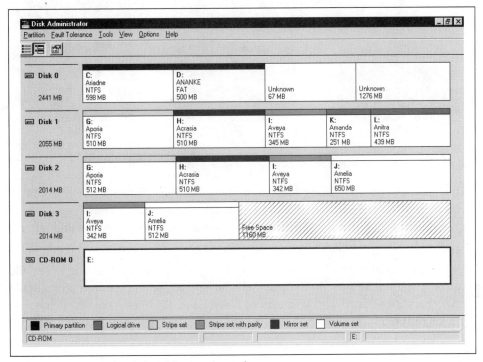

Figure 5-11. A complex disk configuration

We'll consider each of these advanced filesystem facilities individually.

Extending NTFS volumes

Every filesystem within a Windows NT system effectively defines a volume. When more than one partition is used for a single filesystem, the aggregate is known as a *volume set* (illustrated in Figure 5-12).

Creating a volume set is simple with the Disk Administrator:

1. If you want to extend an existing filesystem, then select the corresponding NTFS partition. Any files currently within the filesystem will be preserved.

2. Select areas of free space: one or more for an existing filesystem and two or more for a new volume set. Volume sets may contain up to 32 disk partitions.

3. On the **Partition** menu, select **Create Volume Set** or **Extend Volume Set** as appropriate.

4. Specify the desired size of the volume set in the resulting dialog box.

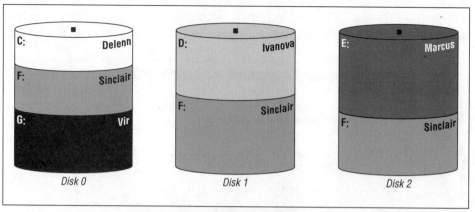

Figure 5-12. Disk configuration including the volume set Sinclair (F:)

When you extend an existing filesystem, the system needs to reboot, and **ChkDsk** runs on that filesystem when the system restarts. Once this is complete, the additional space within the filesystem is available for use. For a new volume set, you still have to create a filesystem by formatting the volume set.

Breaking a volume set is a painful process. You need to backup the entire filesystem and then delete the volume set and create the component partitions as separate entities. Once you create new filesystems, the files from the volume set may be restored as desired.

If any component of a volume set fails, then the entire filesystem becomes unusable and must be recreated and restored. Volume sets are designed for convenience rather than for data integrity. If the latter is important to your system, use one of the fault-tolerant filesystems instead of a volume set.

Filesystems for fault tolerance and performance

As noted before, the Windows NT fault tolerant filesystems are based upon the RAID standard. Physical RAID devices consist of a series of physical disks combined into a single unit, along with additional hardware used to control and access it.

There are six defined RAID levels, which differ in how the multiple disks within the unit are organized and used. Most available hardware RAID devices support all the RAID levels described in Table 5-2 (levels 2 and 4 aren't used in practice). Windows NT provides software-based implementations of RAID levels 0, 1, and 5.

Striped filesystems and fault-tolerant filesystems are managed by the same Windows NT facility (since RAID level 0 is used for the former).

Table 5-2. Commonly Implemented RAID Levels

Level	Description	Advantages
0	Disk striping only (no data mirroring).	Best I/O performance for large transfers. Most efficient storage capacity.
1	Disk mirroring: every disk drive is duplicated for 100% data redundancy.	Most complete data redundancy. Invulnerable to most single disk failures.
3	Disk striping with a parity disk: data is split across component disks, and parity data for each block is stored on a separate disk. The parity data enables reconstruction of all data should any one drive fail.	Data redundancy with minimal overhead. Performs best for large I/O operations.
5	Same as level 3 except that the parity information is split across multiple component disks, in an attempt to prevent the parity disk from becoming an I/O bottleneck.	Data redundancy with minimal overhead. Best rate of I/O operations per second.

Striped filesystems

Disk striping is illustrated in Figure 5-13. Successive chunks of data are written to each of the two disks in turn, and write operations to each disk can occur simultaneously.

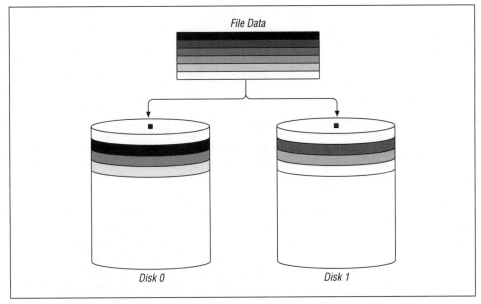

Figure 5-13. A two-way striped filesystem

The following general considerations apply to striped filesystems:

- For maximum performance, the individual disks in the striped filesystem should be on separate disk controllers.

- The partitions selected for striping should be as similar in size as possible. Maximum efficiency and performance is achieved when identically sized partitions in the same physical location on the disk are used as the components of the striped filesystem. If the layouts of the component partitions are different, the size of the smallest one determines the size of the filesystem, and any additional space in the other partitions will be unusable and wasted.

- Disks used for file striping should not be used for any other purpose. Having additional partitions on the same disks as stripe set components will decrease the performance of the striped filesystem.

- In no case should the device containing the system partition be used for disk striping. This is really a corollary of the previous item.

- Although stripe sets can contain up to 32 disk partitions, actual I/O performance improvements are likely to level off significantly before the upper limit. Striped filesystems of 2, 3, and 4 partitions are commonly used. Consider what you hope to achieve carefully and run some preliminary viability tests before creating a production stripe set larger than 8 physical partitions.

A striped filesystem may be created within the Disk Administrator via the following steps:

1. Select two or more regions of free space (up to 32), each on a separate disk.
2. Select the **Partition►Create Stripe Set** menu path.
3. Specify the desired size of the volume set in the resulting dialog box.
4. Format the resulting stripe set to create a filesystem.

Once created, a striped filesystem is transparent to user and application access (except for its performance advantage over an ordinary filesystem). It's not possible to add disks to a stripe set after it is created.

WARNING   In general, the stripe size selected for a striped filesystem is crucial to its performance. The optimal value depends on the typical data transfer characteristics and the typical size of I/O transfer performed by the application programs for which the filesystem is intended. However, Windows NT currently creates striped filesystems using a fixed stripe size of 64 KB, and this value can't be altered by the system administrator.

If any component of a striped filesystem fails, then the entire filesystem becomes unusable and must be recreated and restored. Striped filesystems are designed for performance rather than for data integrity. If the latter is important to your system, use one of the fault-tolerant filesystems instead (see the next subsection).

The Fault Tolerance facility

The Windows NT Server product provides two distinct types of fault tolerant filesystems: disk mirroring and striped sets with parity.

Disk mirroring, via RAID level 1, consists of a filesystem in which two identical copies of the data are maintained at all times. Disk mirroring (using an entire disk) is illustrated in Figure 5-14. The size of a mirrored filesystem is half of the total disk space of its component partitions or the size of the smaller of the two of them if they are different sizes.

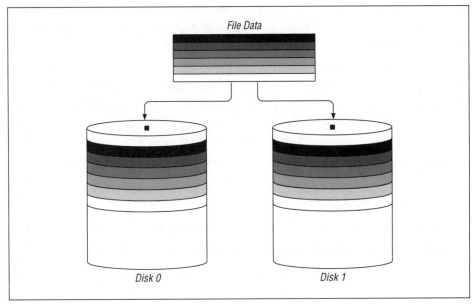

Figure 5-14. Disk mirroring

You can create a mirrored filesystem with the Disk Administrator using the following procedure:

1. Select two areas of free space on two different disks (to form a new mirror set) or a filesystem on an independent partition and an area of free space on another disk (to establish a mirror for an existing filesystem).

2. Choose the **Fault Tolerance➤Establish Mirror** menu path.

3. Specify the desired size of the mirror set in the resulting dialog box.

4. Format the resulting logical partition to create a filesystem.

Once created, the size of a mirrored filesystem cannot be changed.

If one of the disks in a mirror set fails, all of the data is still available. A mirror set may be broken with the **Fault Tolerance➤Break Mirror** menu path, which creates two independent partitions and filesystems, initially containing identical data (provided that both mirror components were intact prior to the operation).

You use the same menu item in the event that one disk in a mirror set fails. Once the mirror set is broken, the working partition retains the drive letter that was assigned to the mirror set, and the nonfunctional partition is marked as an *orphaned partition* and is assigned a new drive letter (if it is accessible at all). You can reestablish mirroring on the remaining partition to a replacement partition when available.

Mirroring the system disk provides fault tolerance for Windows NT itself; this is useful for critical computer systems. However, doing so significantly complicates the recovery procedures in the event that the primary disk fails. See the *Windows NT Server Resource Guide* included in the Resource Kit for server systems for details on the procedures in this event.

Disk striping with parity (RAID 5) is the other fault tolerance option offered by Windows NT. In this scheme, which is illustrated in Figure 5-15, successive chunks of data are stored to each disk in turn. In addition, parity data is generated (via an XOR operation) and stored for every block of the actual data. The parity data rotates among the component disks in the set.

You can create a stripe set with parity in the Disk Administrator as follows:

1. Select three or more areas of free space (the maximum number is 32), each on a separate disk.

2. Choose the **Fault Tolerance➤Create Stripe Set with Parity** menu item.

3. Specify the desired size of the stripe set in the resulting dialog box.

4. Format the resulting logical partition to create a filesystem.

Once created, RAID 5 filesystems cannot be changed in size.

The **Fault Tolerance➤Regenerate** menu item can reconstruct the data from a striped filesystem with parity in which one of the disks has failed.

The FTEdit utility

The Resource Kit also includes the **FTEdit** utility, a tool that can reconstruct the registry entries associated with these advanced filesystem features. For example, if you decide to move disks containing a striped set to another computer after someone's home computer has failed, it's necessary to construct the proper

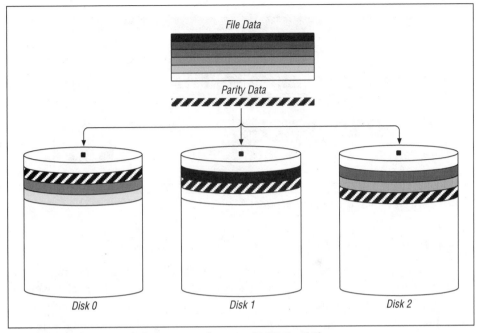

Figure 5-15. Three-way disk striping with parity (RAID Level 5)

registry entries on the new system before the filesystem is accessible. Consult its accompanying documentation for details about **FTEdit**.

Using Removable Disks

FAT and NTFS filesystems may be created on removable disks in Zip, Jaz, and EZ drives and similar devices in the normal manner. Such disks are removable in the normal manner when the FAT filesystem is used. For disks formatted with the NTFS filesystem, Windows NT allows disks to be changed only at boot-time. However, if there are no open files, you can force a dismount by running **ChkDsk /F** on the disk and then pressing the device's eject button. Alternatively, you can use the freely available **unmount** utility discussed earlier in this chapter to unmount these disks (and its **mnt** command to mount their replacements).

Iomega offers a free set of disk tools (illustrated in Figure 5-16) for Windows NT for their Zip and Jaz drives. It is available for download on their web site; consult Appendix B for details.

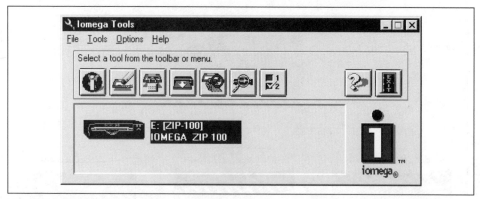

Figure 5-16. The Iomega tools control panel

Network Filesystem Access

In a typical network, files and directories from a variety of systems need to be accessible to network users. In this section, we look at three mechanisms for sharing filesystem resources among a network of Windows NT and other computer systems:

Windows NT shares
> The native facility for sharing disk resources within a Microsoft network.

The Distributed File System
> This facility allows disk resources from a variety of different Windows NT computers to be combined into a single, network-accessible directory tree.

NFS and SAMBA
> Facilities for sharing filesystem resources between Windows NT and UNIX systems.

Windows NT Shares

So far, we've considered disks and filesystems only in the context of a single Windows NT system. In reality, however, such system resources are typically made available to a variety of other systems within the local network. Making a filesystem available to other computers is known as *sharing* it, and shared filesystems or directories are called *shares*. Shares may be accessed by other Windows NT systems and by Windows systems.

Any directory (folder) may be shared. Once shared, the directory, all of the files within it, all of its subdirectories and all of the files and subdirectories within them, and so on to the bottom of that subtree, become potentially available to network users. On NTFS filesystems, however, lower-level files and subdirectories can be protected from network access even if they reside in a shared directory tree, via access control lists (discussed in Chapter 6). On the other hand, it's perfectly acceptable to share a directory that is contained within another shared directory tree (for example, for convenience purposes).

There are several ways of creating a share. The easiest is to right-click on the desired folder and select **Sharing...** from the shortcut menu. The resulting dialog box is illustrated in Figure 5-17.

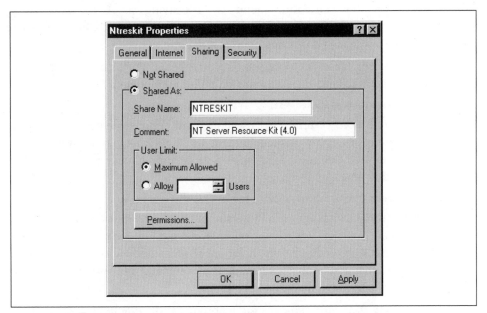

Figure 5-17. Sharing a directory

The two radio buttons at the top of the dialog box control whether the directory is shared or not. When a directory is shared, you must specify a name by which it's accessed from the network (the folder name is prefilled into this field). You may also optionally specify a comment describing the share and its contents.

The **User Limit** area allows you to specify the maximum number of users that may be accessing the share simultaneously. The default is the system maximum (essentially unlimited access); use the **Allow __ Users** field to specify an upper limit.

You can also use the **net share** command to create a shared directory. For example, the following command creates the same share as the preceding dialog box, this time specifying a maximum of 25 simultaneous connections and a slightly different comment:

```
C:\> net share ntreskit=d:\ntreskit /users:25 /remark:"Server Res Kit 4"
```

The **net share** command may also be used to modify the properties of an existing share. For example, the first command removes the upper limit on simultaneous connections from the share named *ntreskit*, and the second command stops that directory from being shared at all:

```
C:\> net share ntreskit /users:unlimited
C:\> net share ntreskit /delete
```

There are several ways of attaching to a shared resource:

- Open it via the **Start►Run** menu by specifying its UNC name (e.g., *vala**ntreskit*). You can also specify a file or subdirectory within the share in the same way: *vala**ntreskit**perl**Install.txt*.

- Use the **net use** command to map it to a drive letter. For example, the following command maps the *ntreskit* share on *vala* to drive letter *J:*

  ```
  C:\> net use J: \\vala\ntreskit
  ```

  The following more complex **net use** command defines drive letter *K:* as the *kona* share on host *pele*, connecting to it as user *Chavez*, requesting a password prompt, and declaring the mapping as *persistent*, meaning that it will be recreated each time the user logs in:

  ```
  C:\> net use K: \\pele\kona /user:chavez * /persistent:yes
  ```

  By default, drive mappings are not persistent. However, the setting of the **/persistent** option is sticky: when the option is specified in a command, whatever setting is selected remains in effect for subsequent **net use** commands until it is explicitly changed. Thus, executing the command **net use /persistent:yes** makes all existing drive mappings persistent.

  The following command removes the mapping for drive letter *J:*

  ```
  C:\> net use J: /delete
  ```

- Right-click on **My Computer** and select **Map Network Drive...** from the resulting shortcut menu. The resulting dialog box is displayed in Figure 5-18.

  This dialog box provides the same functionality as the **net use** command in a graphical mode. The **Disconnect Network Drive...** item on the shortcut menu for **My Computer** may be similarly used to remove existing drive mappings.

Without any arguments, the **net share** and **net use** commands display current outgoing and incoming network connections to shared resources (respectively). For example, the following command lists the shared resources on the local system (*vala* in this case):

```
C:\> net share

Share name   Resource                              Remark
-------------------------------------------------------------------
FLOPPY       A:\
ANANKE       D:\
```

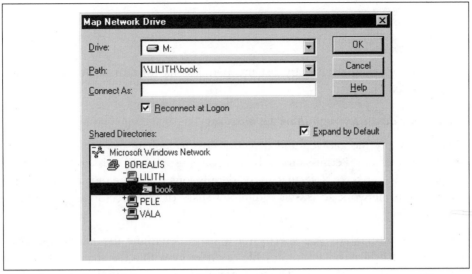

Figure 5-18. Mapping a share to a local drive letter

```
ARIADNE      C:\
CD           E:\                                            Server Res Kit 4
ntreskit     D:\NTResKit
NETLOGON     C:\WINNT\system32\Repl\Import\Scripts  Logon server share
Profiles     C:\WINNT\Profiles
Picasso      LPT1:              Spooled          Picasso
```

The final item in the list of shared resources corresponds to a printer. We consider printer sharing in Chapter 9.

The following command lists the shared resources from remote systems to which the local system is currently connected.

```
C:\> net use
New connections will be remembered.

Status    Local   Remote                Network
-------------------------------------------------------------------
OK                \\Demeter\graphics    Microsoft Windows Network
OK        M:      \\Lilith\book         Microsoft Windows Network
OK        K:      \\Pele\kona           Microsoft Windows Network
```

The first line of output indicates the current setting for the **/persistent** option. On this system, there are three remote disk resources in current use. Two of them are mapped to the drive letters *F:* and *M:*, and the third one (listed first) is being accessed directly.

The **SRVCheck** utility provided in the Resource Kit can be used to list information about shared resources on a specified system:

```
C:\> srvcheck \\pele
\\pele\homes
      .\Everyone
\\pele\kona
      .\Everyone
```

The lines following each entry list the permissions for that share. We consider share permissions next.

Controlling access through share permissions

You can specify the allowed and denied access to a share using its share permissions, set via the **Permissions**... button on the **Sharing** tab of a directory's **Properties** dialog box. Note that these permissions apply neither to local, direct access nor to network access via a different share (if the directory is part of more than one share).

The access permissions you specify for a share determine the *maximum* access level that a user may obtain for any file or directory within the share. In NTFS filesystems, individual file and directory permissions still control access to those objects (discussed in the next section). Share permissions act as an initial access filter for items within NTFS filesystems, a first-level barrier a user must overcome before encountering the file or directory permissions. In contrast, for FAT filesystems, the share permissions provide the only mechanism for limiting access to all of the items within that directory tree.

There are four defined levels of access to a shared directory:

No Access
    Access is denied to everything within the share.

Read
    Allows users to read files and execute programs.

Change
    Allows users to read files, execute programs, and modify and delete files and directories. **Change** access thus gives write access to the share.

Full Control
    Allows all of the access of the **Change** level as well as the ability to change item access permissions and to take ownership of files and directories. This level does not allow a user to change the share permissions themselves; only Administrators may alter share permissions.

By default, *Everyone* is given **Full Control** access to shared directories. This approach uses share permissions as a pass-through filter and relies on properly protected files and directories for access control. A more restrictive set of share permissions makes sense in many contexts.

Figure 5-19 illustrates the dialog box produced by the **Permissions**... button. In this example, share access is group-based. For this share, *ntreskit*, members of the *Chem* and *Phys* groups are allowed complete access to the share, and their file access is determined by the permission sets for the individual items (this share resides on an NTFS filesystem). Members of the group *Baseball* are never allowed to access any file or directory via this share.

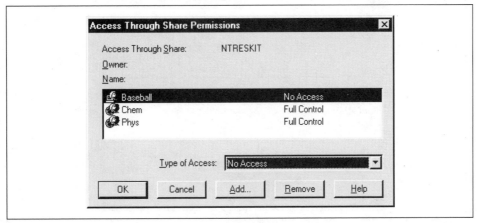

Figure 5-19. Share permissions

What happens if a user is a member of both the *Chem* and *Baseball* groups? In this case, she is denied access to the share. When multiple entries in the list of share permissions apply to a user, any differences among them are resolved as follows:

- If any entry denies the user access (in other words, assigns **No Access**), then the user is denied access.

- Otherwise, the least restrictive access level is granted to the user. For example, if a user was granted **Read** access by one entry and **Change** access by another entry, then that user would be given **Change** level access.

The **Type of Access** field may be used to change the access granted to the current entry. You can remove entries from the share access list with the dialog box's **Remove** button. Pressing the **Add** button allows you to add entries to the list, as shown in the dialog box in Figure 5-20.

Initially, the upper list box contains the list of defined groups. Pressing the **Show Users** adds all user accounts to the bottom of the list. Selecting one or more groups or users and then clicking **Add** adds them to the **Add Names** list in the lower list box. Specify the desired access level for the selected names using the **Type of Access** menu at the bottom of the dialog box. When you click **OK**, the names listed in the **Add Names** list are granted the specified **Type of Access**.

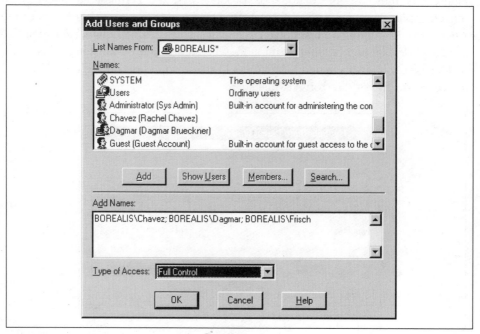

Figure 5-20. Adding entries to share access permissions

Access permissions for local or remote shares may also be specified with the Resource Kit's **RmtShare** utility. It has the following syntax:

```
rmtshare \\server\sharename=drive:path options    Defining a share.
rmtshare \\server\sharename options               Modifying share permissions.
rmtshare \\server\sharename /delete               Deleting a share.
```

Available options include **/remark** and **/users** for specifying comments and maximum number of simultaneous connections (respectively), as for the **net share** command, and these options for specifying share access permissions:

/grant *name:p*

Grants the access specified by the code letter *p* to the specified user or group, where *p* must be one of **r** (Read access), **c** (Change access), **f** (Full Control), or **n** (No Access).

/remove *name*

Remove the specified user or group from the share permissions list (if present). Note that the form **/grant** *user* (without a permission code) performs the same function (although it produces an error message if no matching entry exists).

Multiple instances of both options may be present in a single **RmtShare** command. For example, the following **RmtShare** command adds entries for users *Chavez*

(**Full Control**) and *Dagmar* (**Read** access) and removes any entry for the group *Baseball* from the permission list for the *ntreskit* share on system *vala*:

```
C:\> rmtshare \\vala\ntreskit /grant chavez:f /grant dagmar:r ^
     /remove baseball
```

Hidden shares

If you define a share name with a dollar sign as its final character, you create what is known as a *hidden share*. Such shares are not displayed when users browse the network and so are somewhat invisible to them. However, if a user knows the name of the share, then it will still be accessible to him (provided that the share permissions allow it). The bottom line is that hidden shares aren't inaccessible. Accordingly, hidden shares should never be substituted for proper share access permissions.

Administrative hidden shares are also created by default for system disk partitions and named after the corresponding drive letter. Thus, the automatic administrative share for the *C:* drive is named *C$*. These shares may be accessed only by Administrators. They may be renamed or removed as appropriate for your system.

Sharing CD-ROM drives

CD-ROM drives may be shared like other filesystems via the normal mechanisms. When you share a CD-ROM drive, you make any CD placed into that drive available for network access.

By default, the CD-ROM **autorun** feature is enabled under Windows NT. In this mode, the operating system automatically searches for and runs a program named *AutoRun.Exe* in the root directory whenever a CD is inserted into the drive. You can still browse such CDs using the normal Explorer utility via the **Browse** item on the drive's shortcut menu.

To disable the autorun features for a specific CD, hold down the SHIFT key while inserting it into the CD-ROM drive. To disable the feature altogether, change the Autorun value of the HKEY_LOCAL_MACHINE\System\CurrentControlSet\ Services\CDROM registry key to 0.

The Distributed File System

The Distributed File System (Dfs) is a native Windows NT multicomputer network filesystem facility. It is conceptually similar to the TCP/IP Network File System (NFS) found on UNIX and other computer systems, but is implemented differently. Currently, Dfs is available in a beta version downloadable from the Microsoft web site (*caveat emptor*).

NOTE   The Dfs facility described here is completely separate from (and incompatible with) the DCE facility of the same name supported by some operating systems.

Once set up, the Dfs directory tree appears just like any other share to network users. Components of a Dfs tree may come from Windows NT and Windows 95 systems. The facility also allows alternate paths for its various components for the purpose of load balancing and data redundancy. UNIX users should note that the defined Dfs structure persists across system reboots.

Installing Dfs

The procedure for installing the Dfs software is straightforward:

1. Download, unpack, and install the Dfs files by running the executable (for example, *Dfs-V40-I386.Exe*). The archive is extracted automatically into the directory *%SystemRoot%\System32\Dfs*.

2. Add a new network service from the **Add...** button on the **Services** tab of the **Network** control panel applet. Use the **Have Disk** button on the resulting **Select Network Service** dialog box, specifying the fully qualified path to the *%SystemRoot%\System32\Dfs* directory as the location of the software (e.g., *C:\WinNT\System32\Dfs*). Select the **Distributed File System** item from the **Select OEM Option** dialog box.

3. Specify a share as the root of the Dfs tree in the **Configure Dfs** dialog box (you can also do this later using the Dfs service's **Properties**). You may specify an existing share or create a new one (using an existing or a new directory).

When you exit from the **Network** control panel applet, the system reboots.

Configuring the Dfs tree

Once the system has finished rebooting, you are ready to configure the complete Dfs filesystem. On any given system, the Dfs facility may be used to administer only a single shared Dfs directory tree. However, items within the Dfs tree may themselves be Dfs trees administered by other servers (i.e., Dfs trees may be nested).

The software includes the Dfs Administrator graphical tool (which may be started from the **Start▸Programs▸Administrative Tools (Common)** submenu or with the **dfsadmin** command) and the command-line utility **dfscmd**. We'll consider the graphical utility first.

The components of the Dfs tree appear in the Dfs Administrator's main window. Initially, only the root directory will be listed. Use the **Dfs➤Add to Dfs** menu path to extend the Dfs tree. The resulting dialog is illustrated in Figure 5-21.

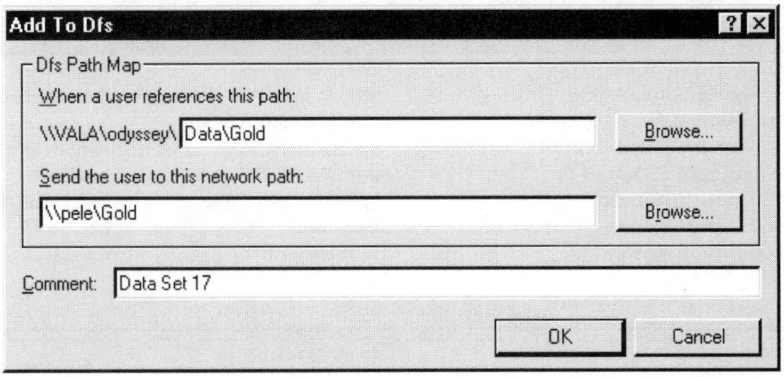

Figure 5-21. Adding a component to the Dfs tree

The first field in the dialog box designates the location for the new component within the Dfs tree, and the second field specifies the name of the share you want to add to the tree. The final dialog field is used for an optional comment describing the component.

In this example, the Dfs tree on *vala* is shared as *odyssey*. In the example dialog box, we place the shared directory named *Gold* on host *pele* as a new subdirectory of the same name in the *Data* subdirectory of the Dfs tree. Note that the subdirectory *Data* is a folder within the directory on *vala* shared as *odyssey* (created in the normal manner) and that it must already exist before a new subdirectory is located within it via the Dfs facility.

Figure 5-22 illustrates a small Dfs tree. As the display indicates, the structure of a Dfs tree is completely arbitrary. In this example, its components come from otherwise unrelated directories on three different systems. The various directories are organized into two groups via the local subdirectories of *vala\odyssey*, named *Software* and *Data*.

The Dfs facility includes the ability to designate multiple paths for a component directory. This capability allows multiple computer systems to provide access to a given set of files. When multiple paths are defined for a component, the Dfs system automatically distributes user requests for items within them among the separate instances of the path. In this way, the Dfs facility provides a simple load balancing scheme in an attempt to prevent any one server from becoming over-

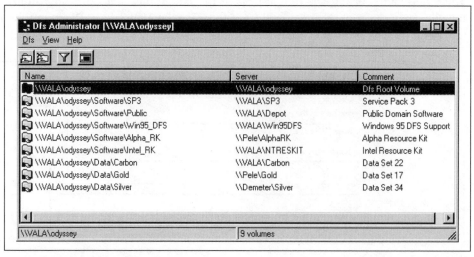

Figure 5-22. A sample Dfs tree

whelmed.* It also provides redundant paths for accessing a given set of files, ensuring that they will still be available to users who need them even if one of the servers storing them becomes temporarily unavailable.

A replica is added to an existing Dfs component within the Dfs Administrator utility by double-clicking on it and then pressing the **Add...** button on its **Properties** dialog box (see Figure 5-23). The resulting dialog box is similar to the one for adding a new Dfs tree component.

Entries in the Dfs Administrator's main window for multiply defined Dfs components indicate the number of defined paths in the window's **Server** column (see Figure 5-24).

NOTE   The Dfs facility provides no mechanism for synchronizing the contents of the multiple instances of one of the tree's components. You can use the Directory Replication Service for this purpose (discussed in Chapter 12).

One component of a multiply defined Dfs path may be removed via the **Remove** button on its **Properties** dialog box. An entire Dfs component may be removed via the utility's **Dfs▶Delete** menu path. This action removes the component from

---

* The load balancing occurs at the highest access level, not at the I/O operation level, so unequal loads still occur whenever the I/O requirements of two users accessing the directory are significantly different.

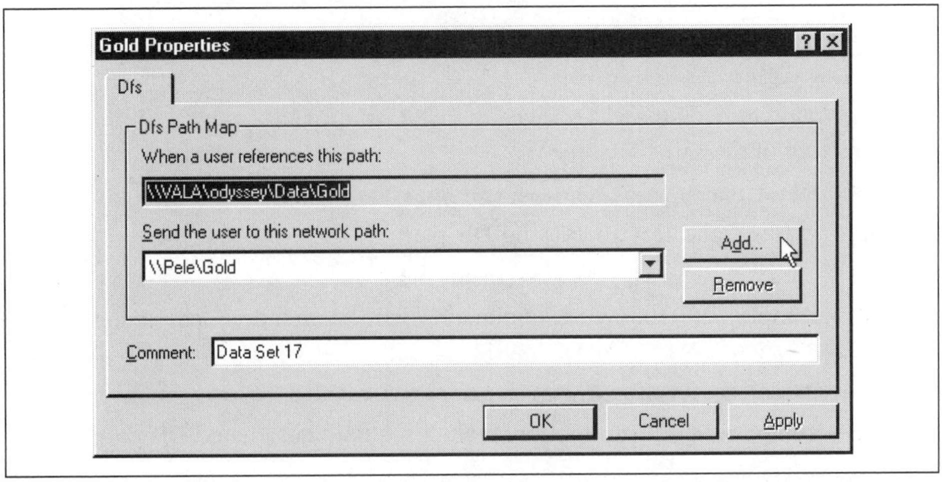

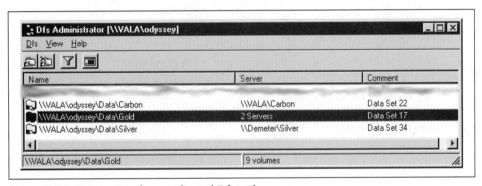

Figure 5-23. Creating a redundant Dfs path

Figure 5-24. Designation for a replicated Dfs path

the Dfs tree, including any defined redundant paths; however, the target directory remains unaffected.

Finally, the Dfs structure can be saved and restored using the Dfs Administrator's **Dfs➤Save As…** and **Dfs➤Load…** menu paths (respectively).

The Dfs Administrator utility operates on the Dfs tree on the local system. The **dfscmd** command can perform most of these same operations on Dfs trees on arbitrary computer systems. It has the following options:

- **/map** is used to add a Dfs tree component. It has the following syntax:

  /map *host**dfs-share**path* *target* [*comment*]

  For example, the following command adds the specified share on host *lilith* as a component of the *Data* subdirectory of the Dfs tree on *vala* that we have been working with:

```
C:\> dfscmd /map \\vala\odyssey\Data\Ore \\lilith\Iron "Data Set 66"
```

- **/unmap** is used to remove a Dfs tree component (including all of its replicas):

  /unmap *host**dfs-share**path*

  The following command removes the *SP2* component from the *Software* sub-directory of the same Dfs tree:

  ```
  C:\> dfscmd /unmap \\vala\odyssey\Software\SP2
  ```

- **/add** adds a replica for an existing Dfs path:

  /add *host**dfs-share**path* *additional-target*

  For example, the following command defines an additional target for the *vala**odyssey**Data**Ore* Dfs path:

  ```
  C:\> dfscmd /add \\vala\odyssey\Data\Ore \\leda\Iron
  ```

- **/remove** removes one component from a multiply designated Dfs path:

  /remove *host**dfs-share**path* *target-path*

  The following command removes the *lilith**Iron* share from the specified Dfs path on *vala:*

  ```
  C:\> dfscmd /remove \\vala\odyssey\Data\Ore \\lilith\Iron
  ```

- **/view** displays the structure of a Dfs tree. By default, only the component names are listed. Use the **/partial** option to display the comments as well or the **/full** option for full component information, including a list of all targets for multiply defined Dfs paths:

```
C:\> dfscmd /view \\vala\odyssey /full
\\VALA\odyssey                              Dfs Root Volume
      \\VALA\odyssey
\\VALA\odyssey\Software\SP3                  Service Pack 3
      \\VALA\SP3
\\VALA\odyssey\Software\Public               Public Domain Software
      \\VALA\Depot
\\VALA\odyssey\Software\Win95_Dfs            Windows 95 Dfs Support
      \\VALA\Win95Dfs
\\VALA\odyssey\Software\Alpha_RK             Alpha Resource Kit
      \\Pele\AlphaRK
\\VALA\odyssey\Software\Intel_RK             Intel Resource Kit
      \\VALA\NTRESKIT
\\VALA\odyssey\Data\Carbon                   Data Set 22
      \\VALA\Carbon
\\VALA\odyssey\Data\Gold                     Data Set 17
      \\Pele\Gold
      \\Demeter\Gold
\\VALA\odyssey\Data\Silver                   Data Set 34
      \\Demeter\Silver
\\VALA\odyssey\Data\Ore                      Data Set 66
      \\Leda\Iron
The command completed successfully.
```

Sharing Filesystems with UNIX Systems

There are two approaches to sharing filesystem resources between Windows NT systems and UNIX systems: make the Windows NT filesystems recognizable to the UNIX systems or make the UNIX filesystems accessible to the Windows NT systems (and many times, you'll want to share filesystems in both directions).

The Network File System (NFS) is the usual facility for sharing disk resources across a local area network on UNIX systems. There are many NFS products available for Windows NT systems, and all of them allow Windows NT systems to function as both NFS servers (filesystems on the Windows NT system can be mounted by UNIX systems) and NFS clients (filesystems from UNIX systems can be mounted on the Windows NT system). Consult Appendix B for product names and vendors.

The freely available SAMBA facility provides another approach to cross-platform filesystem sharing by allowing UNIX systems to support the Server Message Block (SMB) protocol, the native resource-sharing protocol for Microsoft networks. With SAMBA, you can make UNIX filesystems look like shared NTFS file systems to NT systems and access them using the normal **net use** command. Extensions to the facility also allow Windows NT filesystems to be mounted on UNIX systems using its normal **mount** command.

Setting up SAMBA on a UNIX system is straightforward:

1. Download the package from the Internet and unpack it (see Appendix B for the location).

2. Edit the *makefile* and uncomment the lines for the appropriate machine type for your system. Follow the directions in the *makefile* to make any other changes required for your system.

3. Run the **make** commands:

   ```
   # make                          Build the software.
   # make install                  Install the software.
   ```

   The second command installs the software into the target location, which is usually under */usr/local/samba*.

4. Create the SAMBA configuration file, *lib/smb.conf* under the SAMBA directory. Here is a simple version of this file:

   ```
   [global]                        Global settings applying to all exports.
   hosts allow = vala, pele
   hosts deny = lilith
   valid users = dagmar, @chem, @phys, @bio, @geo
   invalid users = root, admin, administrator
   max log size = 2000
   ```

```
[chemdir]                                  Define a directory (share) for export.
path = /chem/data/new                      Local (UNIX) path to be shared.
comment = New Data                         Description of the filesystem.
read only = no                             Filesystem is not read-only.
case sensitive = yes                       Filenames are case sensitive.
force group = chemists                     Map all user access to this UNIX group.
read list = dagmar, @chem, @phys           Windows NT names allowed read access.
write list = @chem                         Windows NT names allowed write access.
```

The first section of the configuration file, introduced by the **[global]** line, specifies global SAMBA settings that apply to all filesystems exported via the facility. Its first two lines specify remote systems that are allowed to access SAMBA filesystems and those that are forbidden from doing so (respectively). The next two lines similarly specify Windows NT users and groups that are allowed and denied access (note that group names are prefixed by an at sign: *@chem*). The final line of this first section specifies the maximum size of the SAMBA log file in KB.

The second section of the sample SAMBA configuration file defines a filesystem for exporting (i.e., a share). In this case, it consists of the local path */chem/data/new*, and it will be accessed by remote systems under the name *chemdir* (defined in the section's header line). This exported filesystem is exported read-write and uses case-sensitive filenames. All incoming access to the filesystem will take place as if the user were a member of the local UNIX *chemists* group. Windows NT user *dagmar* and groups *chem* and *phys* are allowed read access to the filesystem, and members of Windows NT group *chem* are also given write access. Whether or not an individual file may be read or written is still determined by its UNIX file permissions.

You can use the **testparm** command to verify the syntax of a SAMBA configuration file before you install it. See the SAMBA documentation for full details on configuration file entries.

5. Start the SAMBA daemon (server process) by executing the following command (located in the *bin* subdirectory of the SAMBA installation directory):

   ```
   # smbd -D
   ```

6. Connect to the exported filesystem from Windows NT systems via a **net use** command. For example:

   ```
   C:\> net use u: \\dalton\chemdir
   ```

   In general, the SAMBA filesystem may be accessed like any other shared directory.

The **smbstatus** command may be used to display current remote users of local filesystems on the UNIX system:

```
$ smbstatus

Samba version 1.9.16
Service  uid     gid      pid   machine
--------------------------------------------
chemdir  nobody  chemists 14810 vala (193.0.13.4) Mon Jul 14 11:51:07

No locked files
```

In general, SAMBA prompts the user for a password when required. By default, these passwords are sent across the network in unencrypted form (i.e., as clear text). This is an insecure practice that some sites will find unacceptable. SAMBA can be modified to use only encoded passwords as follows:

1. Obtain the *libdes* package from the Internet and build it.

2. Reconfigure the SAMBA *makefile* by uncommenting the lines referring to this package; then rebuild and reinstall the SAMBA software.

3. Add the entries **encrypt passwords = yes** and **security = user** to the global section of the SAMBA configuration file.

4. Use the *mksmbpasswd.sh* script included with the SAMBA package source code to create the initial SAMBA password file. For example:

   ```
   # cat /etc/passwd | /path/source/mksmbpasswd.sh \
     > /usr/local/samba/private/smbpasswd
   ```

   where *path* is the location of the unpacked SAMBA distribution. The *smbpasswd* file should be owned by *root* and have the permissions 600 on the file itself and 500 on the subdirectory *private*.

Once encrypted passwords are enabled, the **smbpasswd** command must be used to change a user's SAMBA password. If the command is installed SETUID *root*, users may change their own passwords; otherwise, the system administrator must update the SAMBA password file as necessary. See the file *docs/ENCRYPTION.txt* in the SAMBA distribution for full details on this feature.

The SAMBA package includes the **smbclient** utility to access remote SMB-based shares from the UNIX system. It uses an interface similar to the FTP facility. A much better approach is provided on Linux systems via the *smbmount* package (written by Tor Lillqvist). It includes a command of the same name that can be used to mount Windows NT shares on the UNIX system. For example, the following command mounts the *depot* share on *vala* as the local directory */nt_stuff:*

```
# smbmount //vala/depot /nt_stuff -U administrator
```

This command makes the connection as the *Administrator* account on the Windows NT system (you are prompted for the proper password).

6

Files and Directories

There are several different kinds of files used on Windows NT systems:

- *Regular files* are files containing data, normally simply called "files." These may be ASCII text files, binary data files, executable program binaries, program input or output, and so on.

- A *directory* is a binary file listing the files it contains (possibly including other directories). Directories are the mechanism for organizing files into subsets of related items.

- A *hard link* is a mechanism that allows several filenames to refer to a single file on disk. A hard link associates two (or more) filenames with the same file—the same entry in the Master File Table—and all of these names are stored in instances of the filename attribute in the file's MFT record. Hard links all share the same disk data blocks while functioning as independent directory entries.

  Hard links are created by the **ln** command in the POSIX subsystem. For example, the command:

  ```
  C:\> ln index.txt hlink.txt
  ```

  creates an entry in the current directory named *hlink.txt* corresponding to the same file as *index.txt*. Since the MFT applies only to the current disk partition, hard links may not span disk partitions.

  In a sense, all files are really hard links. Multiple hard links to the same file are rarely used on Windows NT systems.

- UNIX computer systems provide another type of link, known as a *symbolic link*, to a file. A symbolic link is a file that points to another pathname in the filesystem. Symbolic links may span physical devices, since they refer only to a pathname, not to an actual disk location or MFT record. Windows NT *short-*

cuts are similar to symbolic links in some ways, although there are implementation differences.

A shortcut for an existing item may be created via the graphical user interface by right-clicking on the item and selecting **Create Shortcut** from the resulting menu. This operation will result in a shortcut for the item being created in the same directory. The shortcut's initial name will be *Shortcut to* name.*lnk*, where *name* is the original name of the item, although you may rename it as desired (but be sure to retain the .*lnk* file extension).* Alternatively, you may right-drag an item to a new location and then select **Create Shortcut(s) Here** from the resulting menu to create a shortcut in a different location than the original object. Note that you cannot create a shortcut to an item that does not yet exist.

Shortcuts are designed for use within the Windows NT graphical user interface and do not function in the same way from the command line.

Shortcuts and Hard Links

On Windows NT systems, the two types of links behave similarly, but are not identical. As an example, consider a file *index.txt* to which there is a hard link *hlink.txt* and a shortcut *scut.lnk*. Opening any of these files will view the same data (provided that the associated application understands shortcuts). For both *index.txt* and *hlink.txt*, the disk contents pointed to by the addresses in MFT record will be accessed and displayed. If you double click on *scut*, its contents will be interpreted as a pointer to another file, and this target file will then be accessed as requested.

In directory listings, *hlink.txt* will have identical attributes to *index.txt* (except, of course, its name). Changes made to either file will affect both of them, since they share the same disk blocks. However, moving either file with the **move** command will not affect the other one, because moving a file only involves altering a directory entry. Similarly, deleting *index.txt* will not affect *hlink.txt*, which will still correspond to the same MFT record (and vice versa). If a new file in the current directory named *index.txt* is subsequently created, there will be no connection between it and *hlink.txt*; when the new file is created, it will be assigned a free MFT record.

In contrast, the shortcut *scut* to *index.txt* will behave differently. Shortcuts are always quite small files, while every hard link to a given file is exactly the same size as the original file (e.g., *hlink.txt* is naturally the same length as *index.txt*).

---

* This extension is not be visible from the desktop's graphical user interface.

Changes made by referencing either the real filename or the shortcut will affect the contents of *index.txt*.

Deleting *index.txt* will affect *scut* differently, depending on whether or not there are additional hard links to the file. If *index.txt* is the only hard link to the file (as is almost always the case), deleting it will also break access via the shortcuts; *scut* will point nowhere. In addition, if another file *index.txt* is subsequently recreated in the same location, *scut* will once again be linked to it.

In contrast, if there is another hard link to the file, *scut* will be automatically updated to point to the alternate name (*hlink.txt* in our example). If another file *index.txt* is subsequently created in the same location, *scut* will have no relationship to it.

In either case, deleting *scut* will have no effect on *index.txt*.

File Ownership and Permissions

As we've seen, network access to shared FAT filesystems may be limited by the share permissions. Beyond this control mechanism, FAT filesystems offer virtually nothing in the way of file and directory access controls. Files can be marked with one or more attributes, designating them as read-only, as system files, or as hidden files. However, none of these prevent unwanted access by unauthorized users in any significant way. In general, you should consider everything on a FAT filesystem to be accessible to any local user, as well as to any permitted network user, when the filesystem is shared.

Every file in an NTFS filesystem has an *owner* associated with it: a user account or group to whom it belongs. This is almost always the user that originally created the file. However, system files created when Windows NT was installed are owned by the *Administrators* group, as are other files created by any administrative account. The owner of a file always has the ability to access that file (as we shall see).

NOTE   UNIX users should note that files have just a single owner (which is usually a user account, except in the case of the *Administrators* group). There is no concept of separate group ownership of files under Windows NT.

OnNTFS filesystems, *access control lists* (ACLs) are used to grant and limit access to files and directories. Access control lists are composed of name-permission pairs known as *access control entries* (ACEs). The ACL for a file or directory may be viewed or modified by pressing the **Permissions** button on the **Security** tab of the item's **Properties** dialog box. For example, Figure 6-1 displays the access control list for the file *C:\Boot.Ini*.

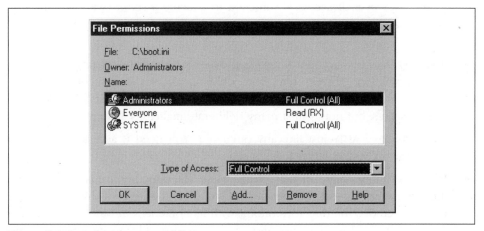

Figure 6-1. Sample access control list

This file is owned by the *Administrators* group. Its access control list contains three entries. Members of the *Administrators* group have **Full Control** of the file, as does the *System* pseudo-user, while everyone else has **Read** access. The entry for *System* indicates operating system-level access to the file.

Windows NT uses the basic permissions described in Table 6-1. It also groups commonly applied subsets of them into named sets (these usually appear in the actual ACE), as is illustrated in Figure 6-1.

Table 6-1. Windows NT Basic Permissions

Permission (Code Letter)	Meaning on a File	Meaning on a Directory
Read (**R**)	View or access the file's contents	List files within the directory
Write (**W**)	Change or delete the file's contents	Add items to the directory
Execute (**X**)	Run an executable image	Change the current directory to that directory
Delete (**D**)	Delete the file	Delete the directory itself
Change Permissions (**P**)	Change the permissions on the file	Change the permissions on the directory
Take Ownership (**O**)	Become the owner of the file	Become the owner of the directory

A few comments on the basic permissions are in order:

- In order to execute a program, you need only **X** access; you do not need **R** access. However, **R** access is sufficient to execute a script (with or without **X** access), and attempting to run a script to which you have only **X** access will fail.

- Allowing **W** access without **D** access prevents a user from deleting a file. However, it will not prevent him from deleting all of the contents of the file (thereby trashing it). Thus, **W** access alone protects against some kinds of user mistakes, but not against many deliberate malicious actions.

- Shortcuts have ACLs just like any other file. You need **R** access to a shortcut to use it to access its target.

- **D** access to a directory allows you to delete that directory if it is empty. If not, then you must have delete permission for all of the items within it as well in order to remove the directory (along with its contents). In other words, delete access to a directory does not allow you to remove files to which you do not also have delete access. Conversely, you can delete any file to which you have **D** access, regardless of whether you also have **D** access for the directory in which the file resides.

- Take ownership (**O**) access allows a user to become the owner of a file or directory. Under Windows NT systems, ownership is taken, not granted or given up. Ownership of an item may be taken via the **Ownership** button on the **Security** tab in its **Properties** dialog box.

By default, file access is independent of the permissions of the various subdirectories in the tree in which it resides. A user can access any file that grants him access by referring to its explicit pathname, even if some directories in the tree leading to it are protected against him.* This functionality is controlled by the **Bypass traverse checking** privilege, which is normally granted to all users. Many security scenarios make turning this off a good idea (and the POSIX standard requires it). See Chapter 10 for more details on system privileges.

Basic permissions may be applied individually or via named sets. The defined permission sets for files are summarized in Table 6-2.

Table 6-2. Permission Sets for Files

Permission Set	Equivalent Basic Permissions
Full Control	RWXDPO *(all)*
Change	RWXD

---

* Experienced UNIX users will see this as "normal" behavior.

Table 6-2. Permission Sets for Files (continued)

Permission Set	Equivalent Basic Permissions
Read	**RX**
No Access	none
Special Access	any desired subset

Permissions defined in ACLs are applied as follows:

- If any applicable entry assigns **No Access** to the user desiring access, that user is denied access to the file.

- Otherwise, the user is granted the access, which is the union (sum) of all ACEs in the ACL which apply to her.

- If no entry applies to the user, she is denied access. This is a corollary of the previous point.

For example, the ACL in Figure 6-2 denies access to the *Boot.Ini* file to user *Dagmar*, regardless of whether she is a member of the *Chem* or *Administrators* groups. User *Chavez* is explicitly granted **Read** access to the file. However, if user *Chavez* is a member of the *Chem* group, then her actual access will be **Change**; if she is also a member of the *Administrators* group, then she will have **Full Control** for the file.

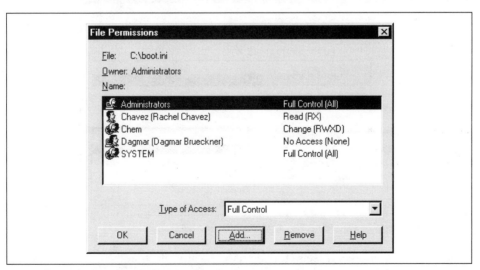

Figure 6-2. An example ACL

Would this ACL really be sufficient to keep user *Dagmar* from accessing the file if she is a member of the *Administrators* group? Only for the amount of time that it takes her to take ownership and change the permissions for the file. ACL settings for the file's owner and for administrators apply only as long as they remain in effect. A file's owner and administrators can always change the permissions on a file or directory, regardless of the ACL settings. Thus, files can be protected even against their owners, but not for long. Similarly, files can be briefly protected even against system administrators, but members of the *Administrators* group can always modify the ownership and ACL for any file or directory.

Access control lists are changed via the **Permissions** button on the **Security** tab of the item's **Properties**; this brings up the **File Permissions** or **Directory Permissions** dialog box, which operates in the usual manner.

The dialog box for a file is pictured in Figure 6-3. It illustrates the method for assigning special access for a user. In this example, user *Chavez*'s ACE gives her **RWX** permissions to the file. This access may be changed by selecting her entry and then specifying the desired permission set in the **Type of Access** field. The items on this menu include the standard named permission sets, the entry **Special Access...** (with an ellipsis), which provides access to a list of basic permissions from which any subset may be chosen, and the entry **Special Access** (no ellipsis), which corresponds to her current permission set. The latter form is included only when an ACE already has a custom (unnamed) permission set.

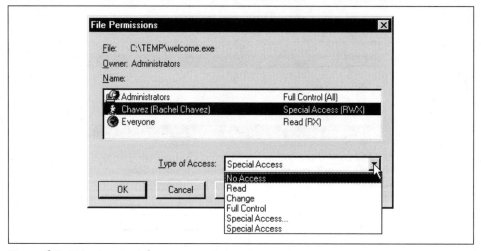

Figure 6-3. Assigning special access permissions to a user

The defined permission sets for directories are illustrated in Figure 6-4 and summarized in Table 6-3. Notice that each ACE in the ACL for a directory contains two permission sets. The first set is used to determine access to the directory itself, and the second set is used only when a new file is created in that directory.

For the directory *C:\Temp*, user *Chavez* can list the contents of the directory, change to it, and add new files. User *Dagmar* can change her current working

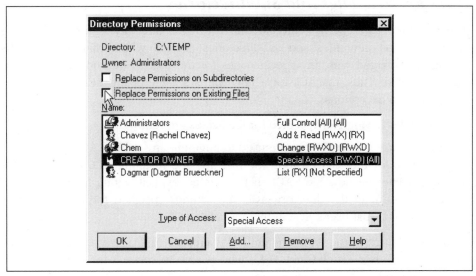

Figure 6-4. Example ACL for a directory

Table 6-3. Permission Sets for Directories

Permission Set	Equivalent Basic Permissions	
	On Directory	New File Defaults
Full Control	RWXDPO *(all)*	RWXDPO *(all)*
Change	RWXD	RWXD
Add & Read	RWX	RX
Add	WX	Not Specified
Read	RX	RX
List	RX	Not Specified
No Access	None	None
Special Directory Access	Any desired subset	N/A
Special File Access	N/A	Any desired subset

directory to this directory and may also list its contents. Members of the *Chem* group can perform all operations on the directory except taking ownership of it and modifying its ACL. Finally, members of the *Administrators* group have full control over the directory (and also happen to own it).

As the upper two fields in this dialog box indicate, when you modify the ACL for a directory, you may also apply the new ACL to its subdirectories and the files within the directory. By default, **Replace Permissions on Existing Files** is checked. Be sure to clear both check boxes if you want to affect only the directory itself.

ACLs for New Files and Subdirectories

The special *Creator Owner* entry in the ACL for a directory is used for setting permissions on new files and subdirectories created within that directory. Its settings are merged with any specific ones for the user in question when a new item is created. Thus, the ACL for a new file is a copy of the ACL for the directory, with two exceptions:

- All entries having **Not Specified** for file access are removed.

- The *Creator Owner* settings are used to augment any explicit ACE in the directory ACL for the user creating the file, and the resulting ACE for the user is placed into the new file's ACL. If there is no explicit setting for the creator's user account in the directory ACL, the settings specified for *Creator Owner* are used for that user's ACE in the new file's ACL.

Figure 6-5 illustrates the ACLs for new files created in *C:\Temp* by user *Chavez* (left ACL) and user *Frisch* (right ACL), who is able to create a file there by virtue of his membership in the *Chem* group.

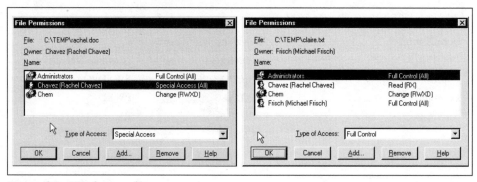

Figure 6-5. ACLs for new files

In both cases, the ACL entry for user *Dagmar* in the directory's ACL is absent from the ACL for the new file, since its new file permissions are **Not Specified**. The ACE for user *Chavez* in the ACL for her file gives her all access permissions (the combination of the **RWX** permissions in her directory ACE and the **All** entry for *Creator Owner*). You can tell that the permissions are formed as a combination because they are labeled as **Special Access**.

For the file on the right (owned by user *Frisch*), the ACE for user *Chavez* is identical to the file permissions specified in her ACE in the directory's ACL. User *Frisch*'s own ACE is constructed entirely from the *Creator Owner* entry in the directory's ACL. The permissions given to group *Chem* are not used to create it even though it is his membership in this group which allows him to create the new file.

ACLs for new subdirectories are handled somewhat differently:

- All entries, including ones with **Not Specified** for their new file part, are copied as is from the directory's ACL into the ACL for the new subdirectory.

- The ACE for the new subdirectory's owner is copied from the entry in the directory's ACL, augmented by the directory permissions part of the ACE for *Creator Owner.*

- When the parent directory's ACL has no entry for the user who is creating the new subdirectory, the directory access part of the ACE in the new subdirectory's ACL for its owner is copied from *Creator Owner,* and the new file default is set to **Not Specified**. The entire entry is also marked with an asterisk, indicating that it will not be propagated to any lower level subdirectories that might subsequently be created by other users.

Figure 6-6 illustrates the ACLs for subdirectories of *C:\Temp* created by users *Chavez* (left ACL) and *Frisch* (right ACL). The ACL for user *Chavez*'s subdirectory contains an entry for her user account; its directory part is the union of the directory part of her ACE for *C:\Temp* and the directory part of the *Creator Owner* ACE, and its file part is copied from her ACE without change.

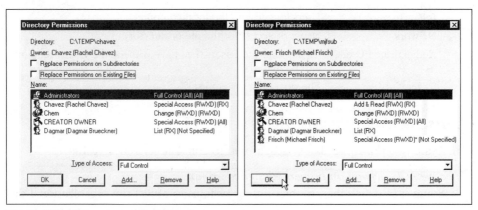

Figure 6-6. ACLs on new subdirectories

Since user *Frisch* has no entry in the parent directory's ACL, the directory part of the entry for user *Frisch* in the ACL for his subdirectory was copied from the ACE for *Creator Owner* in the ACL for *C:\Temp*, and the file part is set to **Not Specified**. The entry is starred, indicating that it will not propagate to lower-level subdirectories.

Here are a few more points about ACLs:

- Deleting a group leaves ACEs for that group untouched in the ACLs on the system. Adding another group of the same name at some later time will not reactivate them. The new group is not the same group as the old one because it has a different internal ID number, and it thus will not inherit the old ACEs. We'll look at a method for cleaning out such stale entries in a bit.

- The NT Backup utility saves and restores ACLs along with the file, as do most commercial backup utilities designed for Windows NT systems.

- By default, ACLs for copied files are created in the normal manner: using the ACL of the target directory as their base. Use the **SCopy** utility in the Resource Kit to copy files and retain their current permission settings.

- Moving a file within the same filesystem (disk partition) does not change its ACL. Moving a file to a different filesystem—which is really an automatic copy and delete operation—results in a new ACL for the file based upon its destination directory's permissions.

- Windows NT provides several special names that can be used for assigning file and directory permissions in ACLs as shown in Table 6-4.

Table 6-4. Special Names for Assigning Permissions

Name	Applies to
Everyone	All users
Interactive	Users logged into the local computer
Network	Network access for the file or directory
Authenticated Users	All authenticated users (i.e., have presented a valid username and password)
System	The operating system itself

Constructing Effective ACLs

There are two principles that will help you to construct effective ACLs:

Effective ACLs depend on properly designed groups

Some sites define the groups on their systems to reflect the organizational divisions of their institution or company: one department will become one group, for example (assuming a department is a relatively small organizational unit). However, this isn't necessarily what makes the most sense in terms of system security.

Groups should be defined on the basis of the need to share files, and, correlatively, the need to protect files from unwanted access. This may involve combining several organizational units into one group or splitting a single organizational unit into several distinct groups. In other words, groups need not mirror "reality" at all if that's not what security considerations call for.

Group divisions are often best structured around projects; people who need to work together, using some set of common files and programs, become a group. Users own the files they use most exclusively (or sometimes a group administrator owns all the group's files), common files are protected to allow group access, and all of the group's files can exclude nongroup member access without affecting anyone in the group. When someone works on more than one project, then he is made a member of both relevant groups.

Be conservative in granting access to resources

In general, grant only the minimum access required to the smallest number of users. For example, don't add a group to an ACL when only one or two of its members need access to the file. In addition, remember that there is seldom a need for *Everyone* to have even read access to large parts of the filesystem.

We conclude our consideration of ACL structure with a few additional examples.

Here is the ACL for user *Chavez*'s home directory:

```
CREATOR OWNER:    Full Control (All) (All)
Chavez:           Special Access (RWXO) (All)
Chem:             Read (RX) (RX)
```

The ACL gives *Chavez* full control over all files and subdirectories she creates within her home directory, but it prevents her from deleting or altering the permissions of the home directory itself. Members of the *Chem* group are also granted **Read** access to the home directory, and this access is inherited by new files and subdirectories she creates. Note that with these permissions, it's unnecessary for *Chavez* to own her home directory.

You may be tempted to add an entry like this one to an ACL:

```
Everyone:         No Access (None) (None)
```

The purpose behind such an entry would be to deny access to everyone who is not explicitly granted access by other ACEs in the ACL. However, its effect is to prevent anyone from accessing the file. Remember that any entry denying a user access prevents his accessing the file, regardless of the settings of other entries in the ACL. In fact, not including an entry for *Everyone* has the desired effect. If no entry in an ACL applies to a user, he is not allowed access to the corresponding file or directory.

UNIX systems always include a shared temporary directory named *tmp* set up so that any user can create files within it and delete these files later, but no user can delete the file belonging to someone else. The following permissions on a directory would provide similar functionality on a Windows NT system:

```
CREATOR OWNER:    Full Control (All) (All)
Everyone:         Special Access (RWX) (Not Specified)
```

Under this scheme, users would have full control of files and subdirectories that they create, but no one else would have any access to them. If you wanted other users to have **Read** access to all files within the scratch directory, use this ACE for *Everyone*:

```
Everyone:          Add and Read (RWX) (RX)
```

With this latter ACE any user would be able to add files to any subdirectory within the tree rooted at the scratch directory, regardless of who created it, unless the subdirectory's owner explicitly protected it against such additions.

Commands to Display and Manipulate ACLs

The Resource Kit provides two utilities for displaying ACLs: **ShowACLs** and **Perms**. The **ShowACLs** command displays the ACLs for a specified file or directory at a level of detail suitable for debugging by system programmers. The **Perms** command is more generally useful, as it displays the permissions for a single user or group for a group of files. Here are some examples:

```
C:\> perms chavez *.doc              Show ACEs on .DOC files for user Chavez.
*RWXDPOA  C:\TEMP\rachel.doc
*R-X----  C:\TEMP\winnie.doc
*R-X----  C:\TEMP\zelda.doc


C:\> perms dagmar *.doc              Show ACEs on .DOC files for user Dagmar.
-------  C:\TEMP\rachel.doc
-------  C:\TEMP\winnie.doc
*RWXDPOA  C:\TEMP\zelda.doc


C:\> perms chem *.doc                Show ACEs on .DOC files for group Chem.
RWXD---  C:\TEMP\rachel.doc
RWXD---  C:\TEMP\winnie.doc
RWXD---  C:\TEMP\zelda.doc


C:\> perms chavez c:\temp /s         Show ACEs on C:\Temp subtree for user Chavez.
RWX----  c:\temp\
*RWXD---  c:\temp\chavez\
*R-X----  c:\temp\claire.txt
*R-X----  c:\temp\Coffee Bean 16.bmp
*RWX----  c:\temp\covers\
*R-X----  c:\temp\covers\armadillo.bmp
*R-X----  c:\temp\covers\mandrill.bmp
*R-X----  c:\temp\covers\blurb.txt
*R-X----  c:\temp\covers\jackal.bmp
*R-X----  c:\temp\funny_joke.exe
*RWXDPOA  c:\temp\rachel.doc
*R-X----  c:\temp\test88.bat
*R-X----  c:\temp\winnie.doc
*R-X----  c:\temp\zelda.doc
```

As the final example indicates, the command's **/S** option causes it to work recursively through all of the subdirectories of the specified items. The asterisk preceding some entries indicates that the specified user owns that item.

Somarsoft's **DumpACL** utility provides more broad-based ACL reports.[*] It works by summarizing groups of files with the same permissions when possible, which sometimes substantially shortens the length of the output. It can report on both local and remote filesystems.

Evaluation versions of this utility are available on the Web (see Appendix B for contact information).

DumpACL has both a graphical and a command-line interface (the latter sends its output to a file). Figure 6-7 shows a report in the graphical format for the *C:\Temp* directory we have been examining (generated via the utility's **Report➤Dump Permissions for File System…** menu path). The command-line version of **DumpACL** can write the same data to a text file in a variety of formats. By default, the report begins with the ACL for the specified directory and includes ACLs for only those files and subdirectories that differ from it.

```
┌─ Somarsoft DumpAcl - \\VALA (local) ───────────────── _ □ X ─┐
│ File  Edit  Search  Report  View  Help                       │
├───────────────────────┬────────────────┬──────────┬─────────┤
│ Path                  │ Account        │ Own Dir  │ File   ▲│
├───────────────────────┴────────────────┴──────────┴─────────┤
│ C:\TEMP\                                                     │
│                                                              │
│ C:\TEMP\              BOREALIS\Dagmar            R X        │
│ C:\TEMP\              BOREALIS\Chem              RWXD   RWXD │
│ C:\TEMP\              BOREALIS\Chavez            RWX    R X  │
│ C:\TEMP\              CREATOR OWNER                     all  │
│ C:\TEMP\              BOREALIS\Administrators o  all    all  │
│                                                              │
│ C:\TEMP\claire.txt    BOREALIS\Chem                    RWXD │
│ C:\TEMP\claire.txt    BOREALIS\Chavez                  R X  │
│ C:\TEMP\claire.txt    BOREALIS\Frisch         o        all  │
│ C:\TEMP\claire.txt    BOREALIS\Administrators          all  │
│                                                              │
│ C:\TEMP\rachel.doc    BOREALIS\Administrators          all  │
│ C:\TEMP\rachel.doc    BOREALIS\Chavez         o        all  │
│ C:\TEMP\rachel.doc    BOREALIS\Chem                    RWXD │
│                                                              │
│ C:\TEMP\zelda.doc     BOREALIS\Administrators o        all  │
│ C:\TEMP\zelda.doc     BOREALIS\Chem                    RWXD │
│ C:\TEMP\zelda.doc     BOREALIS\Will                    all  │
│ C:\TEMP\zelda.doc     BOREALIS\Frisch                  RWXD │
│ C:\TEMP\zelda.doc     BOREALIS\Dagmar                  RWXD │
├──────────────────────────────────────────────────┬──────────┤
│ Processed 11 files in 3 directories               │ 00001   /│
└──────────────────────────────────────────────────┴──────────┘
```

Figure 6-7. ACL report from the Somarsoft DumpACL utility

---

[*] The utility can also produce other sorts of reports. We will make use of some of them in Chapter 12.

Figure 6-8 shows part of a report for the *%SystemRoot%\System32* directory tree. It illustrates the utility's ability to summarize the permissions for groups of files of the same type in a single report entry. After all of the file groups have been listed, the report goes on to list the ACLs for all other files where the ACL differs from that of the top-level directory and from at least one other file of the same type.

```
Somarsoft DumpAcl - \\VALA (local)                                       _ □ ×
File  Edit  Search  Report  View  Help
Path (exception dirs and files)   Account                Own Dir    File
C:\WINNT\system32\

C:\WINNT\system32\                BOREALIS\Administrators  o  all       all
C:\WINNT\system32\                Everyone                    RWXD      RWXD
C:\WINNT\system32\                CREATOR OWNER                         all
C:\WINNT\system32\                BOREALIS\Server Operators   RWXD      RWXD
C:\WINNT\system32\                SYSTEM                      all       all

C:\WINNT\system32\*.acm           BOREALIS\Administrators  o            all
C:\WINNT\system32\*.acm           Everyone                             R X
C:\WINNT\system32\*.acm           BOREALIS\Server Operators            RWXD
C:\WINNT\system32\*.acm           SYSTEM                               all

C:\WINNT\system32\*.bas           BOREALIS\Administrators  o            all
C:\WINNT\system32\*.bas           Everyone                             R X
C:\WINNT\system32\*.bas           BOREALIS\Server Operators            RWXD
C:\WINNT\system32\*.bas           SYSTEM                               all

C:\WINNT\system32\*.dat           BOREALIS\Administrators  o            all
C:\WINNT\system32\*.dat           Everyone                             R X
C:\WINNT\system32\*.dat           BOREALIS\Server Operators            RWXD
C:\WINNT\system32\*.dat           SYSTEM                               all

C:\WINNT\system32\*.TSP           BOREALIS\Administrators  o            all
C:\WINNT\system32\*.TSP           Everyone                             R X
C:\WINNT\system32\*.TSP           BOREALIS\Server Operators            RWXD
C:\WINNT\system32\*.TSP           SYSTEM                               all

C:\WINNT\system32\$winnt$.inf     Everyone                             all
C:\WINNT\system32\$winnt$.inf     BOREALIS\Administrators  o

C:\WINNT\system32\access.cpl      BOREALIS\Administrators  o            all
C:\WINNT\system32\access.cpl      Everyone                             R X
C:\WINNT\system32\access.cpl      BOREALIS\Server Operators            RWXD
C:\WINNT\system32\access.cpl      SYSTEM                               all

C:\WINNT\system32\ACLEDIT.DLL     BOREALIS\Administrators  o            all
C:\WINNT\system32\ACLEDIT.DLL     Everyone                             R X
C:\WINNT\system32\ACLEDIT.DLL     BOREALIS\Server Operators            RWXD

Processed 1535 files in 45 directories                            00001
```

Figure 6-8. ACLs summarized for groups of files

The graphical utility also has the ability to search the reports it generates and to filter the display, limiting it to items of interest. We will consider the latter feature in Chapter 11.

The freely available Security Manager (written by Martin Weindel) provides a file browsing environment to display ACL information (illustrated in Figure 6-9). The ACL for the selected directory (left list area) or file (upper-right list area) is displayed in the bottom-right section of the window. The **Classification** area provides a summary of the number of distinct ACLs used for the files within the current directory. In this case, there are only 2, one used for 2 files and another used by 11 files. Each ACL is identified by the alphabetically first filename that uses it. Clicking on one of the **Security Types** highlights those items in the file list using that ACL. Thus, in our example, it is easy to see that all the *.BMP* files in the specified directory use the same ACL.

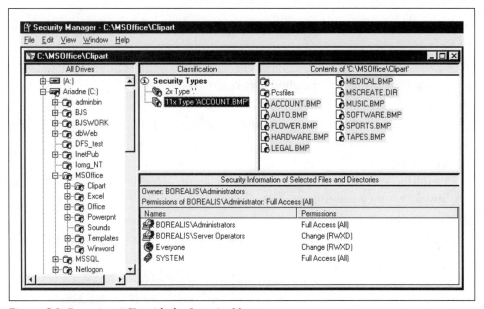

Figure 6-9. Browsing ACLs with the Security Manager

The Windows NT **CACLS** utility may be used to display and modify ACLs. It has the following syntax:

```
cacls file(s) [options]
```

Without any options, the command displays the ACL for the specified files:

```
C:\> cacls *.doc
C:\TEMP\rachel.doc BUILTIN\Administrators:F
                   BOREALIS\Chavez:F
                   BOREALIS\Chem:C

C:\TEMP\winnie.doc BOREALIS\Chem:C
                   BOREALIS\Chavez:R
                   BUILTIN\Administrators:F
                   BUILTIN\Administrators:F

C:\TEMP\zelda.doc BUILTIN\Administrators:F
                  BOREALIS\Chavez:R
                  BOREALIS\Chem:C
                  BOREALIS\Dagmar:F
```

Some of the **CACLS** command options specify how the command works in general:

/E Edit the current ACL (the default is to replace it in its entirety—and not merely to replace any entries the command explicitly changes). In most cases, you will want to include this option.

/T Propagate changes to files and subdirectories of a specified directory.

/C Continue applying changes even after an error.

The command's remaining options specify the content of the various ACEs in the ACL:

/D *name*
> Deny all access to the specified user or group.

/R *name*
> Remove any ACE for the specified user or group. This option is valid only in combination with **/E**.

/G *name:code*
> Grant the specified access to the user or group given in *name*, in addition to any access they currently possess.

/P *name:code*
> Replace the current access for the specified user or group with that given in *code*.

The valid code letters are **R** for **Read** access, **C** for **Change** access, and **F** for **Full Control**. In addition, the **/P** option accepts the code letter **N** for **No Access** (which makes it equivalent to **/D**).

Let's consider some examples. The following command grants **Read** access to the *Phys* group and changes the access for the *Chem* group to **Change** for the file *Zelda.Doc*:

```
C:\> cacls zelda.doc /e /g phys:r /p chem:c
```

As the command illustrates, multiple distinct options may be specified. Note that if the *Phys* group already has any access level that includes the permissions in the **Read** access set (**RX**), its ACE won't change. In contrast, the access for the *Chem* group is changed from whatever its current value is to **Change** (or a new ACE with this access level is created for the group if none currently exists).

Be aware of the difference between the previous command and this one:

```
C:\> cacls zelda.doc /g phys:r /p chem:c
```

When the **/E** option is omitted, the new ACL will have entries only for the two groups whose access is specified in the command, since the entire ACL for the file is replaced by **CACLS**.

You may also specify multiple users or groups with the applicable options. For example, the following command grants **Read** access to the *Chem* and *Phys* groups and **Full Control** to user *Chavez*:

```
C:\> cacls zelda.doc /g phys:r chem:r chavez:f
```

Using **/D** and **/G** in succession is legal but not a good idea, since doing so effectively attempts to add permissions to the **No Access** set:

```
C:\> cacls zelda.doc /e /d dagmar
C:\> cacls zelda.doc /e /g dagmar:c
C:\> cacls zelda.doc
C:\TEMP\zelda.doc BOREALIS\Dagmar:(DENY)(special access:)
                                    WRITE_DAC
                                    WRITE_OWNER
                                    FILE_DELETE_CHILD
                   BOREALIS\Dagmar:C
   . . .
```

The confusion in this output mirrors the corruption in the ACL. In fact, if you attempt to view the file's ACL via its **Properties**, you get an error message like that in Figure 6-10.

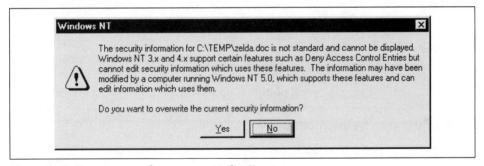

Figure 6-10. Error message from a corrupted ACL

It's best to answer **No** to this prompt (otherwise the entire ACL is cleared), and to use the following command to fix the bad ACE:

```
C:\> cacls zelda.doc /e /p dagmar:c
```

The following command removes any ACEs for the group *Bio* from all files and directories in the filesystem accessed as drive *C*:

```
C:\> cacls C:\ /t /c /e /r bio
```

The **CACLS** utility provides a basic command-line facility for manipulating ACLs, but it has many restrictions. The most serious of these are its inability to assign arbitrary permission sets to an ACE and its limitation on a single file specification. Keith Woodard has written a set of utilities for manipulating ACLs that he distributes as shareware. The package is called the *NT Command Line Security Utilities* (*NTSec* for short), and it includes the following ACL-related utilities (among others):

listacl
> Display ACLs

grant
> Assign permissions to users or groups on files

revoke
> Remove permissions from users or groups on files

igrant
> Assign permissions to users or groups on directories

irevoke
> Remove permissions from users or groups on directories

swapacl
> Transfer existing permissions from one user or group to another

saveacl
> Save ACLs and file ownerships to a binary file

restacl
> Restore ACLs and file ownerships from a **saveacl** file

setowner
> Change the ownership of files or directories

Let's consider some examples of these utilities in action (we assume that the system administrator is running them in all cases). The following command displays the ACLs for the *.DOC* files in *C:\Temp*:

```
C:\> cd C:\Temp & listacl *.doc

C:\TEMP\rachel.doc
    Owner: Chavez
    Chavez                        (RWXD)
    Administrators (lg)           (All)
    Dagmar                        (RXO)
    Will                          (RPO)
C:\TEMP\winnie.doc
    Owner: Administrators (lg)
    Chavez                        (RWXD)
    Dagmar                        (RX)
    Administrators (lg)           (All)
C:\TEMP\zelda.doc
    Owner: Administrators (lg)
```

```
Chavez                          (RWXD)
Dagmar                          (RX)
Administrators (lg)             (All)
```

The following command gives user *Dagmar* **RWOP** access to the indicated file:

```
C:\> grant dagmar:rwop rachel.doc
Granting permissions to: BOREALIS\dagmar(user)
C:\TEMP\rachel.doc
```

The following command illustrates the full syntax of the **grant** command. It replaces any current permissions held by the three specified users with those listed in the command for all files (but not subdirectories) whose names begin with the letter c and have a non-empty file extension, except the file *Claire.Doc*:

```
C:\> grant -replace dagmar:rwx chavez:rwxdop will:all c*.* ^
          -x claire.doc
Granting permissions to: BOREALIS\dagmar(user)
Granting permissions to: BOREALIS\chavez(user)
Granting permissions to: BOREALIS\will(user)
C:\TEMP\closet.txt
C:\TEMP\Coffee Bean 16.bmp
```

Both *Will* and *Chavez* are granted **Full Control** of the files by the command.

The **-x** option is valid for all of these commands, and specifies a list of items to be excluded from the command's operation. Its argument is one or more file specifications, which may contain wildcards.

NOTE   Command options are preceded by a hyphen rather than a forward slash and must be entered in lowercase letters.

This command revokes write access for user *Dagmar* from the specified file:

```
C:\> revoke dagmar:w rachel.doc
C:\TEMP\rachel.doc
```

The **igrant** and **irevoke** commands operate similarly on directories. Both allow you to specify both directory permissions and file default permissions. For example, the following command gives user *Chavez* full control of *C:\Temp* and all of its subdirectories (the **-r** option says to recurse into all subdirectories), and sets her default file permissions for new files to **RWX**:

```
C:\> igrant -r chavez:all,rwx c:\temp
Granting permissions to: BOREALIS\chavez(user)
c:\TEMP
c:\temp\chavez
c:\temp\covers
```

The following command removes write access from the default file permissions part of user *Dagmar*'s ACE for *C:\Temp*, leaving her directory access part unchanged (indicated by the hyphen placeholder):

```
C:\> irevoke dagmar:-,w c:\temp
c:\TEMP
```

The **swapacl** command may be used to change the user or group associated with an ACE to a different one. For example, the first command assigns *Dagmar*'s ACEs to user *Viveca* for all files in the current directory, and the second command gives the ACEs for group *Bio* to user *Will*:

```
C:\> swapacl Viveca Dagmar *
Swapping BOREALIS\dagmar (user) ACLs with BOREALIS\viveca (user)
. . .
C:\> swapacl -r Bio Will C:\Temp
Swapping BOREALIS\bio (group) ACLs with BOREALIS\will (user)
. . .
```

The **saveacl** command saves the ownerships and permissions of files and directories to a binary data file. For example, this command saves this data for the entire Windows NT system directory tree to the file *NT_ACL*, excluding files with the extension *.TMP* or *.BMP* and the *Profiles* subtree:

```
C:\> saveacl -r C:\WinNT nt_acl -x *.tmp *.bmp C:\WinNT\Profiles
```

Ownerships and permissions are saved by pathname. This facility allows you to clone the permissions on one system onto a different system. For example, the following command applies the ownerships and permissions saved by the previous command on the local system where it's executed (*pele* in this case):

```
Pele>> restacl nt_acl
```

Files whose permissions were saved on *vala* but not present on *pele* are ignored.

Finally, the **setowner** command allows you to assign ownership of a file or directory to any desired user, as in this example:

```
C:\> setowner dagmar rachel.doc
Changing ownership to BOREALIS\dagmar (user)
C:\TEMP\rachel.doc
```

The package also includes commands for displaying and modifying share permissions: **sharelistacl**, **sharegrant**, and **sharerevoke**. Here is an example of the first of these:

```
C:\> sharelistacl \\vala\profiles
Permissions for share: \\vala\profiles
    Everyone              (All)
```

This share allows full access to everyone (relying on the underlying file permissions to prevent unauthorized access). The other two commands can modify share permissions from the command line.

7

Backups

Any user of any computer system figures out sooner or later that files are occasionally lost. These losses have many causes: users may delete their own files accidentally, a power failure can corrupt an important database file, a hardware failure may ruin an entire disk, and so on. The damage resulting from these losses can range from minor to very expensive. To guard against them, one primary responsibility of a system administrator is planning and implementing a backup scheme that periodically saves all of the files on the systems for which she is responsible. It is also the administrator's responsibility to see that backups are performed in a timely manner and that backup tapes (or other media) are stored safely and securely. This chapter begins by discussing backup strategies and options and then turns to the tools that are available for making them.

Planning a Backup Schedule

Developing an effective backup strategy is an ongoing process. You usually inherit something when you take over existing systems, and start out doing the same thing you've always done when you become responsible for new systems. While this may work for a while, such an approach all too often ends up in chaos, with no viable policy ever replacing the outdated one. The time to develop a good backup strategy is right now, starting from however you are approaching things at the moment.

Ultimately, backups are insurance. They represent time expended in an effort to prevent future losses. The time required for any backup schedule must be weighed against the decrease in productivity, product schedule slippage, and so on if the files are needed but are not available. The overall requirement of any backup plan is that it be able to restore the entire computing core within an acceptable amount of time in the event of a large-scale failure while at the same time not sacrificing too much in the way of convenience in either what it takes to get the backup done or how easy it is to restore one or two files when a user deletes them accidentally. The approaches one might take in the abstract when considering just disaster recovery or just day-to-day convenience in isolation are often very different, and the final backup plan will need to take both of them into account (and will accordingly reflect the tension between them).

There are many factors to consider in developing a backup plan. The following questions are among the most important:

What files need to be backed up? The simplest answer is, of course, everything. But while everything but scratch files and directories needs to be saved somewhere, it doesn't all have to be saved as part of the formal backup procedures. For example, since the Windows NT operating system is delivered on CD-ROM, there may not be a pressing need to back up the system files (although you may choose do so anyway for reasons of convenience).* However, it is a good idea to be cautious and to err on the side of backing up too many files. If you overlook something important, chances are it will be the first file to be lost.

Where are these files? This question involves both considering where the important files are and identifying the systems that hold important data. The type of system on which the important data reside also needs to be taken into account (we'll consider developing a backup plan for a heterogeneous network in a bit).

Who will back up the files? The answer may depend on where the files are. For example, many sites assign the backup responsibility for server systems to the system administrator, but make users responsible for files that they keep on their workstation's local disks. This may or may not be a good idea, depending on whether all of the important files really get backed up under such a scheme.

What resources are available for performing backups? Both the number and characteristics of available output devices, such as their media capacity and write speed, and the specific software packages that are present on the systems in question are important factors in developing an effective backup plan.

Where, when, and under what conditions should backups be performed? This refers to the computer system on which the backup will be performed, which obviously need not be the same as the system where the files are physically located. Similarly, in an ideal world, all backups would be performed after hours on idle filesystems. That's not always practical in the real world, however.

---

* However, the more patches you have applied to the operating system, the more helpful a recent backup will be if you have to restore the system disk. In addition, backing up the system disk can make it easier to restore libraries required by application programs, which are typically stored in the system directory tree even when the application itself is installed on a different disk.

How often do these files change? This information will help you decide both when and how often to perform backups and the type of schedule to implement. For example, if your system supports a large ongoing development project, then the files on it are likely to change frequently and will need to be backed up at least daily and probably after hours. On the other hand, if the only volatile file on a system is a large database, its filesystem might need to backed up several times every day, while the other filesystems on the same system would be backed up only once a week.

Backup facilities designed for the Windows NT environment are generally designed to perform these different types of backups:

Full backups
> All of the files within some predefined set are copied to tape (or other media), and they are all marked as backed up. This archive attribute is cleared for a file whenever it is modified.

Copy-only backups
> All of the files within the set are copied, but none of them are marked as backed up.

Differential backups
> All files in the set that have been modified since the most recent full backup are copied but not marked as backed up.

Incremental backups
> All files in the set that have been modified since the most recent backup of any type are copied and marked as backed up.

How do differential and incremental backups differ? Suppose you perform a full backup on Monday. On Tuesday, both types of backup will include any files that have changed since Monday. On Wednesday, however, a second differential backup will include all files changed since Monday while a second incremental backup will include only those changed since Tuesday.

Incremental backups mark the saved files as backed up while differential backups do not. Thus, an incremental backup and a differential backup are identical when run as the first backup following a full backup. Differential backups inevitably increase in size over time while the size of successive incremental backups depends solely on the volatility of the filesystem.

I personally prefer differential backups to incremental backups for two reasons: there are only two sets of tapes to be restored in the event of a major failure, and its easy to find the location of a required file (usually on the most

---

* This type of backup is the traditional UNIX and mainframe meaning of the term *incremental backup*. However, the Windows world defines that term differently (as we're about to see).

recent differential). However, very active sites, where many files are changing constantly, may find that only incremental backups are practical, despite their inconvenience when you need to restore an individual file.

Windows NT does not include the concept of incremental backup levels, as do many other operating systems.

Daily backups
    All files in the set that were modified today are backed up, but none are marked as archived.

The frequency and types of backups that you decide should be performed depends on how volatile the files within them are. Most sites will want to use a schedule that combines full and differential or incremental backups. A good rule of thumb is that you should do a full backup whenever the size of the incremental or differential backup is getting close to that of a full backup anyway. Sometimes, this means doing full backups once a week; other sites need to do them only once every month or two.

How quickly does an important missing or damaged file need to be restored? Backups protect against both widespread and isolated file loss, and the timeframe in which key files need to be back online must be taken into account. The number of key files, how widely spread they are throughout a network, and how large they are will also influence matters. Your site may only have one irreplaceable file, but you'll need to plan differently depending on whether it is 100 KB or 10 GB in size. (Note that losing even a single 1 KB file can wreak havoc if it's the license file, without which the central application program won't run.) In the first case, you won't want to have to read through a five-tape backup set in order to restore just the one file. Considerations such as these will help you to divide the data to be backed up into subsets of manageable size.

Where will the data be restored? Will the backup files be used only on the system from which they were made, or is there an expectation that they could be restored to a different system in an emergency?

Once you have gathered all of the data about what needs to be backed up and the resources available for doing so, a procedure like the following can be used to develop the detailed backup plan itself:

• Begin by specifying an ideal backup schedule without considering any of the constraints imposed by your actual situation. List what data you would like to be backed up, how often it needs to be backed up, and what subdivisions of the total amount make sense.

• Now compare that ideal schedule to what is actually possible in your environment, taking the following points into consideration:

— When the data is available to be backed up: Backing up open files is always problematic—the best you can hope for is to get an uncorrupted snapshot of the state of the file at the instant that the backup is made—so ideally backups should be performed on idle systems. This usually translates to after normal working hours.

— How many tape drives (or other backup devices) are available to perform backups at those times and their maximum capacities and transfer rates: In order to determine the latter, you can start with the manufacturer's specifications for the device, but you will also want to run some timing tests of your own under actual conditions to determine realistic transfer rates that take into account the system loads, network I/O rates, and other factors in your environment. You will also need to take into account whether or not all of the data is accessible to every backup device.

At this point (as with any aspect of capacity planning), there is no substitute for doing the math. Let's consider a simple example: a site has 150 GB of data that all needs to be backed up once a week, and there are three tape drives available for backups (assume that all of the data is accessible to every drive). Ideally, backups should be performed only on weeknights between midnight and 6 A.M. In order to get everything done, each tape drive will have to back up 50 GB of data in the 30 hours that the data is available. That means that each tape drive must write 1.4 GB of data per hour to tape.

This is well within the capabilities of many current tape drives when writing local data.* However, much of the data in our example is distributed across a network, so there's a chance that data might not be available at a fast enough rate to sustain the tape drive's top speed. Some backup programs also pause when they encounter an open file, giving it a chance to close (30 seconds is a typical wait period); when there are a lot of open files in a backup set, this can substantially increase how long the backup takes to complete.

In addition, we have not made any allowances for incremental backups between full backups. Thus, this situation seems to strain the available resources.

• Make modifications to the plan to take into account the constraints of your environment. Our example site is cutting things a bit too close for comfort, but they have several options for addressing this:

— Adding additional backup hardware (a fourth tape drive)

---

* In practice, of course, you would also need someone to change tapes in the middle of the night (or an autoloading tape device).

— Decreasing the amount of data to be backed up or the backup frequency: for example, they could perform full backups only every two weeks for some or all of the data

— Increasing the amount of time available for backups (for example, performing some backups on weekends or doing incremental backups during the early evening hours)

• Test and refine the backup plan. Actually trying it out frequently reveals factors your on-paper planning has failed to consider.

• Review the backup plan on a periodic basis to determine if it is still the best solution to your site's backup needs.

Backup Options in a Heterogeneous Environment

When important data is distributed among different kinds of systems within a network or site, backups become more complicated. There are several ways of handling such a situation:

Back up everything from Windows NT systems
This requires either making the data on the foreign systems accessible to a Windows NT system (for example, by using SAMBA on a UNIX system) or purchasing backup software that supports all of the system types from which data must be saved.

Back up everything from a different operating system
For example, you could back up data from Windows NT systems to a UNIX system either by accessing the Windows NT files via NFS or SAMBA or by using software on the UNIX system that supports saving data from both types of systems.

Back up everything where it is
In other words, back up the Windows NT data to Windows NT systems and back up the UNIX data to UNIX systems.

Whatever option you choose, the most important thing to remember is that you are developing a single, overall backup plan for the group of systems (or site); make sure that every system is taken into consideration and plays a part in the overall plan, regardless of the operating system it happens to be running.

Backup Media and Tape Devices

There are many different media suitable for storing backed up data. Here's a quick summary of the choices you have available.

Magnetic tape of one sort or another has been the traditional backup medium for decades. In most modern tapes, both the tape and the two reels it moves between are contained completely within a plastic cartridge. The first tape of this type was $\frac{1}{4}$-inch cartridge tape (also known as QIC tapes), which was once the medium of choice for most workstations, and is still in wide use.

Digital audio tapes that are 4mm (commonly called DAT, but the data storage grade is technically known as DDS) are widely used, as are 8mm ("Exabyte") tape drives (8mm drives are now also called DAT drives by hardware vendors, although they actually use tape first intended for video data). Their high capacity—10 GB or more with hardware compression—makes them ideal for unattended backups: you can put a tape in at night, start a command or script to perform a backup, and go home. Their one disadvantage is that these tapes seem even more sensitive to heat than other types.

WARNING 8mm and 4mm tapes come in two grades, one designed for video and audio recording (respectively), and a better, more expensive grade designed for binary data. Be sure to purchase only data quality tapes. Lower quality tapes sometimes work fine, but they are always much less reliable about retaining data, and they may damage tape drive heads in some circumstances.

Digital linear tape (DLT) devices are the high-end tape device of choice. The highest capacity tapes of this type can hold up to 35 GB of data (and twice that amount of raw data when compression is used). The tapes themselves are also significantly more reliable than 4mm or 8mm tapes.

Floppy disk drives are found on most computer systems. Floppy disks are inexpensive and reasonably reliable provided they are stored properly. However, the capacity of a floppy disk is quite small, so they don't present a reasonable option for a primary backup medium. Still, floppy disks do have some limited backup uses: ad hoc saves of a few files, local backups for user workstations, etc.

Removable disks are a viable backup option for some environments and contexts. Removable disks are fully enclosed disk units that are inserted into a drive as needed, and they tend to be significantly more reliable than either tapes or floppy disks. They also generally behave like a hard disk, making backups faster and restorations much easier (since any file can be accessed immediately without the media positioning required by tape). The most popular removable disk drives are the Zip and Jaz drives from Iomega and the EZ drives from Syquest.

Magneto-optical disks have the same width and length as floppy disks but are about twice as thick and hold a lot more data. Magneto-optical disks also come in

3½- and 5¼-inch versions, and their current capacity ranges from 128 MB to about 4 GB (including data compression). Optical disks are purported to be much more stable than any of the purely magnetic media; the stability comes from the fact that they are written magnetically but are read optically, so reading the disk has no degrading effect on the stored data.

Another fairly expensive alternative backup medium is the *write-once CD-ROM*. This device allows a recordable CD (RCD) to be used as a one-time backup destination. Once the RCD is written, the data is permanent and can't be overwritten, since the recorder literally carves the surfaces of the RCD when it writes to it. However, this permanence is a strength rather than a limitation if a permanent archive is what you desire.

There are a variety of devices available designed to make media handling more automated. For example, there are autoloading tape drives—also known as *stackloader* drives—which can feed tapes automatically from a stack of ten or so. Another type of device puts multiple drive units into a box that looks to users like a single tape drive having the combined capacity of all of its components. Alternatively, such a device can be used to make multiple identical tapes simultaneously. Still other units combine both multiple drives and tape autoloading capabilities. Similar devices also exist for optical disks and writeable CD-ROMs.

Storing Backup Media

Properly storing the backup tapes or other media once you've written them is an important part of any backup plan. Here are some things to keep in mind when deciding where to store the ones for your system:

Know where things are

> Having designated storage locations for backups makes finding the right one quickly much more likely. It is also important that anyone who might need to do a restore know where the tapes are kept (you will want to take a vacation occasionally). Installation media and boot diskettes and the like also ought to be kept in a specific location known to those people who need access to them. I can assure you from personal experience that a system failure is much more unpleasant when you have to dig through boxes of tapes or piles of CDs looking for the right one before you can even attempt to fix whatever's wrong.

> Another aspect of knowing where things are concerns figuring out what tape holds the file that you need to restore. Planning for this involves making records of backup contents (as we'll see).

Make routine restorations easy

Backups should be convenient enough so that you can quickly restore a lost file, and tapes should be labeled sufficiently well so that you can find the ones you need right away.

Ideally, you should have a different tape (or set of tapes) for each distinct item in your backup schedule. For example, if you do a backup every day, it's best to have five tapes that you reuse each week; if you can afford it, you might even have twenty tapes that you rotate through every four weeks.

Labeling tapes clearly is also a great help in finding the right one quickly later. Color-coded labels are favored by many sites as an easy yet effective way to distinguish the different sets of tapes. At the other extreme, I visited a site where the backup system they developed prints a detailed label for the tape at the conclusion of each backup.

Write-protect backup media

This prevents them from being accidentally overwritten. The mechanism for doing so varies with different media types, but most of them involve physically moving a plastic dial or tab to some designated position. Which position is the write-protected one varies: for example, 4mm DDS tapes are writeable when the tabbed opening is closed, while 8mm tapes and most removable disks are writeable when it is open.

Environmental considerations

Most backup media like it cool, dry, and dark. High humidity is probably the most damaging environment, especially for cartridge-enclosed media, which are easily ruined by the moisture condensation that accompanies temperature drops in humid conditions. Direct sunlight should also be avoided, and most plastic materials will deform when subjected to the temperature within the trunk of a car or the enclosed passenger compartment on a hot summer day.

Take security into account

In every location where you store backup tapes, the usual physical security considerations apply: the tapes should be protected from theft, vandalism, and environmental disasters as much as is possible.

Off-site backups

These are the last barrier between your system and total annihilation. They are full backup sets that are kept in a locked, fireproof, environmentally controlled location completely offsite. Preparing backups for off-site storage is also one of the few times* when simply making a backup is not enough; you'll need to verify that the data has been written correctly.

---

* Another such time is when you are recreating a filesystem.

You also need to think from time to time about the reasonable expected lifetime of your backup media. Stored under the right conditions, tapes can last for years, but unfortunately, you cannot count on this. Some manufacturers recommend replacing tapes .every year. This is certainly a good idea if you can afford to do so. The way that tapes and removable disks are stored also affects their lifetime: sunlight, heat, and humidity all can significantly shorten it. I always replace tapes that have failed twice, regardless of their age; for some people and situations, a single failure is enough.

Given these considerations, your site may want to consider alternative media for off-site and archival backups. For example, manufacturers of optical disks claim a lifetime of 15 years for this media, based on accelerated aging tests; as of this writing, we won't know for about 11 years whether it is really true or not.

Adding Tape Drives

Before you can use any backup device for backups, you naturally must install and configure it. In the case of tape drives, this involves attaching the device to the computer where it will reside and then installing the required device driver. The latter is accomplished via the **Tape Devices** control panel applet (illustrated in Figure 7-1). Its **Devices** tab lists the installed tape devices (use the **Detect** button to have the system search for newly added ones). The **Properties** button may be used to view the characteristics of the selected device, including its drive number within the system (which will be needed for some backup software).

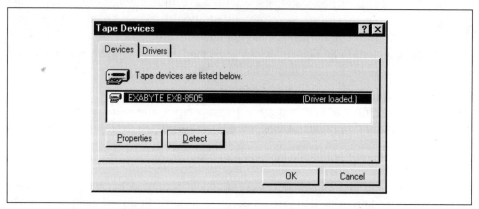

Figure 7-1. The Tape Devices control panel applet

The first time you access a new tape drive with this control panel applet, the operating system will usually prompt you to install the required driver (you will need to insert the Windows NT distribution CD or the floppy disk provided by the drive's manufacturer). Alternatively, you can use the **Drivers** tab of the control panel to add, change or remove device drivers.

WARNING   If your system uses a SCSI tape drive, be sure power is applied to the drive before you turn on the power to the computer itself or its driver may not load properly.

The Windows NT Backup Facility

Windows NT includes a backup facility. It can be accessed via the **Start➤Programs➤Administrative Tools (Common)➤Backup** menu path or with the **ntbackup** command. It requires a tape drive as its backup device, and only users who are members of the *Administrators* and *Backup Operators* groups may use it to back up files other than those to which they have access. This subsection presents an overview of this utility.

Performing a backup with the Windows NT backup facility involves these steps:

1. Start the utility. In the **Drives** window (select **Window➤Drives** to make it visible if necessary) illustrated in Figure 7-2, select the files you want to back up by double-clicking on each desired filesystem in turn and checking the desired subdirectories and individual files from the resulting browser-like lists. When some files from a filesystem have been selected for backup, the corresponding drive will be checked in the **Drives** window. Checking this box manually automatically selects all files in that filesystem for (potential) backup.

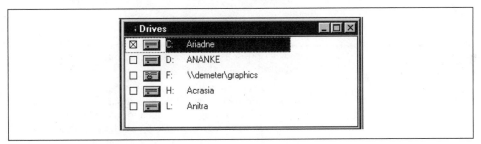

Figure 7-2. Backup facility disk drives window

In order to back up files residing on remote systems, the corresponding filesystems must be mapped to local drive letters (as is the case for drive *F:* in the example).

2. Select the desired tape drive in the **Tapes** window.

3. Press the **Backup** button (or choose **Operations➤Backup...**) to specify the parameters for the backup operation using the **Backup Information** dialog box (illustrated in Figure 7-3). The various fields and check boxes in this dialog box are described in Table 7-1.

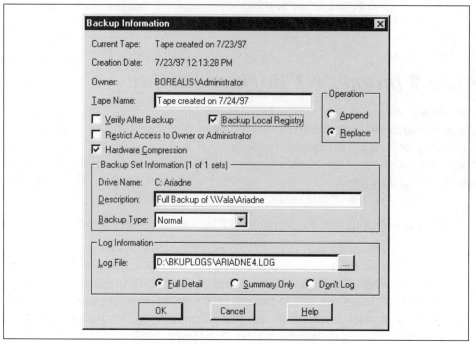

Figure 7-3. Specifying a backup operation

Table 7-1. Backup Operation Options

Field	Meaning
Tape Name	Name/description for the specific tape being written to (defaults to the date made).
Verify After Backup	If selected, a second verification pass is performed on the backup tape, in which every file is compared with the original on disk. The purpose of verification is to ensure against data loss from write errors, and it should be performed for all archival backups.
Operation	**Append** says to add data to the end of the tape, preserving any existing contents. **Replace** says to overwrite any data currently stored on the tape.
Backup Local Registry	If checked, the registry files on the local system are included in the backup (the utility has the ability to save their contents even though they are always open while the system is up).

Table 7-1. Backup Operation Options (continued)

Field	Meaning
Restrict Access to Owner or Administrator	If checked, only the tape's owner or a member of the *Administrators* or *Backup Operators* groups can write files to the tape, restore files from it, or even list its contents. Be aware that it's not hard to get around this, however, and using this feature is no substitute for proper security for backup media (discussed in a bit).
Hardware Compression	This option determines whether or not to use any hardware compression features the device may include. This box should be unchecked if you want to ensure that the tape can be read by any generic tape drive using the same media type, but it also substantially decreases the capacity of the tape.
Description	This is a textual description of the backup set. If more than one backup set is being created, the entire **Backup Set Information** area of the dialog box is scrollable.
Backup Type	Specifies the type of backup: **Normal** (Full), **Copy**, **Incremental**, **Differential**, or **Daily**.
Log File	Selects the file to which the logging information for this backup should be written. If an existing log file is specified, then new logging data is appended to that file.
Log Information detail level	Indicates how detailed the log entry for each saved file should be. **Full Detail** entries include the filename, file attributes, file size, and modification date and time for each file, organized on a directory-by-directory basis, while **Summary Only** entries include only the full pathname for each saved item. The **Don't Log** option prevents all logging.

Once you have specified the settings that you want, pressing the **Backup Information** dialog box's **OK** button will begin the backup.

If files from more than one filesystem have been selected for backup, each distinct group will be saved as a separate *backup set*. Each backup set is stored as a single file on tape.

The following steps are required to restore files from a backup tape:

1. Insert the tape containing the desired files into the tape drive. Then double-click on its entry in the **Tapes** window to load the backup *catalogs* from tape (or select **Operations▸Catalog**). The catalog is a summary file containing information about the files stored within a backup set. When you scan a tape for catalog data, information about all of the backup sets present on the tape is loaded. Figure 7-4 shows the display for a tape containing three backup sets.

2. When the catalogs are all loaded, the available backup sets are displayed in the right side of the **Tapes** window (select **View▸Split** if your **Tapes** windows has only one section). Double-clicking on a backup set loads its table of

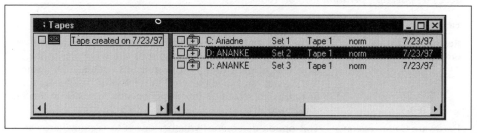

Figure 7-4. Viewing a tape's backup sets

contents and presents a browsing window in which you can select the files you want to restore in the usual manner.

3. Once you have selected the files for restoration, press the **Restore** button (or select **Operations➤Restore...**) to specify the details of the restore operation. The resulting **Restore Information** dialog box is illustrated in Figure 7-5.

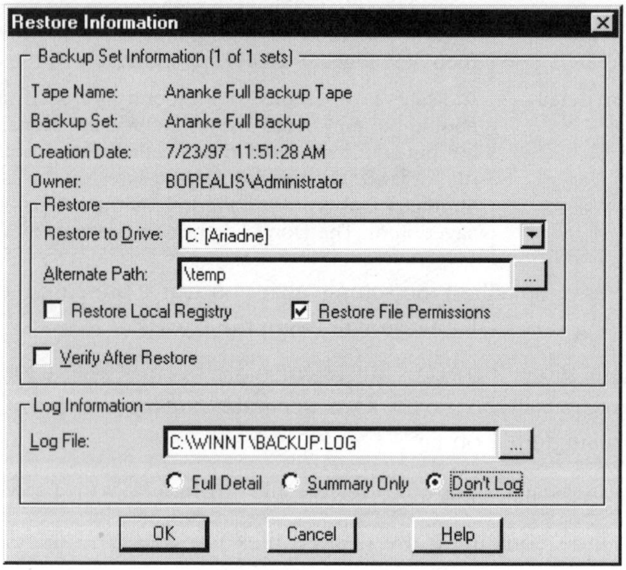

Figure 7-5. Specifying a restore operation

By default, files are restored to their original locations. You can specify an alternate restoration location via the fields in the **Restore** area of the dialog box. Checking **Restore File Permissions** restores ownership and ACL data, along with the file contents; otherwise, the files are owned by the user performing the restore operation and ACLs are created based upon those of the existing directories into which the files are written.

Command-Line Mode

The **ntbackup** utility may also be run in from the command line. This mode is for initiating backups via scripts and for performing unattended backups via the Schedule Service. The command has the following general syntax:

```
ntbackup operation path [options]
```

where *operation* is one of **backup** or **eject**, and *path* is a list of directories to be backed up (separated by spaces).

The **ntbackup** command's options generally correspond to items in the graphical version's **Backup Information** dialog box. These are the most useful options:

/A　Append the backup set to the tape (the default is to replace its current data).

/V　Verify the backup after writing it.

/R　Restrict tape access to its owner and *Administrators* and *Backup Operators.*

/D *label*
　　Specify a description for the backup set (enclose in quotation marks if there are internal spaces).

/B　Back up the local registry in addition to all specified files.

/HC:*onoff*
　　Specify the hardware compression setting (**on** or **off**).

/T *type*
　　Select the backup type: choose one of **normal, copy, incremental, differential,** or **daily**.

/L *path*
　　Indicate the path to the log file for this backup operation (a **Full Detail** log is produced).

/Tape:*n*
　　Use tape drive number *n* (drive number may be viewed with the **Properties** button in the **Tape Devices** control panel applet). By default, the system default tape drive is used.

For example, the following command performs a differential backup for the *C:*, *D:*, and *E:* filesystems, including the local registry files, to the default tape drive using its hardware compression features. The backup set is given the name "Vala_ Fri," the log file for the operation is *G:\BkLogs\Vala_Fri.Log*, and any current data on the tape is overwritten:

```
C:\> ntbackup backup C:\ D:\ E:\ /D Vala_Fri /B /HC:on ^
     /T differential /L G:\BkLogs\Vala_Fri.Log
```

When this command is executed, the **ntbackup** graphical user interface opens to allow for any optional operator input. The GUI terminates automatically once the backup completes. **ntbackup** is thus a driver utility for the graphical backup facility rather than a full-fledged command line backup utility. We look at a sample backup script in Chapter 12.

Locating a File You Need to Restore

When the time comes that a file needs to be restored from backup, it can often take as long to figure out which tape it's on as to perform the restore operation. Summary log files can be useful for determining this information quickly. For example, the following command runs a Perl script named **findit**, which displays the tapes on which the specified file is stored:

```
C:\> perl findit.pl urgent.dat
The file *urgent.dat* is located on the following backup tapes:

Tape            Date
---------------------------------
Ananke_Fri      6/13/97
Ananke_Thu      6/12/97
Ananke_Full4    6/2/97
Ananke_Full3    5/5/97
Ananke_Full2    4/7/97
Archive_15B     3/31/97
Ananke_Full1    3/3/97
```

In Chapter 12, we look at the code for this script in detail.

Disadvantages of the Windows NT Backup Facility

While the Windows NT backup facility works reasonably well for performing basic local system backup and restore operations, it's missing many desirable features of a high-end backup package designed for site-wide use:

- Arbitrary sets of files can't be named and saved for repeated backup but must be respecified each time.
- The command-line utility can't backup arbitrary sets of file at all, only entire directory subtrees.
- Backup set catalogs are stored on tape only, which makes a restoration operation more time consuming.
- Files on remote systems may be accessed only via mapped drive letters.
- Only tape drives are supported as backup devices.
- Only systems running a Windows or Windows NT operating system are supported (unless you use a facility like SAMBA).

You should expect the following features from a high-end commercial backup software package suitable for medium-sized networks and some larger sites:

- The ability to define backups sets as arbitrary sets of files, which can be saved and reloaded into the utility as needed

- A capability for defining and saving standard backup operations settings (including associated file sets)

- A facility for exclusion lists, allowing you to create, save, and load lists of files and directories to exclude from a backup operation (including wildcard specifications)

- An automated backup scheduling facility accessed and controlled from within the backup utility itself

- The ability to specify default settings for backup and restore operations

- The ability to define and initiate remote backup and restore operations

- Support for high-end backup devices such as stackloaders and jukeboxes

- Support for non-tape backup devices such as removable disks

- The capability to perform multiple operations to distinct tape devices simultaneously

- The ability to backup open files or to skip them entirely without pausing (at your option)

- Compatibility with the standard Windows NT backup facility will be important to some sites (so that saved files can be restored to any Windows NT system)

- Optional support for non-Windows NT operating systems

The Seagate Backup Exec and Cheyenne ARCserve products are both excellent backup facilities incorporating most or all of these desirable features. We'll consider the former briefly as an example.

Figure 7-6 illustrates the backup operation options provided by this package (the dialog box on the right is reached via the left one's **Advanced** button). They allow you to specify all of the available parameters for a backup operation. These settings are then saved by name for repeated use.

Figure 7-7 illustrates other dialog boxes used in the process of defining a *job* within this package. A job is simply a specified file set (indicated in the right dialog box in the upper row), a collection of backup operations settings (accessed via the **Job Setup** dialog box's **Edit** button), and an optional execution schedule (see the lower dialog box).

Many very large sites with intensive backup requirements—for example, terabytes of data combined with brief backup windows—will find that even programs such

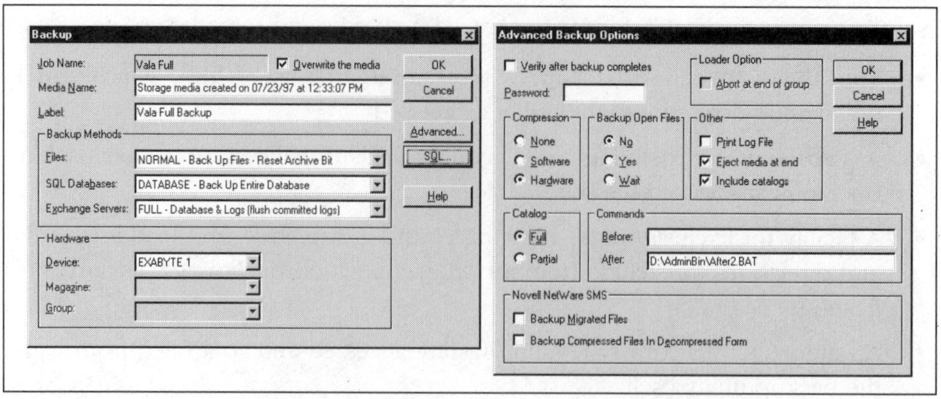

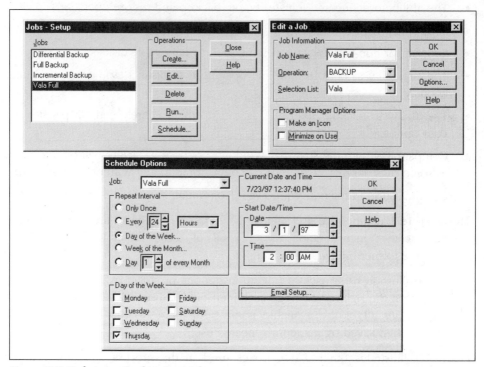

Figure 7-6. Seagate Backup Exec backup options

Figure 7-7. Defining a Backup Exec job

as these are not up to the amount of data that must be handled. For such environments, there are sophisticated network storage management products available, which include additional features like the following:

- Support for multiplexed backup operations, in which multiple data streams are backed up to a single tape device at the same time

- Support for tape RAID devices, in which multiple physical tapes are combined into a single high-performance logical unit via parallel write operations

- Facilities for automatic archiving of inactive files to alternate online storage devices (for example, jukeboxes of optical disks) to conserve disk space and reduce backup requirements

Legato's Networker facility is an example of such a product. Consult Appendix B for sources of additional information about commercial backup packages.

Other Options for Backing Up the Registry

As we've seen, the Windows NT backup utility includes the ability to back up the local registry files. Most commercial backup packages also include this feature.

Alternatively, the Resource Kit includes utilities for saving the registry to an alternate location on disk. The **RegBack** utility may be used to back up open registry hives to disk. It takes the desired output directory location as its argument:

```
C:\> regback F:\REGBACK
saving SECURITY to F:\REGBACK\SECURITY
saving SOFTWARE to F:\REGBACK\software
saving SYSTEM to F:\REGBACK\system
saving .DEFAULT to F:\REGBACK\default
saving SAM to F:\REGBACK\SAM

***Hive = \REGISTRY\USER\S-1-5-21-...
Stored in file
\Device\Harddisk0\Partition1\WINNT\Profiles\Administrator\NTUSER.DAT
Must be backed up manually
...
```

The preceding command backs up the registry to a series of files in the directory *F:\RegBack*. Its output indicates that the subtree of keys corresponding to the current logged-in user can't be backed up automatically. However, the additional command you need to run is displayed as part of the **RegBack** output (omitted above). It will have a form like the following:

```
C:\> regback F:\REGBACK\S-1-5-21-... users  S-1-5-21-...
saving S-1-5-21-... to F:\REGBACK\S-1-5-21-...
```

RegBack doesn't overwrite the target files if they already exist, so be sure to delete any old ones before running the utility, or create a script to perform both operations.

The **RegRest** command can be used to restore registry data saved with **RegBack**. Similarly, the **SaveKey** and **RestKey** utilities can be used to save and restore individual registry values (respectively). Once registry data is saved to disk, it can be backed up normally by any available backup utility.

8

Network Configuration

As we've already seen, managing networking is an inextricable part of administering Windows NT systems. This chapter provides an overview of TCP/IP networking on Windows NT systems. Its goals are two-fold:

- To enable you to perform everyday network management tasks, including adding new hosts to the network, configuring various network services, and monitoring network traffic.

- To enable you to understand all of the most important TCP/IP networking options—including their inherent tradeoffs—so that you will be in a position to evaluate your current network configuration and practices and plan for and manage its future growth.

For book-length discussions of TCP/IP networking, consult Craig Hunt's two excellent books, *Networking Personal Computers with TCP/IP* and *TCP/IP Network Administration* (both published by O'Reilly & Associates).

A bit of history follows: Windows NT supports other standard networking protocols in addition to TCP/IP: IPX/SPX (NetWare), AppleTalk, and SNA (via a separate BackOffice product). In general, discussion of them is beyond the scope of this book.

One other "protocol" does require brief consideration: NetBIOS. On DOS systems, the Basic Input/Output System (BIOS) constituted the operating system's I/O interface. NetBIOS was developed to extend it to I/O operations over a local network. The NetBIOS interface needed a corresponding transport protocol. The first one developed was called the NetBIOS Frames Protocol (NBFP). Currently, in non-TCP/IP environments, NetBIOS traffic uses the NetBIOS Extended User Interface

(NetBEUI) Frame Protocol (NBF); this is the transport protocol used in traditional Microsoft networks. NetBIOS may also be run over TCP/IP (NetBIOS over TCP/IP: NBT). Higher-level services for standard Microsoft networking functionality are provided by the Server Message Block (SMB) protocol.

Vanilla NetBIOS and NetBEUI don't scale well beyond fairly small networks for various technical reasons: they rely on a broadcast-based naming scheme, their packets cannot be routed, they lack networking compatibility with other kinds of computers, and other reasons. Accordingly, methods and standards for running NetBIOS on top of other protocols families, such as TCP/IP were developed. You can run either way on a Windows NT system. If the NetBEUI protocol is installed, local NetBIOS traffic will use its facilities, while standard TCP/IP facilities will use TCP/IP; otherwise, NetBIOS-based facilities will use the TCP/IP networking facilities for communication with other hosts.

NOTE   You must install the NetBIOS protocol if you want to support the standard Microsoft network (computer) browsing features (accessed, for example, by opening the desktop's **Network Neighborhood** icon). It is normally installed by default on Windows NT systems as part of their standard networking facility.

Understanding TCP/IP Networking

The term "TCP/IP" is shorthand for a large collection of protocols and services necessary for internetworking computer systems. In any given implementation, TCP/IP encompasses operating system components, user and administrative commands and utilities, configuration files, and device drivers, as well as the kernel and library support upon which they all depend. Many of the basic TCP/IP networking concepts are not operating-system specific, so we'll begin this chapter by considering TCP/IP networking in a general way.

Figure 8-1 depicts a typical TCP/IP network, including several kinds of network connections. Each computer system on the network is known as a *host* (also known as *nodes* in other networking lexicons). In our example, the systems named for countries are all connected in a local area network (LAN), as are those named for Shakespearean characters.*

The country hosts are connected via an Ethernet. One of the fundamental characteristics of Ethernet is illustrated in the diagram. All hosts on an Ethernet are logically connected to every other host: to communicate with any other host, a

---

* You may wonder whether this is one LAN with two subnets or two LANs. In fact, the term LAN is not precisely defined, and usage varies.

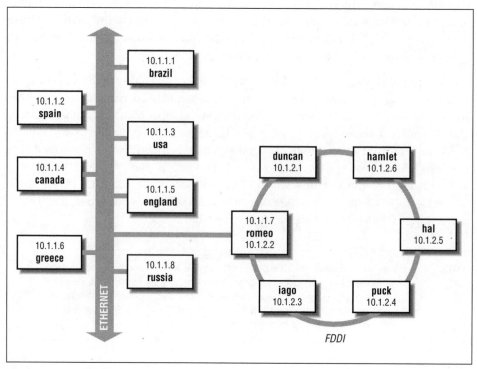

Figure 8-1. TCP/IP local area network

system sends a message out on the Ethernet, where it arrives at the target host in one step (one *hop*). By contrast, for the other network, messages between *duncan* and *puck* must be handled by two other hosts first, thus taking three hops. If this second network ran at the same speed as Ethernet (10 Mbps), then this would be a disadvantage; however, since it is an FDDI network (running at 100 Mbps), more hops are not significant.

The system *romeo* serves as a *gateway* between the two subnets. It is part of both subnets and passes data from one to the other. There are special-purpose computers that are designed to be gateways and nothing else, but many sites only add an additional network interface to a less-used workstation, as in this example.

Names and Addresses

Every system on a network has a *hostname*. This name is unique within the network. Hostnames let users refer to any computer on the network by using a short, easily remembered name rather than the host's network address (described a moment).

Each system on a TCP/IP network also has a *host address*—known as an *IP address*—that is unique for all hosts on the network. When an actual network operation occurs, the hostnames of the systems involved are used to determine their numerical IP addresses, either by looking them up in a table or by requesting translation from a server designated for this task (we'll consider this topic in more detail later in this chapter).

If the system is connected to the Internet, its host address is taken from a range assigned by the Network Information Center to that site. Networks that are not connected to the Internet also generally use network addresses that obey the Internet numbering conventions.

An Internet network address is a sequence of four bytes.* Network addresses are usually written in the form *a.b.c.d*, where *a*, *b*, *c*, and *d* are all decimal integers (e.g. 192.0.10.23). Each component is 8 bits long and thus runs from 0 to 255. The address is split into two parts: the first part identifies the network, the second identifies the host within the network. The sizes of these parts vary. The first byte of the address (*a*) determines the address type (called its *class*), and hence the number of bytes allocated to each part. Table 8-1 gives more specific details about how this works.

Table 8-1. Internet Address Types

Initial Bits	Range of *a*	Address Class	Network Part	Host Part	Max. # Nets	Max. # Hosts/Net
0	1–126	Class A	a	b.c.d	126	16,777,214
10	128–191	Class B	a.b	c.d	16,384	65,534
110	192–223	Class C	a.b.c	d	2,097,152	254
111	224–254	Reserved (*includes multicast addresses*)				

Class A addresses are appropriate for networks with millions of hosts, while Class C addresses are appropriate for a networks with relatively few hosts (fewer than 255). There are few Class A networks; these network numbers are typically reserved for major national networks. Multicast addresses (also sometimes referred to as Class D) are part of the reserved range of addresses. They are used to address a group of hosts as a single entity and are designed for applications like video conferencing.

---

* The Internet address format will change at some point in the near future to accommodate a greater number of hosts than are available under the present scheme. The IP6 standard will expand network addresses to sixteen bytes (128 bits), although it also contains provisions for continued support for present format addresses.

The IP addresses 10.0.0.0 through 10.255.255.255 are one of several ranges that have been reserved for use by private networks (not connected to the Internet).[*] If a site uses 10 for *a*, they might then use *b* and *c* to identify particular subnetworks within a larger network and use *d* to identify an individual host on some subnetwork. For Internet sites, the network is often determined by *a* and *b*, while *c* is used for subnetting, and *d* refers to the host. In any case, you must be consistent with whatever network addressing usage is already established at your site.[†]

NOTE   Many people recommend obtaining an official Internet address for your network even if you never plan for it to be part of the Internet. See the O'Reilly's *TCP/IP Network Administration* for details on the procedures. In many cases, your Internet service provider will also be willing to assist with or perform this process for you.

By convention, the network address 127.0.0.1 is used as a *loopback* address: data sent to it is transmitted back to the same host. The loopback address is mostly used for testing. This address is usually given the hostname *localhost*. Similarly, some host numbers have conventional uses: host 0 refers to the network itself, and host 255 is used for broadcast addresses (specified for messages that are sent to all hosts on the local network).

So far, we've assumed that IP addresses are permanently assigned to each host within a network, but this need not be true. The Dynamic Host Configuration Protocol (DHCP) is a facility that allows IP addresses to be assigned to systems dynamically when they require network access. It is discussed later in this chapter.

A *subnet mask* specifies how the 32-bit IP address is divided between the network part and the host part, and all computers participating in a TCP/IP network have one assigned to them. The subnet mask is a 32-bit value constructed by placing 1 in each bit location for the network portion of the IP address and 0 in all of the bit locations for the host part of the address. Thus, a Class A IP address normally uses a subnet mask of 11111111000000000000000000000000, which is conventionally written as four period-separated decimal integers: 255.0.0.0. Similarly, a normal Class B address uses a subnet mask of 255.255.0.0, and a normal Class C address, a subnet mask of 255.255.255.0.

The subnet mask can also be used to further subdivide one network ID among several local networks. For example, if you use a subnet mask of 255.255.255.192 for a Class C address, you are making the highest two bits of the final address

---

[*] Other ranges are 172.16.0.0 through 172.31.255.255 and 192.168.0.0 through 192.168.255.255. See RFC 1597 for details.

[†] Traditionally, many sites that were not on the Internet used 192 or 193 for *a*.

byte part of the network address (the final byte is 11000000), thereby subdividing that network into four subnets, each of which can have up to 62 hosts on it (since the host ID is coded into the remaining 6 bits).

NOTE   In general, all of the subnet masks within a subnet must be identical (and they are usually the same across an entire network). Be sure to comply with whatever conventions are currently in use at your site.

Media and Topologies

TCP/IP networks can run over a variety of *physical media*. Most current networks use some sort of coaxial cable (thick or thin), twisted-pair cable, or fiber-optic cable.

Network *adapters* provide the interface between a computer and the physical medium comprising the network connection; they usually consist of a single board. Network interfaces support one or more communications protocols, which specify how the computers use the physical medium to exchange data. Most protocols are not media-specific. For example, Ethernet communications—a protocol and not a type of media—can be carried over all four of the media types mentioned previously, and FDDI networks can run over either fiber optic or twisted pair cable. Such protocols specify networking characteristics, such as the structure of the base-level data unit, the way that data moves from host to host across the physical medium, how multiple simultaneous network accesses are handled and resolved, and the like.

All network adapters have a *Media Access Control* (MAC) address, which is a numerical identifier that is absolutely unique to that individual unit (board). For Ethernet devices, MAC addresses are 48-bit values expressed as twelve hexadecimal digits, usually divided into hyphen-separated pairs: for example, 00-00-F8-23-31-91. There are thus over 280 trillion distinct MAC addresses (which ought to be enough even for us). MAC addresses are also commonly referred to as *Ethernet addresses* and occasionally as *hardware addresses*. You can display the MAC address for the network adapters on a Windows NT system using the **ipconfig /all** command or the **GetMAC** command included in the Resource Kit.

Hosts within a local area network can be connected in a variety of arrangements known as *topologies*. For example, the 10.1.1 subnet in Figure 8-1 uses a bus topology in which each host taps into a backbone, which is standard for Ethernet networks. Many times the backbone is not a cable at all but merely a junction box where connections from the various hosts on the network converge, known as a *hub*. The 10.1.2 subnet uses a ring topology.

Networking protocols relating to the physical connection between computers may include a required topology as part of their specification. For example, FDDI networks are composed of two counter-rotating rings (two duplicate rings through which data flows in opposite directions), an arrangement designed to enable a network to easily bypass failed connections (FDDI networks can also include singly attached hosts, which tap into the basic double ring structure).

Nets and Subnets

Individual networks can be organized, subdivided, and joined in a variety of ways, as illustrated in Figure 8-2.

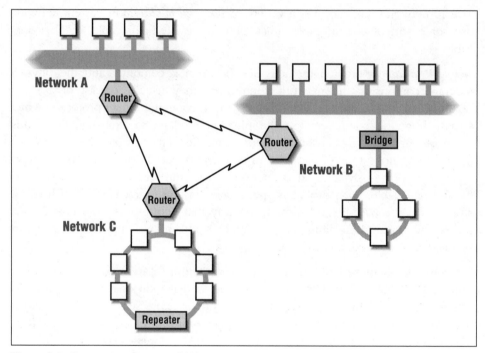

Figure 8-2. Connecting disparate LANs

Networks A, B, and C are geographically separated. In network C, the two hosts at the bottom of the ring are too far apart to be connected directly to one another (all physical media impose a maximum length for an individual cable), so a *repeater* is placed between them. This device simply passes all signals from one wire to the other, thereby connecting the two hosts. More sophisticated repeaters can transfer signals from one media type to another (for example, between twisted-pair and fiber-optic cable).

In network B, the two segments are joined by a *bridge*, a device somewhat more intelligent than a repeater in that it selectively passes only the data destined for the other segment between the two. More complex bridges can filter data in a variety of ways, and some are capable of connecting networks of different types—say, TCP/IP and SNA—by translating the data from one protocol family to the other as it passes it across.

The three networks are connected to one another via *routers*, a still more sophisticated network linking device. In addition to selectively handling data based on its destination, routers also have the ability to determine the current best path to that destination; finding a path to a destination is accordingly known as *routing*. The best routers are highly programmable and can also perform complex filtering on the data they receive, accepting or rejecting it based upon criteria specified by the network administrator. The routers connecting our three networks are arranged so that there are multiple paths to every destination; losing any one of them will cause no harm to communications between the two unaffected networks.

Layers and Protocols

Network communications are organized as a series of layers. With the exception of the one referring to the physical transmission medium, these layers are logical rather than literal or physical. Every network transaction moves down through the layers on its originating system, travels across the physical medium, and then moves up through the same stack of layers on the destination system.

No discussion of any network architecture is complete without at least a brief mention of the Open Systems Interconnection (OSI) Reference Model. Frankly, this description of networking is almost meaningless in terms of actually existing networks, but it is quite helpful in clearly identifying the distinct functions necessary for network communications to occur, even if things are not really divided up this way in real networks. Figure 8-3 shows the layers in the OSI Reference Model and those actually used by TCP/IP; the most important protocols defined for each layer are listed in parentheses.

When a network operation is initiated by a user command or program, it (logically) travels down the protocol stack on the local host (via software), across the physical medium to the destination host, and then back up the protocol stack on the remote host to the proper recipient process. Each layer is equipped to handle data in particular predefined units. The names of these units for the two main transport protocols are listed in Table 8-2. However, the term *packet* is also used generically to refer to any network transmission.

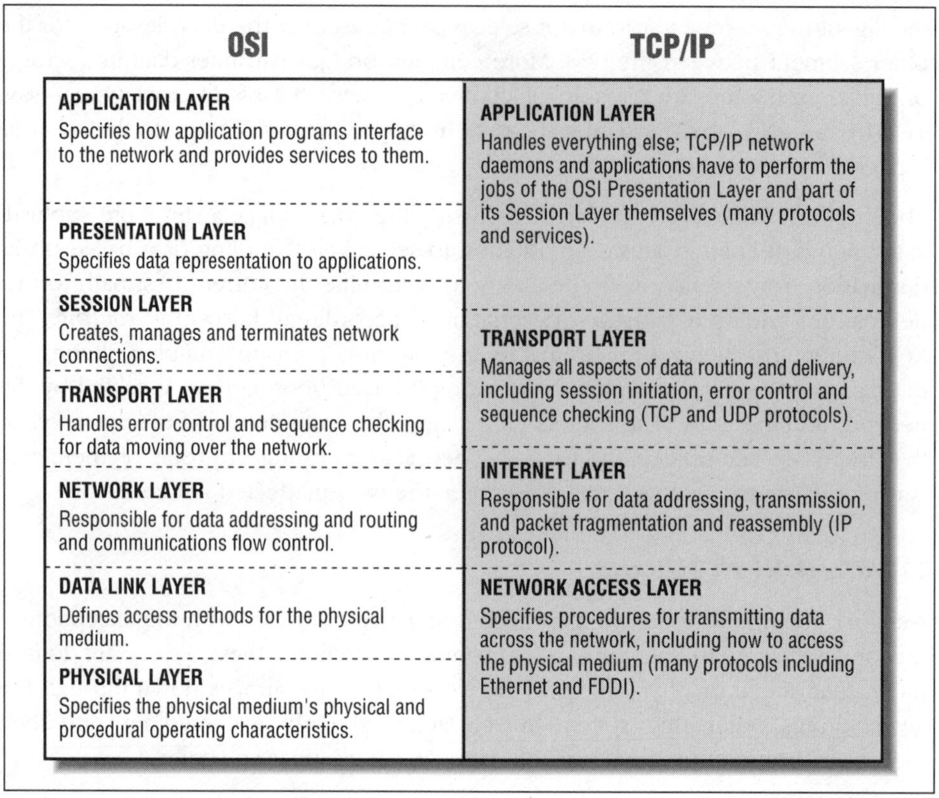

OSI	TCP/IP
APPLICATION LAYER Specifies how application programs interface to the network and provides services to them.	**APPLICATION LAYER** Handles everything else; TCP/IP network daemons and applications have to perform the jobs of the OSI Presentation Layer and part of its Session Layer themselves (many protocols and services).
PRESENTATION LAYER Specifies data representation to applications.	
SESSION LAYER Creates, manages and terminates network connections.	**TRANSPORT LAYER** Manages all aspects of data routing and delivery, including session initiation, error control and sequence checking (TCP and UDP protocols).
TRANSPORT LAYER Handles error control and sequence checking for data moving over the network.	
NETWORK LAYER Responsible for data addressing and routing and communications flow control.	**INTERNET LAYER** Responsible for data addressing, transmission, and packet fragmentation and reassembly (IP protocol).
DATA LINK LAYER Defines access methods for the physical medium.	**NETWORK ACCESS LAYER** Specifies procedures for transmitting data across the network, including how to access the physical medium (many protocols including Ethernet and FDDI).
PHYSICAL LAYER Specifies the physical medium's physical and procedural operating characteristics.	

Figure 8-3. OSI and TCP/IP network architectures

Table 8-2. Data Unit Names

Layer	TCP Protocol	UDP Protocol
Application	stream	message
Transport	segment	packet
Internet	datagram	datagram
Network Access	frame	frame

On the originating end, each layer adds a header to the data it receives from the layer above it (breaking the data into multiple instances of its own units if necessary); similarly, on the receiving end, each layer strips off its own header before passing the data to the next higher layer (combining multiple units together if appropriate), so what is finally received is the same as what was originally sent.

Repeaters, bridges, and routers can be distinguished by how much of the TCP/IP protocol stack they handle. Repeaters operate only at the Network Access layer, bridges use both the Internet and Network Access layers, and routers operate within the three lowest TCP/IP layers. Note that a full network host, which supports all four TCP/IP layers, can accordingly perform the functions of any of these types of devices.

Network Services

Network operations are accomplished by a variety of network *services*, consisting of the software and other facilities needed to perform a specific type of network task. A service is defined by the combination of a transport protocol—TCP and UDP are the most important—and a port: a logical network connection identified by a number. The TCP and UDP port numbering schemes are part of the definition of these protocols.

NOTE   Port numbers are unique only within a given transport protocol; TCP
                  and UDP use the same port numbers.

Various configuration files in the directory *%SystemRoot%\System32\Drivers\Etc* indicate the standard mappings between port numbers and TCP/IP services:

Protocol
> Lists the protocol numbers assigned to the various protocols defined for the TCP/IP family.

Services
> Lists the port numbers assigned to the various TCP and UDP services. Available TCP/IP services on Windows NT systems are listed in Table 8-3.

User and Administrative Commands

Windows NT provides a number of generic TCP/IP user commands, which may be used to access remote systems. The most important of these commands are:

telnet
> Create a character-based (TTY-like) login session on a remote host

ftp
> Copy files to or from a remote host

finger
> Obtain information about a user account on a remote host, which must be running the **Finger** service in order to respond (not included with Windows NT, but there is a freely available version)

System administrators will find the following commands useful:

hostname

Display the name of the local system

ping

Perform a simple network connectivity test

arp

Display or modify the IP-to-MAC address tables

ipconfig

Display information about the system's TCP/IP configuration (useful for determining a system's current IP address when it is a DHCP client)

netstat

Display various network usage statistics

route

Display or modify the static routing tables

tracert

Determine the route to a specified target host

nslookup

Determine the IP address for a hostname via the Domain Name Service

nbtstat

Show current connections and statistics for NetBIOS over TCP/IP

A Sample TCP/IP Conversation

All these concepts come together when we look at a sample TCP/IP conversation. First, we consider what happens when the following generic TCP/IP command is successfully executed:

```
C:\> finger johnm@godot
[godot]
Login name: johnm                In real life: John Montgomery
Directory: /mf/johnm             Shell: /bin/tcsh
Last login Tue Jul 22 13:02 from johnm@verdi
No Plan.
```

This **finger** command (which requests information about a user account on a remote system) causes a network connection to be formed between the local host, which happens to be *vala*, and the remote system *godot*, a UNIX system elsewhere in the network.

The finger service uses the TCP transport protocol (number 6) and port 79. TCP connections are always created using a three-step handshaking process. Figure 8-4 displays a dump of the packet corresponding to the first step, initiated by the local system (created with the **NetXRay** utility from Cinco Networks). The highlighted entry in the top portion of the window displays summary information about the packet, and it indicates that it was transmitted from host *vala* to host *godot*.

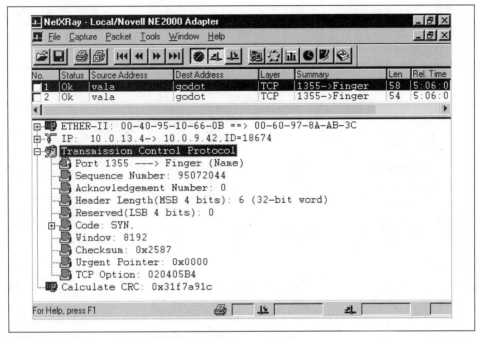

Figure 8-4. First step in a TCP/IP handshake

The second section of this window shows the packet's contents, organized by network layer (remember that each one adds information to the packet as it travels down the protocol stack). The Ethernet area shows the Ethernet addresses of the two hosts (*vala* and *godot* in this case), and the IP area shows their IP addresses. The TCP area contains several important items:

- The ports used by the two systems (line 1 of the TCP section): port 1355 on *vala* and the standard port for the **Finger** service on *godot* (which happens to be 79).

- TCP flags set for this packet (line 6): the SYN flag is set in this case.

- The sequence number for this packet (line 2). The TCP protocol requires that all packets be acknowledged by the receiving host (although not necessarily individually). The SYN (synchronize) flag alone indicates an attempt to create a new network connection, and, in this case, the sequence number is an initial sequence number for the conversation. It will be incremented by one for each byte of data transmitted (and by one at a minimum for each successive packet).

Figure 8-5 shows the next two packets in the sequence, which complete the hand-shake. In the packet on the left (sequence number 1672002085), sent from *godot* back to *vala*, both the SYN and ACK (acknowledge) flags are set. The SYN is the response to *vala*'s SYN, and the ACK is the acknowledgment of the previous packet. The Acknowledgement Number field's contents match the sequence number of the previous packet incremented by 1 (indicating one byte of data received so far). The next packet (on the right) simply acknowledges *godot*'s SYN, and the connection is complete.

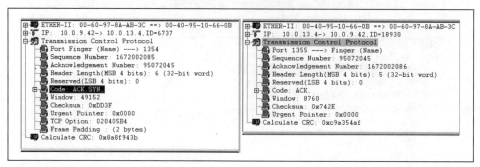

Figure 8-5. Completing the TCP handshake

Now we are ready to actually get some work done. The next packet in the sequence is illustrated in Figure 8-6. This packet sends the data "johnm" to the **Finger** service on *godot* (indicated in the Finger section of the display), and it also acknowledges the previous packet from *godot*. This data is passed up the various network layers, to be delivered ultimately to the proper local process on *godot*.

```
⊞-🔲 ETHER-II: 00-40-95-10-66-0B ==> 00-60-97-8A-AB-3C
⊞-🔲 IP:    10.0.13.4-> 10.0.9.42,ID=19186
⊟-🔲 Transmission Control Protocol
      🔲 Port 1355 ---> Finger (Name)
      🔲 Sequence Number: 95072046
      🔲 Acknowledgement Number: 1672002087
      🔲 Header Length(MSB 4 bits): 5 (32-bit word)
      🔲 Reserved(LSB 4 bits): 0
   ⊞-🔲 Code: ACK,PSH,
      🔲 Window: 8760
      🔲 Checksum: 0x3443
      🔲 Urgent Pointer: 0x0000
⊟-🔲 Finger
      🔲 Data 0000: 6a 6f 68 6e 6d                    | johnm
   🔲 Calculate CRC: 0xf975f46
```

Figure 8-6. Transmitting a request to the remote finger service

godot acknowledges this packet and eventually sends a response. The resulting packet is displayed in Figure 8-7. The output from the local **finger** command on *godot* constitutes the data in this packet. The packet also acknowledges data received from *vala* (5 bytes since the previous packet).

```
ETHER-II: 00-60-97-8A-AB-3C ==> 00-40-95-10-66-0B
IP:  10.0.9.42-> 10.0.13.4,ID=6739
Transmission Control Protocol
    Port Finger (Name) ---> 1354
    Sequence Number: 1672002087
    Acknowledgement Number: 95072051
    Header Length(MSB 4 bits): 5 (32-bit word)
    Reserved(LSB 4 bits): 0
    Code: ACK,PSH,
    Window: 49152
    Checksum: 0xBF8A
    Urgent Pointer: 0x0000
Finger
    Data 0000: 4c 6f 67 69 6e 20 6e 61 6d 65 3a 20 6a 6f 68 6e | Login name: john
         0010: 6d 20 20 20 20 20 09 09 49 6e 20 72 65 61 6c | m     III In real
         0020: 20 6c 69 66 65 3a 20 4a 6f 68 6e 20 4d 6f 6e 74 |  life: John Mont
         0030: 67 6f 6d 65 72 79 0d 0a 44 69 72 65 63 74 6f 72 | gomery..Director
         0040: 79 3a 20 2f 6d 66 2f 6a 6f 68 6e 6d 20 20 20 20 | y: /mf/johnm
         0050: 20 20 20 20 20 20 20 20 20 20 20 09 53 68 65 |            She
         0060: 6c 6c 3a 20 2f 62 69 6e 2f 74 63 73 68 0d 0a 4c | ll: /bin/tcsh..L
         0070: 61 73 74 20 6c 6f 67 69 6e 20 61 74 20 54 75 65 | ast login at Tue
         0080: 20 4a 75 6c 20 32 32 20 31 33 3a 30 32 20 66 72 |  Jul 22 13:02 fr
         0090: 6f 6d 20 6a 6f 68 6e 6d 40 76 65 72 64 69 0d 0a | om johnm@verdi..
         00a0: 4e 6f 20 50 6c 61 6e 2e 0d 0a                   | No Plan...
Calculate CRC: 0x7da75243
```

Figure 8-7. Finger response from the remote system

All that remains is to close down the connection. Conceptually, it proceeds as follows (packets are vastly abbreviated):

```
IP: 193.0.13.4->193.0.9.42
Transmission Control Protocol
Code: ACK, FIN

IP: 193.0.9.42->193.0.13.4
Transmission Control Protocol
Code: ACK

IP: 193.0.9.42->193.0.13.4
Transmission Control Protocol
Code: ACK, FIN

IP: 193.0.13.4->193.0.9.42
Transmission Control Protocol
Code: ACK
```

The FIN flag indicates that a connection is to be terminated. *vala* indicates that it is finished first. *godot* acknowledges that packet and then sends its own FIN, which *vala* acknowledges.

When NetBIOS is being run on top of TCP/IP, a similar process occurs for a command like **net view \\pele**. Figure 8-8 shows the packet from *pele* containing the data from this command that is sent to *vala* (preceding packets from *pele* to *vala* are summarized in the upper part of the window). Notice how the NetBIOS and SMB protocols are subordinate to the TCP protocol.

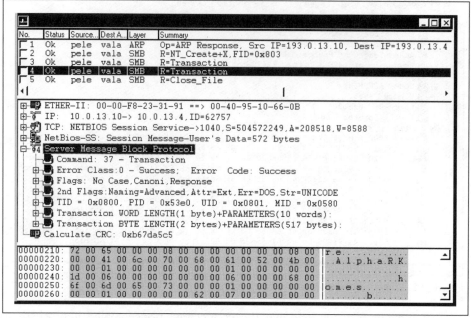

Figure 8-8. NetBIOS running via TCP/IP

When the NetBEUI protocol is installed on a system, packets for such a command bypass TCP/IP, as illustrated in Figure 8-9.

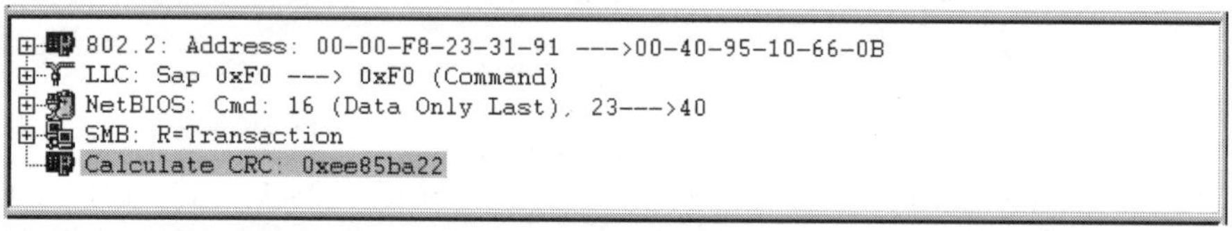

```
⊞🖳 802.2: Address: 00-00-F8-23-31-91 --->00-40-95-10-66-0B
⊞🖵 LLC: Sap 0xF0 ---> 0xF0 (Command)
⊞🖼 NetBIOS: Cmd: 16 (Data Only Last), 23--->40
⊞🖳 SMB: R=Transaction
 🖳 Calculate CRC: 0xee85ba22
```

Figure 8-9. A vanilla NetBIOS/SMB packet

Adding a Host to a Windows NT Domain

To add a new system to a Windows NT domain running TCP/IP, you must complete the following steps:

1. Install and configure the network adapter and identify it to the system, and physically connect the system to the network.

2. Install the TCP/IP networking facility on the system if you did not do so when you installed the Windows NT operating system. Network configuration on Windows NT systems is carried out primarily from the **Network** control panel applet (also accessible via the **Network Neighborhood**'s **Properties**).

3. Assign a hostname and network address to the system (or find out what has been assigned by the network administrator).

4. Create a computer account for the system on the domain's primary domain controller.

5. Install and configure any additional network services that the system requires. This will include deciding on and implementing name service and routing strategies.

6. Test the network connection.

We'll look at each of these steps in some detail.

Configuring the Network Hardware

The first step is to install and configure the network adapter. I use a procedure like the following:

1. Configure any required jumpers on the adapter board to select an appropriate IRQ level and other settings, following the directions in the manufacturer's documentation.

2. Install the adapter board into the computer's CPU cabinet (the power should be off). Connect the system to the network.

3. Boot from a DOS diskette and run the diagnostic utility provided with the adapter to possibly configure and test the adapter board. Only when the board passes all tests at the DOS level do I try to configure it under Windows NT.

4. Reboot the system and tell Windows NT about the adapter via the **Properties...** button of the **Adapters** tab of **Network** control panel applet (illustrated in Figure 8-10). Be aware that you are merely informing the system about the device's settings in this dialog box, not specifying them. When the dialog box first opens, the most common settings for that adapter type are displayed; don't be confused by them and assume that they represent actual settings detected on the device.

You are now ready to install the TCP/IP software.

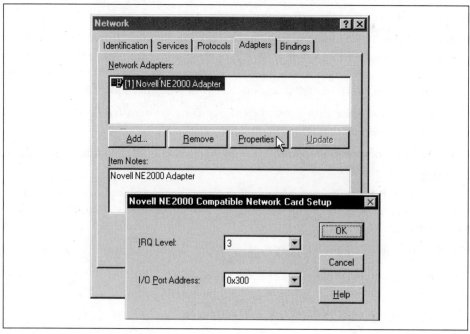

Figure 8-10. Configuring the network adapter

Installing TCP/IP

The **Network** control panel applet's **Protocols** tab (illustrated in Figure 8-11) lists the networking facilities installed on the system and allows you to add new ones. Pressing the **Add...** button brings up a list of available protocols; select **TCP/IP Protocol** to install the TCP/IP networking software. After an initial prompt about whether you want to use DHCP or not (which we will assume you answer with **No** for the moment), you will need to insert the Windows NT distribution CD.

Once the software is installed, closing the control panel applet automatically takes you to basic TCP/IP configuration (which is also always accessible via the **Properties** button on the **Protocols** tab when the TCP/IP protocol is selected). We will cover the various settings in the subsections that follow.

NOTE   As always, you should reapply the latest service pack that is installed when you add a network protocol or service.

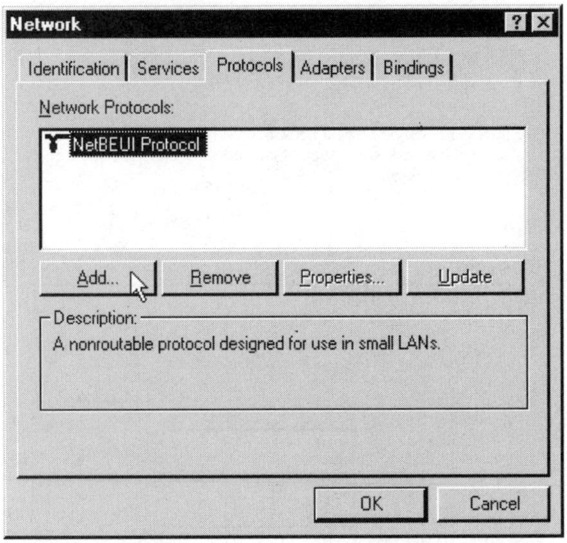

Figure 8-11. The network control panel applet

Basic TCP/IP Configuration

The TCP/IP parameter that you need to specify is the system's IP address, which is accomplished via the **IP Address** tab of the TCP/IP **Properties** dialog box (illustrated in Figure 8-12). The two radio buttons in the dialog box are used to indicate whether the system has a permanent (static) IP address or uses the DHCP facility to obtain one on an as-needed basis. Select whichever setting is appropriate for this system (we'll discuss DHCP in a bit).

After selecting the network adapter from the **Adapter** menu (if more than one is installed in the computer), specify the system's IP address and the subnet mask it will be using in the corresponding fields. Multiple IP addresses for this adapter may be specified with the **Advanced...** button.

The dialog box's final field, **Default Gateway**, is used to specify a gateway host for communications beyond the local network. We consider it later in this chapter.

The other tabs in the **Microsoft TCP/IP Properties** dialog box are used for various name resolution and routing options. We'll examine each of them in the course of this chapter.

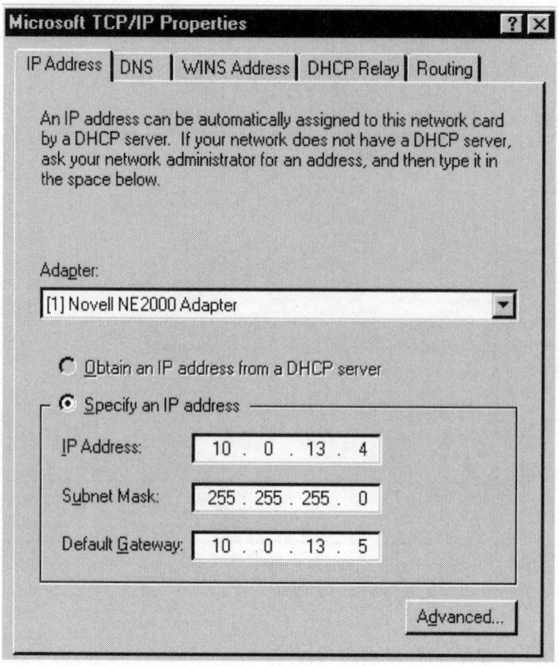

Figure 8-12. IP address configuration

Connecting to the Domain

Before users can log in to a Windows NT domain from the new system, it must be made known to the primary domain controller (PDC).* There are two ways of accomplishing this: from the PDC or from the new system.

On the PDC, you can use the Server Manager to create a computer account for the new system via its **Computer►Add to Domain**... menu path. The resulting dialog box is illustrated in Figure 8-13. After completing the dialog box, pressing the **Add** button adds the system to the domain in the specified capacity.

Alternatively, on the new system, you can use the **Change** button on the **Identification** tab of the **Network** control panel applet to add it to a domain (or to change domains). This brings up the **Identification Changes** dialog box, illustrated in Figure 8-14. Use its lower section to create a new computer account in the desired domain, specifying a username and password for an account with administrative privileges.

---

* This step is not specific to the TCP/IP protocol.

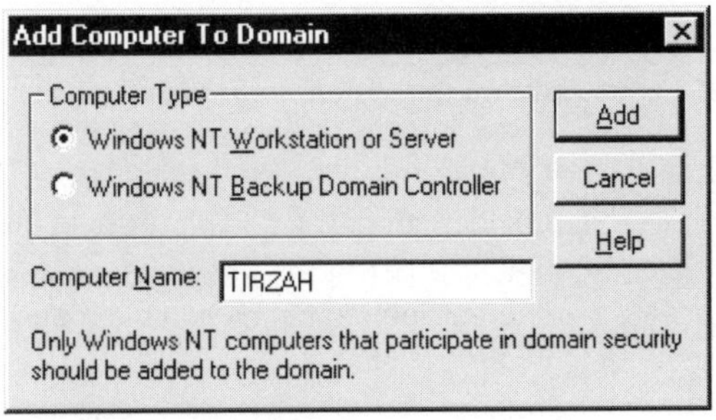

Figure 8-13. Adding a computer to the domain

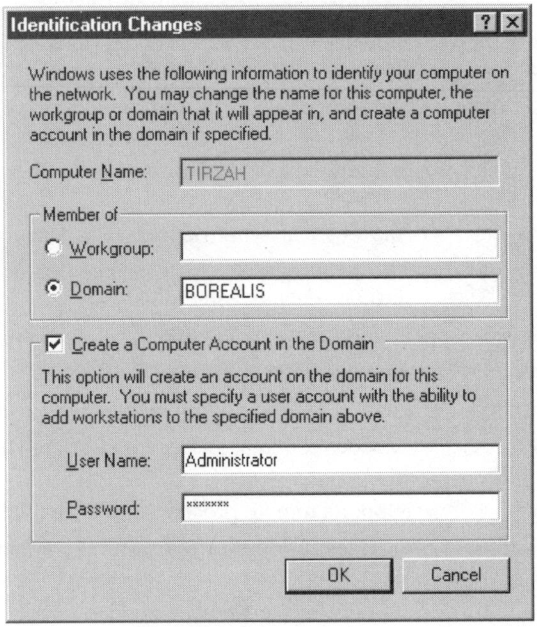

Figure 8-14. Connecting to a domain for the first time

Additional Network Configuration

Depending on the uses for which the new system is intended, it may be necessary to install additional TCP/IP services. Table 8-3 describes the available networking services provided with the Windows NT operating system; the starred items are generally installed by default. Any of them may be installed via the **Network** control panel applet's **Services** tab.

We consider many of these services throughout this chapter.

Table 8-3. Available Networking Services

Service	Description
BOOTP Relay Agent	Allows the system to forward BOOTP broadcast packets across subnets (a pre-DHCP facility that supports remote booting of diskless workstations)
*Computer Browser	Provides support for Explorer-style browsing of networks
DHCP Relay Agent	Forwards DHCP broadcasts to a remote DHCP server in a different subnet (e.g., when the router connecting them will not do so)
Gateway (and Client) Services for NetWare	Provides access to NetWare networks
Microsoft DHCP Server	Assigns IP addresses to requesting computers
Microsoft DNS Server	Provides the IP addresses corresponding to hostnames (includes integration with WINS)
Microsoft Internet Information Server	Provides various web services (includes an FTP server formerly separate under Windows NT 3.5x)
Microsoft TCP/IP Printing	Supports printing to or from foreign TCP/IP hosts via the LPD facility
*NetBIOS Interface	Includes base-level support for NetBIOS (needed by some services)
Network Monitor Agent	Allows for network performance data collection
*Network Monitor Tools and Agent	Allows for network performance data collection and includes data viewing tools
Remote Access Service	Enables dial-up networking (on top of PPP or SLIP)
Remoteboot Service	Provides booting services for diskless workstations
RIP for Internet Protocol	Enables TCP/IP routing between subnets
RIP for NWLink IPX/SPC Compatible Transport	Provides routing services for NetWare (IPX)
*RPC Configuration	Supports remote procedure call capabilities
RPC Support for Banyan	Provides support for RPC calls to computers on Banyan Vines networks
SAP Agent	Support for the NetWare Service Advertising Protocol
*Server	System functions as an NT server (uses the SMB protocol)
Services for Macintosh	Provides connectivity services for Macintosh clients
Simple TCP/IP Services	Adds connectivity-testing related TCP/IP services: Chargen, Daytime, Discard, Echo, and Quote (despite its name, this item is not needed by most systems)
SNMP Service	Implements the Simple Network Monitoring Protocol (used by many general network administration tools)
Windows Internet Name Service	Provides NetBIOS name registration and resolution services, translating NetBIOS computer names to IP addresses
*Workstation	Services required when system functions as a workstation (SMB client)

Other TCP/IP servers

As the preceding list makes clear, Windows NT does not provide the full compliment of TCP/IP services available on UNIX and other computer systems.
However, it is possible to add almost all of the missing services via freely available or commercial software. The Resource Kit includes beta versions of an **rsh**
daemon and a **telnet** server. Consult Appendix B for Internet sources of other
TCP/IP servers for Windows NT systems.

Network Bindings

The **Bindings** tab of the **Network** control panel applet (Figure 8-15) can display
and modify the network *bindings*: defined paths via the various networking
layers, linking hardware, protocols, and services. The display in the figure shows
the network hierarchy from the point of view of the installed network adapters
(there is only one on this system). The same information may also be viewed
from the point of view of networking protocols or networking services.

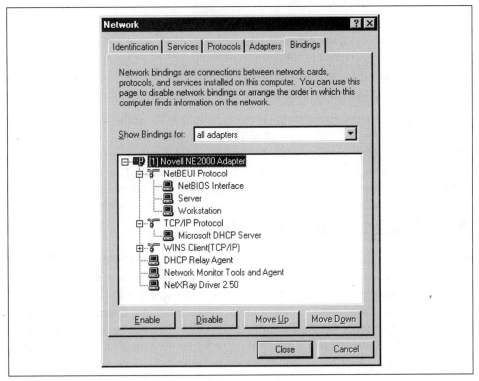

Figure 8-15. Network bindings display

You can use the control panel applet in a variety of ways. For example, if there are multiple adapters installed on the system, you can specify which protocol uses which adapter by disabling unwanted bindings via the protocols-oriented display format. You can also specify the order in which a given protocol or service will use the available network devices by reordering them with the **Move Up** and **Move Down** buttons.

Tools for Testing Network Connections

Testing the network connection is an important part of the configuration process. The first such step is to test the basic network setup and connection with **ping**, a simple command-line utility that tells you whether or not the network connection and its basic setup are working correctly.

Ping takes a remote hostname or an IP address as its argument. For example, the following command determines whether the host *pele* is accessible or not:

```
C:\> ping pele
Pinging pele [10.0.13.10] with 32 bytes of data:
Reply from 10.0.13.10: bytes=32 time<10ms TTL=128
Reply from 10.0.13.10: bytes=32 time<10ms TTL=128
Reply from 10.0.13.10: bytes=32 time<10ms TTL=128
Reply from 10.0.13.10: bytes=32 time<10ms TTL=128
```

From this output, it is clear that *pele* is receiving the data sent by the local system and that the local system is receiving the data *pele* sends back.

Once you have succeeded with **ping**, the next step is to run a command that uses higher levels of the TCP/IP protocol stack (**ping** operates at the IP layer using the ICMP protocol). For example, the **ftp** command can test connectivity to remote systems (which must be running an FTP server facility). The **net time** and **net view** commands are similarly useful for testing SMB protocol-based connectivity.

Name Resolution Facilities

For convenience, high-level user commands generally use hostnames to specify remote locations on the network. Accordingly, the networking software requires the network address of the system using that hostname for the requested operation to succeed. Thus, when a user enters a command like **finger chavez@hamlet**, one of the first things that must happen is that the hostname *hamlet* gets translated to its IP address (10.1.2.6). TCP/IP provides two methods for performing hostname-to-IP address translation (a process also called *name resolution*):

- The IP address can be determined by looking up the hostname in the *Hosts* configuration file. On Windows NT systems, this file is generally stored in the directory *%SystemRoot%\System32\Drivers\Etc.*[*]

- The system can request translation from a server running the Domain Name Service (DNS) in order to determine the IP address.

The same issues often arise when a user enters a command like **net view tirzah** or **dir \\pele\homes\chavez**. These commands rely on the SMB and NetBIOS protocols. NetBIOS operations can obtain IP addresses for specified hostnames via a configuration file, *LMHosts* (stored in the same directory as the TCP/IP *Hosts* file), or via the Windows Internet Name Service (WINS), which provides hostname registration and resolution services for NetBIOS names. On Windows NT systems, WINS can be run in conjunction with DNS, and the two systems are integrated.

The Hosts and LMHosts Files

On TCP/IP networks, the *Hosts* file traditionally contains a list of the hosts in the local network (including the local host itself). If you use this file for your hostname data, you must edit it whenever you add a new system to the network. When you add a new system to an existing network, you will have to edit the *Hosts* file on every system on the local network.

Here is a sample *Hosts* file for a small LAN:

```
# Loopback address for localhost
127.1           localhost
# Our hostname and address
10.1.1.2        spain spain.auroral.com
# Other hosts in the local network
10.1.1.1        brazil
10.1.1.3        usa
10.1.1.4        canada
10.1.1.5        england uk
10.1.1.6        greece olympus achaia
10.0.13.4       vala
192.168.34.77   dalton
```

Lines beginning with # are comments and are ignored. Aside from the comments, each line has three fields: the network address of a host in the network, the host's hostname, and any aliases (or synonyms) for the host. Every *Hosts* file must contain at least two entries: a loopback address for debugging purposes (by convention, 127.1), and the address by which the local system is known to the rest of the network. The other lines describe the other hosts in your local network. After the lines for the loopback address and the local system, the

---

[*] The location of the TCP/IP configuration files is controlled by the HKEY_LOCAL_MACHINE\System\CurrentControlSet\Services\TCPIP\Parameters\DataBasePath registry setting.

example *Hosts* file continues by listing the network addresses for all other systems in the local network. The file may also include entries for hosts that are not on your immediate local network (as its final entry illustrates).

Three hosts have been assigned *aliases* (or synonymous hostnames): the local host is called *spain* and may also be referred to by its full name *spain.auroral.com*. Similarly, *uk* is a synonym for *england*, and *olympus* and *achaia* are synonymous names for the host *greece*. A hostname may have as many aliases as desired; each alias is separated from the previous name by one or more spaces.

Here is a somewhat more complex *Hosts* file:

```
# Loopback address for localhost
127.1           localhost
# Our hostname and address
10.1.1.2        spain spain.auroral.com
# Other hosts in the local network
10.1.1.1        brazil
10.1.1.3        usa
10.1.1.4        canada
...
# gateway to LAN 4 subnet
10.1.1.87       dalton

# hosts in the LAN 4 subnet
192.168.34.77   dalton-gw
192.168.34.2    priestley
192.168.34.4    lavoisier
192.168.34.5    berthollet
```

10.1.1 is one local network, and 192.168.34 is another, separate network. The host *dalton* serves to bridge the two networks; it is connected to both networks, and it is listed as a member of each network in its own *Hosts* file. In this file, one entry has *-gw* appended to "dalton" so that all hostnames will be unique. The *Hosts* files on the other computers in the local LAN will contain only the 10.1.1.87 entry, and those on the other computers in LAN 4 will define *dalton* as 192.168.34.77. This way, every host on both networks will be able to call that computer *dalton*.

The *LMHosts* file serves the same purpose for mapping NetBIOS hostnames to IP addresses. It has a similar basic format to the *Hosts* file, and it is stored in the same directory location. Here is a simple example:

```
10.1.13.1       godot
10.1.13.2       leda
10.1.13.3       demeter
10.1.13.4       vala        #PRE #DOM:BOREALIS
10.1.13.5       janis       #PRE
192.168.34.77   dalton      #PRE

#INCLUDE \\vala\config\lmhosts
```

```
#BEGIN_ALTERNATE
#INCLUDE \\dalton\adminbin\lmhosts
#INCLUDE \\priestley\adminbin\lmhosts
#END_ALTERNATE
```

The first section of the file lists IP addresses and hostnames for several hosts. The **#PRE** comments following some of the entries are actually directives indicating that the corresponding entry should be pre-loaded into the NetBIOS name cache and retained there permanently. The **#DOM** directive identifies *vala* as the domain controller for the *borealis* domain. The second section of the file incorporates the contents of another file into the current *LMHosts* file.

The third section of the file allows for redundant sources for an additional external file to be incorporated within this *LMHosts* file. The **#INCLUDE** directives contained within the **#BEGIN_ALTERNATE** and **#END_ALTERNATE** directives list alternate sources for that include file (which are checked in order, as usual).

Both the *Hosts* and *LMHosts* files may be used in conjunction with their corresponding name resolution service (DNS and WINS, respectively).

The Domain Name Service

The Domain Name Service (DNS) facility relies upon server processes running on various network-accessible systems to provide hostname-to-IP address translations as required by the various systems on the network. DNS organizes groups of systems into units known as *domains*. DNS domains are organized into a single hierarchical structure on an Internet-wide basis, with the defined suffixes constituting the top-level of the tree (*.com*, *.org*, *.edu*, the various two-character country codes, and so on). A DNS domain generally corresponds to an organization. In our examples, we will use the fictional domain *auroral.com*.

NOTE   Keep in mind that DNS domains are completely unrelated to Windows NT domains.

Within a DNS domain, individual systems are referred to by their *fully qualified domain name* (FQDN), consisting of the hostname prepended to the domain name. For example, the system *vala* in our domain would be referred to as *vala.auroral.com*. Domains can be divided into *subdomains*. Thus, the name *viveca.multi.auroral.com* would refer to the host *viveca* in the subdomain *multi* within *auroral.com*. Multiple levels of subdomains are possible, but they are seldom used in practice.

From the DNS server perspective, DNS domains are administered as one or more *zones*, where a zone is simply some pruned subtree of a DNS domain (and the entire domain is a potential subset of itself). The terms "domain" and "zone" are used somewhat interchangeably in many discussions of DNS. For clarity, we will use only the latter term when we are describing the translation data for a collection of systems. Zones may also be subdivided.

WARNING   To further confuse matters, while the Microsoft DNS Administrator tool and its corresponding documentation refer to zones as "zones," they refer to subdivisions of zones as "domains," introducing yet another usage for an already overloaded term.

In this section,* we consider the Microsoft DNS service available on Windows NT server systems. DNS is a vast topic, so we won't be able to cover all of its intricacies. For more information about DNS, including planning a DNS implementation for your site, consult O'Reilly's *TCP/IP Network Administration* and *DNS and BIND* by Paul Albitz and Cricket Liu.

Setting up a DNS client system

We'll begin by looking at setting up a system to use the DNS service for name resolution (if there is also a *Hosts* file on such a system, it will still be checked as well). A DNS Client is also called a *resolver.*

DNS name resolution is enabled via the **DNS** tab of the TCP/IP protocol's **Properties** dialog box (illustrated in Figure 8-16). Its configuration is straightforward.

The **Host Name** field specifies the hostname by which this system will be known to the DNS system. It is generally the same as the system's Windows NT hostname (and making them different is only asking for trouble). The **Domain** field specifies the name of the local domain. The **DNS Service Search Order** contains a list of IP addresses for DNS servers that this system should use for name resolution. Servers are contacted in the order in which they appear in the list box.

By default, required hostnames are assumed to be in the local domain (put another way, the local domain name is applied as a suffix to unknown hostnames). The **Domain Suffix Search Order** may be used to specify additional domains in which to search for a hostname. This feature is not needed in most cases, unless your domain is more than two levels deep. If you do list additional domains here, then the local domain and the listed domains will be searched when attempting to resolve an unknown hostname (in the order in which they appear in the list box), and these will be the only domains checked. In contrast,

---

* Other freely available implementations of DNS are also available for Windows NT systems (including workstations). Consult Appendix B for sources.

† This dialog box contains the same information as is traditionally stored in the *resolv.conf* configuration file on UNIX and other systems.

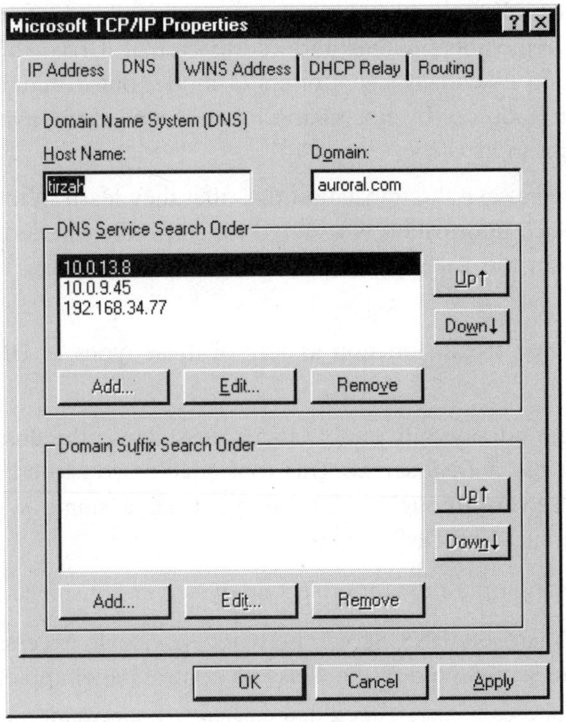

Figure 8-16. Setting up a DNS client

when only the **Domain** field is specified in this dialog box, that domain and all of its parent domains are searched for unknown hostnames.

Setting up a DNS server

A Windows NT server system can also function as a provider of DNS services via the Microsoft DNS Server service of the TCP/IP protocol. There are three kinds of DNS servers:

Primary server

A system that permanently stores authoritative name information for a specific zone, which may range from a local subnet to a wide area of the Internet. It holds the master copy of the configuration files defining hostname-to-IP address translation for the zone.

Secondary server

A system that obtains a set of name information from a primary server when the DNS server process starts up. Thereafter, it can provide the same translations as the primary server. Secondary servers are useful for backup and to distribute the network load created by DNS clients.

Caching-only server

A system that relies on other hosts to determine all unknown hostname translations, but remembers names and addresses that it has learned. Such a host operates in an essentially client-oriented mode, but it minimizes its demands for network resources by not asking for the same name again as long as the name remains in its cache.

All DNS servers save the translation data that they learn in the course of doing their jobs. Such information is retained for a specified period of time and then removed from the cache. The cache is reinitialized every time the server is restarted.

A Windows NT server can function as any of these types of DNS servers, as we shall see.

The DNS Manager administrative tool (also accessible via the **dnsadmin** command) is used to configure a DNS server. This tool enables you to administer all of the Microsoft DNS servers throughout a network from a single system (but cannot affect other non-Microsoft DNS servers).

The steps for setting up a primary or secondary server are similar:

1. Install the Microsoft DNS Server network service if necessary (via the **Add** button in the **Services** tab of the **Network** control panel applet).

2. Select the DNS Manager's **DNS➤New Server**... menu path, and enter the hostname or IP address for the system on which it will run. If the server is already present in the list, then simply select it.

3. Select the **DNS➤New Zone**... menu path. This option is used to both create zones and to define the server as a primary or secondary server.

   — For a primary server, select the **Primary** radio button and then click **Next**. Enter the zone name and zone database filename (which defaults to the zone name with the *.dns* extension added) into the subsequent dialog box. DNS database files are stored in the directory *%SystemRoot%\System32\DNS*.

   — For a secondary server, select the **Secondary** radio button (see Figure 8-17). Then enter the name of an existing zone and its primary server into the **Zone** and **Server** fields (respectively). Alternatively, you may use the hand icon in the lower section of the window to point to an existing zone (drag the hand icon from the dialog box into the tool's main server list window). Click **Next** when you are finished.

   In the next dialog box, enter the local name for the zone (usually just the zone name) and the path to the local data file (which defaults as for a primary server). Click **Next** when you are finished.

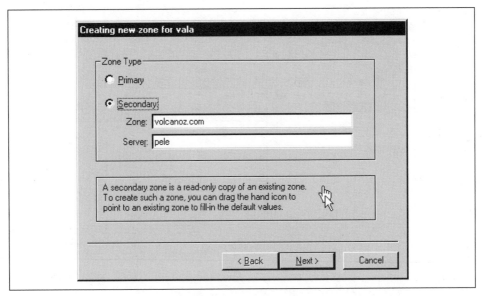

Figure 8-17. Configuring a secondary server

— Finally, list IP addresses of one or more master servers for the zone from which this secondary server should request its initial translation data (the server you specified in an earlier step is pre-filled into the list).

4. If desired, you may now subdivide the zone with the **DNS►New Domain...** menu path. Note that despite its name, this selection creates a subdomain in the currently selected zone, not a new DNS or Windows NT domain.

5. For a new zone, create its associated *reverse-lookup zone*, used to translate IP addresses back into host names. In most cases these zones are assigned names of the form b.a.*in-addr.arpa* where *b* and *a* are the second and first components of local IP addresses: for example, *1.10.in-addr.arpa* would be the reverse-lookup zone for the 10.1 subnet.

6. Add an entry for each host within the zone to the database via the **DNS►New Host...** menu path. Checking the **Create Associated PTR Record** checkbox in the **New Host** dialog box causes a corresponding record to be automatically entered into the reverse-lookup zone at the same time.

7. Add any other DNS records needed for your site via the **DNS►New Record...** menu path, which allows you to enter arbitrary DNS records.

Figure 8-18 illustrates the DNS Manager's main window after a zone has been defined for the *auroral.com* domain. The database records for that zone appear in the right side of the window.

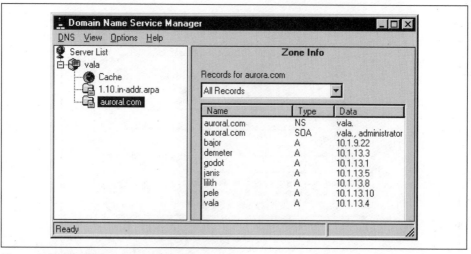

Figure 8-18. The DNS zone auroral.com

Importing existing DNS configuration files

You may also import DNS configuration from another system into the Microsoft DNS server via the following procedure:

1. Stop the DNS server service: **net stop dns**.

2. Copy the zone files and reverse-lookup files to the *%SystemRoot%\ System32\DNS* directory on the system where you want the server to use them. If you want to import the boot and cache files as well, you will have to disable registry-based DNS startup—see the next subsection.

3. Restart the DNS server service: **net start dns**.

4. Start the DNS Manager tool and select the appropriate system (creating a new server if necessary).

5. Create a new zone corresponding to the data you want to import, specifying the appropriate zone file in the **Zone File** field. You may then go on to create the corresponding reverse-lookup zone and import its data file.

If you add entries manually to the zone database files in *%SystemRoot%\ System32\DNS*, the new information is generally recognized. However, two caveats apply: first, you have to create the associated reverse-lookup record manually as well, and second, the forward and reverse translation records may not be linked properly, so subsequent changes to the host's record within the DNS Manager tool will not always update the associated PTR record properly.

Configuring a caching-only DNS server

By default, the DNS server facility is installed in caching-only mode. If your network is connected to the Internet, then no further configuration is required. If not, modify the DNS cache file as indicated in step 4 below. I prefer to run a caching-only server in manual mode. Here are the steps for setting one up:

1. Stop the DNS Server service if it is running (**net stop dns**).

2. Disable DNS startup from the Windows NT registry by setting the EnableRegistryBoot value of the HKEY_LOCAL_MACHINE\System\CurrentControlSet\ Services\DNS\Parameters key to 0. Once you have done so, initialization information will be taken from the file named *Boot* in *%SystemRoot%\ System32\DNS.*

3. Create a boot file like this one:

```
directory %systemRoot%\System32\DNS
cache . cache.dns
```

The first line specifies the default location from which to apply relative pathnames (including empty ones) within the remainder of the file. The second line specifies the name of the DNS cache file. Note that the second entry in the line—a period—is required.

4. Set up a cache file (named *Cache.dns*) that points to one or more authoritative DNS servers for your domain. If you are connected to the Internet, then these will be the Internet's root name servers; these are provided in the default cache file provided with Windows NT and may also be obtained from *ftp.rs.internic.net/domain/root.cache.* If your network is not connected to the Internet, then the file should contain entries for the local root servers. For example, this file specifies the host with IP address 10.1.13.4 as the DNS server for the zone *auroral.com*:

```
; Cache file
; Zone          Timeout      IN RecType  Data

    .             2163095040   IN  NS      auroral.com.
auroral.com.      2163095040   IN  A       10.1.13.4
```

5. Restart the DNS Server service (**net start dns**).

Additional DNS server configuration

There are many other DNS parameters that may be specified. In this subsection, we will briefly consider a few of the most important ones.

Parameters specific to a DNS zone may be set using the zone **Properties**, accessed by selecting the zone and choosing the **DNS►Properties**... menu path or by right-clicking on the zone. The **SOA Record** tab of the **Zone Properties** dialog box allows you to specify several timeout periods (see Figure 8-19) for the zone's servers.

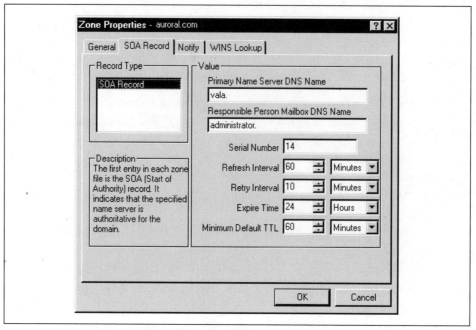

Figure 8-19. Specifying parameters for a DNS zone

- The **Refresh Interval** field indicates how often a secondary server should recheck the accuracy of its data with a primary server.

- The **Retry Interval** field indicates how long a secondary server should wait after a refresh attempt has failed before trying to contact the unresponsive server again.

- If a secondary server continues to be unable to refresh its data, the **Expire Time** field indicates when it will stop responding to DNS queries because its data is too old to be reliable.

- The **Minimum Default TTL** field indicates how long a receiving name server is allowed to cache the data it learns as a result of any specific DNS query (known as the *time-to-live* interval).

The zone Properties dialog box's **Notify** tab lists secondary servers to notify automatically whenever the database for the primary server changes.

Systemwide properties for a specific server system are set via the server's **Properties** (accessed by selecting the server and then choosing the **DNS►Properties...** menu path or by right-clicking on the server name). These are the most important tabs in the resulting **Server Properties** dialog box:

- The **Interfaces** tab lists additional IP addresses used by that host on which the name server will listen.

- The **Forwarders** tab specifies a list of hosts which can be contacted for name resolution outside of the local domain (see Figure 8-20).

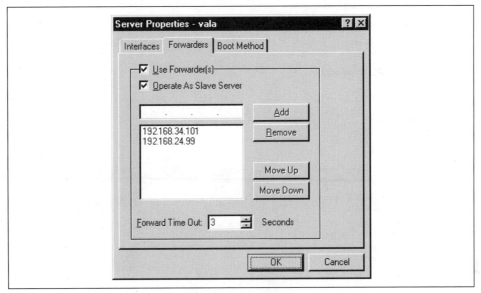

Figure 8-20. Accessing DNS servers beyond the local domain

If **Use Forwarders** is checked, then the listed systems will be contacted first to resolve names that cannot be translated locally. If **Operate As Slave Service** is also checked, then only the designated systems are used to forward name resolution requests beyond the local domain. This setting is designed to filter DNS requests beyond the local domain through a few designated systems. The final field in the dialog box specifies the timeout period before going on to the next forwarder in the list.

The Windows Internet Name Service

The Windows Internet Name Service (WINS) is a dynamic hostname-based addressing scheme used on Microsoft LANs supporting NetBIOS network operations. It is integrated with DNS via the Microsoft DNS Server, allowing WINS clients to resolve DNS names.* WINS translates NetBIOS names to IP addresses using a process like the following (which is simplified somewhat):

1. A client computer contacts the WINS server system, giving it its hostname and IP address and asking to be added to the database. Its request is accepted if

---

* The two facilities are rumored to be completely merged in Windows NT Version 5.0.

the specified name and address aren't in active use by another system, and it's granted exclusive use of that name for a period of time known as a *lease*.

2. When the client system shuts down, it contacts the WINS server and releases the name it has registered.

3. When its lease period is 50% gone, the client system attempts to renew it with the WINS server. It keeps trying until it is successful or the lease period expires; in the latter case, it registers its name with an accessible WINS server.

Configuring a WINS client

A Windows NT system is configured to use the WINS facility for NetBIOS name resolution via the **WINS Address** tab of the TCP/IP protocol **Properties** (illustrated in Figure 8-21).

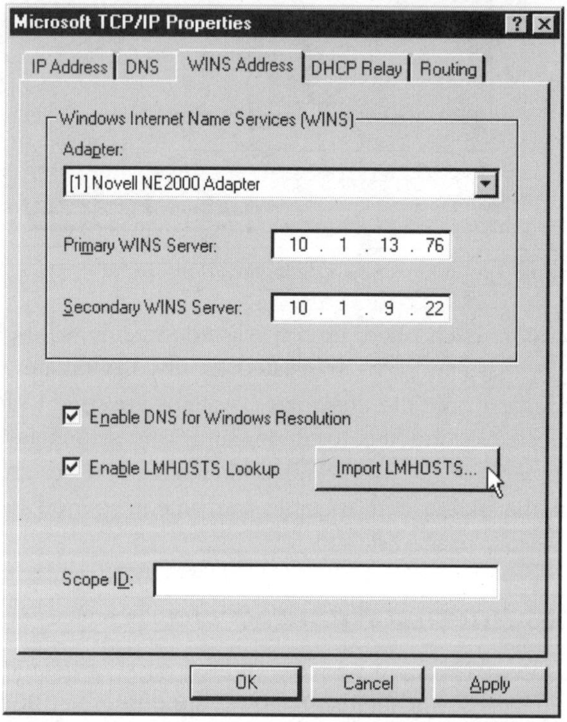

Figure 8-21. Configuring a WINS client

After specifying the network adapter to use for WINS queries, specify the IP addresses of the primary and secondary WINS servers this system should contact for name resolution services.

If **Enable DNS for Windows Resolution** is checked, the system will use DNS name resolution services (via the Microsoft DNS Server facility) to resolve a name if WINS is unable to do so. If **Enable LMHOSTS Lookup** is checked, the local *LMHosts* file is also searched for hostname translations. Pressing the **Import LMHOSTS...** button copies the information from a different file that you specify into the local *LMHosts* file, *replacing* its current contents (if any).

Configuring a WINS server

The following procedure prepares a system to operate as a WINS server:

1. Add the Windows Internet Name Service network service, if necessary, to that system (using the **Add** button in the **Services** tab of the **Network** control panel applet).

2. Start the WINS Manager administrative tool (also accessible via the **winsadmn** command). Select the appropriate WINS server from the list, adding it if necessary.

3. Use the **Mappings►Static Mappings...** menu path to define any static name mappings used within the network. These are hostname–IP address pairs, which are assigned to systems on a permanent basis.

4. Use the **Server►Configuration...** menu path to specify operating parameters for the WINS server (see Figure 8-22).

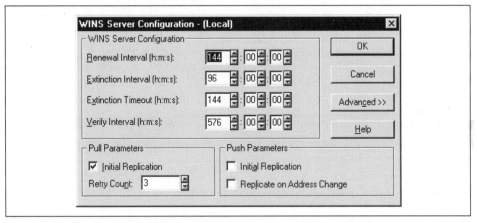

Figure 8-22. Configuring the WINS server

The most important fields of the WINS server configuration dialog box are:

— The **Renewal Interval** field specifies the lease period for a WINS client.

— The **Extinction Interval** field indicates how long a released database entry is held before it is marked as extinct (assuming that no other system requests that name).

— The **Extinction Timeout** field specifies how quickly extinct entries are removed from the WINS database during a *scavenging* operation (which is requested with the WINS Manager's **Mappings▶Initiate Scavenging** menu option).

— The **Initial Replication** checkboxes in the **Pull Parameters** and **Push Parameters** areas indicate whether the server always sends information to or requests information from its replication partners at startup (discussed later).

— The **Replicate on Address Change** checkbox in the **Push Parameters** area specifies whether the server always informs its push replication partners when an entry in its database changes (including the creation of a new entry).

5. Use the **Server▶Replication Partners…**menu path to specify other systems with which this server will periodically exchange name resolution data. A system to which this server sends its data is known as a *push partner*, and a system from which this server receives data is called a *pull partner*. A remote system can operate in one or both modes.

Figure 8-23 illustrates the **Replication Partners** dialog box for a single partner, along with those used to configure push partners and pull partners (accessed via the corresponding **Configure…** button in the **Replication Options** area).

You may add and delete replication partner systems with the **Add…** and **Delete** buttons. You may force an immediate replication operation for a selected system with the **Replicate Now** button. The buttons in the **Send Replication Trigger Now** area can be used to request a push or pull operation individually. If **Push with Propagation** is checked, a push partner will be directed to send any new information it receives as a result of the operation to all of its own pull partners.

The **Push Partner Properties** dialog box allows you to specify how many changes must be made to the WINS database before the server notifies this push partner about them (the **Update Count** field). The **Pull Partner Properties** dialog box indicates the first time a request for data is sent to this pull partner and how often updates are requested thereafter.

Other useful features of the WINS Manager administrative tools are the following:

• The **Mappings▶Show Database…** menu path displays the current database entries for the selected server.

• The **Backup Database…** and **Restore Local Database…** items on the **Mappings** menu to save the current contents of the WINS database and restore a previously saved file into the active database (respectively).

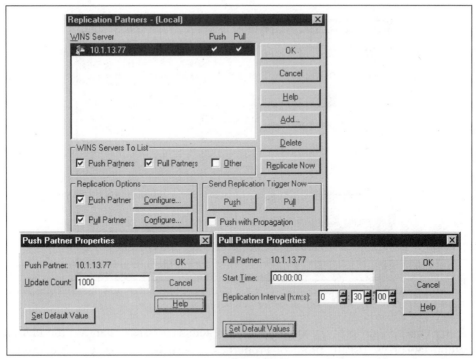

Figure 8-23. Configuring replication partners for a WINS server

The Resource Kit contains several command-line utilities for administering the WINS facility, including **winscl** and **winschk**; the latter can be used to verify the consistency of the WINS database.

WINS integration with DNS

WINS server integration with DNS is enabled with the DNS Manager using the **Zone Properties** dialog box's **WINS Lookup** tab (illustrated in Figure 8-24). When the **Use WINS Resolution** checkbox is selected, the Microsoft DNS Server submits hostnames to the specified WINS servers when it cannot resolve them itself.

Dynamic IP Address Assignment with DHCP

While its purpose is somewhat different than the two name resolution facilities we have examined so far in this section, the Dynamic Host Configuration Protocol (DHCP) facility performs a related function. It is used to assign IP addresses to network hosts dynamically. This facility is designed to decrease the individual workstation configuration necessary for a system to be successfully connected to the network. It is especially suited to computer systems that change network locations frequently (e.g., laptops).

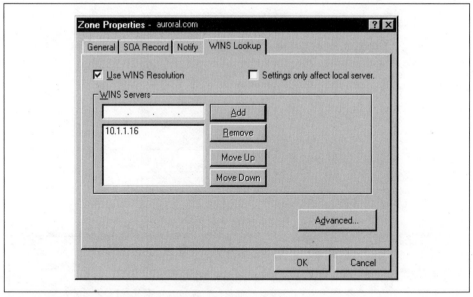

Figure 8-24. DNS server integration with the WINS facility

As we've seen previously, you designate a system as a DHCP client via the **Identifi-cation** tab of its TCP/IP protocol **Properties**. On such systems, you can use the **ipconfig** command to display its current IP address:

```
C:\> ipconfig
Windows NT IP Configuration

Ethernet adapter elpc3r1:

        IP Address. . . . . . . . . : 10.1.13.100
        Subnet Mask . . . . . . . . : 255.255.255.0
```

The output from the **ipconfig** command indicates that this system is currently using the IP address 10.1.13.100.

WARNING   Never use dynamic addressing for any system that functions as a re-
              source server of any kind: this includes not only domain controllers
              but also file servers of all sorts (including via Windows NT shares),
              providers of network services (DNS, DHCP, WINS, RAS, etc.), print
              servers, and so on.

The DHCP facility assigns an IP address to a requesting host for a specified period of time known as a *lease*, using the following process:

1. The requesting (client) system broadcasts a DHCP Discover packet (UDP port 67).

2. DHCP servers reply with a DHCP Offer packet (UDP port 68), containing an IP address, subnet mask, server IP address, and lease duration. The server reserves the offered address until it is accepted or rejected, or a timeout period expires.

3. The client selects an IP address and broadcasts a DHCP Request DHCP packet. All servers other than the successful one release the pending reservation.

4. The selected server sends a DHCP Acknowledge packet to the client.

5. When the lease is 50% expired, the client attempts to renew it. If it cannot do so at that time, it will try again when it reaches 87.5% of lease period; if the second renewal attempt also fails, the client will look for a new server.

As this description indicates, the DHCP facility depends heavily on broadcast messages and so can generate a significant amount of network traffic.

The Microsoft DHCP Server facility is integrated with DNS and WINS on Windows NT server systems.

Configuring a DHCP server

The following steps configure a Windows NT server to function as a DHCP server:

1. Add the Microsoft DHCP Server network service to that system, if necessary (via the **Add** button in the **Services** tab of the **Network** control panel applet).

2. Start the DHCP Manager administrative tool (also accessible via the **dhcpadmn** command). Select the appropriate server from the list, adding it if necessary.

3. Create a new *scope*: a named block of IP addresses that this server is allowed to assign. This can be done via the **Scope►Create...** menu path. The resulting dialog box is illustrated in Figure 8-25.

   The various fields in the dialog box have the following meanings:

   — The **Start Address** and **End Address** fields specify the range of IP addresses that constitute this scope (inclusive).

   — The **Subnet Mask** specifies the subnet mask in use on the network.

   — The fields in the **Exclusion Range** area are used to specify subsets of the previously specified IP address range that are not part of the scope. Use both fields to specify a range of IP addresses or just the **Start Address** field here to specify a single IP address. Excluded addresses appear in the list in the upper right portion of the dialog box.

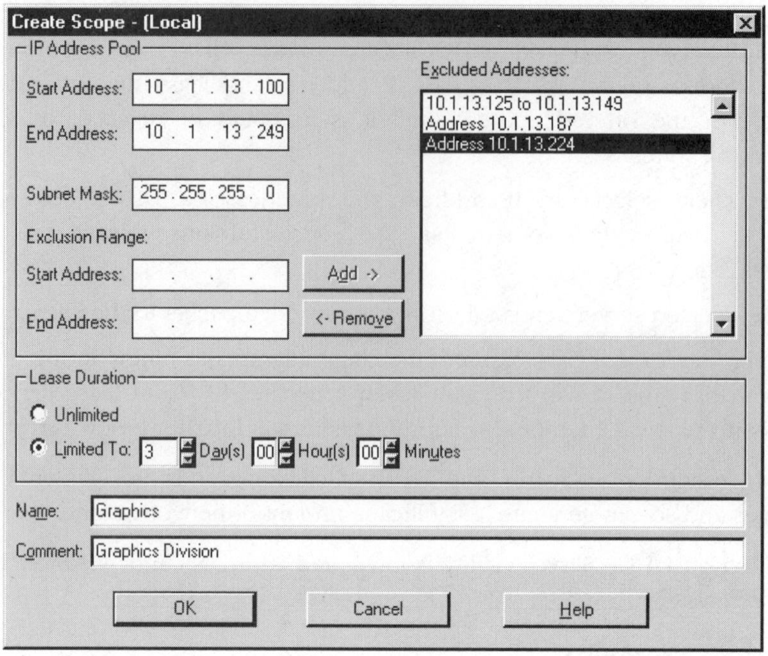

Figure 8-25. Creating a DHCP scope

IP addresses should be excluded if they are assigned (statically) to a specific host or if they are already being administered by another DHCP server. Doing the latter is a way to provide DHCP server redundancy. For example, if you have two DHCP servers, you would divide the available addresses between the two of them.

You may also want to exclude a few addresses for future use (although you can often do so by manipulating the beginning and end of the scope range).

— Specify the lease length in the **Lease Duration** area. Unlimited lease lengths are generally a bad idea (and counter to the purpose of DHCP). A lease duration of days is reasonable in environments with frequent system turnover or a scarcity of available IP addresses, and a lease length of months might be appropriate in a far more stable environment without resource constraints.

— The **Name** and **Comment** fields specify a name and description for the scope.

A DHCP server can administer multiple scopes if desired.

4. The next step in setting up the DHCP server is to *reserve* IP addresses for systems that use static IP addresses. When an IP address is reserved, it is both excluded from general use within the scope and always assigned to a designated system when it requests an IP address. You need to specify reservations for the systems using static IP addresses that receive their IP address from the DHCP facility (for example, a system that might be moved or replaced frequently).

The **Scope►Add Reservations...** menu path defines a new reservation. The resulting dialog box is illustrated in Figure 8-26. Its unique identifier field holds its MAC address.

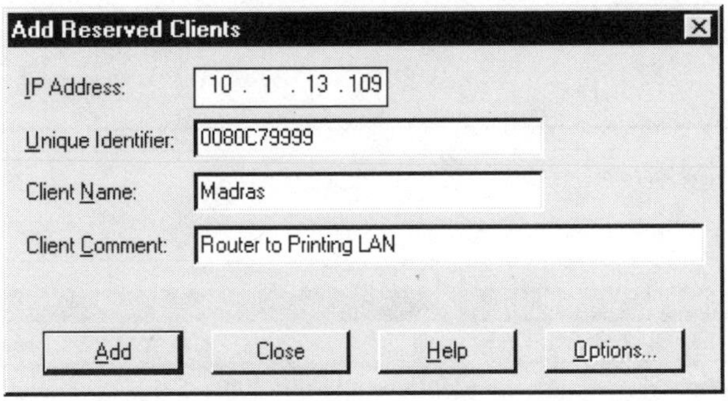

Figure 8-26. Creating a DHCP reservation

5. Set any desired DHCP options. Options can be set either on a global or scope-specific basis, via the DHCP Manager's **DHCP Options** menu. The resulting dialog box is illustrated in Figure 8-27. Select the option you want from either of the lists, and press the **Value** button to set its value.

Figure 8-28 displays the main DHCP Manager window after the server has been configured with a single scope. DHCP options appear in the right half of the window.

Some functions of the DHCP Manager may also be performed via a command-line interface with the **dhcpcmd** command included in the Resource Kit.

DHCP with subnets

If you want systems on a local subnet to receive IP addresses from a server on a separate subnet, then one of the following conditions must be met:

*   If a router connects the two subnets, it must include support for DHCP/ BOOTP Relay (broadcast packets normally dropped by routers and not forwarded).

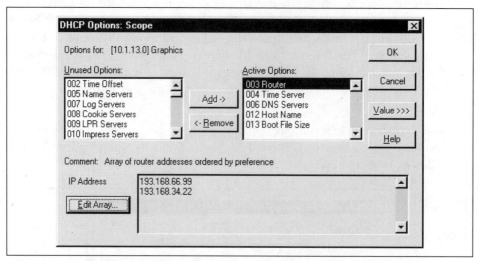

Figure 8-27. Setting DHCP options

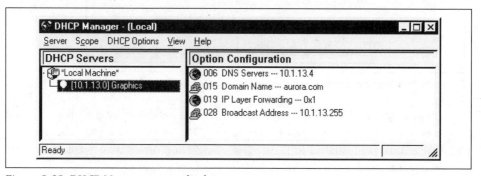

Figure 8-28. DHCP Manager server display

- The DHCP Relay Agent must be installed on a system within the subnet not containing the DHCP server. This network service provides a software solution to the same problem.

Once installed, the DHCP Relay Agent is configured via the **DHCP Relay** tab of the TCP/IP protocol **Properties** (illustrated in Figure 8-29). The DHCP servers to which the system will forward DHCP requests are listed in the **DHCP Servers** list box and are specified via the buttons below it.

Servers are contacted in the order in which they're listed in the display. The **Seconds threshold** field specifies the number of seconds to wait for a response from a server before going to the next one in the list. The **Maximum hops** field indicates the maximum number of hops that may be taken to reach a DHCP server.

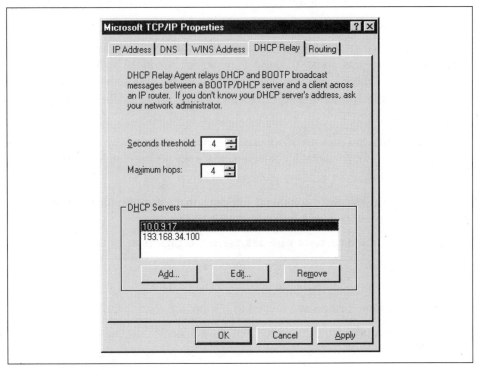

Figure 8-29. Configuring the DHCP relay facility

Routing Options

Routing is the process by which a packet finds its way from its source system to its final destination. As with hostname resolution, there are a number of options for configuring routing within a local network:

- If the LAN consists of a single, isolated Ethernet network, no explicit routing is usually needed, since all of the hosts are immediately visible to one another. Gateways to adjacent Ethernet LANs may be listed in each system's TCP/IP protocol **Properties**. The default gateway is specified in the **Default Gateway** field of the **IP Address** tab, and this dialog box's **Advanced** button may be used to specify additional gateway hosts.

- More complex static routing may be set up by issuing explicit **route** commands.

- Distinct LANs can be linked by routers (or gateway hosts that can function as routers) that can dynamically determine the best route to a given destination.

The Windows NT version of the **route** command has the following syntax:

```
route [options] cmd dest [mask netmask] gateway [metric]
```

where *cmd* is one of **add**, **delete**, **change**, or **print**. *Dest* specifies the destination corresponding to this route (usually a network), *netmask* specifies the subnet mask to use, *gateway* specifies the gateway host (or router) that provides a connection to the specified destination, and *metric* specifies the number of hops to the destination.

The **route** command has two options: /F clears all gateway entries from the routing tables, and /P defines (or refers to) a persistent route (which survives system reboots).

For example, the following command indicates that the route to the 10.1.9 subnet is through the gateway with the IP address 10.1.13.5:

```
C:\> route /P add 10.1.9.0 mask 255.255.255.0 10.1.13.5
```

This route persists across system boots and specifies a subnet mask of 255.255.255.0.

The command **route print** may be used to display the routing tables:

```
C:\> route print
Active Routes:

     Network Address          Netmask  Gateway Addr    Interface  Metric
           0.0.0.0          0.0.0.0       10.1.13.5      10.1.13.4       1
         127.0.0.0        255.0.0.0       127.0.0.1      127.0.0.1       1
          10.1.9.0    255.255.255.0       10.1.13.5      10.1.13.4       1
         10.1.13.0    255.255.255.0       10.1.13.4      10.1.13.4       1
         10.1.13.4  255.255.255.255       127.0.0.1      127.0.0.1       1
       10.1.13.255  255.255.255.255       10.1.13.4      10.1.13.4       1
         224.0.0.0        224.0.0.0       10.1.13.4      10.1.13.4       1
   255.255.255.255  255.255.255.255       10.1.13.4      10.1.13.4       1
```

The columns of the display indicate the destination address, its subnet mask, the IP address of the gateway for that destination, the IP address of the network adapter within the local system to use for communication with that destination, and the number of hops to that destination. This display shows the routes for a simple network. It contains a route to a single other network, the 10.1.9 subnet. All the other entries are standard ones used for any LAN and ones corresponding to the system's own LAN.

Consult O'Reilly's *TCP/IP Network Administration* for further information about setting up static routing.

NOTE   As of this writing, Microsoft has just made available a new facility (code-named "Steelhead") that combines routing and dial-up networking (RAS) services within a single facility. It also incorporates the DHCP Relay facility examined earlier in this chapter.

Enabling IP Forwarding

Normally, systems will not forward IP packets received that are not addressed to the local system (it simply discards them). If you want a Windows NT system to function as a gateway between two subnets, you will need to enable IP forwarding. This can be done using the **Routing** tab of the TCP/IP protocol **Properties** (Figure 8-30).

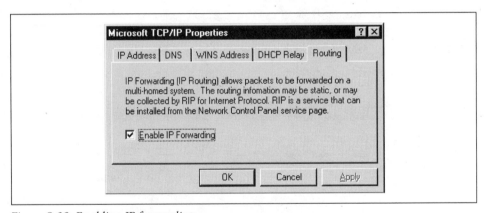

Figure 8-30. Enabling IP forwarding

Configuring the Remote Access Service

The Windows NT operating system provides the Remote Access Service (RAS) for dial-up networking access for remote computer systems.* This facility allows a remote user to dial into a Windows NT server and connect to its local network as a full-fledged network host; the various network protocols are implemented over the serial line connecting the remote system to the server. RAS is a complicated facility worthy of a book-length treatment on its own. This section provides an overview of installing and configuring a RAS server on a Windows NT server system.

---

* RAS runs on top of either PPP or SLIP, standard networking protocols for serial lines.

The following steps are required to enable the RAS network service on a Windows NT server system:

1. Install one or more modems onto the system. This is accomplished with the **Modems** control panel applet. In most cases, allowing the system to detect the modems automatically works fine. In those rare cases where the system cannot determine your modem type, select the corresponding entry from the list of manufacturers and modem models.

   Once the modem is added to the system, you can specify standard settings, such as its maximum speed, parity, and flow control scheme using the **Properties** button.

2. Install the Remote Access Service network service, using the **Add** button in the **Services** tab of the **Network** control panel applet. After the required software is copied to the system disk, the installation process will guide you through the remaining basic RAS configuration steps.

3. Select a device in the **Add RAS Device** dialog box (Figure 8-31). If necessary, you can install a modem or an X25 device at this time using the corresponding buttons.

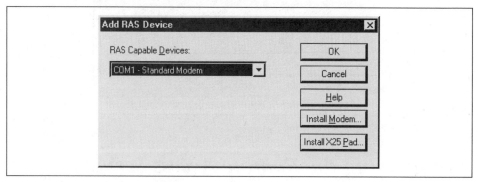

Figure 8-31. Designating a modem as an RAS device

4. The next dialog box forms the heart of the RAS setup process (Figure 8-32). You may add additional ports to the RAS configuration using its **Add...** button, and configure a port with the **Configure...** button. The **Clone** button may be used to copy a port, including its configuration information. Finally, the **Network** button allows you to configure RAS networking parameters.

5. Port configuration is accomplished using the **Configure Port Usage** dialog box (Figure 8-33). You use this dialog box to specify whether a port accepts incoming calls, allows outgoing calls, or both.

6. The **Network Configuration** dialog box (Figure 8-34) may be used to specify the allowed networking protocols for outgoing and incoming RAS connec-

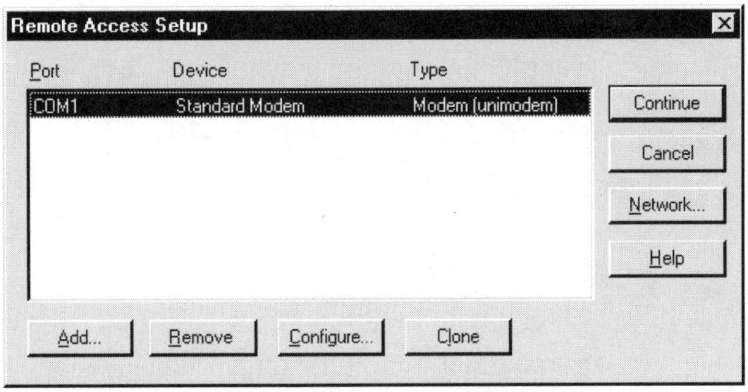

Figure 8-32. The RAS setup control dial-up box

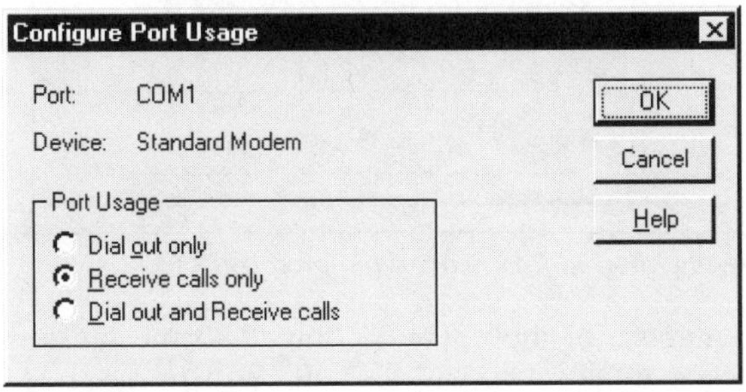

Figure 8-33. Configuring an RAS port

tions from this server and port. The lower section of the dialog box allows you to specify whether user authentication communications are encrypted or not. I don't recommend allowing clear text authentication across a dial-up line.*

The **Enable Multilink** checkbox at the bottom of the dialog box is used to enable *multilink dialing* on the selected port. This facility allows multiple phone lines to be combined into a single logical session with increased effective network bandwidth. This feature must be enabled for all of the ports that participate in the multilink bundle.

7. The **Configure...** buttons on the **Network Configuration** dialog box allow you to specify the range of access for incoming RAS connections. Such users can be given access to the entire network (subject to its usual permissions and

---

* Be aware that the encryption scheme used by the RAS facility is proprietary, however, and doesn't work with most non-Microsoft PPP servers.

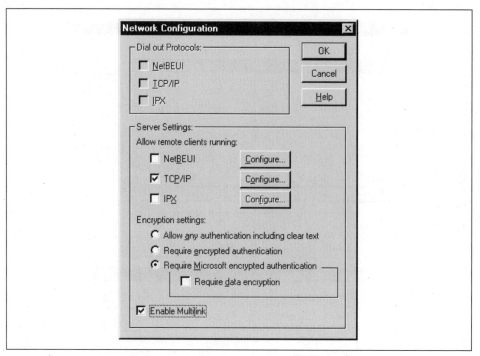

Figure 8-34. Specifying allowed RAS networking protocols

security constraints), or they may be limited to the local system only. Figure 8-35 shows the resulting dialog box for the TCP/IP protocol.

The lower portion of the **RAS Server TCP/IP Configuration** dialog box allows you to select between using the DHCP facility to assign IP addresses to incoming network connections and having the RAS facility assign an IP address itself, taken from the range of IP addresses designated in this dialog box. Using addresses from a static range is recommended if the network adapter on the local system supports more than one IP address. However, if you choose to use DHCP in such a case, subnets normally accessible from the local network adapter via one of its IP addresses, other than the one used for DHCP, will not be available to RAS clients.

8. The final step is to grant RAS access to the appropriate users. This is accomplished using the user properties facility of the User Manager tool (specifically, its **Dialin** button) or via the RAS Administrator administrative tool's **Users➤Permissions**... menu path (the latter utility is also accessible using the **rasadmin** command). A similar dialog results from both routes (Figure 8-36).

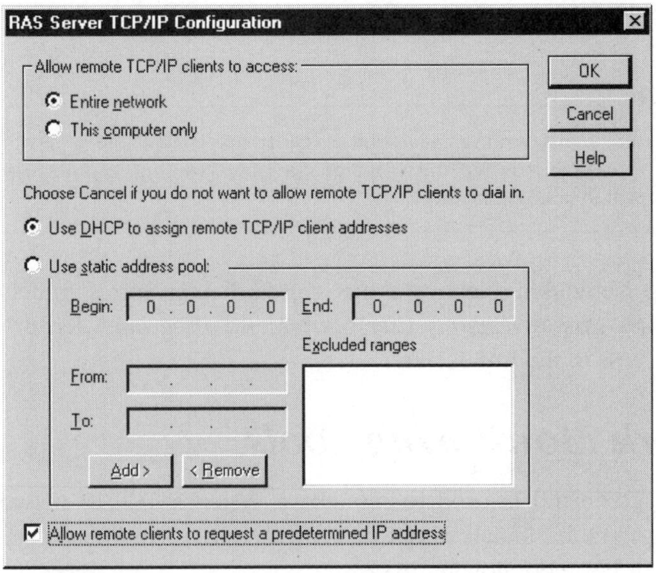

Figure 8-35. Configuring RAS network access for the TCP/IP protocol

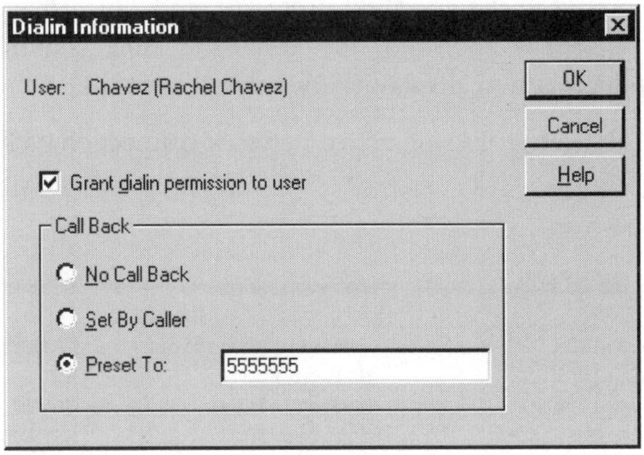

Figure 8-36. Setting RAS access for a user account

The **Grant dialin permission to user** checkbox determines whether the user may dial into the domain using the RAS facility. The **Call Back** area allows you to enable mandatory call-back for this user, either to a specified telephone number in all cases (**Preset To**) or to a telephone number that the user specifies at connection time (**Set By Caller**). Preset call-back numbers are more secure, but the latter setting is needed when the user can't know the appropriate telephone number in advance (for example, when traveling).

The RAS Administrator tool may also be used to start and stop the RAS service on the local system or a remote system and to view and manipulate current RAS connections.

NOTE   As of this writing, Microsoft has just made available a new facility
              (code-named "Steelhead") that combines routing and RAS services
              within a single facility.

The **Dial-Up Networking** utility in the standard **Accessories** folder (one path is *%SystemRoot%\Profiles\Default User\Start Menu\Programs\Accessories*) provides user-level access to the RAS facility.

Network Monitoring Tools

The **netstat** command is used to monitor a system's TCP/IP network activity. It can provide some basic data about how much and what kinds of network activity is going on. It has the following basic syntax:

```
netstat [options] [interval]
```

The **netstat** command's most useful options are **/S** (produce detailed statistics), **/P** *proto* (limit the output to the specified protocol), and **/R** (display the local routing tables). If an *interval* is specified, the command runs continuously until it is aborted and produces a new display every *interval* seconds.

Without arguments, **netstat** lists all active network connections with the local host:

```
C:\> netstat
Active Connections

   Proto  Local Address          Foreign Address          State
   ...
   TCP    vala:1025              demeter:nbsession        ESTABLISHED
   TCP    vala:1091              dalton:ftp               ESTABLISHED
   TCP    vala:1100              hamlet:finger            CLOSE_WAIT
   TCP    vala:nbsession         demeter:1026             ESTABLISHED
   TCP    vala:nbsession         lilith:1037              ESTABLISHED
   TCP    vala:nbsession         pele:1037                ESTABLISHED
```

At the current time, the local system (*vala*) has active NetBIOS connections to *demeter* (two separate connections), *lilith* and *pele* (all of which correspond to shared filesystem resources). Someone is also running a **finger** command to host *hamlet* (which is almost finished), and an FTP session to *dalton*.

Netstat's **/S** option produces a more detailed set of network-related statistics:

```
C:\> netstat /S
IP Statistics          Overall TCP/IP traffic statistics
   Packets Received                      = 1552
   Received Header Errors                = 0
   Received Address Errors               = 0
   Datagrams Forwarded                   = 0
   Unknown Protocols Received            = 0
   Received Packets Discarded            = 0
   Received Packets Delivered            = 1552
   Output Requests                       = 1172
   Routing Discards                      = 0
   Discarded Output Packets              = 0
   Output Packet No Route                = 0
   Reassembly Required                   = 0
   Reassembly Successful                 = 0
   Reassembly Failures                   = 0
   Datagrams Successfully Fragmented     = 0
   Datagrams Failing Fragmentation       = 0
   Fragments Created                     = 0

ICMP Statistics        Used by ping and for routing
                            Received    Sent
   Messages                    42         25
   Errors                      0          0
   Destination Unreachable     18         1
   Time Exceeded               0          0
   Parameter Problems          0          0
   Source Quenchs              0          0
   Redirects                   0          0
   Echos                       8          16
   Echo Replies                16         8
   Timestamps                  0          0
   Timestamp Replies           0          0
   Address Masks               0          0
   Address Mask Replies        0          0

TCP Statistics         Connection-oriented data
   Active Opens                          = 42
   Passive Opens                         = 24
   Failed Connection Attempts            = 17
   Reset Connections                     = 3
   Current Connections                   = 7
   Segments Received                     = 827
   Segments Sent                         = 806
   Segments Retransmitted                = 51

UDP Statistics         UDP data
   Datagrams Received      = 545
   No Ports                = 170
   Receive Errors          = 0
   Datagrams Sent          = 288
```

One use for this display is to check the various error counts. Clearly, this network is working extremely well, since all of them are 0. Small numbers of errors over time are normal and nothing to be concerned about. How small is small? Error levels above a very few percent of the total network traffic need further investigation and may indicate flaky or failing network hardware.

The Network Monitor administrative tool (also accessible via the **netmon** command, which is located in the *Netmon* subdirectory of *%SystemRoot%\System32*) provides a graphical display of the same data (see Figure 8-37). You initiate the network statistics display with the **Capture►Start** menu path or the F10 key. Its display is subdivided into four windows; moving counterclockwise from the upper-left corner, the windows currently display three bar graphs indicating the overall network usage and traffic levels, a list of active connections of remote systems with the local host (systems are identified by MAC address), detailed total I/O statistics for each active connection, and overall network statistics data (in numerical format) since the capture operation began.

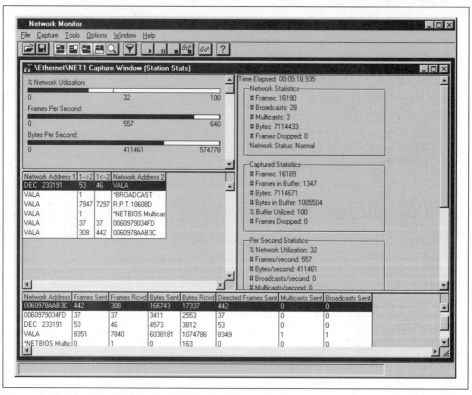

Figure 8-37. The Network Monitor administrative tool

Data collected with the Network Monitor may be saved to a file and viewed again at a later time. See the documentation for more information about its data capturing facilities.

These facilities can provide you with a snapshot of a system's current network activity and load. We will consider network monitoring for performance purposes in Chapter 11.

Managing Domain Controllers

We conclude this chapter on network configuration by considering how to manage the domain controllers within a domain. A server system can be designated as a primary or backup domain controller when the Windows NT operating system is installed.

The Server Manager administrative tool (also accessible with the **srvmgr** command) may be used for a variety of high-level system management tasks:

- Sending a message to all of the users on any system in a domain
- Starting and stopping Windows NT services on any system in a domain
- Managing shares on any system in a domain
- Displaying the current usage for shared resources for any system in a domain
- Managing the directory replication facility
- Adding and removing systems from a domain

Most relevant to our current consideration are its features for configuring and synchronizing domain controllers.

Synchronizing the Data on Backup Domain Controllers

The data on backup domain controllers (BDC) is automatically synchronized with that on the Primary Domain Controller (PDC) on a periodic basis. When a new backup domain controller is added to a domain, a full synchronization of the complete contents of the domain databases is performed. Thereafter, partial synchronization operations are performed whenever possible. You can force a partial synchronization using the Server Manager's **Computer►Synchronize with Primary Domain Controller** menu path.

The PDC maintains a list of changes to its data in a buffer known as the *change log*. When a BDC requests data synchronization, it sends it all of the changes from the change log that have been added since the previous synchronization. The change log is a circular buffer, overwriting the oldest entries when it is full. If an entry that has not been sent to a BDC is overwritten, the PDC performs a full synchronization with that system the next time it requests data. Such synchronizations are time consuming and best avoided if at all possible. If they are occurring consistently, the change log may need to be increased in size (its default size is 64 KB, which corresponds to about 2,000 changes).

You can change the size of the change log by editing the ChangeLogSize value of the HKEY_LOCAL_MACHINE\System\CurrentControlSet\Services\Netlogon\Parameters registry key (you may need to add the key, which is type REG_DWORD). This value specifies the size of the change log buffer in bytes. Reboot the system to put the new setting into effect.

Modifying Domain Controllers

It is easy to move a workstation or stand-alone server to another domain: simply delete its computer account from its current domain and use the **Change** button on the **Identification** tab of the network **Properties** to specify its new domain.

Performing this and related actions for domain controllers is generally more complicated. We'll consider several of them.

Adding a new backup domain controller is most straightforward if you decide to do so when you install the Windows NT operating system. At that time, designate the system as a BDC. You can then add a computer account for the new system via the Server Manager's **Computer➤Add to Domain...** menu path. The resulting dialog is illustrated in Figure 8-38.

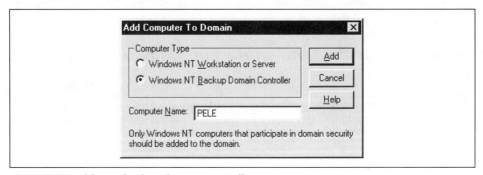

Figure 8-38. Adding a backup domain controller

Converting an existing server system within a domain to a BDC is more tedious:

1. Delete its computer account from the domain.

2. Reinstall Windows NT on the target system, designating it as a BDC.

3. Add the computer back into the domain.

As you can see, it is much, much easier to designate a system as a BDC right from the start.

An existing BDC can be promoted to the domain's primary domain controller using the Server Manager's **Computer▶Promote to Primary Domain Controller** menu path. If the current PDC is accessible at the time, it will automatically be demoted to a BDC. If the PDC is unavailable at that time, you will have to demote it manually when it comes back online (**Computer▶Demote to Backup Domain Controller**, a menu path available only when a lame duck PDC is selected).

Replacing the system serving as the PDC uses a similar strategy:

1. Perform a full backup of the PDC.

2. Install the Windows NT operating system on the new computer, designating it as a backup domain controller. Install any required software for the system in the normal manner.

3. Restore files from the PDC backup to the new system as appropriate. You may have to restore some registry hives to transfer all of the customization of the old system to the new one (although recreating them by hand may be easier).

4. Add the new system to the domain as a BDC.

5. Wait a few hours to ensure that all data has been transferred, and then promote the BDC to the PDC. The old PDC will be demoted automatically.

6. Remove the system that previously served as the PDC from the domain (if desired).

9

Print Services

Printers are system resources that are typically shared among the various systems and users within a network. We'll begin our consideration of them by looking at what happens when a user prints a document on a local printer (the process of sending a print job to a printer is sometimes referred to as *spooling*).

Suppose user *Chavez* decides to print a short letter from a word processing program. The following events must occur before the printed page appears at the printer:

- The information in the word processing document is translated into a form (language) that is understood by the printer. This is typically handled by the printer driver, possibly in conjunction with the application software.

- A print *job* is created for the page and handed off to the printing subsystem. If *Chavez* is allowed to print to the printer she has specified, the job goes into a print *queue* corresponding to the particular printer (or printer type) that *Chavez* has chosen, where it waits its turn to print.

- When the job reaches the top of the queue, the printing subsystem sends it to an actual printer device. The printer may be physically connected to the same computer as the one where *Chavez* originated the job, to a different computer on the network, or to the network itself.

- The printer receives the print job and produces a printed page based upon the data within it.

The system administration tasks associated with the printing subsystem include adding and configuring new printers and print queues, and monitoring and manipulating print queues and the pending jobs within them. We begin this chapter by considering the basic process of adding a printer to a Windows NT system, then go on to consider managing print queues, and conclude by considering the setup and configuration of printers in several special sets of circumstances.

Adding a Printer

The following steps are required to add a new printer to a Windows NT system:

1. Connect the printer to the computer and configure the port to which it is attached (if necessary). If you are using a parallel printer (the most common type), it might be necessary to enable support for bidirectional communication for the corresponding parallel port via the computer's setup program. This option might be labeled "Bidirectional" or "ECP mode" or "ECP/EPP" mode; you should usually select ECP if ECP and EPP are separate choices. Make sure that you are using a bidirectional-capable cable (IEEE 1284-compliant).

2. Windows NT provides an **Add Printer** wizard, which is easy to use (start it using the **My Computer▸Printers▸Add Printer** icon). This tool allows you to specify printers and to create print queues for use with them. We will consider each of its dialog boxes in turn.

3. The first dialog box (illustrated in Figure 9-1) asks you whether the new printer is to be administered locally or remotely (**My Computer** vs. **Network**, respectively). For a local printer, we select **My Computer**.

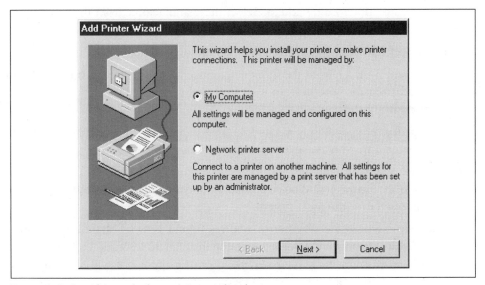

Figure 9-1. Specifying whether a printer is local or remote

4. Next, you are asked to identify the port to which the printer is attached. The example in Figure 9-2 indicates a printer attached to the second parallel port on the local system.

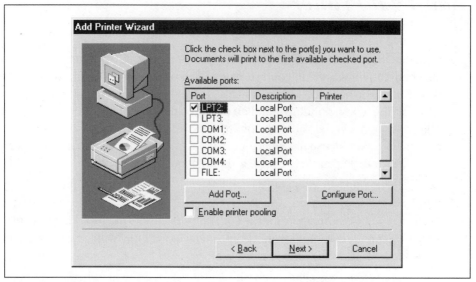

Figure 9-2. Specifying the printer port

5. The next dialog box requires you to specify the manufacturer and model of the specific printer being added. Select the manufacturer from the left list box and then select the appropriate model from the right list box (see Figure 9-3).

   If your printer is not listed, you have two options:

   — Obtain a driver from the printer manufacturer (often available for download from the Internet) and use this dialog box's **Have Disk**... button to load it.

   — Specify a type closely related to and supported by your printer (many printers can emulate several standard printer types).

6. The next dialog box allows you to assign a name to the printer (*Degas* in our example in Figure 9-4). You can also optionally make the new printer the default printer for the local system.

7. You will now indicate whether or not this printer is to be shared. If you indicate that it is, you may enter a name for the shared resource (which defaults to the first word of the printer name). In our example, we will share the new printer, also under the name *Degas* (see Figure 9-5).

   The lower portion of this dialog box is used to install printer drivers for other operating systems that may be downloaded to such systems as needed (print

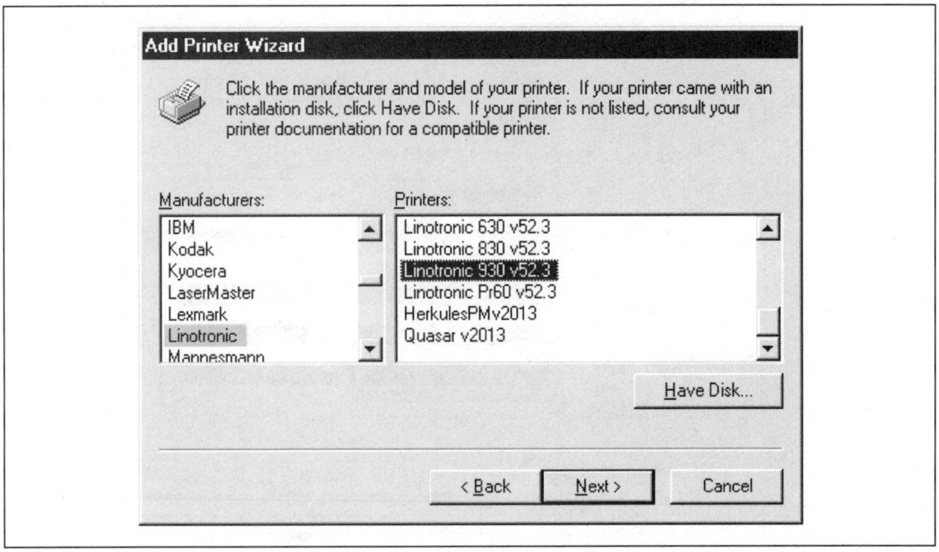

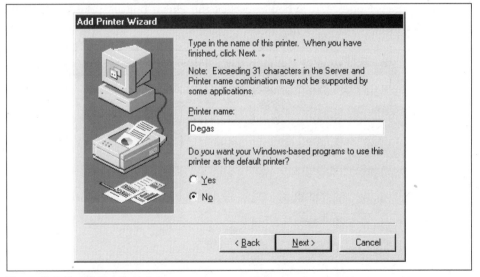

Figure 9-3. *Specifying the printer model*

Figure 9-4. *Specifying the printer name*

clients must determine whether their system has the latest driver when initiating a print job). If you select any items from the list, you will be prompted
to insert the distribution CD for each one.

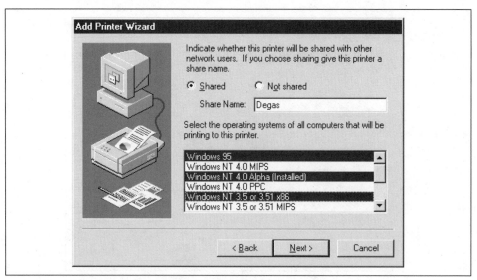

Figure 9-5. Sharing a printer with other operating systems

8. The final dialog box gives you the option of printing a test page to the new printer (see Figure 9-6). When you click the **Finish** button, printer installation will be complete.

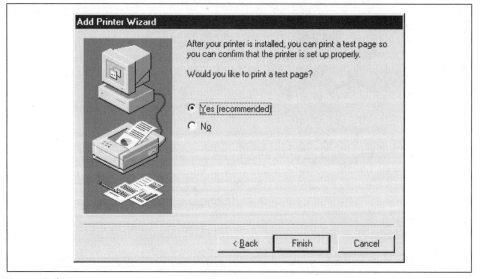

Figure 9-6. Printing a test page

As you might expect, you can change the settings for an existing printer via its **Properties**.

What this process has done is to identify the location of a printer device to the system and create a queue for it. There is no reason that the process can't be repeated in order to create another queue for the same printer (the only item that must change is the printer name). The two queues can then be given different properties.

Sharing an Existing Printer

The **Sharing**... item on the printer's shortcut (right click) menu allows you to change the sharing status of an existing printer. The resulting dialog box is similar to the corresponding one from the **Add Printer** wizard (Figure 9-5). Using this item, you may later designate a printer as shared or remove network access to a shared printer.

Setting Printer Permissions

Printers have permissions lists similar to those for filesystem shares. They may be viewed and modified via the **Permissions** button on the **Security** tab of the printer's **Properties**. Figure 9-7 shows the resulting dialog box.

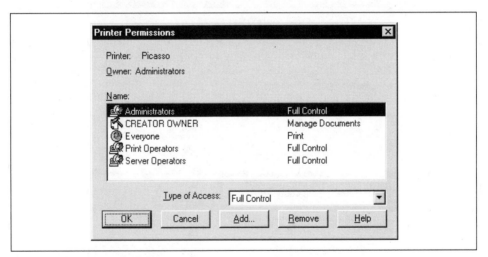

Figure 9-7. Printer permissions

The permissions defined for printers are listed in Table 9-1. They may be assigned to users and groups using the same process as for files and shares.

Table 9-1. Printer Permissions

Permission	Meaning
Full Control	Perform any printer configuration or management function (including printing documents).

Table 9-1. Printer Permissions (continued)

Permission	Meaning
Print	Send documents to this printer and control one's own print jobs.
Manage documents	Manipulate print jobs belonging to any user (this permission doesn't include printing to the device or printer configuration).
No Access	The user/group may not use the printer or affect any print job or the printer configuration.

Figure 9-7 lists the default permissions for a new printer: anyone can submit a print job to it, system administrators and two operator groups have full control of it, and the user who created it can manage print jobs in this queue.

Printer Scheduling Properties

The **Scheduling** tab of a printer's **Properties** may be used to specify how and when jobs may be added to that queue and are sent from the queue to the printer. Its dialog box is illustrated in Figure 9-8.

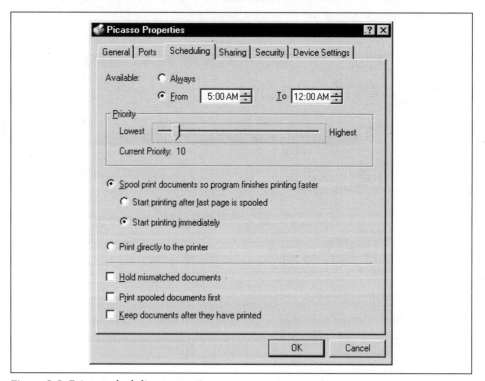

Figure 9-8. Printer scheduling properties

The following items may be specified in this dialog box:

- **Available** area: specifies when items from this print queue will be sent to the printer. At other times, users may submit jobs to the queue, which will be held until the specified time. When a job is created, it inherits the current availability settings of the corresponding print queue.

- **Priority** area: specifies the default priority level assigned to jobs in this print queue. Priority levels range from 1 to 99, with higher numbers indicating jobs that will print sooner.

- Spooling settings: The area in the middle of the dialog box contains three options for how documents are transmitted to the printer. Jobs may be sent directly to the printer (selected via the bottom radio button in this section of the dialog box) or they may be spooled (held in the queue and sent according to their relative priorities); the latter is recommended for all devices except ones that don't support spooling.

  Spooled jobs are handled in one of two ways: if the printer is not otherwise occupied, printing may begin once the first page of the document is spooled, or the spooling subsystem may wait until the entire document has reached the queue before beginning to print it. The first approach returns control of the originating application to the user much sooner if it does not support background printing.

- The **Hold mismatched documents** check box specifies whether the spooling subsystem compares the current setup of the printer against that specified in each print job and automatically holds jobs for which they do not match. The default is unchecked.

- The **Print spooled documents first** check box controls what happens when a job is in the process of being queued at the moment the spooler is ready to send the next job to the printer. If this box is checked, then such jobs will be ignored if there are any pending jobs in the queue. If it is unchecked (the default), then a higher-priority job in the process of being spooled will print before waiting jobs with lower priorities.

- The **Keep documents after they have printed** check box specifies whether or not the copies of documents stored in the print queue are deleted after the corresponding job finishes printing. By default, it is unchecked, and print job files are automatically deleted (of course, the original documents are unaffected).

Setting Global Spooler Properties

The **My Computer►Printers►File►Server Properties** menu path allows you to specify global properties for the entire spooling subsystem. Its **Advanced** tab allows you to specify the location of the spooling scratch directory (see Figure

9-9) and to change various settings related to error logging (to the normal Event Viewer facility) and error notification messages to the system administrator.

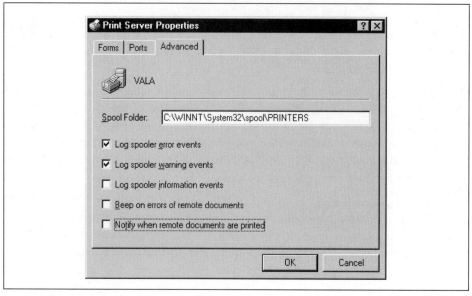

Figure 9-9. Global spooling subsystem properties

The **Notify when remote documents are printed** check box is selected by default; it is responsible for those annoying message boxes that appear every time a remote document prints. Unchecking it eliminates them.

For dedicated print server systems, another setting you will probably want to alter is the run priority setting of the spooling service process, which sends print jobs to the print devices, favoring it over other requests for CPU resources. This is accomplished using the System Policy Editor. Select its **File▶Open Registry** menu path, and then double click on the **Local Computer** icon. Navigate to the **Scheduler Priority** setting of the **Windows NT Printers** setting group and check the corresponding check box. Use the **Priority** menu in the lower section of the dialog box to set the priority to **Above Normal** (see Figure 9-10). The System Policy Editor is discussed in detail in Chapter 10.

This setting changes the value of the SchedulerThreadPriority value of the HKEY_ LOCAL_MACHINE\System\CurrentControlSet\Control\Print key. The SpoolerPriority* value of the same key (type REG_DWORD) similarly specifies the priority class of the print spooler process. Its normal setting is the **Normal** priority class

---

* This value replaces the PriorityClass setting used with previous versions of Windows NT (and still present in the registry).

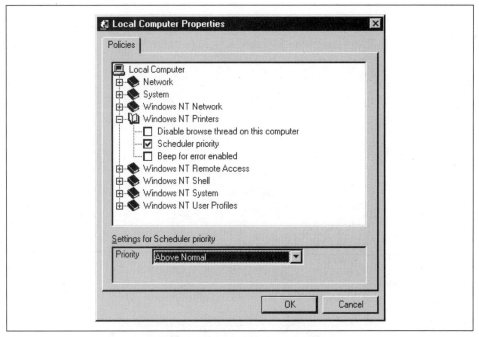

Figure 9-10. Specifying the priority level of the print scheduler process

(corresponding to a setting of 0). A value of 1 sets it to the **High** priority class and a value of 0xFFFFFFFF sets it to the lowest priority class. You must create this registry key if you want to change the default value.

Manipulating Print Jobs

The other important aspect of printer administration is monitoring the status of the various print queues and devices on the network and modifying individual jobs within them.

The contents of a print queue can be displayed by double clicking on its icon in the **Printers** folder, which produces a list of jobs and their current status. Selecting a job and then choosing the **Document➤Properties** menu path displays the job's properties (Figure 9-11).

Information about the job appears in the upper portion of the dialog box, and users may use the **Priority** and **Schedule** areas to modify the job's in-queue priority and time restrictions on when it may print (respectively). In the latter case, the settings you specify must conform to any restrictions currently set for the printer itself.

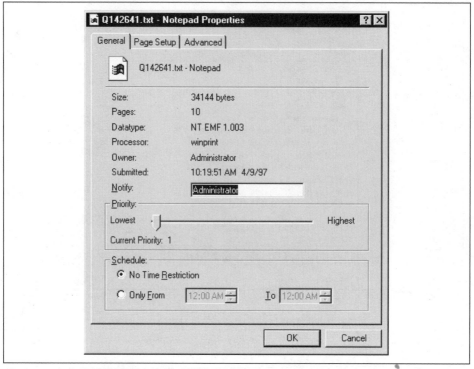

Figure 9-11. Print job properties

A selected job may also be paused or canceled using other items on the **Docu-ment** menu (see Figure 9-12). The **Resume** item is used to continue the printing of a paused job from its current point, and the **Restart** item will reprint a current print job from the beginning. A job may be removed from the print queue with the **Cancel** item or by pressing the **Delete** key.

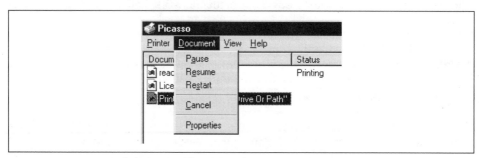

Figure 9-12. Commands for manipulating a print job

Similarly, the **Printer►Pause Printing** menu item may be used to pause a print queue after the current job completes (a check mark next to the menu item indicates that it has been selected, and selecting it a second time will resume the queue). Use the **Printer►Purge Print Documents** menu path to clear out the entire contents of a print queue.

The **net print** command may be used to perform these same tasks from the command line for any Windows print queue on any network-accessible system. For example, the following command displays the jobs in the queue *Picasso* on system *vala*:

```
C:\> net print \\vala\picasso
Printers at \\vala

Name                       Job #      Size       Status
-----------------------------------------------------------------
picasso Queue              3 jobs                *Printer Active*
    ADMINISTRATOR              8     4596310      Printing
    CHAVEZ                     9       23453      Waiting
    WILL                      10     1264456      Waiting
The command completed successfully.
```

This print queue is currently printing a job, and there are two others waiting.

The command has the following syntax when used to manipulate a print job:

net print *host**printer n* /*cmd*

where *n* is the job number of the job you want to modify, and *cmd* is **hold**, **delete**, or **release** (all are options preceded by a forward slash).

Finally, the **PQCount** freeware utility (written by Scott Lemieux) may be used to create a quick status display for a print queue. It takes a hostname as its argument. For example, the following command produces the display for system *vala* shown in Figure 9-13.

```
C:\> pqcount \\vala.
```

Figure 9-13. The PQCount utility display

The display is automatically updated periodically. Clicking on the display window provides access to its **File** menu, from which you may close the display.

This program relies on the *Admin$* administrative share for access to print subsystem information. You can create this share if it does not exist via the Server Manager's **Computer➤Shared Directories...** menu path.

Advanced Printer Configuration

In this section, we consider procedures for setting up printers and print queue in a variety of special circumstances.

Creating a Network Printer

Network printers are created by the **Add Printer** wizard using the same general process as for local printers. The **Network printer server** radio button should be selected in its initial dialog box (see Figure 9-1). You then need to specify the network location of the printer in the **Connect to Printer** dialog box (Figure 9-14).

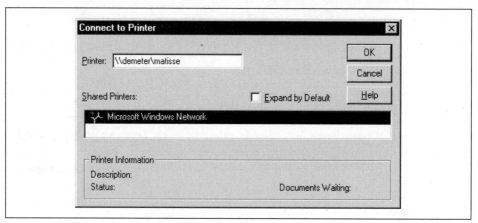

Figure 9-14. Specifying a printer on a remote system

You may use the browsing window in the middle of the dialog box to select the desired printer, or you may enter its name directly into the **Printer** field, as in our example. The remote printer may reside on a Windows NT system or on a Windows system.

Creating a Queue for a Network Printer

Alternatively, you may choose to create a local print queue, whose properties you can specify as desired, for a remote printer. This is accomplished by creating a new local printer (select **My Computer** in the first dialog box of the **Add Printer** wizard) and then defining a local port pointing to the network location.

Selecting the **Add Port...** button on the **Add Printer** wizard's ports dialog box allows you to create a new local printer port (see Figure 9-15).

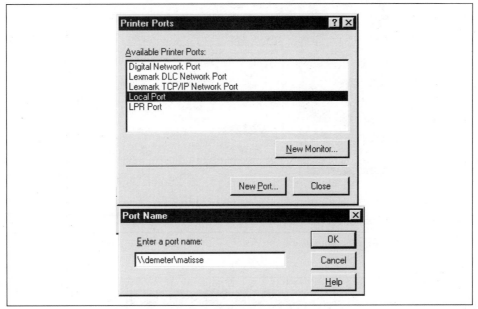

Figure 9-15. Defining a new port for a network printer

Choose the **Local Port** port type and select the **New Port...** button. Then enter the hostname and share name for the remote printer into the resulting **Port Name** dialog box (the lower dialog box in Figure 9-15).

Once the port is defined, you may select it from the list as usual (see Figure 9-16) and continue with the printer creation process.

Once created, local queues for remote printers appear differently from remote printers in the **Printers** folder. For example, in the display in Figure 9-17, both printers refer to the printer *matisse* on host *demeter*, but *Degas* looks like any other local printer.

Combining Several Printers

A *printer pool* is a single print queue that serves multiple physical print devices. You can create a printer pool by checking the **Enable printer pooling** option on the **Add Printer** wizard's ports dialog box and then selecting multiple ports from the list (see Figure 9-18). All of the printers in the pool must be of the same type, or be capable of emulating the same common type.

Print jobs sent to a printer pool are printed on the first available printer.

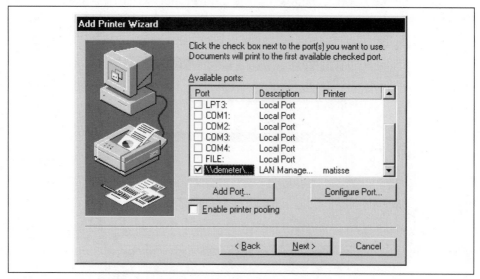

Figure 9-16. Selecting the new port

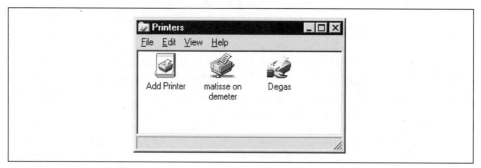

Figure 9-17. Two queues for the same remote printer

Printing to UNIX Systems

Print queues may also be created that send print jobs to printers located on network-accessible UNIX systems supporting BSD print spooling. To take advantage of this feature, the Microsoft TCP/IP Printing network service must be installed (it is not, by default); you can do so in the usual way from the **Services** tab of the network **Properties**.

Once you have done so, create a new local printer with the **Add Printer** wizard. You will need to define a new port for the remote UNIX printer. Create a port of type **LPR Port** and then enter the name of the remote UNIX system and the desired printer into the resulting **Add LPR compatible printer** dialog box (see Figure 9-19).

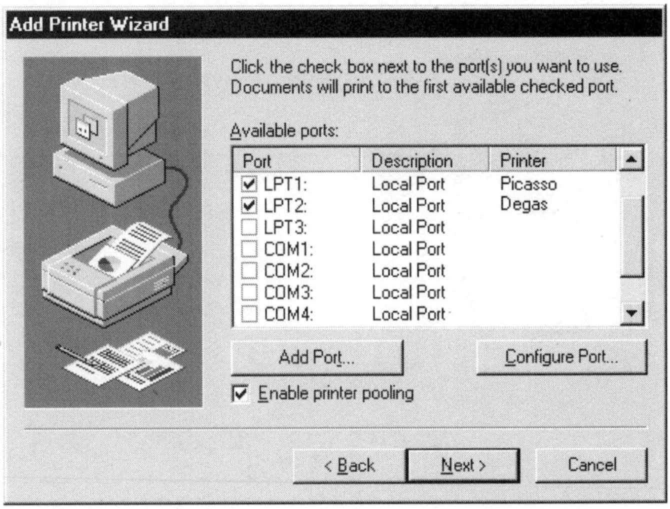

Figure 9-18. Creating a printer pool

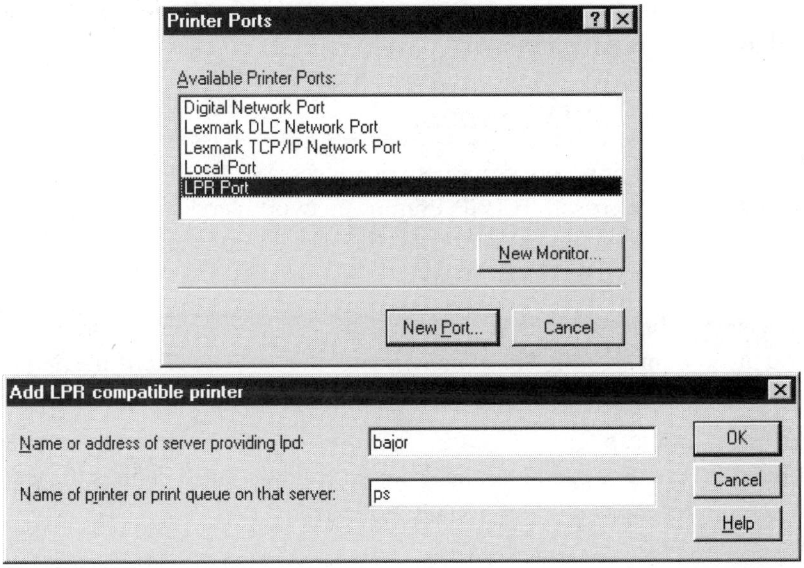

Figure 9-19. Creating an LPR printer port

Once the port is defined, it may be selected from the list of ports (see Figure 9-20), and you may continue with the normal printer creation process.

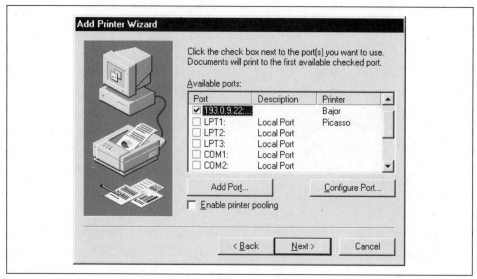

Figure 9-20. Selecting the port for a remote UNIX printer

Once the printer is defined, it may be selected in the normal manner by any application. The Resource Kit also contains native Windows NT versions of the UNIX **lpq** and **lpr** for users who prefer them.

Printing from UNIX Systems

Accepting incoming print jobs from network-accessible UNIX systems also requires installation of the Microsoft TCP/IP Printing network service. Once it is installed, the following steps allow a Windows NT system to accept jobs from UNIX systems:

1. Execute the **net start lpdsvc** command to start the incoming print job server. You may want to add this command to the *AutoExNT.Bat* file if you have installed that facility (see Chapter 2).

2. Set up a printcap entry on the UNIX system in the normal manner for a remote printer. For example, the following simple entry defines the *pic* printer as the printer *Picasso* on the remote node *vala:*

   ```
   pic:lp=:rm=vala:rp=picasso:
   ```

   If you plan to accept incoming print jobs from UNIX systems, it is imperative that you select a printer name that complies with UNIX requirements.

NOTE   Currently, the Solaris operating system sometimes requires Sun patch number 103959 to print successfully to remote Windows NT printers. This patch modifies the print server to provide full compliance with RFC 1179.

PostScript printing glitches

Setting up print spooling to and from remote UNIX systems is easy. Doing so correctly does not always guarantee that jobs will print correctly, however; just that they will arrive at their destination. Unfortunately, the printing part can be a nightmare and cannot always be made to work.

Problems tend to arise in two main cases: with PostScript printers and with printers that are not supported or poorly supported by Windows NT. Some PostScript printers also work fine, but many don't; the symptom when they don't is that you get pages of raw PostScript text instead of the proper output. PCL printers can exhibit the same symptom.

For incoming jobs, the only recourse is to force the spooling subsystems to treat all LPD-based jobs as raw print files (to be passed on to the printer unexamined and unmodified). To do so, add the SimulatePassThrough value (type REG_DWORD) to the HKEY_LOCAL_MACHINE\System\CurrentControlSet\Services\LPDSVC\Parameters registry key and set it to 1. This setting is used on a system-wide basis and cannot be limited to a specific print queue.

For outgoing jobs, try printing to a file instead of directly to the remote UNIX printer, and then use the **lpr -o l** command to spool the file as type binary to the remote printer. For example, the following command sends the file *apple.PS* to a remote printer on *bajor*:

```
C:\> lpr -s bajor -P ps -o l apple.PS
```

If this command is successful, ensure that the data type of the print queue corresponding to the remote printer is set to **RAW**. This is specified in the Datatype value of the registry key HKEY_LOCAL_MACHINE\System\CurrentControlSet\Control\Print\Printers*printer_name*, where *printer_name* is the name of the print queue for the remote UNIX printer.

The following Knowledge Base articles may be helpful in troubleshooting printer problems between Windows NT and UNIX systems:

- Q163551, "Troubleshooting Printing Problems in Windows NT 4.0"
- "TCP/IP Printing Troubleshooting" (available at *www.microsoft.com/NtWksSupport/content/nttroubleshoot/print/tcpprt.htm*)

- Q124735, "How Windows NT LPD Server Implements LPR Control Characters"

- Q132460, "Troubleshooting Windows NT Print Server Alteration of Print Jobs"

- Q150930, "LPD Server Adds and Prints Control Codes"

- Q123107, "LPR Does Not Print PostScript Files Correctly"

- Q121737, "TCP/IP Printing Supports Only Berkeley Style Daemons (RFC 1179)"

See Appendix B for information on accessing the Microsoft Knowledge Base.

Deleting Unwanted Printer Ports

The **File➤Server Properties** menu path in the **Printers** folder allows access to the properties of the spooling subsystem. Its **Ports** tab may be used to add, delete, and reconfigure printer ports.

10

Security

System security considerations have already come up at many points in this book: for example, when we considered user passwords and access control lists. This makes sense, since system security practices and techniques are most effective when they are inextricably intertwined with the ordinary tasks of system administration. Although we've chosen to discuss some security topics in isolation within this chapter, keep in mind that you can't maintain such a separation in real life.

We begin with a general consideration of system security and then look at a variety of topics relating to securing Windows NT systems. Later sections discuss system policies, user rights, and system security auditing.

NOTE   This chapter will undoubtedly strike some readers as excessively paranoid. The general approach I take to system security grows out of my experiences working with a large manufacturing firm designing its new products entirely on CAD/CAM workstations, and with a variety of fairly small software companies. In all of these environments, a significant part of the company's future products and assets existed solely in an online form. Naturally, protecting them was a major system administrative focus, and the choices that are appropriate for such sites may be very different from what makes sense in other contexts. This chapter presents the available options for securing a Windows NT installation. It's up to you and your site to determine what you need.

Prelude: Some Bits of History

Before turning to the specifics of securing and monitoring Windows NT systems, let's take a brief look at some well-known security problems from the relatively recent past:

- On NTFS filesystems, access control lists specify permitted file access, and files without an ACL were designed to be inaccessible to everyone. However, under Windows NT version 3.51, if a user removed the ACL associated with a file, then any user could delete that file.

- The Windows NT user interface includes extensive browsing capabilities of shared network resources. For example, users can browse the network and view the available shared filesystems and printers. This feature relies on the use of *anonymous connections*: connections to remote systems that aren't required to present the normal user authentication data (username and password). However, anonymous connections can also be exploited by an unscrupulous ordinary user in order to learn a substantial amount of information about a remote system: the name of its administrative account, the names of all shared filesystems (including hidden shares), and other information from its system registry. This is the so-called "Red Button" bug, named after the program that demonstrated its existence and seriousness (see Figure 10-1).

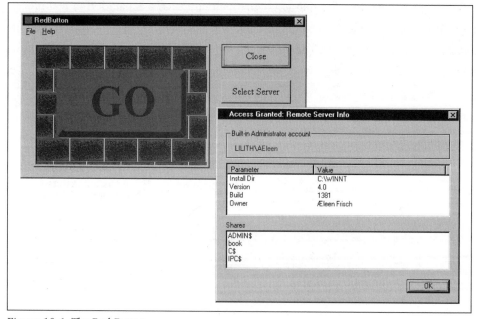

Figure 10-1. The Red Button

- The Windows NT operating system includes many facilities designed to make kernel debugging easier. Such items are designed to be limited to users and processes with administrative access to the system. However, due to a bug in a system service (which did not check the validity of the address where it stored the result it returns), one of them could be enabled by programs running from an ordinary user account. A nefarious user could take advantage of this to create a program that would ultimately allow him to add himself to the *Administrators* group. (There are currently several known variations of this exploit.)

- The Windows NT distribution CD contains the **RollBack** utility, a tool designed primarily to enable computer manufacturers to preinstall the operating system on new systems, and for limited sorts of initial system configuration by system administrators. However, if an unscrupulous person runs the utility on an existing Windows NT system, the operating system will need to be restored from a backup or reinstalled from scratch.

What do all of these items have in common? They all illustrate the fundamental Windows NT view that the system exists in a trustworthy environment of reasonable people; in its most basic design, ease-of-use ultimately takes precedence over security. In all four of these cases, some part of Windows NT failed to anticipate or check for unintended uses of its facilities or for circumstances that could "never" occur. Seeing these problems merely as bugs that have been fixed misses the point: such a view is inherent in the Windows NT operating system. If this attitude does not match reality in your environment, you have a lot of work to do to overcome it, and you can expect that task to be ongoing.

Thinking About Security

Security discussions often begin by considering the kinds of threats facing a system. I'd like to come at this issue from a slightly different angle by focusing first on what needs to be protected. Before you can address any security-related issue on your system, you need to be able to answer the following questions:

- What are you trying to protect? What valuable asset might be lost?

- Who are you trying to protect it from, how hard are they willing to work to get it, and how much money are they willing to spend?

If you can answer these questions, you go a long way toward identifying and solving potential security problems. One way to approach them is to imagine discovering one morning that your entire computer system or network had been stolen during the previous night. Having this happen would upset nearly everyone, but for many different reasons:

- Because of the monetary cost; what is valuable is the computer as a physical object (*loss of equipment*).

- Because of the loss of sensitive or private data, such as company secrets, or information about individuals (one type of *loss of data*).

- Because you can't conduct business—the computer is essential to manufacturing your product or providing services to your customers (*loss of use*). In this case, the computer's business or educational role is more important than the hardware per se.

Of course, there are many other causes of all three kinds of losses besides theft. For example, data can also be stolen by copying it electronically or by removing the medium on which it is stored, as well as by stealing the computer itself. There is also both physical and electronic vandalism. Physical vandalism can mean broken or damaged equipment (as when thieves break into your office, get annoyed at not finding any money, and pour the cup of coffee left on a desk into the vents on the computer and onto the keyboard). Electronic vandalism can consist of corrupted or removed files, or a system overwhelmed by so many garbage processes that it becomes unusable.

Which concerns are relevant to you govern the threats you need to be prepared for. Physical threats include not only theft but also natural disasters (fires, pipes bursting, power failures from electrical storms, and so on). Data loss can be caused by malice or accident, ranging from deliberate theft and destruction, to user and administrator errors, to program bugs wreaking havoc. Thus, preventing data loss means taking into account not only unauthorized users getting on to the system and authorized users on the system doing things they're not supposed to do, but also authorized users doing things they're allowed to, but didn't really mean or want to. And, occasionally, it means cleaning up after yourself.

Once you've identified what needs to be protected, as well as the people, acts, and events from which it needs to be protected, you'll be in a much better position to determine what concrete steps to take to secure your system or site. For example, if theft of the computer itself is your biggest worry, then you need to think more about locks than about how often to make users change their passwords. Conversely, if physical security is no problem but data loss is, then you need to think about ways to prevent it, from both accidental and deliberate acts, and to recover it quickly should it occur despite all of your precautions.

The final complication is that security inevitably varies inversely with convenience: the more secure a system, the less convenient it is to use, and vice versa. You and your organization need to find the right set of tradeoffs for your situation. For example, isolated systems are easier to make secure than those on networks, but few people want to write a tape to transfer files between two nonnetworked systems.

Threats can come from a variety of sources. External threats range from electronic joy-riders who stumble into your system more-or-less at random, to purposeful hackers who have specifically targeted your system (or another system that can be reached by a path including your system). Internal threats come from legitimate users attempting to do things that they aren't supposed to, with motivations ranging from curiosity and mischievousness, to malice and industrial espionage. You'll need to take different steps depending on which kind of threats are most applicable to your site.

In the end, good security, like successful system administration in general, is largely a matter of planning and habit: designing responses to various scenarios in advance and faithfully, scrupulously carrying out the routine, boring, daily actions required to prevent and recover from the various disasters you've foreseen (or failed to foresee). Although it may seem at times like pounds, rather than ounces, of prevention are needed, I think you'll find that they are far less burdensome than even grams of cure.

Security Policies and Plans

Many sites find written security policies and plans helpful. By "security policy," I mean a written statement for users of what constitutes appropriate and unacceptable uses of their accounts and the data associated with them.

I'll refer to a written description of periodic security-related system administration activities as a "security plan." At some sites, the computer security policy is part of a more comprehensive security policy; similarly, an administrative security plan is often part of a more general disaster recovery plan.

Security policies

Security policies are most effective when users read, understand, and agree to abide by them at the time they receive their computer accounts, usually by signing some sort of form (retaining a copy of the written policy for future reference). For employees, this usually occurs when they are hired, as part of the security briefing they attend some time during the first few days of employment. In an educational setting, students can also be required to sign the written security policy when they receive their accounts or even attend a mandatory computer security awareness session before a student receives an account for the first time.

A good computer security policy covers these areas:

- Who is allowed to use the account (generally no one but the user herself). Don't forget to consider spouses, significant others, and children as you formulate this item.

- Password requirements and prohibitions (e.g., don't reveal it to anyone, don't use a password here that you have ever used anywhere else and vice versa). It is also worth pointing out that no one from the computing or system administration staff will ever ask for a password by phone or in person.*

- Proper and improper use of local computers and those accessed via the Internet. This can include not only prohibitions against hacking, but also whether personal use of an account is allowed, whether commercial use of a university account is permitted, policies about erotic or pornographic images being kept or displayed online, and similar issues.

- Conditions under which the user can lose her account. This item can also be somewhat broader and include, for example, when a job might be killed (when the system needs to go down for maintenance, when a job is overwhelming the system, and so on).

- Rules and guidelines about what kinds of use are allowed on which computers (for example, whether game playing is allowed, where large jobs should be run, and the like).

- Consent to monitoring of all aspects of account activity by system administration staff as needed for system or network security, performance optimization, general configuration, and accounting purposes.

- How printed output is to be disposed of, whether it can leave the building or site, and similar issues for tapes and other media.

Some sites need more than one policy for different classes of users. When you formulate or revise a written security policy, it may be appropriate to run it by your organization's legal department.

Security plans

Formulating or revising a security plan is often a good way to assess and review the general state of security on a system or network. Such a plan should address some or all of the following issues:

- General computer access policies: what general classes of users are present on the system, along with the access and privileges that they are allowed (or

---

* Gaining access to a computer system by tricking a legitimate user into revealing her password or other information is known as *social engineering*. Users need to be educated about the common sorts of scams that may be attempted by the bad guys.

are denied). Describing this will include noting the purpose and scope of the various user groups.

- Optional system security features that are in effect (password aging and other restrictions, user account retirement policies, and so on).

- Preventive measures in effect (for example, the backup schedule, actions to be performed in conjunction with operating system installations and upgrades, and other related activities).

- What periodic (or continuous) system monitoring is performed and how it is implemented.

- How often complete system security audits are performed and what items they encompass (see Appendix B for works on this topic).

- Policies and strategies for actively handling and recovering from security breaches.

Like any important policy or procedure, the security plan needs to be reviewed and updated periodically.

Lines of Defense

I find it helpful to think of the various security facilities provided by a computer system or operating system in terms of the various "lines of defense" that could potentially be set up to protect your system from the various losses it might experience.

Physical security

The first line of defense is limiting physical access to your computer. The most security-conscious installations protect their computers by eliminating all network and dial-up access and then strictly limiting who can get near them. At the far extreme are those systems in locked rooms (requiring a password be entered on a keypad, in addition to the key for the lock, in order to get in), isolated in restricted access areas of installations with guarded entrances (usually military or defense-related). To get onto these systems, you have to get into the site, into the right building, past another set of guards in the secure part of that building, and finally into the computer room before you even have to worry about having a valid password on the system. Such an approach effectively keeps out outsiders and unauthorized users; security threats then can come only from insiders.

Although this extreme level of physical security is not needed by most sites, all administrators will face some physical security issues. Some of the most common include:

- Preventing theft and vandalism by locking the door or locking the equipment to a table or desk. If these are significant threats for you, you might also need to consider other aspects of the computer's physical location. For example, the best locks in the world can be worthless if the door has a glass window in it.

- Limiting access to the console and the CPU unit to prevent someone from crashing the system and rebooting it to single-user mode. Even if your system allows you to disable single-user mode access without a password, there still may be issues here for you. For example, if your system is secured by a key position on its front panel, but you keep the key in the top middle drawer of your desk (right next to your file cabinet keys), or inserted in the front panel, this level of security is effectively stripped away.

- Controlling environmental factors as much as is realistically possible. This concern can include considering special power systems (backup generators, line conditioners, surge suppressors, and so on) to prevent downtime or loss of data, and fire detection and extinguishing systems to prevent equipment damage. It also includes simple, common sense policies like not putting open cups of liquid next to a keyboard or on top of a monitor.

- Restricting or monitoring access to other parts of the system, like terminals, workstations, network cables (vulnerable to tapping and eavesdropping), and so on.

- Limiting access to backup tapes. If the security of its data is important to your system, backup tapes need to be protected from theft and damage as well as the system itself.

Passwords

If someone gains access to the system, or you have voluntarily given up complete physical security, passwords form the next line of defense against unauthorized users and the risks associated with them. As we discussed before, *all accounts should have passwords* (or be disabled).

The weakness with passwords is that if someone breaks into an account by finding out its password, he has all the rights and privileges granted to that account and can impersonate the legitimate user as desired (as can a nefarious program).

File permissions

File permissions form the next line of defense, against both bad guys who've succeeded in breaking into an account and legitimate users trying to do something they're not supposed to. Properly set up file protection can prevent many potential problems. However, if someone succeeds in logging in via an administrator account, in most cases, system security is irreparably compromised. In such cases, the administrative focus must shift from prevention to detection: finding out what has been done to the system (and repairing it) and determining how the system was compromised—and plugging that gap.

Encrypting data

There is one exception to the complete loss of security if an administrator account is compromised. For some types of data files, encryption can form a fourth line of defense, providing protection against even privileged accounts. The freely available Pretty Good Privacy (PGP) package, designed for securing electronic mail messages, may also be used to encrypt files. There are many commercial encryption packages available.

Backups

Backups provide the final line of defense against some kinds of security problems and system disasters. A good backup scheme almost always enables you to restore the system to something near its previous state, or to re-create it on new hardware if some part of the computer itself is damaged. However, if someone steals the data from your system but doesn't alter or destroy it, backups are irrelevant.

Backups provide protection against data loss and filesystem damage only in conjunction with frequent system monitoring, designed to detect security problems quickly. Otherwise, a problem might not be uncovered for a long time. If this occurs, then backups would simply save the corrupted system state, making it necessary to go back weeks or months to a known clean state when the problem finally is uncovered, and restoring or re-creating newer versions of files by hand.

Security begins and ends with people

Getting users to care about security takes time and effort. In the last instance, a system is only as secure as its most vulnerable part, and the system's users are a part that it is important not to forget or neglect.

When users cause security problems, there are three main reasons: ignorance, laziness, and evil:

- Ignorance is the easiest to address. Developing formal and informal training tactics and procedures is something that happens over time. Users also need to be reminded of things they already know from time to time.

- Laziness will always be a temptation—for system administrators as well as users—but you'll find it will be less of a problem when users have bought in to the system security goals. This requires both support from management—theirs as well as yours—and the organization as a whole and a formal commitment from individual users. In addition, an atmosphere that focuses on solutions rather than on blame is generally more successful than raw intimidation or coercion. When people are worried about getting in trouble, they will tend to cover up problems rather than fix them.

- Consideration of the third cause will have to wait. Creating a corporate culture that encourages and fosters employee loyalty and openness rather than deceit and betrayal is the subject of another book, as is recognizing and neutralizing malefactors.

C2 Security

As its marketing literature proudly proclaims, the Windows NT operating system can be configured to provide what is commonly called *C2 security* (more technically, the Windows NT operating system is C2-certifiable). Various U.S. government official security levels—D, C1, C2, B1, B2, B3, and A1—are defined in a series of books known as the *Trusted Computer Security Evaluation Criteria* (TCSEC). The books are colloquially referred to by the color of their covers. The Orange Book describes single system security. The Red Book attempts to interpret the Orange Book in a network context. The Blue Book attempts to apply the Orange Book to other subsystems not considered by the original. Of the defined levels, C2 is the lowest (least secure) level of official security that anyone actually cares about.

Any operating system that supports C2 security includes the following design features:

- Discretionary control of objects:
  - All objects are owned by a specific user.
  - Their owners have control over who is able to access them.
- User identification and authentication (usually accomplished via usernames and passwords, which must be presented for system access).
- No object reuse: numerical user IDs and group IDs for deleted user accounts and groups are never used again, and a new user or group with the same name as a deleted account receives an unrelated ID and has no relationship to the name's previous incarnation.
- A security-related auditing facility.

One requirement of C2 security states that access to the system (or the secure part of the system) can be granted only after a predefined key sequence is entered. On Windows NT systems, this key sequence is the CTRL-ALT-DEL combination, which a user must press in order to access the login screen. Since this scheme is designed to prevent (or lessen) the risk of password-stealing via trojan horse programs masquerading as the official login sequence, users need to be informed of the key sequence's purpose and instructed to never respond to any login screen which appears without having summoned it in this way.

The Resource Kit includes the **C2Config** command, which displays the system's current compliance with the requirements of C2 security and allows you to modify some aspects of the system configuration accordingly.

Securing a Windows NT System

In this section we will consider a wide variety of issues related to system and network security in the Windows NT environment.

User Authentication Revisited

We looked at passwords and other user account controls in some detail in Chapter 3. The importance of choosing effective passwords cannot be over-stressed. Easy-to-crack passwords can be the weak link that compromises the security of an entire network or site.

There are password-cracking programs available for Windows NT. These programs can be used by a system administrator to determine how susceptible users' passwords are to program-based attacks (although they can obviously also be put to more nefarious purposes). They include:

- Midwestern Commerce's **ScanNT** program, a commercial password-cracking package.

- The freely available **Crack** facility (which originated on UNIX systems).

- The freely available **PwDump** utility, which can display the encoded (hashed) passwords from a local or remote Windows NT system. For example:

  ```
  Administrator:500:FB5F514FCC69FA43AAD3B435B51404EE:...:Sys Admin,
  Built-in account for administering the computer/domain::
  Guest:501:NO PASSWORD********************:...:Guest Account,
  Built-in account for guest access to the computer/domain::
  Chavez:1017:A7EE2C19007ED676FF17365FAF1FFE89:...:Rachel Chavez:
  \\pele\homes\Chavez:
  ...
  ```

  Despite the tantalizing second entry in this example, this utility is not useful for looking for blank passwords because the "NO PASSWORD" string appears only when an account has never been assigned any password.[*]

---

[*] One useful side effect of running **PwDump** is a list of numeric user IDs.

The existence of utilities like **PwDump** underlines the need for properly securing the user account databases. Even encoded passwords can constitute security risks in a Windows NT environment, because of the way the operating system validates passwords over the network. The process proceeds according to a challenge/ response scheme:

1. The server sends a *nonce* (random nonsense) message to the client.

2. The client encrypts the nonce and user account name using the encoded password and sends the result and the clear text username back to the server.

3. The server validates the client's response, again using the encoded user password.

In theory, such network transactions are not as subject to spoofing as some of the alternatives. However, they are still subject to session hijacking: the bad guy sends a forged challenge to the server and then waits for a real request by the same user; when he gets it, he sends a challenge to the user and intercepts the response, which he can send on to the server (this sort of attack is known as a "man in the middle" attack). If the bad guy has the hashed passwords for various user accounts, then he does not even have to wait for a legitimate network request by a real user, because he can impersonate the user immediately.

WARNING   Most Telnet and FTP facilities generally transmit clear text passwords across the network and accordingly present a security risk if the corresponding packets are viewed ("sniffed") by bad guys.

Renaming the administrator account

The consequences of a poorly chosen password for an administrative account are even more serious than those for normal user accounts. Once such an account has been compromised, the integrity of every system to which the account has access is suspect.

One piece of advice that is frequently repeated is that the name of the *Administrator* account ought to be changed in order to make it harder for the bad guys to know where to focus their attack. While doing so might have some minor benefit in this respect, do not let it lull you into a false sense of security. As the Red Button bug makes clear, it's easy to find out the name of a renamed administrator account. In some circumstances, merely running the **nbtstat** command reveals it. I'll repeat my previous advice regarding securing administrative accounts:

• Ensure that all administrative accounts have secure passwords. Consider using passwords of ten characters or more.

- Create individual accounts for multiple system administrators (copying *Administrator* as needed).

- Use an unprivileged (or less privileged) account for nonadministrative work.

Smart cards

There are other approaches to user authentication, aside from passwords. Instead of supplying something she knows at login time (her password), a user can also be validated based on something she is, that is, some unique and unchanging physical characteristic, such a fingerprint or retina image. *Biometric* devices validate a person's identity in this way. They are commonly used to protect entrances to secure installations or areas, but are seldom used solely to authenticate users on a computer system.

A third approach is to validate the user is based upon *something she has.* That something, known generically as a *token,* can in the abstract be as simple as a photo ID badge. In the context of login authentication, *smart cards* are what is used most often. Smart cards range from more or less credit-card size to about the same size as a small calculator, and like a calculator they generally have a keypad and an LED display in which a number appears. Users are required to enter a number from the display in addition to their normal password when they log in to a protected computer.

Most smart cards require the user to enter a personal identification number (PIN) before the card will operate, to provide some protection if the card is lost or stolen. (Smart cards are also often designed to stop working if anyone tries take them apart or otherwise gain access to their protected memory.)

After that point, smart cards can work in several different ways. In the most common mode of operation, the user is presented with a number when he tries to log in, known as a *challenge.* He types that number into his smart card, and then types the number it displays, the *response,* into the computer. The challenge and response values are generated cryptographically.

Under another scheme, the number to give the computer appears automatically after the proper PIN is entered. In this case, the card is synchronized with software running on the target computer; the most elaborate cards of this type can be synchronized with multiple hosts and can also operate in challenge/response mode in order to access still other computers. A second variation on this theme are cards that automatically generate new numeric passwords as often as every 60 seconds. Whatever the details of how they are generated, numeric passwords generated without an explicit challenge may only be used once.

Smart cards provide an effective and relatively low cost means of substantially increasing login authentication effectiveness. While they do not replace well-chosen user passwords, the combination of the two can go a long way toward securing a computer system against user-account-based attacks. See the *Computer Security Products Buyer's Guide* in Appendix B for information about smart card vendors.

Search Path Issues

Search paths provide a convenient way of specifying locations of command executables, but they simultaneously raise a serious security issue. The danger inherent is search paths is that if they are not set up properly, an unscrupulous user may be able to substitute her own executable for the real one corresponding to a Windows NT command or utility. Any user who runs the substituted file will perform whatever actions the malefactor has chosen. Taking these steps will minimize the risk of such trojan horse substitutions:

- Directory order within a search path is important. More specifically, make sure system directories come first within a search path.

- Directories where commands are located should not be writeable by everyone. System directories should not be writeable by anyone other than administrators. Similarly, no user-specific directories in search paths should be writeable by anyone other than that user. (As we'll see, the out-of-the-box Windows NT configuration fails to meet this criterion in several ways.)

- Directories where users commonly work (and make their current directory) should be checked regularly for suspicious executable files. This is necessary because files in the current directory are used before those in the directories in the search path.

As always, take extra care with *Administrator*'s search path since the consequences of a security breach with that account are so severe.

Filesystem Issues

We discussed access control lists at some length in Chapter 6. As we noted, ACLs are the primary mechanism for protecting files and directories from unauthorized access and modification. Accordingly, improperly set up ACLs can seriously compromise system security. In general, be cautious in granting access to files and directories; I try to err on the side of caution rather than convenience.

Should you get rid of Everyone?

The entries for *Everyone* in ACLs require special attention. For example, the Red Button bug we looked at earlier takes advantage of system access granted to *Everyone* as part of its strategy. Based upon concerns like this, a strong argument can be made that the existence or use of *Everyone* in permissions is fundamentally a bad idea: that it is simply too broad a classification and will inevitably result in unforeseen side effects as it interacts with all of the complexity of the Windows NT environment.

You have three choices for addressing the issues raised by the existence of *Everyone* within the installed file permissions on Windows NT systems:

- Examine the entries for *Everyone* in all of the filesystem's ACLs and modify (or eliminate) them to remove any unnecessary security holes.

- Replace the *Everyone* group by the new built-in group *Authenticated Users* (added in a hot fix to Service Pack 2 and in Service Pack 3), which corresponds to all users who have been authenticated by the system by presenting a valid username and password. Modify all ACLs to use the new group (again removing unnecessary access as you do so).

- Create a new group having all of the users in the domain as its members. This group will then function as an explicit *Everyone* group. It can be set up in a couple of ways:

    — As a global group to which you add each user as his account is created.

    — As a local group whose members are all of the global groups in which users are normally placed. In this case, you modify the group only when you create a new global group (which usually happens much less frequently than adding a new user).

    Once the group is defined, you would again replace the entries for *Everyone* in all ACLs with ones for the new group, removing unnecessary access as you do so.

    You can also create multiple groups of this type if there is more than one sort of general user from a security perspective within your environment.

If you decide to replace *Everyone* within ACLs, you will also want to do so in share permissions, printer permissions, and other security access contexts.

WARNING   The *Interactive* and *Network* built-in groups can pose some of the same problems as *Everyone*.

Important files and directories to protect

As installed, the Windows NT filesystem is far from secure. Random users have write access to important files and directories. Table 10-1 lists important directories and files whose ownership and permissions may require modification, depending on the needs of your site; it assumes that the Windows NT operating system is installed in *C:\WinNT.* This information assumes that traverse checking is disabled (as is the default).

Table 10-1. Important Files and Directories to Secure

Item	Permission Recommendations for *Everyone*
Directories	
C:	List permission is most appropriate if you don't want users to automatically inherit access to subsequently created top-level subdirectories.
C:\WinNT	**Read** permission is usually sufficient for *%SystemRoot%* and most of its subdirectories (but exceptions are noted below).
C:\WinNT\System32	**Read** permission is usually sufficient for this important directory as well (**Change** is the default setting).
C:\WinNT\System32\Config	Ordinary users need **List** access, at most, to this directory, and an argument can be made for eliminating access altogether.
C:\WinNT\System32\Spool\Printers	**Change** access is required for users to submit and manipulate their own print jobs. This may be accomplished via the *Creator Owner* ACE. In some circumstances, denying users read access to other users' spool files is necessary, so *Everyone* should have either **Read** or **List** access to the directory accordingly.
C:\WinNT\System *C:\WinNT\PIF*	Once again, **Read** permission is usually sufficient for these Windows-related subdirectories.
C:\WinNT\Repair	This subdirectory holds the files used to create an Emergency Repair Diskette, including copies of the user accounts database, which holds the encoded passwords. When Windows NT is first installed, only the *Administrator* password is present in this copy, but if you update the ERD information, then all user account information is present. Ordinary users should not have any access to this directory and its file (i.e., no entry in the ACL).
C:\WinNT\Profiles	Users need **Add** and **Read** permission to this directory if mandatory, presetup profiles are not in use (so that a subdirectory for their profile can be created after their first login). However, you should reduce this if you are using mandatory profiles so that users cannot add to or modify the contents of this directory.
C:\WinNT\Profiles\All Users *C:\WinNT\Profiles\Default User*	Users need **Read** access to these items, but should not be able to make modifications anywhere within these subdirectory trees.

Table 10-1. Important Files and Directories to Secure (continued)

Item	Permission Recommendations for *Everyone*
C:\WinNT\Profiles\Administrator	Ordinary users shouldn't have access to the *Administrator's* user profile.
other subdirectories of *C:\WinNT\Profiles*	Each user requires **Full Control** to his or her own user profile subdirectory tree, but normally no other ordinary user should have any access to someone else's user profile tree.
C:\Temp	All users need to be able to create and delete files within this directory, since it is used as a scratch directory by many application programs, and thus will need at least **RWX** access to the directory. *Creator Owner* needs **Change** or **Full Control** access so that users can remove the files they create.
Other directories holding executable files	Ordinary users need **List** or **Read** access to these directories, but must not have the ability to modify them or any of the files within them.
User home directories	Each user needs to have **RWXO** access to his home directory, at a minimum. This level of access prevents users from changing the permissions on their home directory (and potentially granting access to people they shouldn't) and from deleting it; less restrictive access may also be appropriate in some environments. The directory also needs a *Creator Owner,* specifying **Change** or **Full Control**, so that users may add files and subdirectories.
Groups and Types of Files	
C:.**	Ordinary users should not be able to modify or delete any of the system files stored in the root directory of the system partition. In some environments, even **Read** access to these files can be an unacceptable security risk.
C:\WinNT*.Exe *C:\WinNT\System32*.DLL* *C:\WinNT\System32*.Exe*	Users need **Read** access to these files to run commands and programs, but they should not have write access to any of them. A malevolent user with write access to a system executable or shared library would be able to substitute a different, nefarious program for the real one.
C:\WinNT\System*.Drv *C:\WinNT\System*.DLL*	Once again, ordinary users should have **Read** access to these files, but not write access.

You should treat the information in Table 10-1 as a starting list of items to check and monitor on the systems at your site. Be aware that it is not comprehensive, and that there are probably other important directories at your site.

The following strategy makes assigning permissions to the Windows NT system files straightforward and efficient:

- Decide on the minimum level of access. Then, apply this level to the *%System-Root%* directory and propagate these settings throughout the entire tree.

- Modify files and subdirectories for which you have decided on different permissions after the base-level permissions are set, adding, modifying, or removing ACEs from their ACLs as appropriate.

For example, the following commands implement some of these recommendations using the ACL-related utilities we discussed in Chapter 6:

```
C:\> irevoke -r Everyone:all,all %systemroot%
C:\> igrant -r -replace Everybody:rx,rx %systemroot%\system32
C:\> igrant -r -replace Everybody:rwxd,rwxd ^
        %systemroot%\system32\spool\printers
C:\> irevoke Everybody:all,all %systemroot%\repair
 ...
```

These commands remove the *Everyone* entries from all ACLs for the system directories and then add ACEs for a group named *Everybody* to several of them. Once you have decided on the permissions you want to use at your site, it is easy to create a script containing the appropriate commands, which can be run on every system and on new systems as they are installed.

You can use the **DumpACL** utility to look for permissions problems within the filesystem. Using its command-line mode can be helpful in this regard. For example, the following commands produce a report on the entire filesystem, storing it in the file *ACLs.Txt*, and then search the resulting data for entries where *Everyone* has **Full Control** access:

```
C:\> dumpacl /rpt=dir=c:\winnt /outfile=acls.txt /saveas=tsv
Wait for the command to finish (it runs in the background).
C:\> type acls.txt | grep Everyone | grep all
c:\winnt\system32\drivers\etc\hosts        Everyone          all
```

The first command prepares a report on the *C:\WinNT* subtree, saving it to the specified file in tab-separated value format (note that **DumpACL** does not have the option of sending its reports to standard output). The second command uses the **grep** string search command, included in the POSIX utilities in the Resource Kit. These commands reveal that the *Hosts* file on this system has inappropriate permissions.

Registry Key Ownership and Permissions

Like files and directories, registry keys have owners and permission settings. As you would expect, the same sorts of security issues arise with them. Note that ownership and permissions are set at the registry key level (and not on individual values or settings).

WARNING   Consider the consequences carefully before you make modifications
to registry key ownership and permissions. Limiting access may result in unintended side effects and loss of normal system functionality. Before you make changes, test them on a nonproduction system.

Table 10-2 lists the defined access permissions for registry keys.

Table 10-2. Registry Key Permissions

Access Permission	Effect
Full Control	Shorthand for all permissions
Query Value	Determine a key's current setting
Set Value	Modify a key's current setting
Create Subkey	Add a subkey to a key
Enumerate Subkey	View the subkey tree under a key
Notify	Enable auditing of changes to a key
Create Link	Create link to this location within the registry
Delete	Remove the key
Write DAC	Modify the permissions settings for a key
Write Owner	Take ownership of a key
Read Control	View a key's security settings

There are two defined permission sets for registry keys:

Read

Corresponding to the combination of **Query Value**, **Enumerate Subkeys**,
Notify, and **Read Control**. This permission set thus allows users to search and
query the registry but not to modify anything within it.

Full Control

Corresponding to all available permissions.

The **Security►Permissions...** menu path in the Registry Editor may be used to
view and modify registry key permissions. An example is illustrated in Figure 10-2.

The **Registry Key Permissions** dialog box is similar to the one used to set ACLs. Its
Type of Access field specifies the access allowed for the selected user or group,
one of **Read**, **Full Control**, and **Special Access** (the latter allows you to assign arbitrary sets of basic permissions). The **Add...** and **Remove** buttons enable you to
add or delete entries as usual.

The *Everyone* group poses the same sort of security risks within the registry as it
does within the filesystem, and you have the same options regarding it: tightening

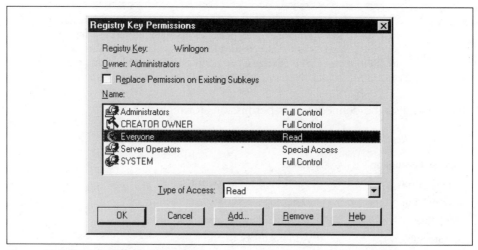

Figure 10-2. Registry key permissions

the current settings or replacing it with *Authenticated Users* or a new group of your own construction. Keys that require special attention are ones whose values specify the location of executable files or shared libraries (DLLs).

The **DumpACL** utility can also be used to search for potential security problems among the registry key permissions via its registry permissions reporting mode (obtained using its **Report►Dump Permissions for Registry...** menu path during an interactive session). The **Search►Filter...** menu path may be used to display only report entries matching certain desired criteria. For example, the dialog box settings in Figure 10-3 may be used to limit the display to entries for which group *Everyone* can modify the current setting or delete the key.

Remote registry access

Previous versions of Windows NT allowed any user to access the registry on a remote system. This proved to be an unacceptable security practice, so under version 4.0, by default only administrators are allowed to do so.

Remote access to the registry is controlled by the HKEY_LOCAL_MACHINE\ System\CurrentControlSet\Control\SecurePipeServers\winreg registry key.* The permissions on this key specify users who are allowed to access the registry remotely. The default permissions assign **Full Control** to *Administrators* and contain no entries for other users or groups. You can add other items to these

---

* If this key doesn't exist, you can create it. In addition, create a value named Description (type REG_ SZ), and set it to "Registry Server" (include the space).

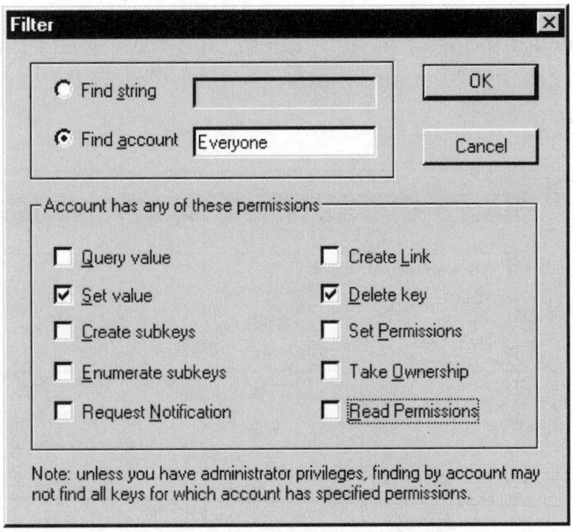

Figure 10-3. Filtering DumpACL's Registry permissions report

permissions as needed for system services (for example, the print spooler or replicator services) or system administration requirements at your site.

The AllowedPaths subkey of the winreg key is used to specify registry locations for which these restrictions do not apply.

Disabling anonymous registry access

You can choose to disable registry access by anonymous connections.* This is accomplished by adding the RestrictAnonymous value to the HKEY_LOCAL_MACHINE\System\CurrentControlSet\Control\Lsa registry key (type REG_DWORD) and setting it to 1.

Disabling anonymous registry access results in the loss of some functionality. For example, users from other (untrusted) domains will not be able to retrieve lists of users for your domain (for example, when adding entries to an ACL). See article Q143474 in the Knowledge Base for more information.

TCP/IP Port Filtering

The Windows NT implementation of TCP/IP networking includes a limited facility for restricting incoming network access by port and protocol. This facility is part

---

* The ability to do so was introduced as the "sec-fix" hot fix to Service Pack 2 and is included in Service Pack 3 (and later).

of the TCP/IP protocol **Properties** (accessed via the **Protocols** tab of the **Network** control panel applet). Once the **Microsoft TCP/IP Properties** dialog box is open, click the **Advanced** button on its **IP Address**, and then select the **Enable Security** check box and click its **Configure** button to reach the **TCP/IP Security** dialog box (illustrated in Figure 10-4).

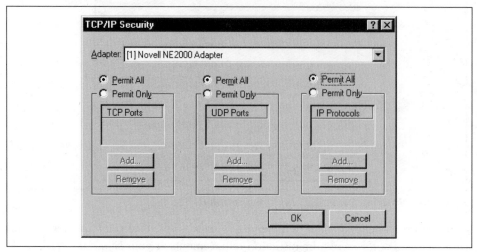

Figure 10-4. TCP/IP port filtering

This facility is vaguely similar to the well-known UNIX TCP **Wrappers** package, but it is considerably less sophisticated. As the figure makes clear, the dialog box provides only the ability to specify a list of allowed ports or protocols. If you decide to use this feature, consult a list of well-known TCP/IP ports, and enter all of those required by your system into the appropriate list boxes.

NOTE   Usually, port filtering facilities allow you to specify a list of items for which network access will be denied, since this list is generally much shorter; such an approach also eliminates the risk of accidentally disabling a service you intended to keep because you forgot to include a required port or protocol. The designer of this dialog box obviously never had to use it.

Viruses

Viruses are programs that insert themselves into other programs, often legitimate ones, producing noxious side-effects when their host program is later executed. Computer viruses are a much greater issue in microcomputer environments than in other computing environments. Windows NT inherits that legacy.

There are currently several types of viruses of which you need to be aware:

Master Boot Record viruses
Programs that infect the MBR, potentially rendering a system unbootable.

DOS and 16-bit Windows viruses
The most prevalent type; Windows NT systems are susceptible to many of them.

Macro viruses
These viruses infect documents produced by application programs, such as word processors and spreadsheets.

Windows NT-specific viruses
As of this writing, no viruses that specifically target Windows NT systems are known, but it is just a matter of time until someone creates one. The often-repeated statement that the Windows NT operating system is immune to viruses is a myth.

Scanning the system for viruses is an important part of system security maintenance. The following recommendations ensures that the process is as effective as possible:

- Use Windows NT-native virus checking software (in other words, packages specifically designed for the Windows NT environment).

- Subscribe to a virus update service so that your software can address new threats as they are uncovered.

- Monitor security-related mailing lists for news about viruses and other security issues.

- Obtain multiple virus checking programs. This is often a good idea, because they have different strengths and weaknesses. It is not unusual for different programs to perform differently when attempting to detect and repair the same virus.

There are many Windows NT virus checking packages, some of which can be used to scan an entire local area network. Some of the most popular are Inoc-uLAN (Cheyenne), McAfee Anti-Virus (McAfee), the antivirus components of the Norton NT Tools (Symantec), and Carmel Software Engineering's NTAV package. See Appendix B for details.

Common sense advice for securing software downloaded from the Web

Adhering to the following procedures will help minimize the risk of virus infections and other risks from software obtained from the Web:

- When possible, build the application from source code you have reviewed.

- Scan incoming software for viruses every time.

- Use an isolated system to test the new software.

- Install the software as an unprivileged user.

- Test the software as an unprivileged user.

- Install services as an unprivileged user, if possible. In any case, always create a new user account with the minimum privileges to run the service.

Windows NT System Policies

System policies provide another mechanism for specifying various aspects of a user's work environment. System policies are a more powerful and effective way than user profiles to limit what a user can see and do from his desktop and access within a system. As such, they are more appropriate for implementing and enforcing a security policy.

There is always a system policy in effect, even if you never examine or modify it. You can view the current settings and create customized system policies using the System Policy Editor administrative tool (also accessible via the **PolEdit** command included in the Resource Kit). Its main window is illustrated in Figure 10-5.

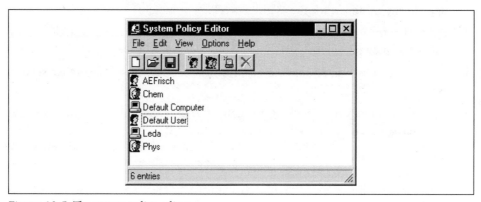

Figure 10-5. The system policy editor

Items on the utility's **File** menu are used to specify the system policy to be examined and modified:

Open Registry

View or modify the system policy inherent in the local system registry. Use this only when you do not want to use the system policy on a different system or apply it to anyone other than local interactive users.

Open Policy...

View or modify a system policy stored in a file.

New Policy

Create a new system policy (to be stored in a file).

Connect...

Specify the host whose system policies you want to modify.

Each of the icons in the System Policy Editor's main window represents a set of registry settings controlling system access and user behavior. The **Default Computer** and **Default User** icons apply to general computers and users (respectively) throughout the scope of the system policy. Other icons that may be present represent settings that apply to specific users, groups, and computers. Settings can be copied by cutting and pasting them from one icon to another.

If more than one set applies to a given user, contradictions among them are resolved as follows. Settings in a user-specific set always take precedence over all settings for groups. However, if a user has no named set applying to her, but is a member of more than one group for which there are specific settings, settings are applied according to the order specified via the **Options➤Group Priority...** menu item (see Figure 10-6).

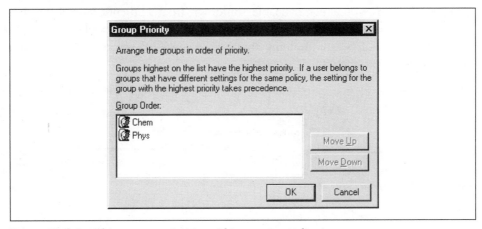

Figure 10-6. Specifying group priorities within a system policy

Double-clicking on an icon in the main window of the System Policy Editor reveals a series of setting options arranged in a hierarchical manner under several top-level categories. Figure 10-7 illustrates the defined categories for computer (left dialog box) and user/group sets.

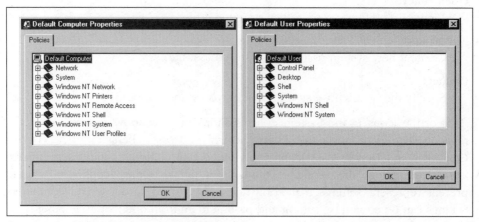

Figure 10-7. Top-level system policy categories

Expanding an individual category reveals a list of settings (or subcategories). When a setting is selected, additional information and fields may appear in the lower area within the dialog box.

Figure 10-8 illustrates how individual settings appear within the System Policy Editor, depending on their state. Settings that have never been specified appear dimmed (grayed-out), like the **Enable shutdown from Authentication dialog box** setting in the example. Settings that are turned on appear with a checked box to the left of their label, and items that are turned off appear with a blank (unchecked) box to the left of their label.

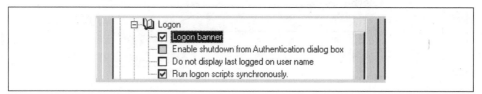

Figure 10-8. User policy setting states

The difference between an unused setting and a disabled setting is important. Unused settings have no effect on system access or behavior. However, cleared check boxes always have some effect. For example, the cleared check box in Figure 10-8 means that the name of the last logged-in user *will* be displayed in the logon dialog box. Similarly, if the check box for the Logon banner settings was unchecked, then no prelogin message would be displayed (even if one was defined). Checked and unchecked settings override those in the system registry, while unused ones default to the current registry setting.

NOTE	Successive clicks within the same check box cycle between the checked, unchecked, and dimmed settings.

Important User Policy Settings

There are a multitude of system policy settings that apply to individuals or groups of users. Table 10-3 lists the most important.

Table 10-3. Important User-Specific System Policy Settings

Setting	What It Prevents Users from Doing
Control Panel▶Display▶Restrict display	
Deny access to display icon	Modifying any aspect of display via its control panel applet
Hide **Screen Saver** tab	Disabling or reconfiguring the screen saver (e.g., removing password protection)
Desktop	
Wallpaper	Displaying an unacceptable image on the desktop
Shell▶Restrictions	
Remove **Run** command from **Start** menu	Running commands, except by double-clicking on icons (although the icon for a DOS prompt also needs to be removed)
Remove folders from **Settings** on **Start** menu	Accessing the **Control Panel** and **Printers** folders (directly)
Remove **Taskbar** from **Settings** on **Start** menu	Adding items to the **Start** menu and customizing the task bar via this facility
Remove **Find** command from **Start** menu	Searching for files
Hide drives in **My Computer**	Viewing the available drives on the computer
Hide **Network Neighborhood**	Browsing the local network via this icon
No **Entire Network** in **Network Neighborhood**	Viewing subnets beyond the local network via the **Network Neighborhood** icon
Hide all items on desktop	Accessing any of the usual desktop icons and their associated facilities
Disable **Shut Down** command	Shutting down or rebooting the computer
Don't save settings at **Exit**	Saving any modifications users make to their user environment during a login session (except in settings like public computer labs, it is rather mean to allow users to make modifications but not to save them)
Windows NT Shell▶Restrictions	
Only use approved shell extensions	Using unapproved shell extensions

Table 10-3. Important User-Specific System Policy Settings (continued)

Setting	What It Prevents Users from Doing
Disable context menus for the taskbar	Using the taskbar's context menu
Remove common program groups from **Start** menu	Using items stored in the common program groups
Remove **Map Network Drive** and **Disconnect Network Drive** options	Creating or removing mappings of network shares to local drive letters
Windows NT System	
Parse *Autoexec.Bat*	Deciding whether or not the *AutoExec.Bat* file is parsed for PATH commands
Run logon scripts synchronously	Running commands before their login script has finished executing
Disable **Task Manager**	Viewing or terminating processes via the **Task Manager**
Show welcome tips at logon	Deciding whether or not the Welcome Tips facility runs automatically at login

The following items under the **System►Restrictions** category are not as useful as they might seem at first:

Disable Registry editing tools
> Checking this setting prevents users from running the copy of **RegEdt32** on the local system. However, it won't prevent anyone from running a copy on a Windows NT distribution CD or a copy of the executable that has been given a different name.

Run only allowed Windows applications
> This setting lets you specify a list of acceptable executable files which the corresponding users are allowed to run. However, *any* file having one of these names may be run, so the names of forbidden programs may simply be changed to acceptable names.

Important Computer Policy Settings

Table 10-4 lists the most important computer policy settings, again arranged in groups under the corresponding category path.

Table 10-4. Important Computer-Specific System Policy Settings

Setting	Effect
System►Run	
Run	Specifies items to run at login time
Windows NT Network►Sharing	
Create hidden drive shares	Prevents users from creating hidden shares (via the terminal $ in the share name)

Table 10-4. Important Computer-Specific System Policy Settings (continued)

Setting	Effect
Windows NT Printers	
Scheduler priority	Specifies the relative priority of the print scheduler with respect to other system processes
Windows NT System►Logon	
Logon banner	Specifies the use and contents of a system message preceding the login dialog box
Enable shutdown from **Authentication** dialog box	Specifies whether the **Shut Down...** button appears in the login dialog box
Do not display last logged on user name	Determines whether the **User name** field is prefilled in the login dialog box
Run login scripts synchronously	If enabled, user login scripts must complete executing before users are given access to the system

Applying a System Policy to Multiple Systems

The **Network►System policies update** setting of a system policy (including that for the local registry) specifies where the system policy information for a system is located. Aside from strictly local system policies, there are two methods for obtaining a system policy from a remote server:

- In automatic mode, the system policy must be saved in a file named *NTConfig.Pol*, which is stored in and available from the *Netlogon* share from the primary domain controller. The settings for this update method are illustrated in Figure 10-9.

  The **Load balancing** check box specifies whether or not to consult backup domain controllers, as well as the PDC, when the system attempts to obtain the system policy file (checked means that BDCs are contacted in an effort to distribute the network load). The directory replication facility can be used to automatically copy system policy files to the BDCs (see Chapter 12).

  By default, Windows NT systems are set for automatic system policy updates without load balancing.

- Manual updates may be made from any network-accessible file. Figure 10-10 illustrates the setting that specifies a custom system policy file for the local system, *MrgPol.Pol*, residing in the *Policy* share on system *vala*.

  The **Display error messages** field specifies whether an error message should be displayed to a user if the system policy file is unavailable when he logs in (in this case, the settings from the most recent login session by any user on that system are used).

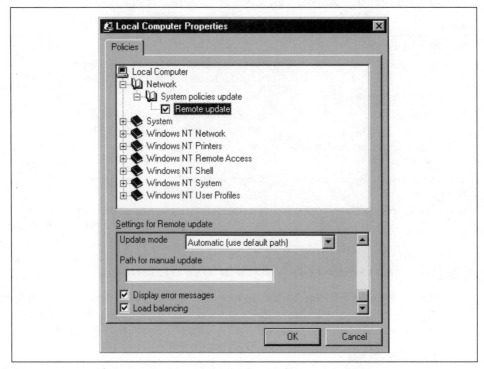

Figure 10-9. Specifying an automatic system policy update

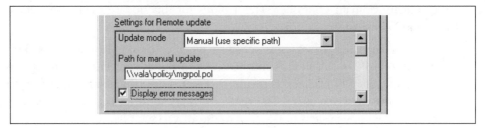

Figure 10-10. Specifying a manual system policy update

In general, system policy files should be owned and writeable only by administrators. Ordinary users will need **Read** access to them.

User Rights

In addition to the access permissions on files and other system resources and the constraints imposed by any system policy in effect, permitted and forbidden user actions are also defined by *user rights*. These rights apply to some specific action or class of action within the system or domain as a whole, regardless of the specific object toward which the action is directed (if any).

WARNING   While user rights control many sorts of user actions within a system or domain, they aren't comprehensive or definitive in all cases. In particular, be aware that administrators—members of the *Administrators* group—can always perform certain activities essential to their job, regardless of user rights settings.

User rights may be viewed and modified from the User Manager administrative tools via their **Policies►User Rights** menu path. Figure 10-11 shows the resulting dialog box.

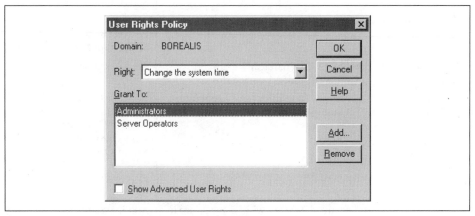

Figure 10-11. Viewing and assigning user rights

The **User Rights Policy** dialog box displays the holders of a specific user right (indicated in the **Right** menu). The **Grant To** area lists the users and groups to whom this right has been assigned.

User rights are divided into *basic* and *advanced* user rights, based primarily on the likelihood of a right's needing to be granted to users in addition to those who hold it by default (where advanced rights are primarily intended for application programs and will be assigned manually only rarely).

Table 10-5 describes all of the defined user rights, along with the groups to which they are assigned by default. Remember that the *Power Users* group is found only on workstations and the *Server Operators* and *Print Operators* groups are found only on servers.

Table 10-5. Windows NT User Rights

User Right	If You Have This Right, Then You Are Able to ...	Groups Holding by Default
Basic User Rights		
Access this computer from the network	Use shared resources via the network	Everyone, Administrators, Power Users
Add workstations to domain	Define a system as part of the domain	None
Backup files and directories	Access or modify any file or directory on the system, regardless of its ACL setting	Administrators, Backup Operators, Server Operators
Change the system time	Modify the time setting of the system's *internal* clock	Administrators, Power Users, Server Operators
Force shutdown from a remote system	Shut down a remote server *(not implemented)*	Administrators, Power Users, Server Operators
Load and unload device drivers	Dynamically load and unload device drivers	Administrators
Log on locally	Log in to the system interactively	Account Operators, Administrators, Backup Operators, Print Operators, Server Operators Everyone (on workstations)
Manage auditing and security log	Specify which objects are to be audited when auditing is enabled (which must be done by an administrator)	Administrators
Restore files and directories	Access or modify any file or directory on the system, regardless of its ACL setting	Administrators, Backup Operators
Shut down the system	Shut down the local system (when logged-in interactively)	Administrators, Server Operators Everyone (on workstations)
Take ownership of files or other objects	Assume ownership of files, directories, and other file-system objects, regardless of their access permissions	Administrators
Advanced User Rights		
Act as part of the operating system	Execute with operating system–level system access	None

Table 10-5. Windows NT User Rights (continued)

User Right	If You Have This Right, Then You Are Able to ...	Groups Holding by Default
Bypass traverse checking	Ignore directory permissions when accessing a file by full pathname	Everyone
Create a pagefile	Create and modify paging files	Administrators
Create a token object	Create a token object	None
Create permanent shared objects	Create shared operating system–level objects (not filesystem shares)	None
Debug programs	Execute with certain system debug bits set	Administrators
Generate security audits	Generate security audits	None
Increase quotas	Modify resource quotas *(not implemented)*	Administrators
Increase scheduling priority	Modify a process's execution priority upward	Administrators, Power Users
Lock pages in memory	Force memory pages to remain resident in real memory	None
Log on as a batch job	Register with the system as a batch job (designed for applications)	None
Log on as a service	Register with the system as a service (designed for applications)	None
Modify firmware environment values	Change firmware parameter values (hardware-dependent)	Administrators
Profile single process	Measure performance data for a single process *(not implemented)*	Administrators, Power Users
Profile system performance	Measure performance data systemwide	Administrators
Replace a process-level token	Adjust aspects of a process's environment	None

As with file access permissions, user rights are best assigned to groups rather than to individual users, and additional rights should be granted sparingly and with care.

The freely available utility **Grant.Exe** (written by Andreas Hansson) allows you to assign user rights from the command line.

Security Across Domains: Trust

Although a single domain can theoretically support tens of thousands of users, there are a variety of reasons that you might want to subdivide even a much smaller domain:

For security reasons
> Separate domains provide natural security boundaries between groups of users and their respective data and resources.

For performance reasons
> Although a single domain can support a large number of users, subdividing it sometimes results in improved performance.

To divide administrative responsibilities
> Creating multiple domains instead of a single one can allow administrative duties to be split among different members of the administrative staff in a straightforward manner.

In general, users can only access files and other shared resources from domains in which they have a valid user account (unless they are accessible to *Everyone*). However, the resources within a given domain can be made available to authenticated users from a specified other domain via a mechanism known as *trust*.

Trust is a one-way relationship between two domains in which the trusting domain agrees to recognize users and groups from the trusted domain just as it does its own. Users and global groups from a trusted domain can be assigned user rights, file and directory permissions, share permissions, and printer permissions, and can be members of local groups in the trusting domain. The trusting domain is also known as a *resource domain* (since it makes its resources available to users from the other domain), and the trusted domain is also known as an *account domain* (since it is the location of the user accounts for the trusted foreign users).

Trust is not a reciprocal relationship. The fact that domain A trusts domain B does not mean that domain B trusts domain A; if the latter relationship is desired as well, it must be set up explicitly and separately.

The trust relationships among multiple domains are often organized in some sort of hierarchical structure. The simplest such organization consists of a central account domain—the *master domain*—with one or more satellite resource domains (often referred to as the *single master domain model*). In this scheme, the set of user accounts and groups from the master domain is made available to the subordinate domains (but not vice versa). All user accounts are defined in the master domain, allowing for centralized user administration, and shared resources are located in the satellite domains.

Larger user communities may employ multiple master account domains, each with a set of associated satellite resource domains (the so-called *multiple master domain mode*). Once again, user accounts are defined and managed only in the master domains, and shared resources are located and managed in the resource domains. Reciprocal trust relationships are set up between each pair of master domains, effectively creating a single metadomain, which can support large numbers of users. Under this scheme, trust flows outward from the master domains, and trust relationships are not set up between individual resource domains. Despite its separate name, this strategy is really just an extension of the single master domain model to a large number of user accounts.

Figure 10-12 illustrates some of the possible trust relationships that may be set up among the various domains within an organization. The account domain *Borealis* has three subordinate resource domains, illustrating the single master domain model. Similarly, the account domains *Inferno, Purgatorio,* and *Paradiso* illustrate the multiple master domain model: they have two-way trust relationship set up among all three pairs of domains, and each has a one-way trust relationship defined for each of the three resource domains. Access rights flow in the opposite direction to trust.

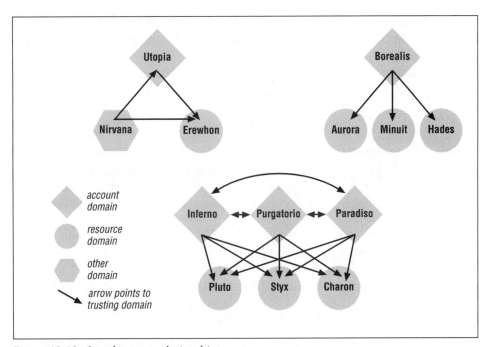

Figure 10-12. Complex trust relationships

The resource domain *Erewhon* trusts its account domain *Utopia*. However, the relationship between *Utopia* and *Erewhon* and the domain *Nirvana* is different.

Trust flows in the opposite direction in this case, meaning that *Utopia* trusts *Nirvana* but not vice versa. Thus, *Nirvana's* users may be granted access to resources in *Utopia* and *Erewhon*, but its own resources and data remain inaccessible to foreign users. (In many cases, the trust relationship to *Utopia* won't be needed if all the resources required by *Nirvana's* users are located in the resource domain *Erewhon.*)

As with reciprocal trust, transitive trust is not automatic: the fact that domain A trusts domain B and domain B trusts domain C does not mean that domain A trusts domain C. If this latter trust relationship is desired, it must be set up explicitly.

The previous statement is far more significant from an administrative point of view than it is from a security viewpoint. Trust just makes it easy for users from one domain to use the resources in another domain, and a lack of trust does not in itself prevent them from doing so if they know a valid account name and password in the target domain (and sometimes even when they don't, as in the case of anonymous connections). A Windows NT system does not distinguish between access requests from "inside" (originating on a system that is part of the domain) and "outside" of the local domain.

The significance of this fact is that even if the system administrator for a domain has chosen not to set up a trust relationship to another domain, his system's security is nevertheless intimately dependent on the security of any domain with network access to his domain, since if an account within such a domain is successfully attacked, it could be used as the origination point for an attack on his own domain.

Taken to its logical conclusion, this line of reasoning suggests that anytime two systems are connected via a network, their security, to some extent, becomes intertwined. In the end, your system's security may be no better than that of the least-protected system on the network. See Dan Farmer and Wietse Venema's documentation to their *Satan* network scanning facility for a full discussion of implicit transitive trust (listed in Appendix B).

Establishing Trust

Trust relationships are established via the User Manager's **Policies➤Trust Relationships** menu path. Pressing one of the **Add** buttons on the resulting dialog box will bring up one of the two dialog boxes in Figure 10-13.

The **Add Trusting Domain** dialog box is used in the domain that will be granting access to the other domain's users (left illustration in Figure 10-13). The system administrator must enter the name of the domain that will trust her domain and any password into the dialog box. Then, the system administrator of the other

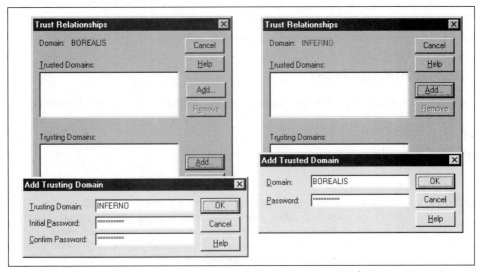

Figure 10-13. Setting up a trust relationship (Inferno trusts Borealis)

domain must add her domain to his list of trusted domains, specifying the same password (right illustration in Figure 10-13).

Trusting domains operate via a hidden user account and a secure communications channel. The initial password set by the system administrator is automatically changed periodically and is never needed again.

Existing trust relationships can be monitored with the **NLMon** utility in the Resource Kit.

Creating a Transdomain Group

In some circumstances, you may want to create a group that contains user accounts from more than one domain. Doing so requires that a two-way trust relationship exists between the two domains. The following is the most administratively efficient method of doing so:

1. Create a global group in each domain that will hold members of the transdomain group from that domain. In some cases, an appropriate group may already exist.

2. Add the appropriate local domain users to the designated group in each domain.

3. Create a local group in each domain, whose only members are the global groups from each domain.

The advantage of this approach is that you only have to set up the transdomain group once. Its membership from each domain can be entirely maintained within that domain by adding or removing users from the domain's global group.

Alternatives to Trust

Matching user accounts for the same user in two or more domains provides an alternative to a full trust relationship when only a few users need access to both domains. The user must enter his password in the remote domain if it differs from the one in his home domain.

NOTE   Once trust is enabled between domains, it's always in effect, even for users already holding matching accounts in the target domain. All requests for access by such users employ the usual mechanism when trust is in effect—requiring communication between domain controllers for the two domains—and the matching account in the target domain is ignored.

Security Auditing

We examined the Event Viewer administrative tool in Chapter 1 in the context of system error messages. This same utility can also be used to display security-related messages generated by the Windows NT auditing subsystem.

A security auditing facility is a required part of the U.S. government C2 and higher security levels. On Windows NT systems, security auditing is not enabled by default. Audit policies are set on a per-computer basis via the User Manager administrative tool's **Policies▸Audit...** menu path. System auditing can generate a large amount of data quickly, so you'll need to keep an eye on the size of the auditing log files.

Enabling Security Auditing

The **Audit Policy** dialog box is used to enable general classes of security auditing (see Figure 10-14). Table 10-6 describes the defined audit classes. For each audit class, you can audit successes, failures, or both.

Deciding what to audit can be the trickiest part of setting up the Windows NT security auditing subsystem. Your site's security policy may be of help in identifying which events are of interest to you and therefore ought to be recorded. How you plan to use the data collected by the auditing facility determines in large part, how much data you need to collect.

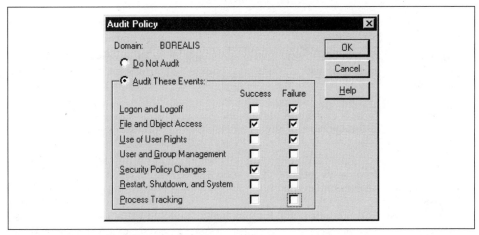

Figure 10-14. Specifying the system security audit policy

If you only want to use the auditing facility to check for suspicious activity on the system, you can limit auditing to a few classes (mostly failures). However, if you want to be prepared to conduct a full investigation of any suspected security-related incident at all times, then you need to collect much more data (since you can't know in advance exactly what will be important). Table 10-6 provides some guidelines as to which audit classes are most appropriate for various purposes.

Table 10-6. Windows NT Security Audit Classes

Audit Class	Description	Minimum Audit Recommendations
Logon and Logoff	Records primary and secondary (network) logins and logouts.	Audit failures. Audit successes to generate data which *may* be useful for after-the-fact security investigations.
File and Object Access	Records access to objects controlled via ACLs and similar permissions (includes printers and shares). You must turn on auditing for files and directories of interest using the **Security** tab of their **Properties**.	Audit all events for files and directories of special interest.
Use of User Rights	Records any action that requires a user right. Note that the **Backup** and **Restore** user rights aren't audited by default; they generate staggering amounts of data each time a backup is performed. If you want to enable auditing of the Backup and Restore rights, change the setting of the FullPrivilegeAuditing value of the HKEY_LOCAL_ MACHINE\System\CurrentCon-trolSet\Control\Lsa registry key to 1.	Audit failures; successes are less interesting than you might think, since most normal activities involve invoking user rights.

Table 10-6. Windows NT Security Audit Classes (continued)

Audit Class	Description	Minimum Audit Recommendations
User and Group Management	Records instances of adding, modifying, or deleting user accounts or groups.	Audit successes and failures, if unauthorized changes to user account data are a concern or threat.
Security Policy Changes	Records changes in the auditing policy or reassignment of any user rights.	Audit successes and failures. Successes are important for this class, since they should occur only rarely.
Restart, Shutdown, and System	Records system booting, shutdown, and other system events.	Audit failures. Audit successes as well if you are interested in tracking this kind of information.
Process Tracking	Records detailed system-level information about processes.	Audit failures, if desired. Audit successes to generate data that may be useful in after-the-fact incident investigations.

The **AuditSet** program from Midwestern Commerce allows you to set the audit policies on multiple computers via a single operation.

Enabling security auditing for files and directories

Turning on auditing for files and directories of interest is accomplished with the **Auditing** button on the **Security** tab of their **Properties** (illustrated in Figure 10-15). You can specify the types of access attempts to be recorded (which correspond to the basic permissions). Be selective when you choose the files and directories for which you want to enable security auditing, limiting them to those for which unauthorized access presents an important security breach (for example, the files in *%SystemRoot%\System32\Config*).

Managing the Security Log

Settings for the security log file are specified in the Event Viewer via its **Log➤Log Settings...** menu path. The resulting dialog box is illustrated in Figure 10-16. Select the Security log in the **Change Settings for** menu, and use the other fields in the dialog box to specify a maximum size for the raw audit log file, as well as the facility's behavior when the log becomes full.

You can clear the security log file via the Event Viewer's **Log➤Clear All Events** menu path. You will have the option of saving the log's current contents to a file when you do so. Somarsoft's **DumpEvt** utility may also be used to extract and save events from the security log and remove them from the raw log file. It has the advantage that it may be executed from a script or via the Schedule service

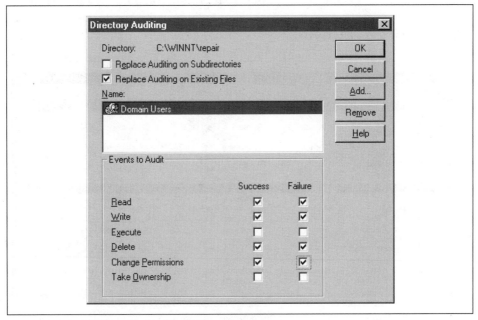

Figure 10-15. Enabling file-level security auditing

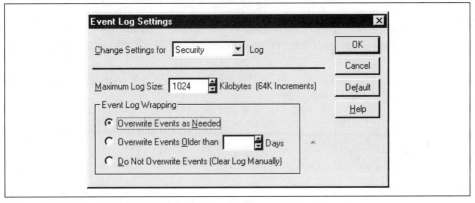

Figure 10-16. Specifying the settings for the security audit log file

for automatic log file maintenance. This topic is discussed in more detail in Chapter 12.

Viewing the Security Log

The Event Viewer's **Log►Security** menu path may be used to view security-related events in that tool's main window. Figure 10-17 shows a typical slice of a security log. Each record holds the data for one event, including its date and time, audit class, event type (a numeric ID), and the user and computer system that generated it. The icon at the far left of each entry indicates whether it is a success event (the key icon) or a failure event (the lock icon).

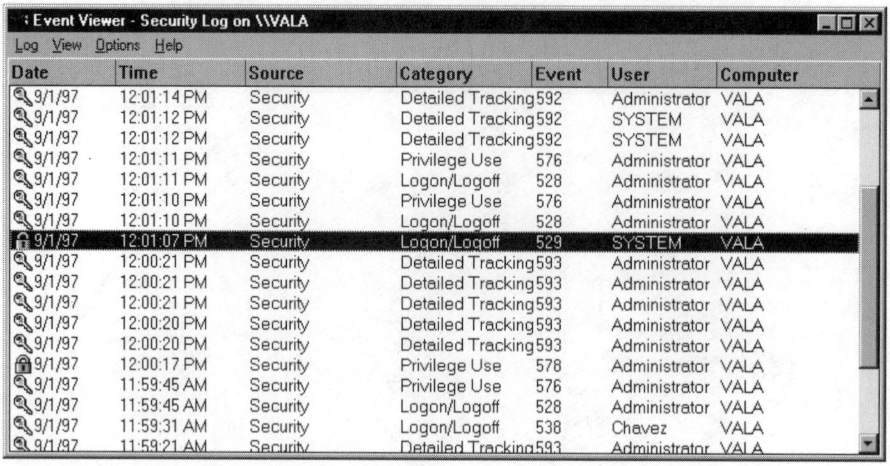

Date	Time	Source	Category	Event	User	Computer
9/1/97	12:01:14 PM	Security	Detailed Tracking	592	Administrator	VALA
9/1/97	12:01:12 PM	Security	Detailed Tracking	592	SYSTEM	VALA
9/1/97	12:01:12 PM	Security	Detailed Tracking	592	SYSTEM	VALA
9/1/97	12:01:11 PM	Security	Privilege Use	576	Administrator	VALA
9/1/97	12:01:11 PM	Security	Logon/Logoff	528	Administrator	VALA
9/1/97	12:01:10 PM	Security	Privilege Use	576	Administrator	VALA
9/1/97	12:01:10 PM	Security	Logon/Logoff	528	Administrator	VALA
9/1/97	12:01:07 PM	Security	Logon/Logoff	529	SYSTEM	VALA
9/1/97	12:00:21 PM	Security	Detailed Tracking	593	Administrator	VALA
9/1/97	12:00:21 PM	Security	Detailed Tracking	593	Administrator	VALA
9/1/97	12:00:21 PM	Security	Detailed Tracking	593	Administrator	VALA
9/1/97	12:00:20 PM	Security	Detailed Tracking	593	Administrator	VALA
9/1/97	12:00:20 PM	Security	Detailed Tracking	593	Administrator	VALA
9/1/97	12:00:17 PM	Security	Privilege Use	578	Administrator	VALA
9/1/97	11:59:45 AM	Security	Privilege Use	576	Administrator	VALA
9/1/97	11:59:45 AM	Security	Logon/Logoff	528	Administrator	VALA
9/1/97	11:59:31 AM	Security	Logon/Logoff	538	Chavez	VALA
9/1/97	11:59:21 AM	Security	Detailed Tracking	593	Administrator	VALA

Figure 10-17. Viewing security data with the event viewer

Double-clicking on an event brings up the **Event Detail** dialog box for that event. For example, Figure 10-18 displays the details for an event similar to the one highlighted in Figure 10-17. This is a failed login event, indicating the reason for the failure, the username and domain name provided during the failed attempt, and other data about the event. Note that the event type code is displayed in the field somewhat confusingly labeled **Event ID**, at the top of the second column in the upper portion of the dialog box.

The **Previous** and **Next** buttons at the bottom of the dialog box may be used to step through the events in the event log sequentially.

Case Studies

It is important to become familiar not only with the tools provided for security auditing but also with the sort of data that they produce. You need to have a good feeling for what ordinary system events look like so that you will be in a position to spot abnormalities and potential problems quickly. In this section, we will examine the key events generated by several normal and unusual security-related events.

Normal login and logoff

Figure 10-19 illustrates the security audit events that are generated by a normal successful login to a Windows NT domain. Two events are generated by this

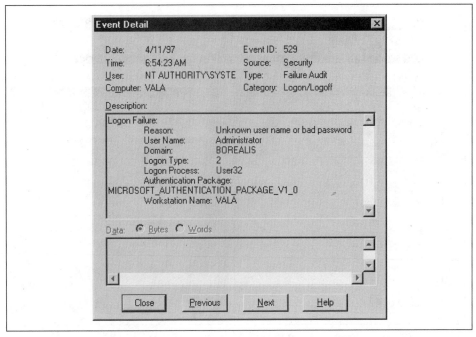

Figure 10-18. Detailed event view

action. In our example, the two events corresponding to user *Chavez* are typical of those you will see for an interactive login. The lower part of the illustration contains the detail views for these two events.

The event on the right corresponds to the successful login itself (event type 528). The detailed information indicates that user *Chavez* logged in to the domain from the system *Lilith*. The **Logon Type** field's value is 3, indicating that it is some sort of network-based login; local logins are assigned type 2. The **Logon ID** field can be used to match distinct events generated by this same login session (for example, its corresponding logout event).

The event on the left (event type 576) may look ominous, but the listed privilege is always granted to login processes, and the event is completely normal.

Figure 10-20 illustrates the events that can be generated when matching user accounts in two domains have different passwords. In this case, the user *Administrator* opened a file browser window for a share in another domain.

Note that all of the failed events (indicated by the lock icon) occurred before the dialog box requesting a valid username and password was presented to this user. They result from the operating system's usual practice of presenting the current username and password to the target domain as authentication information. The

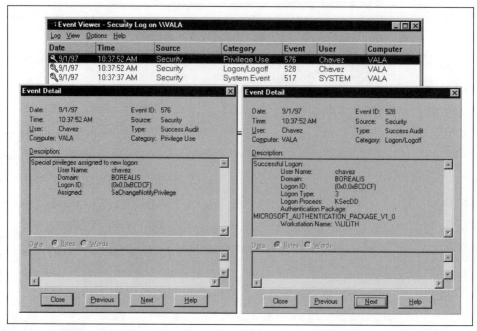

Figure 10-19. Events generated by a normal login

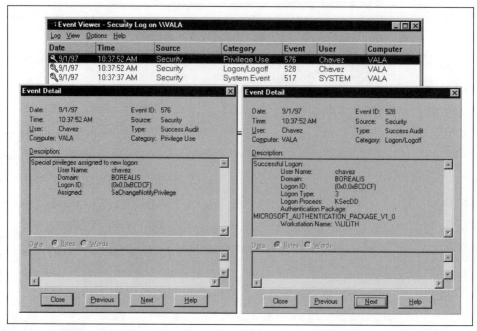

Figure 10-20. Events generated by a password mismatch

moral here is that even login failure events can result from perfectly ordinary practices.

Password policy change

The event in Figure 10-21 illustrates the key event (type 643) resulting from a successful change to the domain password policy. The details provide the name of the user who made the change, but few details on the nature of the change itself. Events such as this one occurring at unexpected times usually require investigation.

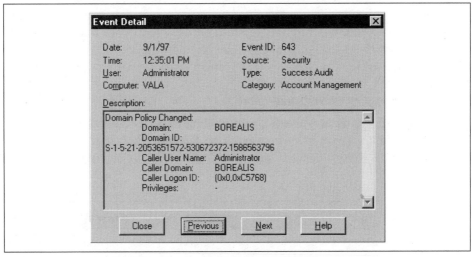

Figure 10-21. Successful change to the domain password policy

Modifying a user account

Figure 10-22 shows two different events resulting from a single change to a user account setting. The event on the left (type 642) is typical of the key event generated when changes to user accounts are being audited. It indicates the name of the account that was changed, *Dagmar* in this case, as well as the user who performed the operation, although it doesn't indicate what setting was changed.

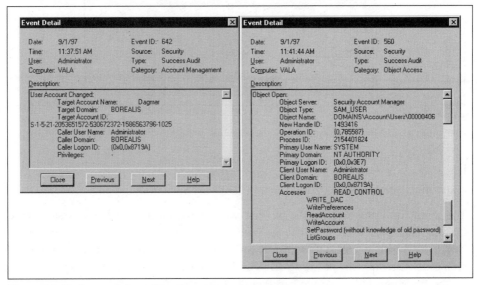

Figure 10-22. Successful modifications to a user account

The event on the right indicates what the same event looks like if user account auditing is disabled, but file auditing for the user account database file is enabled. This event (type 560, typically the key fi le access event type) indicates the SAM database was written to, but it doesn't identify the account that was changed by name. A failed attempt to change a user account looks similarly cryptic.

Changing the system security audit policy

Figure 10-23 shows the key event corresponding to a change in the system security auditing policy (type 612). In contrast to the preceding user account–related events, this one is very detailed and would allow you to determine easily what had been changed.

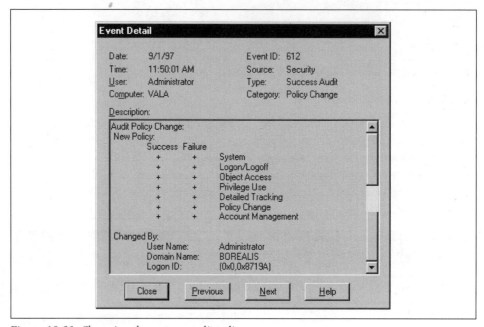

Figure 10-23. Changing the system audit policy

Assigning a user right

Figure 10-24 shows the key event generated when a user right is granted to an additional user or group (type 608).

The event indicates the user right that was granted via its internal system name (in our example, it is the right to **Take Ownership** of files or other objects), as well as the user or group to whom it was granted. The latter is given via the corresponding internal user or group ID. The last four digits of this string are displayed by the **PwDump** utility, so we can identify this as user *Chavez*:

```
C:\> pwdump | grep 1017
Chavez:1017:A7EE...:BCB3....:Rachel Chavez::
```

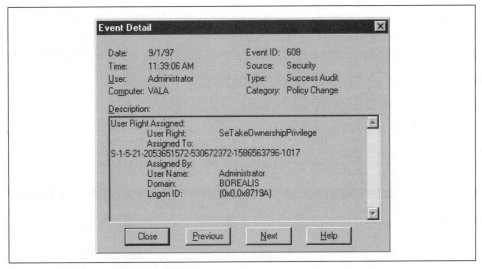

Figure 10-24. Assigning a user right

This example uses the **grep** command included in the POSIX utilities in the Resource Kit to search the output from **PwDump**.

Events relating to file access

Normal file access operations produce large numbers of security log events. Figure 10-25 illustrates the events generated by a successful change to a file's access control list; security auditing of all access has been enabled for the file in question.

The six events beginning with the highlighted event are generated merely by opening the file's **Properties** dialog box, before any changes have been attempted. The events above the highlight result from navigating to the **Security** tab and opening, modifying, and saving the new ACL.

Figure 10-26 gives a detailed view of the key event (type 560). It indicates the file that was modified (**Object Name** field), the user who made the change, and the fact that it is an ACL modification event (**Accesses** field), whose value in this case is WRITE_DAC.

A file access failure event is illustrated in Figure 10-27 (again, the event type is 560). In this case, user *Chavez* has unsuccessfully attempted to read the file *C:\Boot.Ini*. Once again, the keywords in the **Accesses** field indicate the types of file access that have been attempted.

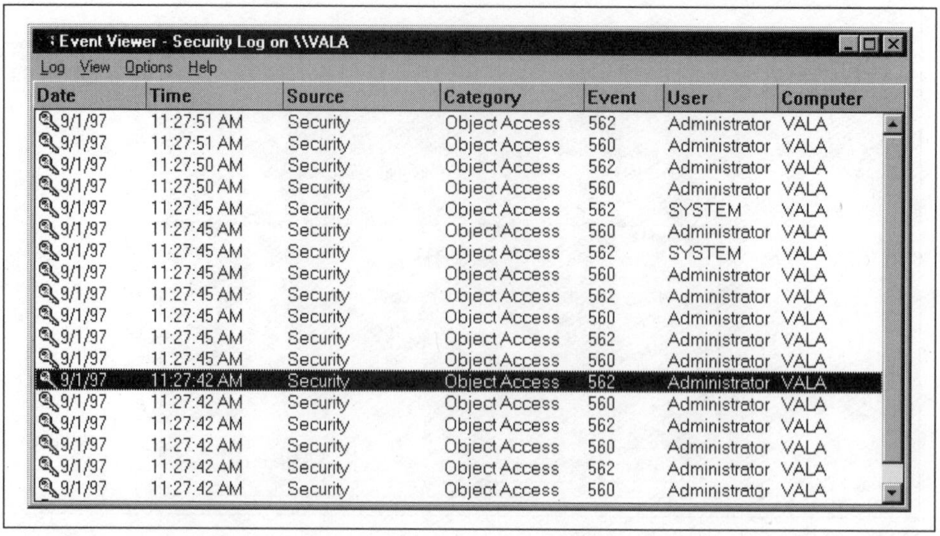

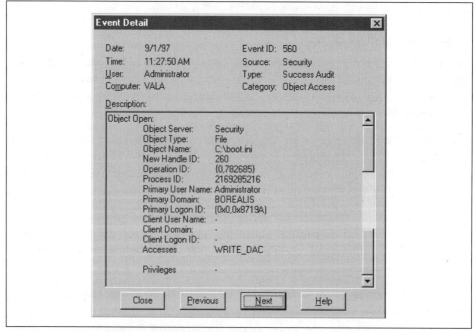

Figure 10-25. Events corresponding to an ACL modification

Figure 10-26. Event detail for modifying an ACL

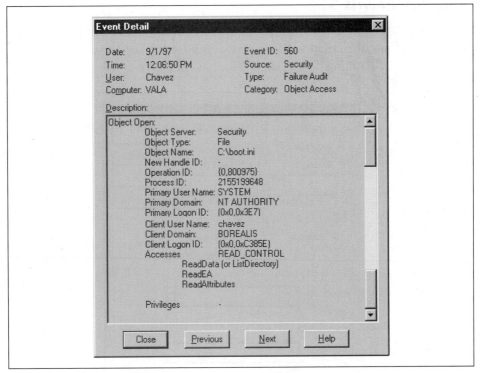

Figure 10-27. Event corresponding to a file access failure

"Missing" Audit Events

Sometimes, you may look in vain for the audit records corresponding to actions you know have occurred. There are several common types of what appear to be missing audit events, each with their own causes and explanations:

- If you haven't enabled security auditing for a file or directory of interest, no audit events will be generated for unsuccessful attempts to access or modify that item. To record such events, you must enable auditing for the item. Also, remember that only items on NTFS filesystems can be audited.

- Failed login events in which the user has entered an invalid password are not recorded in the audit log for the PDC. Rather, such events are recorded in the event log for the computer system at which the failure occurred (and then only when auditing has been enabled for that system in its standalone mode).

- Failed login attempts in which an invalid username is entered are not always recorded (there may be a hotfix for this bug).

Filtering Events

The Event Viewer includes a simple facility for filtering the events that appear in the event list and the detail window; it's accessed using the **View►Filter Events...** menu path. The resulting dialog box is illustrated in Figure 10-28.

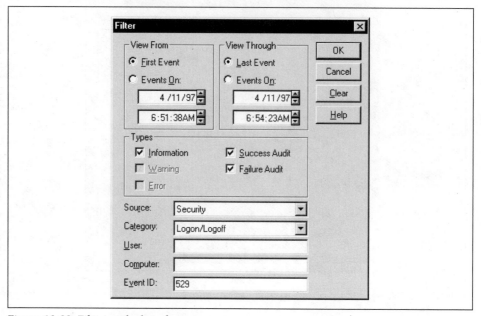

Figure 10-28. Filtering the list of events

This dialog box allows you to specify the events of interest in a variety of ways, including by date (the **View From** and **View Through** fields), success or failure (check boxes in the **Types** area), security audit class (**Category** field), user who performed the corresponding action (**User** field), originating system (**Computer** field), and event type (**Event ID** field).

In Chapter 12, we consider strategies for coping with the security event logs from multiple systems

11

Performance Optimization

This chapter describes the tools and facilities Windows NT offers for managing CPU, memory, disk, and network resources, including some of the limitations inherent in the Windows NT approach. The first part of the chapter provides an overview of system performance considerations. Next, we discuss in detail managing the various system resources, and conclude with an overview of capacity planning.

A large part of managing any computing resource is knowing how to interpret its current status, and so we'll spend some time looking at ways to monitor resources and track their use over time.

Thinking About Performance

Why is everything so slow? is probably second on any system administrator's things-I-least-want-to-hear list (right after *Why did the system crash again?!*). Like system reliability, system performance is another of those areas visible only in its absence. Unfortunately, no one is likely to compliment or thank you for getting the most out of a system's or network's resources. Performance-related complaints can take on a variety of forms, ranging from sluggish interactive response time, to a job taking too long to complete, to one that can't run at all because of insufficient resources.

System performance depends on how efficiently its resources are applied to the current demand for them by the various jobs in the system. The most important resources from a performance perspective are CPU, memory, disk I/O, and network I/O, although other device I/O can also be relevant in some contexts. How well a system is performing at any given moment is the result of both the total demand for the various resources and how well the competition for them among processes is being managed. Accordingly, performance problems can arise from a number of causes, including both a lack of needed resources and ineffective control over them. Addressing a performance problem involves identifying what these resources are and figuring out how to manage them more effectively.

When the lack of a critical resource is the source of a performance problem, there are a limited number of approaches to improving the situation. Put simply, when you don't have enough of something, there are only a few options: you can get more of it, you can use less of it, or you can ration the amount you do have. In the case of a system resource, this can mean obtaining more of it (if that is possible), reducing job or system requirements to desire less of it, having its various consumers share the amount that is available by dividing it between them, having them take turns using it, or otherwise changing the way it is allocated or controlled.

For example, if a system is short of CPU resources, the options for improving things may include some or all of the following:

- Adding additional CPU capacity by upgrading the processor, adding additional processors, or adding another computer to handle part of the workload.

- Taking advantage of currently unused CPU capacity by scheduling some jobs to run during times when the CPU is lightly loaded or even idle.

- Reducing demands for CPU cycles by eliminating some of the jobs that are contending for them.

- Using process priorities to explicitly allocate CPU time among processes that want it, favoring some of them over the others.

- Employing a batch system to ensure that only a reasonable number of jobs run at the same time, making others wait.

- Modifying the behavior of the operating system to affect how the CPU is divided among multiple jobs.

It is often necessary to distinguish between raw system resources like CPU and memory, and the control mechanisms by which they are accessed and allocated. For example, in the case of the system's CPU, you don't have the ability to allocate or control this resource as such (unless you count taking the system down). Table 11-1 lists the most important control mechanisms associated with CPU, memory, and disk I/O performance.

The Tuning Process

The following process offers the most effective approach to addressing system performance issues.

Table 11-1. Resource Control Mechanisms Available Under Windows NT

Physical Resource	Associated Logical Resource	Available Control Mechanisms
CPU	Time quantum	Process priorities, thread priorities
Memory	Pages	Process working sets, workload profile settings, cache management settings
Disk	Files/data blocks	Device and bus speeds, striped filesystems, disk access patterns, file placement
Network	Packet throughput	Media characteristics, protocol selection, workload profile settings

Define the problem in as much detail as you can. The more specific you can be about what is wrong (or less than optimal) with the way things currently are, the more likely it will be that you will be able to find ways to improve them. Ideally, you'd like to move from an initial problem description like "system response time is slow" to a much more detailed one: "large ad-hoc database queries can take up to several minutes to complete on this server."

A good description of the current performance issues implicitly states your performance goals. In this case, the performance goal is clearly to improve the response time for users running large database queries. It is important to understand such goals clearly, even if it is not always possible to reach them (in which case, they are really wishes more than goals).

You won't be able to define the performance problem unless you have a clear sense of what is normal for the process and system in question. Performance problems are, by definition, deviations from the norm, so you must be able to distinguish between normal and abnormal system behavior and conditions. In many cases, addressing a performance problem requires learning and even defining the range of "normal behavior" for a particular system, network, or task. It also can include educating users as to what they can and cannot reasonably expect; managing performance often includes managing user expectations.

Determine the cause or causes of the problem. In order to do so, you'll need to answer questions like these:

- What is running on the system (or, when the performance of a single job or process is the issue, what else is running)? You may also need to consider the sources of the other processes (for example, batch jobs).

- When or under what conditions does the problem occur? For example, does it occur at certain times of the day or under certain resource usage patterns?

- Has anything about the system changed that could have introduced or exacerbated the problem?

- What is the critical resource that is adversely affecting performance? Answering this question involves finding the performance bottleneck for the system's workload; later sections of this chapter discuss the tools and utilities that enable you to find bottlenecks. Here is a brief outline of how these investigations generally proceed:

  — Is the system or process CPU bound? If so, is the entire system overloaded or is the shortage limited to the process in question?

  — If there is no shortage of CPU resources, is memory the culprit? Is the system paging (indicating a systemwide shortage of memory)?

  — If memory resources are adequate, consider whether the system or process is I/O bound. Is disk I/O or network I/O the rate-determining component leading to the performance problem?

For example, if we examined the system with the database query performance problems, we might find that the response time problems only occurred when the size of the database log files have grown to a large size, when the number of ordinary database users exceeds a certain level, or when another program is being compiled on the same server. By watching what happens when a user tries to run such a query under those conditions, we could also figure out that the critical resource is system memory and that the system is paging (more on this later in the chapter).

Formulate explicit performance improvement goals. This step involves transforming the implicit goals (wishes) that were part of the problem description into concrete, measurable goals. Again, being as precise and detailed as possible will make your job easier.

In many cases, tuning goals need to be developed in conjunction with the users affected by the performance problems, and possibly with other users and management personnel as well. System performance is almost always a matter of compromise and tradeoffs, because it inevitably involves deciding how to apply and apportion the finite available resources. Tuning is easiest and most successful where there is a clear agreement about the relative priorities and importance of the various competing activities on the system.

To continue with our example, setting achievable tuning goals will be quite difficult unless it is decided whose performance is more important. In other words, it is probably necessary to choose between how snappy interactive response time is for ordinary database users, how quickly the compilation job finishes and how long a large ad hoc query will take. Remember that the status quo has already been demonstrated not to work.

Decided one way, the tuning goal could become something like this: improve response time for large ad hoc queries as much as possible without affecting interactive response time for ordinary database users. Compilations can be delayed somewhat in order to keep the system from paging.

Design and implement modifications to achieve those goals. Figuring out what to do is the trickiest part of tuning a system. We'll look at what the options are for various sorts of problems in upcoming sections.

It's important to tune the system as a whole. Focusing only on part of the system workload gives a distorted picture of the problem and is unlikely to lead to a solution since system performance is ultimately the result of the interactions among everything on the system.

Monitor the system to determine how well the changes worked. The purpose here is to evaluate the new system status and determine whether or not the change has improved things as expected or desired. The most successful tuning method introduces small changes to the system, one at a time, allowing you to thoroughly test changes and judge their effectiveness—and to back each change out again if it makes things worse instead of better.

Return to the first step and begin again. System performance tuning is inevitably an iterative process; even a successful change will often reveal new interactions to understand and new problems to address. Similarly, once the bottleneck caused by one system resource is relieved, a new one centered around a different resource may very well arise.

WARNING   Before we proceed to more specific consideration of the various system resources, consider this quotation from an IBM performance tuning guide for AIX systems: *the analyst must resist the temptation to tune what is measurable rather than what is important.* Basically, this maxim reminds us that the tools Windows NT provides for observing system behavior offer one way of looking at the system, but not the only way. What is important to watch and tune on your system may or may not be trivially accessible to either monitoring or modification. At the same time, it's also necessary to keep this important corollary in mind: *resist the temptation to tune something just because it is tunable,* which is really just another way of saying *if it isn't broken, don't fix it.*

Important hardware specifications

A key part of successful performance optimization is knowing what your system and its components are capable of. On Windows NT computer systems, the following hardware characteristics are generally the most important contributors to overall performance and should be considered carefully when new hardware is selected.

- The processor architecture and clock speed are the most important factors affecting CPU capacity. Within a processor family, higher clock speeds provide faster performance. For Intel-based systems, more processors with more advanced architectures generally provide better performance than earlier models with the same clock speed (for example, a 200-MHz Pentium Pro system will outperform a 200-MHz Pentium system for most tasks).

  The presence and amount of level 2 cache memory on a system also affects its performance. Larger amounts usually result in better performance.

- Since a memory shortage is the most common cause of performance problems, the most important performance-related memory characteristic is the total amount present on the system. In terms of selecting specific memory modules, the access speed (e.g., 60 vs. 70 nanoseconds) is the key characteristic that distinguishes them (although the differences between the available options are often very minor).

- Disk I/O performance depends on the characteristics of both the hard disks themselves and the disk adapters (controllers) to which they are connected. If your system's workload requires high disk transfer rates, consider using SCSI disks instead of IDE disks since the maximum performance for high-end SCSI devices is several times that of the best IDE disks.

  SCSI devices can be confusingly labeled, and the designations SCSI vs. SCSI II vs. SCSI III, although well defined, are not always used consistently in vendor marketing materials. Key characteristics of SCSI devices and controllers are:

  — Bus speed: 5 MB/s vs. 10 MB/s for "fast SCSI" devices and controllers.

  — Bus width: 8 bits vs. 16 bits for "wide SCSI" devices and controllers (doubling the bus width doubles the performance).

  — "Ultra" and "ultra wide" SCSI devices and controllers effectively double the clock speed, again resulting in a twofold performance increase.

  Other important SCSI controller characteristics include the "width" of the interconnects between the adapter and the device controller and CPU (32-bit cards and buses provide more performance than 16- or 8-bit ones) and whether the adapter is a *bus mastering* controller. Bus mastering controllers manage the I/O bus, themselves rather than relying on the system's CPU to do so, thereby freeing those CPU resources for other tasks.* Cache present on the controller can also improve its I/O performance.

  Disks of the same bus speed, width, and type are distinguished by their seek times (how long on average it takes the disk head to move to a desired location on disk), which is a function of their revolutions-per-minute value (lower

---

* If your system has a high-end SCSI controller installed, be sure its advanced features are enabled (they often come disabled by default). You can use the vendor-supplied hardware setup program to make sure.

seek times and higher RPMs result in better performance). The size of built-in disk buffers can also affect disk performance.

- Network adapter characteristics have similar considerations to disk controllers. For a given network medium, card/bus width is usually the most important factor (32-bit cards are best), and bus mastering controllers are preferable.

Performance Monitoring Tools

Processes are to system performance what files are to system security: the central entity over which the system administrator has control. Managing system resources is, to a great extent, equivalent to managing processes. Windows NT provides the ability to monitor process execution and, to a limited extent, specify their execution characteristics. This section discusses the tools available for monitoring and controlling process execution.

We considered some of the more important process monitoring tools earlier in Chapter 4, including the Task Manager graphical tool and the **TList**, **PStat**, and **PMon** command-line utilities. The **PViewer** and **PView** utilities in the Resource Kit provide more detailed information about individual processes. Figure 11-1 illustrates the **PViewer** display.

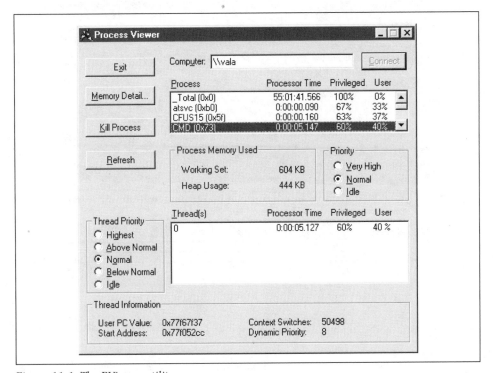

Figure 11-1. The PViewer utility

The process of interest is selected via the **Computer** field and the process list
beneath it. The other areas of the display indicate the process's memory usage,
the process and thread priority classes, the threads that compose the process and
dynamic information about the selected thread. You can modify the priority class
for the process by selecting one of the radio buttons in the **Priority** area.*

Figure 11-2 illustrates the display generated by the **Pview** utility. The desired
process is selected via the drop-down menu in the upper-left part of the window.
The display also contains process and thread priority settings (the former may be
modified), as well as a detailed set of memory usage statistics for the process. The
Times area displays the total elapsed time, kernel CPU time (system time) and
user CPU time (labeled **E**, **K**, and **U**, respectively) that the process has accumulated so far.

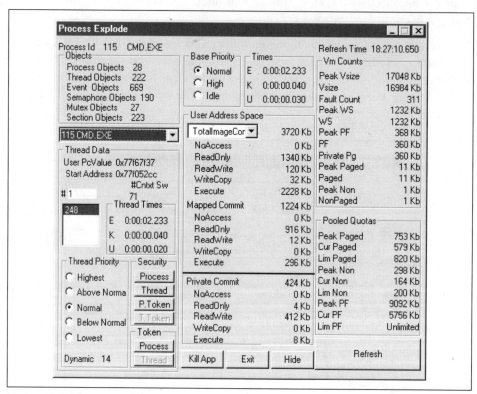

Figure 11-2. The PView utility

---

* The radio buttons in the **Thread Priority** area are intended for display purposes only; they have no effect
on thread priorities.

The Performance Monitor Facility

The Windows NT Performance Monitor facility provides the ability to display and track a variety of system performance statistics. The tool may be executed via the **Start➤Programs➤Administrative Tools (Common)➤Performance Monitor** menu path of the **perfmon** command. The utility can track and plot the values of various system resource statistics known as *counters*. Counters are of three types: instantaneous values of a system statistic, averaged values over some unit time period, or the difference between two statistics. Sets of counters can be created and saved for repeated use via the tool's **File➤Save Settings** menu items.

Objects that can be tracked include various attributes of the system itself, each component processor, real and virtual memory, cache, individual processes or threads, the paging files, and network interfaces and protocols.

NOTE	Physical and logical disk usage counters may also be monitored. However, they must be enabled first by executing the **diskperf -ye** command; these counters are disabled by the command's **-n** option. The system must be rebooted for any change to take effect.

The Performance Monitor operates in several modes. The most important distinction is between data collection, known as *logging*, and data viewing in three different perspectives: *chart, alert,* and *report*. Logging consists of collecting and recording specified system performance data over a specified time period for later analysis. Data viewing can be performed on live data or from data collected previously, and the performance data can be displayed in graphical or textual form.

The items on the **View** menu select the active operating mode.

Displaying performance data

As an example, we will construct a simple chart of current system CPU usage. To begin, we select **View➤Chart** (and possibly **File➤New Chart** to clear the current display). Next, we indicate the counters that we want to track by selecting the **Edit➤Add to Chart...** menu item, which brings up the dialog box illustrated in Figure 11-3.

The available counters are grouped by object, so we begin by selecting the processor object in the **Object** field. Then we select three counters from the **Counter** list in turn: % Processor Time, which indicates total system CPU usage, % Privileged Time (total kernel CPU time), and % User Time (total user CPU time), clicking on the **Add** button after each one. The fields at the bottom of the dialog box may be used to scale the raw data and to specify the appearance of

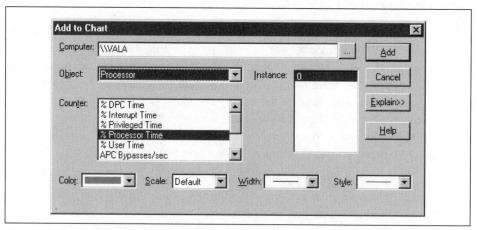

Figure 11-3. Adding performance counters to a chart

the line corresponding to the current counter in the chart. The resulting chart is illustrated in Figure 11-4.

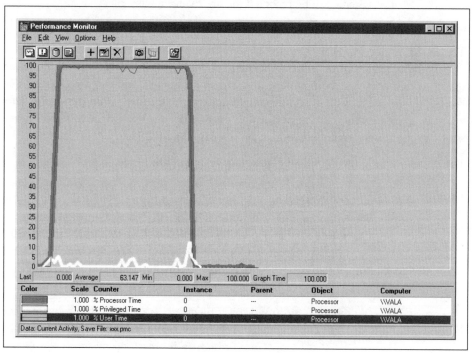

Figure 11-4. Sample CPU performance chart

In this example, total system CPU usage is indicated by the thick gray line. User CPU time—the amount of CPU time spent executing processes (real work)—is indicated by the thin black line, and kernel time (CPU time spent by the operating system servicing processes) is represented by the medium white line. Over this interval, the system was initially idle, then became completely busy (100% total CPU usage) for a while, and finally became idle again. The entries at the bottom of the chart provide a legend, and double-clicking on any entry lets you change that counter's appearance within the chart.

As it happens, the busy period corresponds to the execution of a CPU-intensive process. While it was running, this process consumed almost all of the CPU resources as indicated by the small amount of kernel CPU time and correspondingly high amount of user CPU time over the period of 100% CPU usage.

The Performance Monitor tool can also produce numerical reports. Figure 11-5 shows one such report.

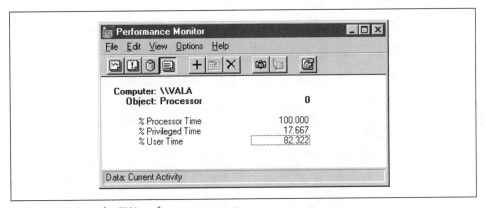

Figure 11-5. Sample CPU performance report

Collecting performance data

Data logging is specified by selecting the **View▶Log** menu item and then choosing the objects whose counters you want to record using the **Edit▶Add to Log...** menu item, which results in the dialog box in Figure 11-6. Select each item in turn and click the **Add** button.

The **Options▶Log** menu item is used to specify the location of the log file and update interval. Pressing **Start Log** initiates data collection (see Figure 11-7). The same dialog may be used to halt data collection; the **Start Log** button toggles to **Stop Log** when logging is running.

While data collection is proceeding, you can use the **Options▶Bookmark...** menu item to mark and label interesting points within it.

You can automate data collection using tools provided in the Resource Kit:

- Install the **DataLog** service using the **InstSrv** utility.

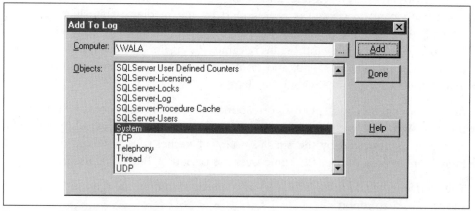

Figure 11-6. Specifying the objects to log

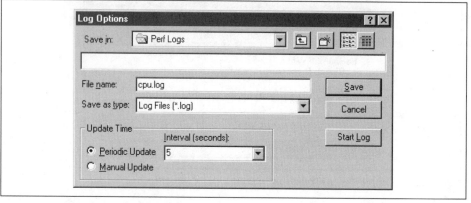

Figure 11-7. Specifying log file settings

- Set up an appropriate Performance Monitor settings file.

- Use the **Monitor** utility to stop and start logging. This command can, of course, be used in conjunction with the Scheduler facility to automate the process completely.

Finally, saved performance data may be viewed in the Performance Monitor, using its **Options►Data From...** menu item. The normal charting and report generation facilities of the utility will be available for the recorded data. In addition, you can specify a subset of the total data for analysis, via the **Edit►Time Window...** menu item. Figure 11-8 illustrates the resulting dialog box.

The bar in the upper portion of the dialog box indicates the time range to be charted or reported on. By default, the entire range of data is included. You can specify a subset by dragging either end of the bar to the desired point (or using

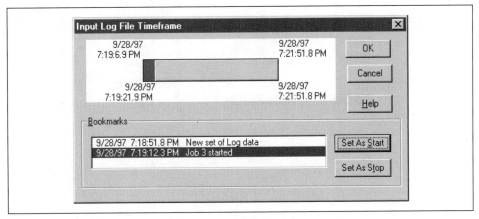

Figure 11-8. Selecting a time range from logged data

the left and right arrow keys). In our example, a portion of the data at the beginning of the recording session is being omitted (indicated by the black bar in the illustration). You may also use any defined bookmarks as the starting or stopping points, using the list box and buttons in the lower portion of the dialog box.

Defining performance-based alerts

The Performance Monitor tool also has the capability of generating an alert message within the utility if a specified system resource condition occurs (for example, if a counter drops below or exceeds some threshold). A specified command may also be run when such an event occurs if desired.

Alerts are defined using the **View➤Alert** and **Edit➤Add to Alert...** menu items; Figure 11-9 shows the dialog box produced by the latter.

In this example, we specify that the script *E:\SysBin\PF.Bat* be run whenever the current usage of the overall system paging space exceeds 90% of its total capacity.

Managing CPU Resources

CPU usage is usually the first factor that you consider when tracking down a performance problem or just trying to assess the current system state in general. We'll begin this section with an overview of the Windows NT process scheduling scheme, and then consider how to analyze CPU usage and address CPU resource shortages.

Windows NT Process Scheduling

In Chapter 4, we considered the distinction between processes and threads under Windows NT. Users initiate processes to get work done, and these processes are

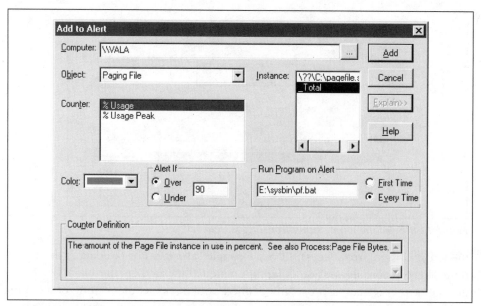

Figure 11-9. Adding a performance-based alert

composed of one or more threads. Processes usually consist of a single thread; generally they only have two or more threads associated when they run in parallel across multiple heads in a multiprocessor system. Threads are the entities that are actually executed by the operating system.

Windows NT uses a *priority-based round-robin scheduling algorithm* to distribute CPU resources among multiple competing threads. Each process has a base priority class assigned to it, indicating its general level of importance with respect to other processes within the system. The defined priority classes are **Low**, **Normal**, **High**, and **RealTime**.

Each thread has a numeric base priority specifying its importance relative to other threads, which is derived from the priority class of the process that owns it. Windows NT thread priorities range from 1* to 31, with higher numbers indicating more important threads. The **Low** priority class corresponds to a level of 4, the **Normal** priority class to a level of 7, and the **High** priority class to a level of 13. Priority numbers above 16 are used for real-time processes.

Threads also have an execution priority assigned to them, an integer value that is dynamically recomputed frequently, taking into account factors such as how recently the thread has executed. This dynamic priority level is always within two levels of the thread's base priority.

---

* Priority level 0 is reserved for use by the operating system.

Although there may be many threads simultaneously present on the system, only one thread actually uses each CPU at any given time. Whenever the CPU is free, the scheduler selects the most favored thread to begin or resume executing; this is the thread with the highest execution priority that is ready to run.

Once a thread begins running, it continues to execute until it needs to wait for an I/O operation to complete, receives an interrupt (for example, a user kills it or the system suspends it because a higher priority thread is ready to run), otherwise voluntarily or involuntarily gives up control of the CPU, or exhausts the maximum execution *quantum* (time slice). Once the current thread stops executing, the scheduler will again select the most favored thread on the system and start or resume that job.

Multiple threads at the same priority level are placed into a run queue for that priority level. Whenever the CPU is free, the scheduler starts the thread at the head of the highest priority run queue. When the thread at the top of a run queue stops executing, the next thread moves to the front.

The scheduler modifies thread execution priorities on an ongoing basis. For example, a thread's execution priority is lowered whenever it ceases executing. On workstations, threads receive a priority boost after returning from a wait (of +1 on return from disk I/O and +5 on return from keyboard input). In addition, the scheduler eventually provides priority boosts for CPU-starved threads and random boosts to low priority threads to avoid their monopolizing a critical system resource (thereby creating a bottleneck for other threads).

You can configure the scheduler to boost the priority of the thread corresponding to the system's foreground process, in order to ensure acceptable interactive response time. This setting may be accessed from the **System** control panel applet's **Performance** tab (Figure 11-10). It is also accessible via the **Properties** dialog box of **My Computer**.

The slider in the dialog box's **Application Performance** area allows you to specify two levels of foreground process boosting. The middle (unlabeled) position will favor the foreground process over background processes, but still provide some CPU resources to the latter, while the **Maximum** position provides the best interactive response time for the foreground process.

Analyzing CPU Usage

There are many different ways of obtaining a quick snapshot of current overall CPU activity. For example, you can consult the **Performance** tab of the Task Manager utility (Figure 11-11). In this example, the system is currently idle (3% current CPU usage), but it was fully busy in the recent past (indicated by the **CPU Usage History** graph).

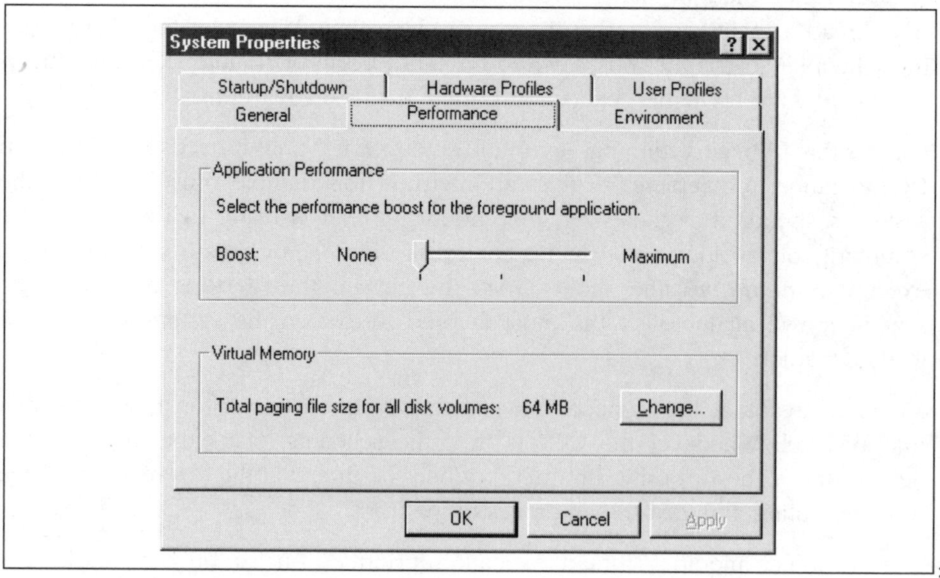

Figure 11-10. Boosting the priority of the foreground process

The **QSlice** utility in the Resource Kit displays CPU usage by process (Figure 11-12). System time—CPU time consumed by the operating system performing activities on behalf of user processes (such as I/O operations and display updates)—is indicated by the white bars, while user time (CPU time spent doing processes' actual work) is indicated by the black bars.

On this system, the available CPU time is currently being divided primarily among three processes: the **QSlice** utility itself (which is mainly consuming system time) and two Perl programs.

The following Performance Monitor counters are useful in analyzing system CPU usage:

*Processor: % Processor Time**
The percentage of CPU capacity in use.

Processor: %User Time
The percentage of CPU capacity consumed by user processes performing actual work.

Processor: %Privileged Time
The percentage of CPU capacity consumed by the operating system while servicing user processes and threads. When this counter is a large fraction of

---

* The notation is *object:counter.*

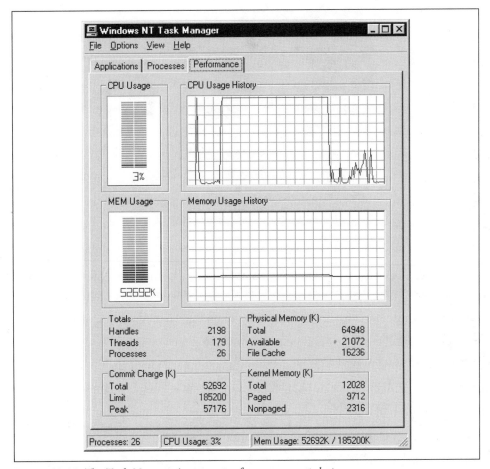

Figure 11-11. The Task Manager's system performance snapshot

the total CPU time used, excessive system overhead may be reducing the performance of user processes.

System: Processor Queue Length

The number of threads that are ready to run, but have to wait until another thread finishes. A long queue length indicates a CPU resource shortage.

System: Context Switches/sec

The number of times the current executing thread changed per second. Context switching is a normal part of the Windows NT scheduling algorithm. However, excessive levels can indicate that system overhead is degrading process performance.

The method for determining whether a single job is CPU-limited or not is somewhat different. When there is a significant difference between the CPU time and

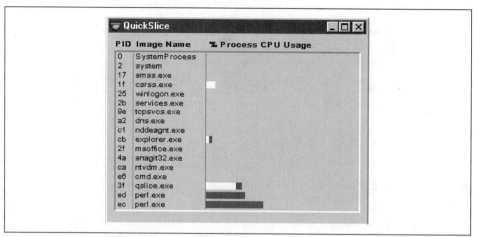

Figure 11-12. The QSlice utility

the elapsed time taken for a job to complete on an otherwise idle system, then some factors other than a lack of CPU cycles are degrading its performance.

The following Performance Monitor counters are useful in analyzing single process CPU usage:

Process: %Processor Time

Process: %User Time

Process: %Privileged Time

> These counters have the same meaning as those for the Processor object, but their scope is limited to the specified process.

Process: Elapsed Time

> The total time that has passed since the process began executing.

Thread: Priority Current

> Indicates the thread's execution priority.

Thread: Context Switches/sec

> This statistic indicates how often the thread is starting, pausing, and resuming execution. High start-and-stop levels require further investigation to determine the causes of the context switches.

Let's consider some actual performance data from a fully loaded system. Figure 11-13 displays performance data for a system running seven CPU-intensive jobs, five at **Normal** priority and two at **Low** priority. The graph displays the values of % Total Processor Time (thick black line), % Total Privileged Time (thin black line), and Processor Queue Length (white line) counters. As you might expect, interactive response time during the period charted was very poor.

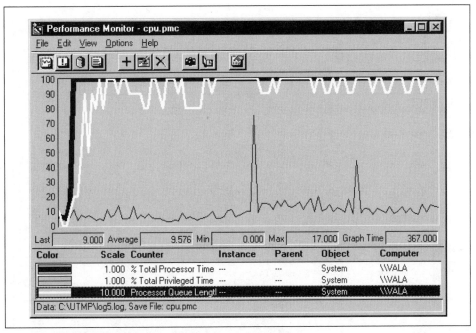

Figure 11-13. Performance data from a CPU-starved system

Throughout the period covered by the chart, total system CPU usage is at 100%. However, for most of the time, system time remains quite low, indicating that the CPU resources are being used by the processes to perform their computations. After an initial build-up, the run queue length fluctuates around two levels, which correspond to the execution of the **Normal** priority processes only (the higher level) and the execution of one or both of the **Low** priority processes as well. It's clear that the poor interactive response time is due to a shortage of available CPU cycles.

There are two large spikes in the plot of system time. These correspond to when the operating system finally got around to responding to a mouse click made by the system's user, which resulted in updates to the display and a corresponding consumption of CPU time by the operating system.

Figure 11-14 illustrates the Task Manager's **Process** tab midway during the same period of time. The seven CPU-bound processes are highlighted. Note that the accumulated CPU times for each of them vary, as one would expect, based on their process priority class. The process that started first (PID 75) has gained a minor performance advantage over the other **Normal** priority processes.

High levels of CPU usage are not a bad thing in themselves (quite the contrary, in fact, when they mean that the system is accomplishing a lot of useful work). The

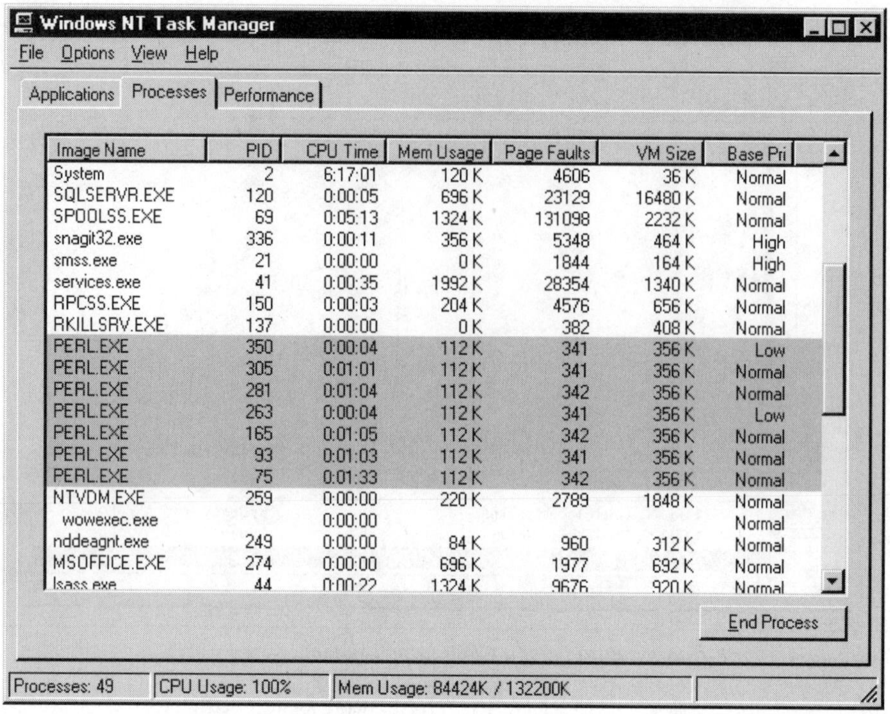
Windows NT Task Manager
File Options View Help
Applications Processes Performance
Image Name PID CPU Time Mem Usage Page Faults VM Size Base Pri
System 2 6:17:01 120 K 4606 36 K Normal
SQLSERVR.EXE 120 0:00:05 696 K 23129 16480 K Normal
SPOOLSS.EXE 69 0:05:13 1324 K 131098 2232 K Normal
snagit32.exe 336 0:00:11 356 K 5348 464 K High
smss.exe 21 0:00:00 0 K 1844 164 K High
services.exe 41 0:00:35 1992 K 28354 1340 K Normal
RPCSS.EXE 150 0:00:03 204 K 4576 656 K Normal
RKILLSRV.EXE 137 0:00:00 0 K 382 408 K Normal
PERL.EXE 350 0:00:04 112 K 341 356 K Low
PERL.EXE 305 0:01:01 112 K 341 356 K Normal
PERL.EXE 281 0:01:04 112 K 342 356 K Normal
PERL.EXE 263 0:00:04 112 K 341 356 K Low
PERL.EXE 165 0:01:05 112 K 342 356 K Normal
PERL.EXE 93 0:01:03 112 K 341 356 K Normal
PERL.EXE 75 0:01:33 112 K 342 356 K Normal
NTVDM.EXE 259 0:00:00 220 K 2789 1848 K Normal
wowexec.exe 0:00:00 Normal
nddeagnt.exe 249 0:00:00 84 K 960 312 K Normal
MSOFFICE.EXE 274 0:00:00 696 K 1977 692 K Normal
lsass.exe 44 0:00:22 1324 K 9676 920 K Normal
End Process
Processes: 49
CPU Usage: 100%
Mem Usage: 84424K / 132200K

Figure 11-14. Accumulated CPU time for the seven processes

mere presence of high CPU usage numbers means nothing in isolation. However, if you are tracking down a system performance problem, and you see such levels of CPU use consistently over a significant period of time, then you will determine that a shortage of CPU cycles is one factor contributing to that problem (it may not be the total problem, however, as we shall see).

Addressing CPU Shortages

As we've seen, a CPU shortage is caused by too large a workload for the capacity of the system. This may be the result of too many jobs, as in the previous example, or even a single CPU-hogging job.

When an overcommitment of CPU resources is the source of a performance bottleneck, there are two options for addressing the situation: rationing the available CPU resources and providing additional CPU capacity.

If you want to favor some jobs over others, you can explicitly divide the existing CPU resources using process priorities. You can modify the priority class of an existing process by right-clicking on it in the Task Manager's **Processes** display.

However, assigning any process to the **RealTime** class can easily overwhelm the system and make it unusable.

If there is simply more demand for the CPU resources than can be met on the system, you'll need to reduce consumption or increase CPU capacity in some way:

- Move some of the load to a different (presumably less heavily loaded) system.

- Execute some jobs at a different time (during off-hours via a batch system, for example).

- Upgrade the system to a more powerful processor, providing additional CPU resources to service the workload. Be aware that you can do so within or across processor families: if the fastest Intel processors are not adequate to your needs, consider a server using an Alpha processor as a replacement.

We look at ways of deploying CPU resources on a networkwide basis when we discuss capacity planning later in this chapter.

The Start command

Windows NT provides the **Start** command for explicitly initiating processes. It is useful for starting a process at a specific priority level. It has the following syntax:

```
Start [title] [options] command [arguments]
```

where *command* is the command to be executed, which can be either a Windows NT command or a script; any specified arguments are passed to the command when it is executed. If included, the *title* parameter becomes the title bar text for the resulting window.

Start has a variety of options; the following are the most important:

/B   Run the process in the background

/Low, /Normal, /High, /RealTime
   Specify the process priority class

/D*path*
   Specify the working directory for the process

For example, the following command runs the program named **G98** at **Low** priority in the background:

```
C:\> Start /B /Low G98 Test178.GJF
```

Managing Memory Use

Memory resources have at least as much effect on overall system performance as the distribution of CPU time. To perform well, a system needs to have adequate memory, not just for the largest jobs it will run, but also for the overall mix of jobs typical of its everyday use. For example, the amount of memory that is sufficient for the one or two big jobs that run overnight might provide only a mediocre response time under the heavy interactive use a system is expected to support in the daytime; on the other hand, an amount of memory that supports a system's normal interactive use might very well result in quite poor performance when larger jobs are run. Thus, both sets of needs should be taken into consideration when planning for and evaluating system memory requirements.

A component of the Windows NT operating system known as the *Virtual Memory Manager* (VMM) is responsible for allocating and managing system memory. On systems without virtual memory, a process must have an amount of contiguous physical memory equal to its current image and data requirements in order to run. Virtual memory systems take advantage of the fact that most of this memory isn't actually needed all the time. Information is read in from disk only as needed. The system automatically maps the *virtual addresses* (the relative address of a text or data location with respect to the beginning of the process's image in memory) used internally by the program to real physical memory locations. When the process accesses a part of its executable image or its data that is not currently in memory, the kernel reads in—*pages in*—what is needed from disk, sometimes replacing other pages that the process no longer needs.

So, for a large program that spends most of its time in, say, two routines, only the part of its executable image containing them need be in memory while they are running, freeing up the memory the rest of the program's image segment would occupy on a nonvirtual memory computer for other uses. This is true whether the two routines are close together or far apart in the executable. Similarly, if a program uses a large data area, all of it needn't be resident in memory simultaneously if the program doesn't access it all at once.

When there is not enough physical memory on the system for all of the processes currently running, the VMM will apportion the total physical memory among them dynamically. When a process needs a new page read in and there are no free or reusable pages, then the VMM must *steal* a page that is being used by some other process. In this case, the previous contents of the physical page may need to be stored; if so, it is *paged out*: written out to a paging file on disk. If that page is again required, then it must be paged back in, possibly forcing out another page.

Despite the strong negative connotations the term has acquired, *paging* is not always a bad thing. When an appreciable portion of the available system resources are spent page-faulting under such conditions, all processes will execute much less efficiently. In the worst case, *thrashing* can occur, where the system spends all its time managing the virtual memory, and no real work gets done; all CPU time is spent as kernel time, and no CPU cycles are actually used to advance the execution of any process.

The VMM incorporates a number of modern virtual memory management techniques in an effort to maximize the efficiency of the system's memory resources:

- Demand paging: Pages are loaded into memory only when a page fault occurs. The Windows NT VMM uses a *clustering* technique in which a few pages surrounding the faulted page are also loaded in the same operation, in an effort to avoid future page faults.

- Copy-on-write page protection: Whenever possible, only a single copy of identical pages in use by multiple processes is kept in memory. Duplicate, private copies of a page are created only if one of the processes modifies it.

- Automatic working set adjustment: The VMM trims process working sets when memory is scarce (a process's *working set* is the amount of physical memory it is using at any given time), beginning with processes that have working sets larger than their minimum working set value. Similarly, the VMM automatically increases the working set for a process that is paging when memory is available to do so.

- When memory is short, the VMM takes memory pages being used by current processes (selected via a first in, first out algorithm, which reuses the oldest pages first). However, such pages are simply initially marked as free, and are not replaced with new data (*reclaimed*) until the last possible moment. In this way, the owning process can reaccess them without a disk read operation, if they are still in memory when they are required again.

Server vs. Workstation Memory Management Differences

There are some important internal tuning differences between the server and workstation versions of the Windows NT operating system, many of which relate to memory management:

- The memory threshold defining a "large" system is 32 MB for a workstation, 64 MB for a server system (on Intel systems).

- Additional worker threads for the operating system are created on large server systems.

- Data is written out to disk more often on workstation systems than on server systems (see the next section).

- More aggressive trimming of processes' memory occurs on small workstation systems than on other system types.

- The thread execution quantum is longer on server systems than on workstation systems.

- A priority boost is given at thread wake-up by the scheduler on workstation systems.

- System components allocate and consume more memory on servers than on workstations.

Monitoring System Memory Use

You can obtain a quick snapshot of current memory usage via the Task Manager's **Performance** tab (Figure 11-11). Its **MEM Usage** displays a bar graph of the percentage of physical memory that is currently in use, as well as the total amount of available physical memory after the operating system's requirements are fulfilled. The window also displays a graph of recent overall memory usage and statistics about the total and currently available amounts of physical memory and kernel memory usage.

The freely available **WMem** utility (written by Steven Chervets) also provides overall system memory status data in a compact form (Figure 11-15). The first line of its display shows the percentage of physical memory currently in use (as a number and as a bar graph), as well as the total number of bytes in use. The second line similarly shows the percentage of paging space that is currently in use and the total bytes consumed. The example display indicates that this system has plenty of both.

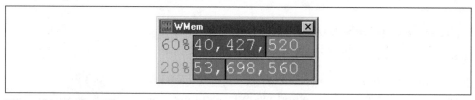

Figure 11-15. The WMem utility

The Performance Monitor facility may also be used to study system and process memory use. The following counters will provide an overall view of memory usage on the system:

Memory: Available bytes
   Amount of physical memory currently available for allocation.

Memory: Page Reads/sec or Memory: Page Input/sec
Memory: Page Writes/sec or Memory: Page Output/sec
   These counters indicate the number of operations and number of pages per second read from or written to disk to satisfy page faults and memory management needs. These counters are generally more useful than the Memory: Page Faults/sec counter, since it includes all page faults, including ones resolved without any disk activity.

Process: Page File Bytes (Total Instance)
Total number of bytes in use in all paging files.

For a disk-level view of paging activity, monitor these counters:

Logical Disk: Disk Reads/sec
Logical Disk: Disk Writes/sec
These counters indicate the number of operations to or from disk per second. By comparing them to the paging rates, you can determine how much of the disk I/O activity is due to paging.

The following counters are useful for monitoring the memory usage at the single process level:

Process: Page Faults/sec
The number of page faults generated by the process per second.

Process: Working set
The amount of physical memory currently used by the process. Tracking this counter over time can reveal process memory requirements and how they are affected by other concurrent activity on the system.

Process: Page File Bytes
The amount of page file space consumed by pages belonging to the process.

We'll examine many of these counters in the next example (which is a bit more complicated than the previous one). During the period we are examining, we began by saving a 32-MB Word file to disk. Then we started the same CPU-intensive job we ran earlier, and finally we opened an Excel document; the system was otherwise idle. The CPU and memory usage data for these activities are plotted in Figure 11-16. The black line shows the total amount of available memory (in MB), and the white line shows the total system CPU usage.

The left half of the figure up to the plateau in the available memory line corresponds to the file save operation. This process intermittently required a fair amount of CPU time, and system CPU consumption decreased to almost nothing once the save completed. At the same time, the process released an amount of memory about the same size as the file being written to disk.

The leftmost asterisk in the diagram corresponds to the start of the CPU-intensive job. Available memory is essentially unchanged, but CPU usage goes to 100%. The right asterisk in the diagram indicates the initiation of the Excel application. There is a slight decrease in the amount of available memory as it starts up.

Figure 11-17 displays paging statistics over the same period. We have again plotted the total available memory as a reference. The white line here indicates the Page Reads/sec counter, and the thin black line plots Page Writes/sec.

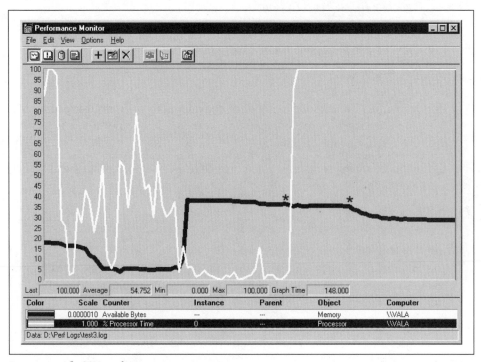

Figure 11-16. CPU and memory consumption

Write operations to the paging file occur only during the second half of the file save operation, coinciding with a low amount of available memory. Disk read operations to satisfy page faults occur throughout the time period we are investigating. The largest peak occurs as the Excel application starts up, as its executable image is brought into memory from disk. Such page faults are a completely normal part of process initiation and do not indicate a performance problem on the system.

The white line in Figure 11-18 illustrates paging file usage over the same time period (the total available memory line is again included for reference). There is a slight rise in usage toward the end of the save operation, corresponding to the nonzero Page Writes/sec counter we saw in the previous figure. However, total page file usage remains low throughout this time period.

Figure 11-19 compares the page file I/O counters to the same total disk I/O counters. The left graph plots Page Reads/sec (black line) and Disk Reads/sec (white line). Note how the two counters mirror one another. This indicates that essentially all of the disk read operations were in service of page faults.

By contrast, the plots for Page Writes/sec (gray line) and Disk Writes/sec (white line) in the right graph are quite different. There are a substantial number of disk

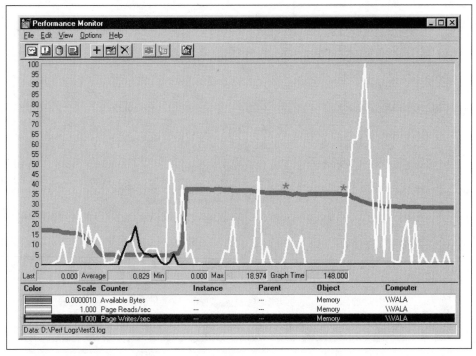

Figure 11-17. Paging statistics

writes during the file save operation (as we would expect), as well as a few others during the other activities.

All in all, it is clear that this system is performing in a consistent manner with its workload and that the paging activity we see does not indicate a problem. Memory is scarce only for one brief period, during the latter part of the file write operation (which is a typical effect of any large disk write). Any degradation of interactive response time must be attributed to the user's overly ambitious use of the system's finite resources.

We next consider a system with a serious memory shortage. This system has only a single job running on it, but the job's memory requirements exceed the total system capacity by a considerable amount. Figure 11-20 illustrates the CPU usage for this system. Total CPU usage is indicated by the thick gray line, and system time is plotted as the thin black line. For most of the period under observation, system time comprises virtually 100% of the total used CPU time, indicating that almost all of it is being used for operating system operations on behalf of the process. Clearly, little real work is being done.

Figure 11-21 displays memory and paging statistics over the same period. It's a busy chart, but a close examination quickly reveals what is consuming the system

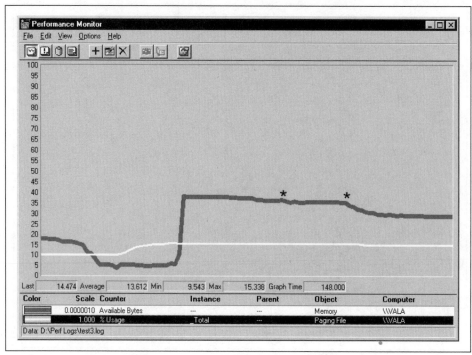

Figure 11-18. Paging file usage

time: paging. The gray line in the chart indicates page file usage, which steadily increases for most of the observation period. At the same time, available memory (plotted as the white line) remains more or less constant over the same period. The VMM's attempts to increase the amount of available memory by writing pages to disk is unsuccessful.

This conclusion is reinforced when we consider the paging I/O statistics. The thick black line shows the value of the Pages Output/sec counter, and the dashed black line plots the Pages Input/sec counter. Both values are high for most of the observation period. This system is clearly thrashing, spending all its time paging and no time advancing the computation being attempted by the user process.

Managing the System Paging Space

It is important to keep an eye on system paging space usage on an ongoing basis, expanding it if it becomes consistently scarce. Under Windows NT, paging is performed to one or more designated paging files on disk. The default paging file is *C:\PageFile.Sys*, and you may add additional paging files as needed.

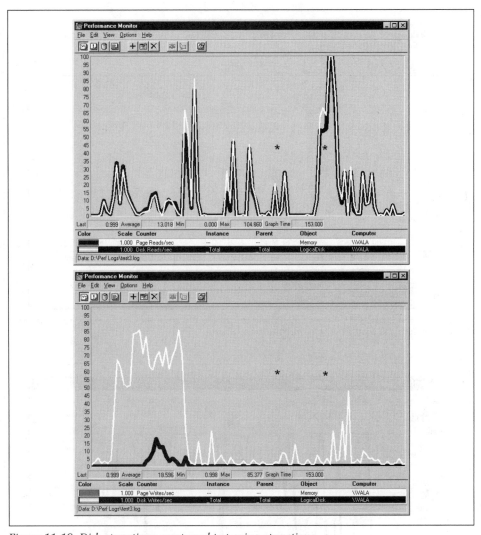

Figure 11-19. Disk operations compared to paging operations

NOTE   Splitting the available paging space across separate disks (ideally on
            separate disk controllers) can improve system performance when
            paging activity is significant. However, you should be sure it's the
            disk I/O you want to favor before doing so (see the next section).

You should plan on a total system paging space of one to two times the amount
of physical memory on the system. The lower end of this range is appropriate for
systems with the normal modest memory requirements typical of primarily interac-

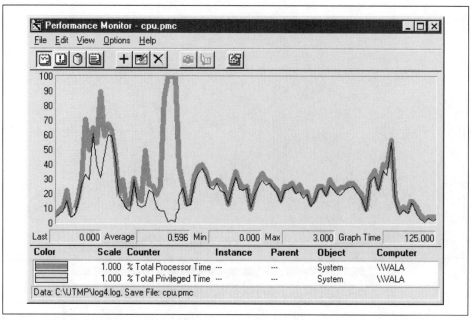

Figure 11-20. CPU usage on a memory-starved system

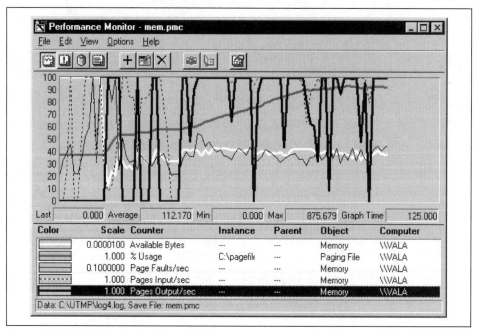

Figure 11-21. Memory and paging statistics

tive systems, and the higher range is appropriate for compute servers expected to run multiple jobs with significant memory requirements.

If the system workload requires more paging space than this, adding more' memory will significantly improve performance. Virtual memory came into existence because disk has been historically much cheaper than memory (which was very expensive). While this is still true, now memory is also cheap, so trading off disk for memory is no longer a good deal or a sensible practice.

Page file settings are accessed via the **System** control panel applet's **Performance** tab. Pressing its **Change** button results in the dialog box in Figure 11-22. The existing paging file on each disk is shown in the list box at the top of the dialog box. Settings for the selected disk are indicated in the **Paging File Size for Selected Drive** section below it. When you create or modify a paging file, you specify its initial size and the maximum size to which it may grow. Pressing the **Set** button applies the current settings. Decreasing the current size of any paging file requires a system reboot.

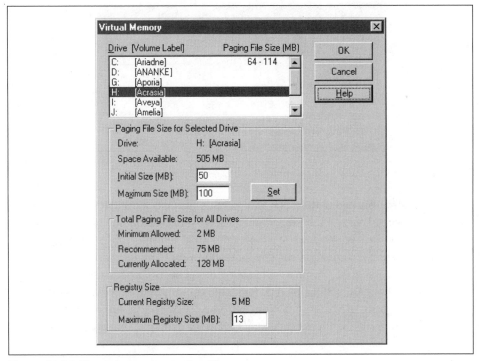

Figure 11-22. Managing system paging files

The **Total Paging File Size for All Drives** section of the dialog box gives statistics on the total amount of paging space on the system. The **Recommended** value should not be taken too literally. In my experience, it tends to be a bit low for most systems, especially active servers.

The Filesystem Cache

As is the case for many modern operating systems, Windows NT uses any available memory as a data cache for disk I/O operations, in an effort to maximize I/O performance.* Recently accessed data is kept in memory for a time, in case it is needed again, as long as there is sufficient memory to do so. This setting affects the performance of local processes and network system access operations.

On a server system, you can specify the extent to which the system favors user processes or the data cache when allocating available memory. This setting is accessed via the **Properties** of the Server network service. The resulting dialog box is illustrated in Figure 11-23, and its selections have the meanings described in Table 11-2.

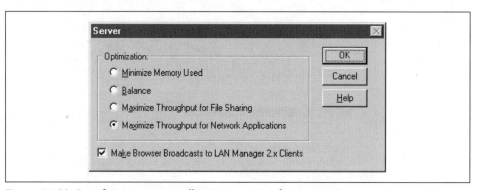

Figure 11-23. Specifying a memory allocation strategy for a server

Table 11-2 also lists the settings of two registry values, identified by Mark Russinovich, associated with each selection; they may be set manually to achieve the same behavior on workstation systems. The first registry value, HKEY_LOCAL_MACHINE\System\CurrentControlSet\Control\Session manager\Memory Management\LargeSystemCache, controls whether the cache or processes are favored in allocating memory (a setting of 1 favors the cache). The second registry value, HKEY_LOCAL_MACHINE\System\CurrentControlSet\Services\LanmanServer\Parameters\Size, further specifies the system's memory management profile.

---

* The relevant Performance Monitor counters for analyzing cache performance are Memory: Available Bytes, Memory: Cache Bytes, Cache: Copy Read Hits %, and Memory: Cache Faults/sec.

Table 11-2. Available Memory Allocation Strategies

Selection	Meaning	Corresponding Registry Settings	
		LargeSystemCache	Size
Minimize Memory Used	Favor local processes in allocating memory. Assumes only minimal network-based system usage (10 connections or fewer).	0	1
Balance	Maintain a balance between memory allocated for local and network processes. Designed for a system with up to 64 network connections also having some nontrivial local use.	0	2
Maximize Throughput for File Sharing	Favor the data cache over the memory requirements of local processes. Designed for a system that functions primarily as a network file server.	1	3
Maximize Throughput for Network Applications	Allocate memory to support a large number of network connections. Designed for application-based server systems on large networks (e.g., database servers).	0	3

Russinovich and Cogswell have also created the **CacheMan** utility for further fine tuning Windows NT memory management. It is illustrated in Figure 11-24. The fields are documented by Russinovich and Cogswell as follows:

CcFirstDelay
Delay before writing back a page after first access

CcIdleDelay
Idle period to wait before writing back dirty pages

CcCollisionDelay
Delay by this amount if writeback is not possible

CcTargetCleanDelay
Standard delay before writing back dirty data

CcDirtyPageThreshold
Maximum number of dirty pages to allow in cache

CcDirtyPageTarget
Desired number of dirty pages in cache

CcAvailableMaxDirtyWrite
Maximum number of dirty pages to write back at a time

CcAvailablePagesThreshold
Require at least this many pages available

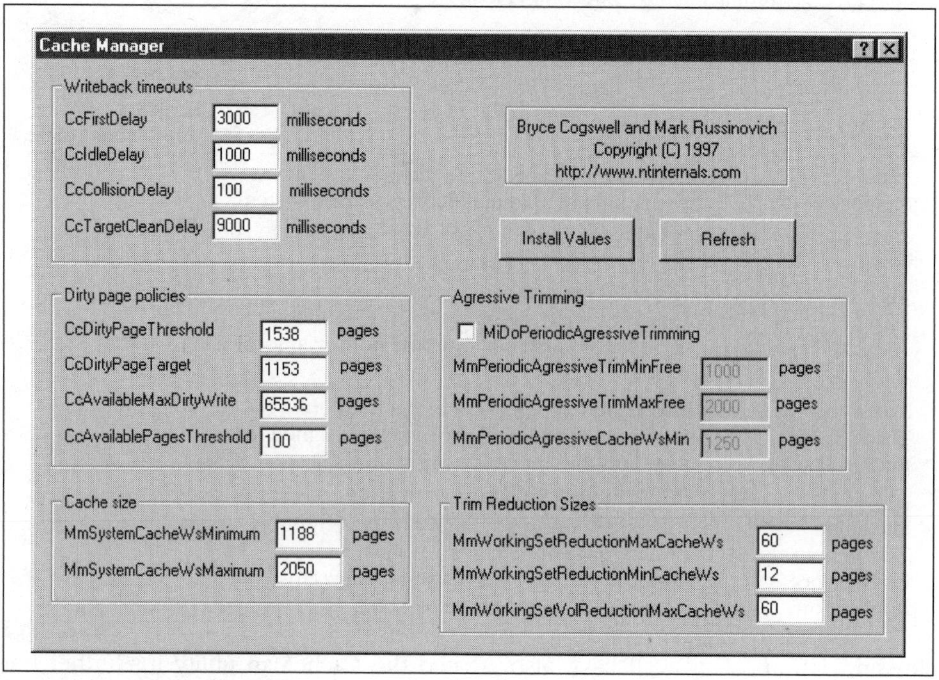

Figure 11-24. The CacheMan utility

MmSystemCacheWsMinimum

Minimum size of the working set of the cache

MmSystemCacheWsMaximum

Maximum size of the working set of the cache

MmDoPeriodicAgressiveTrimming

Aggressively reduce working sets of all tasks

MmPeriodicAgressiveTrimMinFree

Trim working set of cache if available pages greater than this amount

MmPeriodicAgressiveTrimMaxFree

Trim working set of cache if available pages less than this amount

MmPeriodicAgressiveCacheWsMin

Trim cache to this amount periodically

MmWorkingSetReductionMaxCacheWs

Trim cache by this amount if larger than maximum size

MmWorkingSetVolReductionMaxCacheWs

Trim cache by this amount if larger than maximum size during volume reduction

You can potentially use this tool to fine tune Windows NT cache memory management. However, any changes should be made with caution and be thoroughly tested on a noncritical system before they are made on important production systems.

Optimizing Disk I/O Performance

Disk I/O is the third major performance bottleneck that can affect a system or individual job. In this section we look at some of the factors than can affect disk I/O performance, as well as some sample performance data.

The first major factor affecting overall disk performance is the way that disks are divided among the available disk controllers. Placing disks on multiple disk controllers is one way to improve I/O throughput rates. In configuring a system, be sure to compare the maximum transfer rate for each disk adapter with the sum of the maximum transfer rates for all of the disks that it will control; placing too large a load on a disk adapter will do nothing but degrade performance. A more conservative view states that you should limit total maximum disk transfer rates to 75% to 80% of the top adapter speed.

The next step, after a system's hardware configuration, is to plan data distribution among the available disks: in other words, what files go on which disk. The basic principle is distributing the anticipated disk I/O across controllers and disks as evenly as possible (to prevent any one resource from becoming a bottleneck). In its simplest form, this means spreading the files with the highest activity across two or more disks.

So, if you expect most of a system's I/O to come from user processes, distributing the files they are likely to use across multiple disks usually works better than putting everything on a single disk. Similarly, if the system is intended to support multiple large simulations, placing the data for different programs or jobs on different disks (and ideally on separate controllers) minimizes the extent to which they interfere with one another. Placing heavily accessed files on a network rather than local drives is almost always a guarantee of poor performance. Finally, it's almost always a good idea to use a separate disk for the operating system (provided you can afford to do so) in order to isolate the effects of the operating system's own I/O operations from user processes.

The final disk performance factor that we will consider is the physical placement of files on disk. The following general considerations apply to the relationship between file access patterns, physical disk location, and disk I/O performance:

- Filesystem fragmentation degrades I/O performance. Fragmentation results when the free space within a filesystem is scattered in small chunks, rather than fewer large ones of the same total size. This means that files themselves become fragmented (noncontiguous), and access times to reach them become correspondingly longer.

Filesystem fragmentation tends to increase over time. Eventually, it will be necessary to defragment the filesystem. There are currently several commercially available utilities designed for this purpose.

- Sequential access of large files (i.e., reading or writing, starting at the beginning and moving steadily toward the end) is most efficient when the files are contiguous: made up of a single, continuous chunk of space on disk. It may be necessary to defragment or even rebuild a filesystem to create a large amount of contiguous disk space.

- Disk I/O to large sequentially accessed files is also improved by disk striping (see Chapter 5 for information about disk striping without parity).

- Placing large, randomly accessed files (e.g., databases) in the center portions of disk drives (rather than out at the edges) yields the best performance. Random data access is dominated by *seek times*—the time taken to move the disk heads to the correct radius along the platters—and seek times are minimized when the data is in the middle of the disk; it increases at the inner and outer edges. If you are dividing a large disk into several partitions, you can create one comprising the central portion and place the appropriate files into the filesystem for that partition.

- If you plan to use a fault-tolerant filesystem, selecting the appropriate kind for the disk access patterns you anticipate can optimize its I/O performance. Disk mirroring provides good performance for I/O characterized by small transfers, while disk striping with parity optimizes the number of I/O operations per second.

- Be aware that there may be several options for implementing fault tolerance, with differing performance implications. For example, if you wish to provide a fault-tolerant filesystem for a database file, you may select a hardware RAID device (assuming you can afford it), Windows NT software-based RAID 1 or 5, or the mirroring facility provided by the database application. You need to understand how all of the facilities work to make the best selection. In this example, the best software-based solution is usually RAID, implemented by the Windows NT operating system, since the data mirroring facilities provided by many database applications operate sequentially (i.e., only one copy of a data block is written at a time), rather than in parallel.

Monitoring Disk I/O Performance

The following Performance Monitor counters are useful for analyzing disk I/O performance. Note that many of them may be viewed for the system as a whole or for one or more disks of interest and that they all apply to both the Logical Disk and Physical Disk objects:

% Disk Time

Percentage of time that the disk drive is busy reading or writing.

Current Disk Queue Length

The number of pending I/O requests at the current time.

Avg. Disk sec/Transfer

The average time taken by a disk transfer. If desired, this counter may be subdivided by the Avg. Disk sec/Read and Avg. Disk sec/Write counters to track reading and writing rates separately.

Disk Read bytes/sec and Disk Write bytes/sec

The rate at which data is read from or written to the disk (in bytes per second).

Figure 11-25 displays performance data collected during two successive copy operations of the same 10-MB file. The thick gray line plots the Current Disk Queue Length counter, while the black and white lines plot total system disk write and read rates, respectively. The two copy operations are indicated by the two large peaks in the plot.

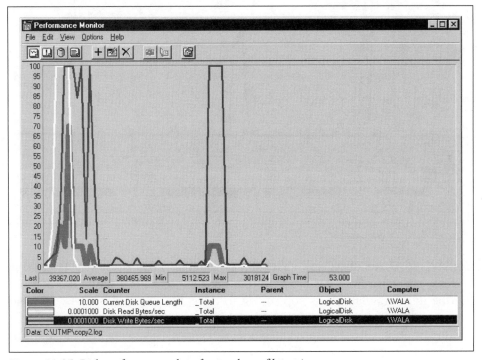

Figure 11-25. Disk performance data for two large file copies

You might have expected that the data for the two copy operations would be identical, but this is not the case. During the first one, disk read and write rates are high. By contrast, there is almost no disk read activity during the second copy. There is plenty of available memory, so the file contents have remained in the disk cache from the first operation, eliminating the need to read them in from disk. The second copy operation also completes much more quickly than the first one, since its write operations do not have to compete with read operations for system I/O capacity (indicated by the much lower disk queue lengths throughout the second copy).

Figure 11-26 compares total disk activity to paging-related I/O operations for the period we are investigating. From this data, it is clear that little of the I/O activity we are seeing is due to paging.

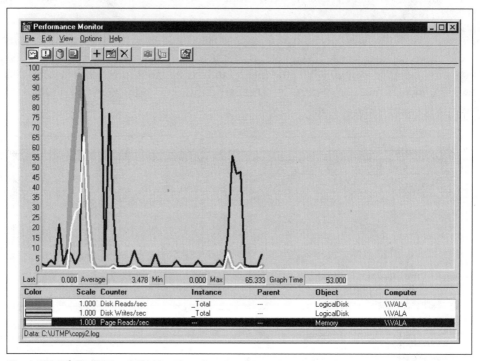

Figure 11-26. Paging activity

Figure 11-27 tracks disk usage for each filesystem individually via their Disk Transfers/sec counters. From this chart, we can see that the source file resided on disk *C:* (the thick gray line), was copied first to drive *K:* (indicated by the white line) and was then copied to drive *J:* (the black line).

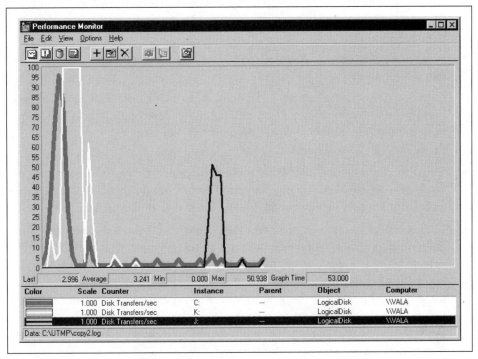

Figure 11-27. I/O performance by logical disk

Network Performance

In the Windows NT environment, network performance is usually as important as single system performance. However, good network performance depends on well-tuned servers, specifically their CPU, memory and disk I/O performance. Network performance also depends on a well-designed division of responsibilities and tasks among the various servers and other systems within the network.

Here are some points and recommendations regarding network performance under Windows NT:

- Make sure that important network servers are configured with sufficient memory. File servers should also be configured and tuned for optimum disk performance.

- Select networking protocols with the expected workload and desired performance in mind. Choose the fastest protocol available when there is a choice for a particular function (usually TCP/IP). Also, install only those protocols that you are actually using on the various systems to minimize networking overhead requirements.

- Adjust network bindings to reflect your network performance goals and typical usage patterns, placing more important protocols above less important ones (see Chapter 8).

- Select the appropriate workload profile setting for each server in a network (see Figure 11-23).

- Network hardware selection is an important factor contributing to network performance. For example, 32-bit bus mastering network adapters provide the best throughput. Slow network adapters on key systems can contribute to poorer overall network performance.

- Network performance problems must be diagnosed by examining the network as a whole. Performance data and error rates from many systems need to be compared to determine the nature and scope of the problem.

- Network performance degradation over time can be reliably identified and diagnosed only via systematic testing. If you suspect that network performance problems have recently arisen or increased, devise some standard operations that you can use to observe and quantitatively measure it (a transfer of a large file is a good one to start with). Perform the test on an idle or lightly loaded network and then under the actual usage conditions. Trying the same test using varying source and destination systems can also enable you to pinpoint the sources of performance problems.

Monitoring Network Performance

We considered the **netstat** command and the Network Monitor tool in Chapter 8. Both of them can be used to monitor current network activity. For example, the following **netstat** command may be used to monitor overall system network activity using the TCP protocol:

```
C:\> netstat /S /P tcp
TCP Statistics

    Active Opens                   = 39
    Passive Opens                  = 164
    Failed Connection Attempts     = 0
    Reset Connections              = 1
    Current Connections            = 3
    Segments Received              = 53923
    Segments Sent                  = 30479
    Segments Retransmitted         = 12
```

The final three entries can give you a general idea of current network activity involving the local system, including the error rate (via Segments Retransmitted). If this number rises above a small percentage of the total traffic, you'll need to investigate where packets are being lost.

The Performance Monitor tool may also be used to monitor network activity. It can monitor multiple systems at the same time; the system of interest is specified via the **Computer** field on the tool's **Add to** dialog boxes. The following counters are the most useful:

Server: Bytes Total/sec

Current rate of network I/O transfers. This counter may also be broken down as Bytes Received/sec and Bytes Transmitted/sec if desired.

Server: Files Open and Server: Files Opened Total

These counters indicate the total number of server files that are currently open and the number of files that have been opened on behalf of network processes. Both of them can provide a general idea of the level of local file and disk I/O occurring via network requests.

Server: Sessions and Server: Logon Total

These counters indicate the total number of network sessions and network logins (full authenticated sessions), respectively. They can give a general idea of the number of user connections to the server.

TCP: Segments Sent/sec, Segments Received/sec and Segments Retransmitted/sec

These counters provide information about current TCP protocol activity by number of segments (as opposed to total bytes). Similarly, various counters of the UDP and IP objects may also be useful for monitoring the network and identifying problems at these networking levels.

Figure 11-28 displays some simple performance data for a single system during a large network file transfer operation (outgoing). The TCP: Segments Retransmitted/ sec counter (the black line) indicates that no network errors are occurring as the data is transferred. The number of network sessions is also constant at a low value (thick gray line), which tells us that network usage is confined to just a few remote systems. The chart also displays the graphs for the TCP: Segments/sec counter (white line), which fluctuates as the file transfer progresses and the Server: Files Open counter, which also increases as the operation proceeds.

Deploying Server Systems

The number and locations of backup domain controllers and other server systems can have a significant effect on overall network performance, and thus on interactive response times and users' perceptions. Figure 11-29 depicts small parts of two Windows NT domains, illustrating some of the factors that ought to be taken into consideration. In this example, assume that domain B trusts domain A.

The illustration includes two of the subnets that make up domain A. Notice that there is a BDC on each of the separate network segments. This placement prevents communications with a domain controller required by Windows NT

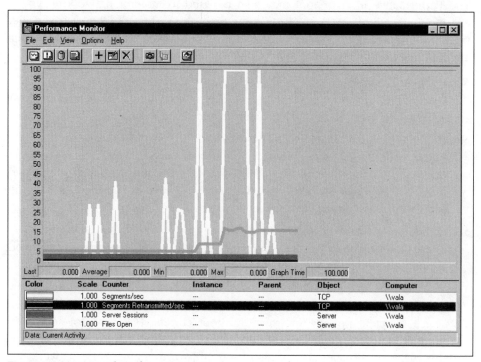

Figure 11-28. Network performance data

systems from becoming a performance bottleneck for either subnet. It also minimizes administrative traffic between the two subnets, limiting it in most cases to
communication between the BDC and the PDC.

Having a server system on the second subnet in domain A is not strictly necessary
for network connectivity; for example, the two subnets could be connected by a
high performance, full-featured router. However, placing a server system on each
subnet improves performance for many sorts of network operations. Ideally, there
should be a server process on each subnet, providing for each major network
facility: DNS, WINS, DHCP, the Browser Service (discussed in the next subsection), and so on, although a single properly configured computer could handle
most or all of them for many subnets.

The second point about server placement becomes clear when we examine
domain B. In addition to its own PDC and BDC, a BDC for domain A is also physically located within the domain. Of course, it is really a member of domain A, but
locating it on the same local network as the systems in domain B once again minimizes the administrative traffic generated by communication between the two
domains. Whenever a domain controller of domain B requires user validation data
for domain A, it can obtain that data by contacting a system on the local network,

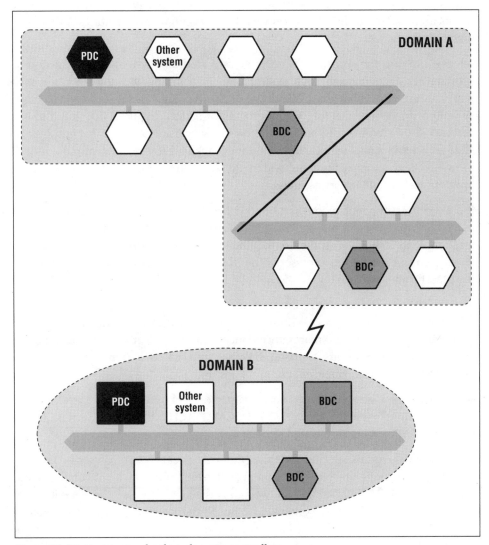

Figure 11-29. Positioning backup domain controllers

rather than having to communicate directly with domain A, which would take significantly longer. If the trust relationship between these domains were two-way, then placing a BDC for domain B somewhere within domain A would also be beneficial.

Configuring the Browser Service

The Windows NT Browser Service is the facility that provides the information displayed in network browse lists in dialog boxes: lists of printers, remote shares, and so on. The reliability and performance of network browsing can be significantly affected by the browser-related configuration settings of systems within the network.

Information for the Browser Service is provided by systems that function as browser servers, although such systems can be running Windows NT server or workstation software or even Windows or Samba. The *master browser* maintains an authoritative *browse list* (the set of information required for the Browser Service). This system distributes the browse list to one or more *backup browser* systems on the same subnet. There is one backup browser system for every 32 browser client systems. Systems within the domain announce their existence to browser systems via broadcast messages.

If a domain consists of more than one subnet, then a master browser and one or more backup browsers will exist for each distinct subnet. Information from each master browser will be gathered together by the *domain master browser* and distributed to each master browser within the domain. This role is usually filled by the PDC for the domain.

Systems are selected as master browser and backup browsers automatically by the Browser Service via a process known as a *browser election*. Browser elections occur under a variety of circumstances, including whenever any system requiring information cannot locate a master browser and when a domain controller or other preferred master browser system comes up.

Whether or not a system can become a master or backup browser depends on two registry values under the HKEY_LOCAL_MACHINE\System\CurrentControl-Set\Services\Browser\Parameters registry keys:

- MaintainServerList specifies whether the system can be a browser or not. The allowed settings are **No**—the system will never serve as a master or backup browser, **Yes**—the system is allowed to serve as a browser, the default setting for Windows NT server systems, and **Auto**—the system is a *potential browser*, capable of performing as a backup browser if it is needed, the default value for Windows NT workstation systems.

- IsDomainMaster specifies whether the computer is a preferred master browser or not—**TRUE** specifies a preferred master browser. By default, this value is set to **FALSE**.

Browser elections are decided on the basis of several criteria: systems running Windows NT are preferred over those running other operating systems, and server systems are preferred over workstation systems. Elections among server systems distinguish among themselves in this decreasing order of preference: the PDC, servers running WINS, a preferred master browser (IsDomainMaster=**TRUE**), the current master browser, an allowed master browser system (MaintainServer-List=**Yes**), and any current backup browser system. All else being equal, the system with the lowest alphabetically ordered hostname will win.

Whenever a browser election takes place, it is repeated one to several times until an equilibrium configuration is reached. Repeated browser elections can affect both browsing and overall network performance, so avoid them if possible. You can do so by setting the preceding registry values to appropriate settings for various systems within the domain:

- Select preferred master browsers for all subnets, except the one containing the PDC, and set IsDomainMaster appropriately. If you so designate one system within a subnet, then it should always become the master browser, but many elections may be necessary when it is unavailable. If you designate more than one system as a preferred master browser, browser elections will occur whenever one or both of them reboot, but you will avoid the chaos that can occur when the usual master browser is down.

- You should select a server system as the preferred master browser system whenever possible.

- Make sure that there are sufficient systems capable of serving as backup browsers (one is needed for every 32 clients) by setting their MaintainServer-List values to **Yes** or **Auto**.

- In order for a subnet's master browser to be able to service requests for its information from systems on other subnets, both of the following conditions must be met:

- The router connecting the subnets must forward UDP port 137, assigned to the NetBT Name Service. This allows the client's broadcast message to reach the subnet's master browser.

- Alternatively, the client system must be capable of contacting the remote system directly by obtaining its IP address via the WINS facility: either via a WINS server or by looking it up in the *LMHosts* file (the client will have previously determined the proper system via the domain master browser).

- The master browser on the subnet must be capable of obtaining the remote system's IP address via the WINS facility: either via a WINS server (often itself) or an *LMHosts* file (which should contain information for all systems on all other subnets within the domain).

- It must also be able to determine the IP address of the PDC via a WINS server or a #DOM entry in the *LMHosts* file.

   If either condition is not met, then the subnet may exhibit the nasty habit of "disappearing" for significant periods of time from the perspective of other subnets within the domain. Clearly, the simplest way to fulfill them is to make sure that every master browser is a WINS server (or has local access to one).

NOTE   If there are systems running LAN Manager version 2.x on the net-
           work with which you want to provide browsing interoperability, the
           Make Browser Broadcasts to LAN Manager 2.x Clients checkbox in
           the Server **Properties** dialog box must be checked (see Figure 11-23).

The Resource Kit includes the **BrowMon** graphical tool and the **BrowStat**
command-line utility for examining the Browser Service within a domain.

Capacity Planning

In this section, we consider some of the quantitative aspects of server capacity
planning. When making decisions about the configurations of key computer
systems, there is no substitute for doing the math.

CPU

The preceding two subsections contained information about server placement
within networks. In general, avoid overloading server systems with too many
tasks. For example, except for the smallest domains, it is unrealistic to expect a
single system to function as the PDC, a file server, a printer server and the
provider of standard network services. If possible, the system serving as the PDC
should be dedicated to that function and not be expected to perform any other
function within the network.

Designating separate systems as special purpose servers is a good way to avoid
overloading any of them with too much work. The file servers should be separate
from the print server, which should be distinct from the systems offering network
services. Be aware that print spooling requires a significant amount of CPU
capacity.

Monitoring system performance under simulated system and network loads
approximating the expected usage allows you to determine how much work a
system is capable of handling and what services may be combined within a single
server.

Memory

It never pays to scrimp on the amount of memory on a system. When deciding on
the amount of memory for a new or existing system, take the following items into
consideration:

- The Windows NT operating system itself requires at least 16 MB of memory. Allow 24 MB or even 32 MB for the operating system, if you can afford it. Memory is not the place to economize.

- To this starting value, add the amount of memory required by applications you expect to run on the system. In general, this item takes the following form for *each* application the system runs simultaneously: *memory/user * #sessions*. For example, if you expect 100 simultaneous database sessions, each using about 50 KB, then you'll need 5 MB of memory to support them.

- Add any additional memory requirements needed by the applications. For example, the SQL Server database server itself requires 5 MB of memory.

- Increase the total you compute by 2% to 5%

You can determine a process's *minimum working set*—the minimum amount of memory that it requires to execute successfully—by starting the process on an idle system, initiating Performance Monitor logging, and then running the **ClearMem** utility from the Resource Kit, which steals memory from all current processes until they reach their minimum size. Once **ClearMem** completes, you can examine the logged performance data and determine the process's final working set size. Use this figure as a lower bound for the amount of memory needed by the process, keeping in mind that its optimal performance may occur with a higher value.

Print servers benefit from generous amounts of physical memory since this process is memory-intensive.

Disk

In general, you should buy the fastest disks and disk controllers that you can afford for key server systems. When determining disk space requirements for a system, keep the following points in mind:

- The Windows NT operating system requires about 100 MB of disk space itself.

- The total amount of recommended paging space is one and a half to four times the amount of physical memory. However, the minimum recommended page file size for a small memory system is 30 to 40 MB.

- Add the disk space requirements of the application programs you plan to run, including permanent storage for their executable and data files and any execution scratch space they may require.

- Take into account any fault tolerance features you plan to use, which will increase the disk space needed to create a filesystem of a given size.

Additional Server Considerations

*   When planning for the number of BDCs within a domain, the rule of thumb is one BDC for every 1,500 users.

*   Microsoft cites a figure of 40 MB as the maximum practical size for the SAM user account database. Under "normal" circumstances, this corresponds to a limit of about 26,000 users per domain. However, your site will find it beneficial to subdivide a domain long before that level is reached.

*   A Remote Access Service (RAS) server is limited to 255 simultaneous connections.

*   Windows NT systems are limited to 16 LAN interfaces (network adapters).

*   The maximum number of printers that can be efficiently managed by a "typical" server system is somewhere in the range of 35 to 60, depending on the system's CPU and memory resources.

12

Automating System Administration

This chapter discusses techniques for automating many Windows NT system administration tasks. In general, such automation offers many advantages over performing such tasks by hand, including:

Greater reliability

Tasks are performed in the same (correct) way every time. Once you have automated a task, its correct and complete performance no longer depends on your alertness or your memory.

Guaranteed regularity

Tasks can be performed according to whatever schedule seems appropriate and need not depend on your availability or even your presence.

Enhanced system efficiency

Time-consuming or resource-intensive tasks can be performed during off-hours, freeing the system for users during their normal work hours.

Automation can be accomplished by several mechanisms, including writing scripts or other programs, taking advantage of standard or commercial automation facilities, such as the Windows NT Schedule Service or any of the available batch processing packages, and installing additional facilities to make a job easier and less labor-intensive.

NOTE   By "automation" I don't always mean a completely hands-off solution to a problem. For example, it can be helpful to create a script to perform a certain task in the desired manner, even if you run the script manually as necessary.

Creating Scripts for System Administration

In this section, we consider a variety of scripts designed to address various Windows NT administrative tasks, as well as some important facilities that can also make system administration easier. The scripts that a system administrator may be called on to write are of two main types:

- Those designed to make system administration easier and more efficient, often by automating some process or job.

- Those that provide necessary or helpful tools for users and are not otherwise available to them.

We will look at scripts intended for both contexts.

We use the freely available Perl scripting language for the scripts in this chapter. While Windows NT provides many GUI administrative tools and a few command line utilities (and a few more in the Resource Kit), it lacks many features necessary for system administration automation. In addition, the Windows NT command language is limited in its scope and functionality.

Perl addresses many of the deficiencies of standard Windows NT scripting.[*] The following are among its most useful features:

- Perl makes it easy to combine native tools with a powerful command language.

- Parsing and processing user input and textual output is easy.

- Arithmetic is easy (it's not really even possible in the native Windows NT command language).

- Perl provides built-in pattern matching via regular expressions.

- Perl provides associative arrays for managing and manipulating textual key-based data.

A discussion of the Perl language is beyond the scope of this book. Consult Appendix B for the standard works on Perl (as well as for Internet sources for obtaining the software).

---

[*] Python and Tk/Tcl are also good choices available for the Windows NT environment.

Perl Resources for Windows NT

In addition to the standard Perl language, there are a number of "standard" Perl modules designed for the Win32 environment (i.e., Windows NT and Windows 95) that are part of the basic Perl distribution. Table 12-1 lists these modules.

Table 12-1. Win32 Perl Modules

Win32 Module	What Component Routines Do
Win32::ChangeNotify	Monitor changes to filesystem
Win32::Eventlog	Read and save event log entries
Win32::File	Manipulate DOS file attributes
Win32::IPC	IPC support for other modules
Win32::Mutex	Manipulate MUTEX objects
Win32::NetAdmin	Determine PDC, create/display/modify user accounts, administer groups
Win32::NetResource	Map drive letters to shares and manipulate shares
Win32::Process	Create/kill/suspend/resume process, get/set process priority class, get process status, wait for process to complete
Win32::Registry	Display/modify registry key/value settings
Win32::Service	Query and manipulates services
Win32::Semaphore	Manipulate semaphores

There are some additional Perl extension routines that support Win32 systems, and other contributed modules designed for the Windows NT environment. We consider an important example of the latter later in this chapter.

The remainder of this section consists of Perl scripts designed to perform useful tasks and to illustrate techniques for creating scripts to automate system administration.

Finding a File's Backup Set

We begin with a simple Perl utility to search the standard log files created by the Windows NT Backup facility. This script isn't really Win32-specific in any way. Here is an example of how the script, named *findit.pl*, is used:

```
C:\> perl findit.pl urgent.dat
The file *urgent.dat* is located on the following backup tapes:

Tape            Date
--------------------------
Ananke_Fri      6/13/97
Ananke_Thu      6/12/97
Ananke_Full4    6/2/97
Ananke_Full3    5/5/97
```

```
Ananke_Full2     4/7/97
Archive_15B      3/31/97
Ananke_Full1     3/3/97
```

The utility searches the log files in a designated directory and lists the corresponding tape name and date whenever it finds a match.

Here is the first part of the Perl script:

```perl
# findit.pl

if  ($ARGV[0] eq "") { exit; }  # could add a usage message here
$searchfile=$ARGV[0];

$dir =  $ENV{"LOGLOC"};
opendir LOGDIR, $dir or die "Can't access backup log directory";
@allfiles = readdir LOGDIR;
closedir LOGDIR;
&printheader;
$nonefound=1;
```

The script exits if no argument is provided when it is invoked. Next, it determines the location of the designated log file directory by translating the LOGDIR environment variable. It then opens the directory and reads its contents into the array *@allfiles.*

The heart of the script is a loop over the files in the directory. Each file is opened, and the tape name is extracted from the save set header lines. Then the various lines in the file are examined and processed in turn, as the comments within the script explain:

```perl
foreach $file (@allfiles) {
    if ($file =~ /^.*.Log$/) {
        open(NEXTLOG,$file) or next;
        $tapename = substr($file,0,-4);
        while (<NEXTLOG>) {
            # Ignore everything after the verify pass header line
            if ($_ =~ /Verify Status/) { goto MOVE_ON; }
            # Extract the tape name if the proper line
            elsif ($_ =~ /^Tape Name/) {
                @junk = split;
                $tapedate = substr ($junk[5], 0, -1);
                }
            # Start of a new directory within the save set (save name)
            elsif ($_ =~ /^ Directory/) {
                ($junk, $currdir) = split;
            # We could check the directory here if searching for a pathname.
                }
            # Otherwise it's a regular entry, so check for
            # the desired file name
            elsif ($_ =~ /[AP]M$/) {
                ($thisfile,$size,$filedate,$filetime,$ampm) = split;
                if ($thisfile =~ /$searchfile/) {
```

```
                    print "$tapename\t$tapedate\t\t$currdir\n";
                    $nonefound=0;      # We found a match
                    }
                }
            }
MOVE_ON: close(NEXTLOG);  # Close the file and restart the loop
        }
    }
    print "No matches found\n" if $nonefound;
```

This script determines if each line in the file is of interest by comparing its initial contents to several character strings. If one of them matches, relevant information is extracted from the remainder of the line. Otherwise, the line is assumed to be a normal file entry in the backup log and is searched for the desired filename.

All that remains is the simple subroutine *printheader*:

```
sub printheader {
    print "Tape\t\tDate\t\tDirectory\n";
    print "---------------------------------------------------\n";
    }
```

This script could be easily extended to print the directory location corresponding to each matching entry within the log files, and to search for a full path as well as a simple filename, by initially separating its argument into directory and filename portions and comparing the former to the value of *$currdir*.

Listing User Rights

This script, *ur.pl*, illustrates the combination of Perl logic and scripting features in conjunction with native Windows NT commands. It uses the **DumpACL** utility (Somarsoft) we examined in Chapter 6 and the **ShowGrps** command from the Resource Kit to produce a list of user rights that have been assigned to a specified user.

Here is an example of its use:

```
C:\> perl ur.pl chavez
User Right                      Gained via
----------------------------------------------
Add workstations to domain      Chavez
Bypass traverse checking        Everyone
Login locally                   Chem
Login via network               Everyone
```

The script displays each right held by the user and the entity through which it is obtained (user or local account, global or built-in group).

Here is the beginning of the script, which checks for an argument and translates it to uppercase:

```
# ur.pl

if ($ARGV[0] eq "") { die "Usage: ur.pl name"; }
$name=$ARGV[0]; $name =~ tr/a-z/A-Z/;
```

Next, the script runs the **DumpACL** command, sending its output to the file *rights.out*:

```
system("dumpacl /rpt=rights /outfile=rights.out /saveas=csv");
sleep 3;   # This is a kludge
```

The script then determines the user's group memberships by examining the output of the **ShowGrps** command, storing them in the associative array *$has* (using the *$group* variable as its key):

```
open GROUPS, "showgrps $name |" or die;
while (<GROUPS>) {
    if ($_ =~ /^Error:/) { goto DO_IT; }    # No groups returned
    $i++;
    if ($i > 3) {
        chop;
        s/\\/%/; tr/a-z/A-Z/;
        ($junk,$group) = split("%");
        $has{$group}=1;                      # Save each group name
    }}
close GROUPS;
```

We're now ready to process the rights list output. The script next opens the results of the **DumpACL** command and processes it:

```
DO_IT:
open RF,"rights.out" or die "Can't find rights list.";
print "User Right\t\t\t\tGained via\n\n";
$prev="";  # Holds right just printed (to eliminate duplicates)

# Process the file contents
while (<RF>) {
    $j++;
    if (not ($j <= 3 or $_ =~ ",,")) {
        chop;
        # Parse each entry in the file
        ($junk,$who,$right) = split(",",$_,3);
        $who =~ tr/a-z/A-Z/;
        chop($right);

        # Check for match with username
        if ($who eq $name and $right ne $prev) {
            print "$right\t$who\n"; $prev=$right; }
        # Then check if user is a member of this group
        elsif (exists $has{$who} and $right ne $prev) {
            print "$right\t$who\n"; $prev=$right; }
        }
    }
close RF;
```

For each entry in the output file, the script first checks if the holder field—the second field in each line, stored in the variable *$who*—matches the specified username. If not, it checks if the user is a member of a group with that name by consulting the *$has* array. If a match is found in either case, the right and its holder are printed, provided that this right has not already been included in the output.

Forcing All Users to Change Their Passwords

We discussed the need for requiring all users to change their passwords in Chapter 3. The next script does this using one possible method: the **Global** command from the Resource Kit (to obtain a list of users within the domain) and the **UserSetAttributes** function from the Win32::NetAdmin Perl module.

The script, *newpass.pl*, opens by invoking the Win32::NetAdmin module and generating a user account list for the domain (which in this case we obtain via a hard-coded group name):

```
# newpass.pl

use Win32::NetAdmin;

# These could be arguments
open USERS, "global goodguys Borealis | " or die;
```

The heart of the script is a *while* loop over the user list:

```
while (<USERS>) {
  chop;
  # Get current account attributes for this user
  Win32::NetAdmin::UserGetAttributes("vala", $_, $password,
    $passwordAge, $privilege, $homeDir, $comment, $flags, $scriptPath);

  # Set the password age attribute to 1 second
  Win32::NetAdmin::UserSetAttributes("vala", $_, $password, 1,
    privilege, $homeDir, $comment, $flags, $scriptPath);

  print "Processed user $_\n";
  }
```

The fourth argument of both functions within the Win32::NetAdmin module is the password age: the length of time remaining until the password lifetime expires and must be changed by the user. Setting it to one second effectively expires the password immediately.

Clearly, this is a quick-and-dirty solution for this task. A better approach would be a programmatic equivalent to checking the **User Must Change Password at Next Logon** check box in the **User Properties** dialog box of the User Manager administrative tool, but at the moment no such mechanism exists. The approach we choose here makes a number of assumptions:

- The domain password policy must not force users to login prior to password expiration in order to change it (see the final check box in Figure 3-2).

- The password history features of the password policy should be enabled (otherwise, users could simply reselect their current passwords).

- Passwords remain unchanged until users log in, posing a continuing security risk.

Providing UNIX-Style Utilities: df and quot

UNIX systems provide a couple of useful utilities for displaying system disk usage. In this subsection, we examine Perl scripts that provide similar functionality for Windows NT systems.

Displaying a disk usage summary

All of the information required by a **df** command, which displays used and free space on a filesystem-by-filesystem basis, is clearly available under Windows NT. For example, clicking on a disk icon in the **My Computer** folder will display its usage at the bottom of the window. However, there is no command that will produce the same data in a timely manner.*

We could write a program in C, which executes the required Win32 API calls to obtain this information. However, Perl provides a more practical, much faster to implement alternative. Our strategy is to use the output of the Resource Kit's **ShowDisk** command to identify the filesystems and their types and total capacities within the system and then to perform a very fast **Dir** command to obtain the amount of free space in the filesystem. We can then calculate the amount of space that is in use.

Here is some sample output from this script, *df.pl*:

```
D:\WORK\PERL> perl df.pl

Label    Drive   Total   Used    Free    FS Type
                 MB      MB      MB

Ariadne  C       598     550     48      Normal
ANANKE   D       500     459     41      Normal
Aporia   G       1021    0       1021    Stripe Set
Acrasia  H       510     0       510     Mirror
```

---

* **Dir /S ** displays the total capacity and used space for a filesystem, eventually, but it is a slow and tediously verbose way of getting it.

Aveya	I	686	7	679	RAID 5
Amelia	J	1162	156	1006	Volume Set
Amanda	K	300	286	14	Volume Set
Anitra	L	439	162	277	Normal

The script opens by running the **ShowDisk** command and examining its output:

```
# df.pl

$found_C=0;
open SD, "showdisk |" or die;
while (<SD>) {
    if ($_ =~ /^Disk #0$/) { goto PHASE2; } # We've found all the disks

    # Extract the filesystem type for the current partition
    if ($_ =~ /FT Type\.\./) {
        chop;
        ($junk,$junk,$type) = split(" ",$_,3);
         # Shorten two verbose type names
        $type = "Normal" if ($type =~ /^Not a Fault/);
        $type = "RAID 5" if ($type =~ /^Stripe Set with Parity/);
        }

    # Extract the total size of the current partition
    elsif ($_ =~ /[^t]Length\.\./) { ($junk,$size) = split; }

    # Extract the drive letter assigned to this partition
    elsif ($_ =~ /Drive Letter\.\./) {
        ($junk,$junk,$drive) = split;
        # Avoid duplicate C drive entries
        if ($drive eq "C" and $found_C) { goto PHASE2; }
        if ($drive eq "C") { $found_C = 1; }

        # Accumulate sizes for fault tolerant filesystem components
        $sizes{$drive} =
            ($type =~ /^[SVR]/) ? $sizes{$drive}+$size : $size;
        $types{$drive} = $type;

        # Count the number of components in RAID 5 filesystems
        $raid{$drive}++ if ($type =~ /RAID 5/);
        }
    }
```

This part of the script uses our now-familiar strategy of pattern matching to locate desired lines within the output, which are then parsed to extract the desired information. In this case, the process does some special handling of certain sorts of entries to avoid duplicate data for drive *C:* and to correctly compute the total size for fault-tolerant filesystems (where some of the component disk space is consumed by parity information rather than actual file data). The script uses the associative arrays *$sizes*, *$types*, and *$raid* to store the information it is accumulating for each filesystem. All three of them are keyed via the drive letter (stored in the variable *$drive*).

The next section of the script produces the actual output:

```
PHASE2:
close SD;
print "\nLabel\tDrive\tTotal\tUsed\tFree\tFS Type\n\t\tMB\tMB\tMB\n\n";

# Loop over the drive letters found
foreach $let (keys %sizes) {
  $free=-1;

  # Run a quick DIR command to get filesystem's free space and label
  # (/-c says to omit the usual comma in usage figures)
  open DIR, "dir /w /-c $let:\ 2> junk.junk |" or next;
  while (<DIR>) {
      if ($_ =~ /bytes free/) { ($free,$junk) = split; }
      if ($_ =~ /Volume in drive/) { ($j,$j,$j,$j,$j,$name) = split; }
      }
  $free /= (1024*1024); $free = int($free);  # Convert to integer MB
  close DIR;

  # Convert sizes array to integer MB
  $sizes{$let} /= (1024*1024);
  $sizes{$let} = int($sizes{$let});

  # If filesystem is type RAID 5, then compute the real size
  # from the number of component partitions
  if ($types{$let} =~ /RAID 5/) {
      $sizes{$let} *= (($raid{$let} - 1) / $raid{$let});
      $sizes{$let} = int($sizes{$let});
      }

  # If DIR command failed, then a filesystem doesn't exist on that
  # drive (and $free still = -1), so all space is free
  if ($free < 0) { $free=$sizes{$let}; }

  # Compute used disk space
  $used=$sizes{$let}-$free;

  # Display entry for this filesystem
  print "$name\t$let\t$sizes{$let}\t$used\t$free\t$types{$let}\n";
  }
```

Perl purists will regard this solution as inelegant, but it gets the job done. Recently, new functions have been added to the excellent AdminMisc Perl module, written by Dave Roth, which makes this script much simpler:

```
# df2.pl

use Win32::AdminMisc;

# Get list of local filesystems
@drives = Win32::AdminMisc::GetDrives(DRIVE_FIXED);

print "\nDrive\tTotal\tFree\tUsed\n\t\tMB\tMB\tMB\n\n";
```

```
foreach $let (@drives) {
   # Get total space and free space for each drive
   @size = Win32::AdminMisc::GetDriveSpace($let);

   # Convert to MB, compute used space and print
   $tot = int ($size[0] / (1024 * 1024));
   $free = int ($size[1] / (1024 * 1024));
   $used=$tot - $free;
   print "$let\t\t$tot\t$free\t$used\n";
   }
```

The two functions from the Win32::AdminMisc module make this job simple and straightforward. Here is an example of its output:

```
C:\> perl df2.pl
```

Drive	Total MB	Free MB	Used MB
C:\	598	52	546
D:\	499	4	495
G:\	1019	101	4
H:\	509	505	4
I:\	683	679	4
J:\	1161	1006	155
K:\	300	5	295
L:\	439	273	166

Reporting disk usage by user

It is often useful to have current disk usage broken down by user to see where the disk space is going and who is using a lot of it. The next script, *quot.pl*, provides such information for the directory tree specified as its argument:

```
C:\> perl quot.pl C:\Temp
```

```
C:\Temp:
```

User	KB
Administrators	209
Chavez	87
Dagmar	4

Here is the script, which begins by checking for an argument:

```
# quot.pl

if ($ARGV[0] eq "") { exit; }
$dir=$ARGV[0];

# Extract information from the appropriate "ls -lR" command
# Using OpenNT, the equivalent command is "ls -oR"
open DAT, "cd $dir & ls.exe -oR |" or die;
```

```
while (<DAT>) {
   next if $_ =~ /.*:$/;   # Ignore directory header lines
   @x=split;

   # Accumulate user totals in $tot associative array
   $tot{$x[2]}+=$x[3];
   }
close DAT;
```

The script relies on a UNIX-style **ls -lR** command to obtain file size and ownership data. In this case, we are using the one from the OpenNT product (which in fact uses the arguments **-oR**).[*]

The associative array *$tot*, which is keyed on user account names, holds the running total size of files belonging to each user.

The remainder of the script creates and prints the output table:

```
print "\n$dir:\n\nUser\t\tKB\n--------------------\n";

foreach $user (keys %tot) {
   next if $user eq "";        # Skip any blank username
   next if $tot{$user} == 0;   # Skip zero values

   $tot{$user}/=1024; $tot{$user}=int($tot{$user});   # Convert to KB
   if ($tot{$user} == 0) { $tot{$user} = 1 };

   print "$user\t$tot{$user}\n" if length($user)>6;
   print "$user\t\t$tot{$user}\n" if length($user)<7;
   }
```

Adding New Users

At the conclusion of Chapter 3, we commented on the need for a more flexible user account management tool suitable for handling a great number of users. In this subsection, we examine the *amu.pl* script designed for this purpose. This script makes extensive use of standard Perl features, Windows NT account and group manipulation commands, Win32::NetAdmin module functions (including UserCreate, UserSetAttributes, LocalGroupAddUsers and GroupAddUsers), Win32:AdminMisc module functions (UserGetMiscAttributes, UserSetMiscAttributes and GetLogonName), and some new utility functions written for this utility:

IsGroup($name)

> Returns **G**, **L**, or **N**, depending on whether the item stored in *$name* is a global group, local group, or not a group name.

---

[*] Minor modifications to the parsing strategy may be necessary for different implementations of the **ls** command. For example, if the "group owner" is also included in the output, then the size will have to be extracted as the first field from the substring of each line, beginning at about character 46 (since the group name may consist of one or more words).

UserExists($name, $domain)

> Returns **True** or **False** depending on whether the specified user is a domain user in the specified domain (which defaults to the local domain).

ReallyIsMember($user, $group)

> Returns **True** or **False** depending on whether the specified user is a member of the specified group, taking into account her memberships in global groups that are members of a local group.

This script supports a large number of options, summarized in Table 12-2.

Table 12-2. Options to amu.pl

Option	Meaning and Use
-u *name(s)*	User accounts to create or modify, according to the options that follow
-n *name*	User full name
-d *string*	Account description
-c *string*	User comment
-w *pwd*	Password
-x	User is not allowed to change his password
-g *list*	Specify group memberships
-h *dir*	Specify home directory (created if necessary)
-p *name*	Specify user profile to copy
-s *script*	Specify login script name
-P *codes*	Prompt for items specified via code letters; **-P 0** = stop all prompting
-U *user(s)*	User accounts to create/modify with current options (except as overridden with later options)
-F *file*	Take input from the specified file
-D *file*	Specify an account defaults file
-S *file*	Save all current options to the account defaults file
-R	Don't apply any defaults to the current set of users
-L	Operate on the local system only (domain is the default)
-G *file*	Log all actions to the specified file; **-G 0** = stop logging

The functioning of this script is best explained by looking at several examples. For example, the following command adds or modifies the *Davis, Greene,* and *Forche* user accounts (creating them if they don't already exist), placing the users into the *Chem* and *Bio* groups. If any new accounts are created, other account characteristics are taken from the utility's default values (discussed later):

```
C:\> perl amu.pl -u Davis,Greene,Forche -g Chem,Bio
```

The following command performs the same operation as the previous one, but this time the script prompts for the full name corresponding to each user:

```
C:\> perl amu.pl -u Davis,Greene,Forche -g Chem,Bio -p n
Full name for Davis: Violet Davis
Full name for Greene: Marty Greene
Full name for Forche: Carl Forche
```

The following command again creates or modifies the same three accounts, this time specifying the root of their home directories to be *vala**homes*. However, in this case, user *Forche* is placed only into the *Bio* group:

```
C:\> perl amu.pl -u Davis,Greene -g Chem,Bio -h \\vala\homes ^
        -U Forche -g Bio
```

The command's -U option introduces a second set of user accounts. These users inherit whatever option settings are currently in effect, subject to modifications by any additional options following the user list. In contrast, the -u option introduces a new user set for which all options are reset to their default values before being modified by any following options. You can include as many different user lists on a single command as desired, each with different account attribute settings.

Default user account settings are taken from the file *amu.defs* in the current directory, or a different file may be specified via the -D option. The -R option prevents any file-based default values from being applied to subsequent user sets, until another -D option is encountered.

Input may also be taken from a prepared file using this syntax:

```
C:\> perl amu.pl [-u ... opts1] -F users.new opts2 [-u|U opts3 .... ]
```

This command says to add or modify the first user set (if present) using the settings specified in *opts1*; then take a second set of users from the file *users.new*, applying the options specified in *opts2*; and finally process any additional user sets (or files).

Here is a small sample input file:

```
$SEP=;
$SUBSEP=,
# u f i
Chavez;Rachel Chavez;y
Reese;Terrence Reese
# u g
Gold,Silver,White,Black;Chem,Phys,Everybody
```

The first two lines define the field and list separator characters, respectively. These may be changed at any point in the file. The lines beginning with a number sign indicate the format for the following group of records; the code letters used there have the same meanings as the corresponding script options. This file has user account information specified using two different formats.

NOTE   Options specified on the command line following a **-F** option are used only as defaults. They never override any information entered into the records of the data file itself.

Even more complex uses of the command are possible, but not necessarily recommended.

Script overview

This script is far too lengthy for a line-by-line discussion. However, the following outline indicates the basic structure of this Perl script:

```perl
# amu.pl

use Win32::NetAdmin;
use Win32::AdminMisc;

$user=Win32::LoginName();
if (not ($user eq "Administrator" or
   Win32::NetAdmin::LocalGroupIsMember
  ($server,"Administrators",$user)) { exit; }

# parse the defaults file and set variables accordingly
set_initial_defaults();

# process arguments and set up account additions/modifications
parse_args();

for ($i=0; $i < $num_sets; $i++) {
  @next_set=split(",",$users[$i]);
  foreach $human (@next_set) {
    Check if new account
    Create and run a net user command
    Loop over groups
       Check if a member if it's an existing user
       If not, add user to group
    Assign password
       Pre-expire password
    Assign and create home directory and set ownership/permissions
    Assign and copy login script if personal script being used
    Assign and create user profile if custom one being used
    Log activities if requested
  }}
```

A large part of the work is done by the *parse_args* subroutine, which processes the command's input and sets up a series of arrays holding the specifications for each user account to be added or modified. The script then loops over the account sets specified by the administrator and over each user account, applying the desired settings to each of them.

Monitoring Event Logs from Multiple Systems

We previously considered the Windows NT system event logs in Chapters 2 and 10. In this section, we briefly examine some facilities for dealing with the event logs from multiple Windows NT systems.

The currently available tools use one of three strategies:

Utilities
> Write events of interest to a text file for later processing or filtering

Packages
> Provide a complete system for managing and analyzing the event logs generated within a network (generally commercial software)

Facilities
> Mimic or interface to the UNIX **syslog** facility

Tools of the first type include the filtering features within the Event Viewer administrative tool itself, the **DumpEvt** program from Somarsoft (shareware) and the freely available Perl script **ESentry**.

The latter item is the simplest. This Perl script extracts and displays all error events that have occurred since it was last run for all of the computer systems specified in its configuration file (*ESentry.Ini*). Here is a small sample of its output:

```
Program run by account: Administrator
Program run at time: 876158654 [ 13:24:14 10/6/97 ]
Perlpath:  L:\perl
 Lastrun:  0 [ 19:0:0 12/31/69 ]
 Servers:  vala lilith

Server vala checks out ok
vala, Security log. has 1822 entries.
...

RecordNumber  1
TimeWritten   23:38:18 9/8/97
Source        Service Control Manager
EventID       -2147476648
EventCategory 0
EventType     Error
Computer      VALA
Strings       3Com EtherLink III PC Card Driver
...
```

Each error or warning from the event log of each selected system is displayed in this format. Thus, this script can combine events from a variety of sources, but the problem of separating the important ones from the unimportant ones still remains.

The **DumpEvt** utility can perform a similar function. For example, the following command will dump all records from the security event log on system *lilith,* since the last time the command was run to the file *lilith.dat,* clearing the remote security event log afterward:

```
C:\> dumpevt /logfile=sec /outfile=lilith.dat ^
            /computer=lilith /clear
```

Here are two records from the resulting data file (wrapped due to their length):

```
SEC,10/5/97 11:02:03,Security,538,Success,Logon/Logoff
,BOREALIS\Administrator,VALA,User Logoff:^^  User Name:
    ADMINISTRATOR^^     Domain:         BOREALIS^^  Logon ID:
    (0x0 0xDD3D9)^^     Logon Type:     3^^

SEC,10/5/97 11:02:17,Security,528,Success,Logon/Logoff
,BOREALIS\Administrator,VALA,Successful Logon:^^    User Name:
    ADMINISTRATOR^^     Domain:         BOREALIS^^  Logon ID:
    (0x0 0xDD3EE)^^     Logon Type:     3^^     Logon Process:
    KSecDD^^        Authentication Package:
    MICROSOFT_AUTHENTICATION_PACKAGE_V1_0^^     Workstation Name:
    \\DEMETER
```

The various fields are separated by commas; the event ID appears in the fourth field. The final field contains all of the additional information about the event provided by the Event Log facility; line breaks within it are indicated by double carets (^^). The data is provided in a form suitable for importing into a database or spreadsheet program, where the individual records could be sorted and filtered for further analysis.

The **EventAdmin** product from Midwestern Commerce is at the opposite extreme from these simple, low-cost tools. It attempts to provide a complete multisystem event log analysis environment.

EventAdmin takes data from the event logs on one or more systems and imports it directly into a Microsoft Access or SQL Server database. You can then analyze the data via the standard database product query and reporting facilities. The product also includes several useful reports and predefined queries for the Microsoft Access database environment.

UNIX system administrators may prefer integrating the Windows NT Event Log facility with the similar **syslog** facility. There are several freely available programs for doing so, including the following:

- The **SL4NT** shareware program (written by Franz Krainer) provides a native **syslog** server for Windows NT, somewhat integrated with the standard Event Log and Performance Monitor facilities. It is run as a Windows NT service.

- West Georgia Web Service's **SyslogD** shareware program, another native syslog server for the Windows NT environment. This server may be installed as a Windows NT service.

- The **EvntSLog** program (a shareware program from Adiscon) which sends event log messages to a syslog daemon on a UNIX system, allowing Windows NT system messages to be incorporated into an already-existing central repository and analysis scheme.

The Directory Replication Service

The Windows NT Directory Replication Service is a facility for automatically copying files between systems within a domain. It is designed for distributing user account login scripts and system policies, but you may also use it for your own purposes. The facility automatically copies files from a designated *export* directory tree on a master server (usually the PDC) into designated *import* directory trees on client systems at specified intervals. These directories are conventionally located as the *Export* and *Import* subdirectories of *%SystemRoot%\System32\REPL*. Login scripts are exported and imported via the *Scripts* subdirectories of both locations.

You set up automatic directory exporting from the Server Manager administrative tool by opening the properties of the source system and selecting the **Replication** button on the **Properties** dialog box. This brings up the **Directory Replication** dialog box, illustrated in Figure 12-1.

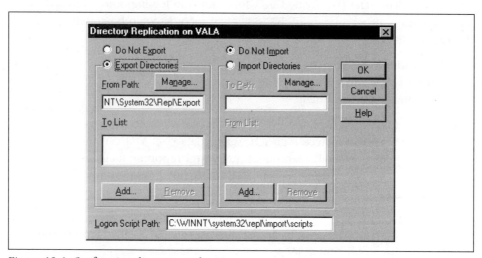

Figure 12-1. Configuring directory replication

Directory exporting is enabled using the **Export Directories** radio button, and the root of the export directory tree is specified in the **From Path** field (the illustration shows the default location). Only a single directory tree may be exported from any given system.

If the **To List** is empty, the directory is automatically exported to all systems within the local domain. If you wish to export to a subset of the systems within the local domain or include systems in another domain, you must specify the names of the desired systems in this list, using its **Add** button. You may select either individual systems or entire domains.

NOTE   Specifying a list of export systems also limits which systems can import the data from this server.

Import computers are configured using the right side of the same dialog box. Selecting the **Import Directories** radio button enables importing via the directory replication service, and the import directory is specified in the **To Path** field. The **From List** field again optionally lists the names of systems from which replicated data will be accepted.

The Directory Replication Service is started and controlled using the **Services** control panel applet. It may be configured for automatic startup, and a special user account may be specified to run the service. This user account must be a member of the *Backup Operators* group.

Directory replication frequency is determined using the various values of the HKEY_LOCAL_MACHINE\System\CurrentControlSet\Services\Replicator\Parameters registry key. These are the most important:

Interval

Specifies how often the service on export systems checks the outgoing directories for changes, in minutes. The default is five, and the maximum value is 60. When changes are found, the server sends an update notice to all of the systems to which it exports, and these systems can initiate an actual data copy operation by responding with an update request.

Pulse

Specifies the repeat interval for the most recent update notice on server systems. Export servers continue to send the change notice continuously (to make sure that no import system fails to receive it) every *Interval ∗ Pulse* minutes. The default setting for Pulse is 3, which means that update notices are sent every fifteen minutes by default (the maximum value is 10).

You must restart the Directory Replicator service for any changes to its parameters to take effect.

You can use the directory replication service to transfer files other than login scripts by adding subdirectories to the export and import directory trees. An individual system can receive replicated data from more than one server. The **Manage** button on the **Directory Replication** dialog box may be used to specify what subset of the directory replication tree is exported or imported for each system, as well as file-locking characteristics during the data-transfer process.

NOTE   You need to configure the system holding the master copies of the user login scripts as both an export and import system so that the scripts are present in their expected location (within the import directory tree) on that system itself.

Quick Start for Experienced UNIX System Administrators

This appendix provides a compact, fast-paced, terse overview of Windows NT system administration designed for experienced UNIX system administrators. It is intended to get you started working under Windows NT and to make it easy to find out how to perform various familiar actions in that environment. Cross references to the main text refer you to fuller discussions of most topics.

This appendix also includes tables listing similar Windows NT commands for a variety of common UNIX commands and corresponding Windows NT locations for standard UNIX directories and configuration files. Its final section provides an overview of freely available and commercial software that provides UNIX-style functionality under Windows NT.

NOTE   Like the rest of this book, this appendix assumes a basic user-level knowledge of the Windows NT environment.

Finding Your Way Around

Logging In

There are a few points about logging in to a Windows NT system that may not be obvious to a UNIX user:

- When you log in to a Windows NT domain, what you are actually logging into is the network, not the specific system at which you happen to be seated.* Domainwide settings for user account attributes, file, directory, and other resource permissions and allowed and forbidden user actions will be in effect, and these global settings supersede those on the local system. Similarly, when you are logged in as the domain *Administrator*, the scope of administrative tools generally defaults to the domain rather than to any single system within it.

- Windows NT is not a multiuser operating system. Only one user may be logged in to a given server or workstation system at a time, although multiple users may use the resources of a given system simultaneously. The final sections of Chapter 4 discuss products that address this deficiency.

- You must enter the CTRL-ALT-DEL key sequence before the login screen will appear. Any screen appearing without your having entered CTRL-ALT-DEL is most likely the product of a Trojan horse program masquerading as the normal login sequence.

- After a system reboot, user logins are allowed at an earlier point in the process than on UNIX systems. In particular, you can't be certain that all system-initialization activities will have completed before a user login occurs. There is no guarantee that standard system activities or ones you designate in a system boot script will have finished prior to the first user login.

The Administrator Account

The superuser account on Windows NT system is named *Administrator* by default (it may be renamed if desired). In fact, any account that is a member of the *Administrators* group has equivalent status. As on UNIX systems, Windows NT administrative accounts are all-powerful; while items may be temporarily protected against administrative accounts, administrators can always modify their protections to gain access to them.

There is no native Windows NT feature comparable to the UNIX **su** facility. There are, however, several add-on **su**-like packages, including the following:

- The Resource Kit includes an **su** facility. However, I can't recommend using it, since the system privileges it requires present an unacceptable security risk.

- The best of the freely available **su** facilities is the **susrv** package by Steffen Krause. See Appendix B for sources for this software.

Since virtually all administrative tasks under Windows NT can be performed only by an administrator, an **su** command is much less useful for full-time Windows NT

---

* To log in locally to the current system, select the system's hostname as the domain in the Windows NT login dialog box.

system administrators than it is for UNIX system administrators. If your administrative duties are intermittent, however, an **su** command may prevent the tedium of repeated logouts and logins between your normal and administrative user accounts.

Windows NT Filesystem Layout

Windows NT system files are concentrated in the Windows NT installation directory subtree, which is usually *C:\WinNT.* The *%SystemRoot%* built-in environment variable always points to the location of the Windows NT tree.

Well-behaved application programs are stored in separate directory trees whose locations are usually designated when they are installed. Some applications are located under *C:\Program Files,* and standard Microsoft Office applications are generally located under *C:\MSOffice.*

The Windows NT filesystem structure is discussed in detail in Chapter 1.

Files Under Windows NT

File ownership and protection are quite a bit different under Windows NT than on UNIX systems. These are the most significant differences:

- Files have only one owner, corresponding to the UNIX user owner. There are no group owners.

- File access is governed by *access control lists* (ACLs), rather than permission bits as on UNIX systems. Here is an example of an access control list:

```
C:\Temp\Test88.Bat
    Owner: Administrators
    Administrators (lg)          (All) Dir Access
    Chavez                       (RX) Dir Access
    Chem (gg)                    (RWXD) Dir Access
    Bio (gg)                     (RO) Dir Access
```

Individual users and groups may be assigned specific access via ACLs. In this example, the user *Chavez*, the global groups *Chem* and *Bio,* and the local group *Administrators* each have been granted access to the file. Everyone else has no access.

- As the preceding ACL indicates, there are more than three base-level permissions that can be granted for files and directories. Windows NT defines six basic permission types (**R**ead, **W**rite, e**X**ecute, **D**elete, take **O**wnership, and change **P**ermissions) and several named subsets of them.

- Network file access is also controlled by an additional protection layer, specified at the exported directory level (*share permissions*).

- File protection for new files and subdirectories flows from the permission settings of the new item's parent directory, not from any setting or entity specified by the creating user (i.e., there is no equivalent to the UNIX *umask*).

See Chapter 6 for details on Windows NT file ownership and permissions.

Processes Under Windows NT

Processes on Windows NT systems are conceptually similar to those on UNIX systems (although there is no real analogue to the fork-and-exec technique). As with many multiprocessor-enabled operating systems, the actual executable entities are threads, one or more of which form a process. Chapter 4 discusses Windows NT processes in detail.

Windows NT supports both foreground and background processes, although there is no way to bring a background process to the foreground while it is executing. Background processes are initiated with the **Start /B** command (see Chapter 11).

Like UNIX, Windows NT employs many daemon processes to provide high-level system services. These are known as *server processes*, and they are generally managed via the **Services** control panel applet (if they can be affected at all).

There are several ways to manipulate existing processes. You'll probably find these two to be the most familiar:

- By using the Task Manager's **Processes** tab
- By using the Resource Kit's **Kill** and **RKill** commands

Process priorities range from 0 to 31, although the range 1 to 15 is what is actually used by normal user interactive (non-real-time) processes.

Windows NT is a virtual memory operating system, and paging to disk takes place to one or more designated *paging files*. These may be configured using the **Performance** tab of the **My Computer**'s **Properties** dialog box (see Chapter 11).

Windows NT includes a **cron**-like facility known as the Schedule Service. It is equivalent to UNIX's **at** and **cron** facilities combined (see Chapter 4).

The closest analogue to the UNIX **syslog** facility is the Event Log facility, which tracks hardware, subsystem, and security-related system messages (see Chapter 2 and Chapter 10). Integration with UNIX syslog facilities can be accomplished via freely available software (see Chapter 12).

System Startup and Shutdown

The system may be shut down or rebooted via the **Shut Down...** on the **Start** menu. Windows NT startup and shutdown are discussed in detail in Chapter 2.

There are no standard system boot scripts, in the UNIX sense. However, the Resource Kit provides the *AutoExNT.Bat* facility for creating a system startup script. The Services facility also specifies processes and facilities to be automatically initiated by the operating system.

There is no built-in equivalent to UNIX's single user mode, but you can create one via the hardware profiles facility (see Chapter 2).

User Accounts

As on UNIX systems, user accounts are identified by a username (which may be more than a single word and up to 20 characters in length). Usernames are not case sensitive (although passwords are). Accounts also have a numeric user ID associated with them, but this value is used only internally and is not visible to users.

Users may be members of one or more groups, all of which are always active and are treated equally by the Windows NT operating system. One of them is designated as the user's primary group, but this setting is used only by the POSIX subsystem. The various types of Windows NT groups are described in Chapter 3.

User accounts also have a number of other attributes that are optionally associated with them, including the following:

- A home directory, generally located on a network shared directory.
- A user profile, specifying an initial graphical user environment (among other things).
- A login script, run whenever the user logs in. The Windows NT login script is very different from those used on UNIX systems (see Chapter 3).
- Valid login periods and computer locations.
- Password change control settings (both individual and systemwide).

Users, groups, and passwords are discussed in Chapter 3.

Disks and Filesystems

Physical disks may be divided into multiple partitions, as on UNIX systems, and a filesystem may be built on each one of them. Each filesystem on a Windows NT system is identified by a unique drive letter (for example, *C:*). Filesystems don't need to be mounted or dismounted by the system administrator; this is handled automatically at system startup and shutdown by the operating system. Disks and filesystems are discussed in Chapter 5.

In addition, Windows NT includes facilities for combining multiple partitions into a single filesystem in several ways:

- By treating them as a single, extendable logical partition.

- By using them in a high-performance, disk-striping configuration.

- By incorporating them into a fault-tolerant filesystem, which includes redundant data information, making it able to survive the failure of one of its component disks.

Filesystems may be shared with UNIX (and other) systems via commercial NFS products or by running the freely available SAMBA facility on the UNIX side. SAMBA provides an interface to the native, SMB-protocol-based file sharing scheme used by Windows NT and other Windows systems (see Chapter 5).

Printing

Printing on Windows NT systems operates in a similar manner to the way it does on Windows 95 systems (it is discussed in Chapter 9). In addition, printing to and from UNIX systems running the BSD spooling system may also be configured.

Networking Basics

Windows NT supports standard TCP/IP networking in addition to other networking protocols such as NetBEUI and IPX. TCP/IP networking on Windows NT systems is discussed in Chapter 8. Many of the major networking protocols and services are present, although traditional configuration file based management is replaced by graphical administrative tools. These are the most important TCP/IP protocols and services:

- The DNS subsystem is quite standard. If you understand its usual configuration files, you will have no problem using the graphical interface provided by Windows NT (although the reverse is not true).

- The DHCP and Bootp protocols are supported. However, not all available DHCP options are implemented in the Windows NT facility.

The following standard facilities are not provided by Windows NT:

- Routing services are limited to static routing tables. However, there are freely available versions of routed and gated.

- NIS: There is a freely available port.

- NFS: Several commercial products provide NFS services for Windows NT systems, enabling them to function as both NFS servers and clients.

In general, there are freely available versions of virtually any standard TCP/IP server that you might want to run. See Appendix B for software archive locations.

Modems

Dial-up access is handled by the Remote Access Service (RAS), which is discussed in Chapter 8. Modems are configured and managed at a hardware level via the **Modems** control panel applet.

Quick Reference Tables

Table A-1 lists the Windows NT commands or facilities that provide similar functionality for a variety of UNIX commands. Both native and third-party (freely available, shareware, and commercial) are listed. UNIX commands that are not included in this table can be assumed to have no close equivalent.

Table A-1. Finding the Windows NT Command You Want

UNIX Command	Similar Windows NT Command or Facility
alias	**doskey**; also included in the freely available **bash** shell (Cygnus GNU utilities) or the Hamilton C shell
apropos	Use the **Index** and **Find** tabs of the **Help** facility (access via the **Start**➤**Help** menu path)
arp	**arp**
at	The Schedule Service and its **at** and **soon** commands
backup	**ntbackup** or **Start**➤**Administrative Tools (Common)** ➤**Backup** for the native Windows NT tape facilities
cat	**type** to display a file; **copy a+b+... c** to concatenate files
cd	**cd**
chgrp	No equivalent, since files don't have group owners.
chmod	File/directory **Properties**➤**Security**➤**Permissions**, the **cacls** command, or various utilities in the *NTSec* package
chown	File/directory **Properties**➤**Security**➤**Ownership** or the **setowner** command in the *NTSec* package
clear	**cls**
compress	**compact** and **expand** for transparent compression. The **WinZip** facility is the most popular compression software. There are also freely available versions of **gzip** and **compress**.
cp	**copy**
cp -r	**xcopy**

Table A-1. Finding the Windows NT Command You Want (continued)

UNIX Command	Similar Windows NT Command or Facility
cp -p	**scopy** in the Resource Kit
cpio	**ntbackup** or **Start➤Administrative Tools (Common)** ➤**Backup** for the native Windows NT tape facilities. The **pax** command can read and write **cpio** tapes.
cron	The Schedule Service and its **at** command.
crypt	Various third-party encryption packages exist (e.g., **pgp** and the Hamilton C shell's **des**), but there is no native facility
date	**date** and **time**
dd	**ntbackup** or **Start➤Administrative Tools (Common)** ➤**Backup** for the native Windows NT tape facilities
df	**du** in the Hamilton C shell package or the Perl script in Chapter 12
diff	**fc** or **comp** commands or **windiff** in the Resource Kit
du	**diruse** in the Resource Kit
dump	**ntbackup** or **Start➤Administrative Tools (Common)** ➤**Backup** for the native Windows NT tape facilities
echo	**echo** (but it is much more limited)
emacs	The native text editor is **Wordpad**; **emacs** has been ported to Windows NT and is widely available.
exportfs	net share
fdisk	**Start➤Administrative Tools (Common)➤Disk Administrator** (or **windisk** command)
fgrep	**find**
find	**Start➤Find➤Files or Folders**...
finger	**finger**
fsck	**chkdsk**
grep	**findstr** or **find**
head	Included in the Cygnus GNU utilities.
hostname	**hostname**
ifconfig	**ipconfig /all** to display information and **Network** control panel➤**Protocols➤TCP/IP Protocol➤Properties**... to configure
kill	**Ctrl-Alt-Del➤Task Manager...➤Processes➤End Process** (**taskmgr** command) or Resource Kit's **kill** command
killall	Resource Kit's **kill** command
last	Some of the functionality is provided by the Resource Kit's **usrstat** command.
ln -s	Create a shortcut to the item (right-click menu)
lpadmin lpc	**My Computer➤Printers** folder➤**Add Printer** and specific printer **Properties** or the **net print** command

Table A-1. Finding the Windows NT Command You Want (continued)

UNIX Command	Similar Windows NT Command or Facility
lpq lpstat	**My Computer►Printers** folder►double-click on printer or use the printer icon in the desktop tray (lower-right corner). Windows NT also provides an **lpq** command for querying LPD-based printers.
lpr lp	**File►Print** in most applications or the **print** command (for text files). Windows NT also provides an **lpr** command for printing to LPD-based printers.
ls	**dir /w**
ls -l	**dir** or **dir /N**
man	**help** *cmd* or *cmd* **/?** or **net help** *cmd* or the Windows NT Help facility (**Start►Help**)
mkdir	**mkdir**
mkfs	**format** and **label**
more *file*	**more <***file*** (set the **MORE** environment variable to **/E** to make the command behave in a UNIX-style fashion).
mount	For local filesystems, mounting is automatic. For network filesystems, see the **net use** command.
mt	Freely available (but limited) **ntape** utility or the **mt** command included with the Hamilton C shell
mv	**move** or **rename**
netstat	**netstat**
newfs	**format** and **label**
nfsstat	**net share** or **net view** (but not NFS)
nice	**start /low	/medium	/high**
nslookup	**nslookup**
od	**xd** command included with the Hamilton C shell.
passwd	**Ctrl-Alt-Del►Change Password...** to change your own password, or **Start►Administrative Tools (Common)►User Manager** (**usrmgr** or **musrmgr** command) or **net user** to change another user's password
ping	**ping**
popd, pushd	**popd** and **pushd**
ps	The Resource Kit's **pstat**, **pulist**, **pviewer**, and **pview** commands provide similar information.
pwd	**cd** (without arguments)
quot	No real equivalent, but see the Perl script in Chapter 12
rcp	**copy** and **xcopy**. Windows NT also provides an **rcp** command for accessing remote TCP/IP systems.
renice	**CTRL-ALT-DEL►Task Manager...►Processes►**right click on process►**Set Priority** (**taskmgr** command), or the Resource Kit's **pviewer** and **pview** commands

Table A-1. Finding the Windows NT Command You Want (continued)

UNIX Command	Similar Windows NT Command or Facility
rlogin	telnet
rm	erase or **del**
rmdir	rmdir
route	route
rsh	telnet or a freely available **rsh** client. Windows NT also provides an **rsh** command for accessing remote TCP/IP systems.
setenv	set or **My Computer➤Properties➤Environment** dialog box
shutdown	Resource Kit **shutdown** command
sleep	Resource Kit's **sleep** command
sort	**sort** (but it is much more limited)
source	call
su	The freely available **susrv** package is the best choice. The **su** facility in the Resource Kit requires far too much privilege.
swap swapon	**My Computer➤Properties➤Virtual Memory➤Change...**
sync	Freely available **ntsync** utility
tail	Included in the Cygnus GNU utilities
tar	**ntbackup** or **Start➤Administrative Tools (Common) ➤Backup** for the native Windows NT tape facilities or the Cygnus GNU utilities for a real **tar** utility. The **pax** command can also read/write tar tapes.
telinit	shutdown
time	Resource Kit's **timethis** command
top	Resource Kit's **pmon** command
touch	Included in the Cygnus GNU utilities.
traceroute	tracert
umask	No real equivalent, since default file protections flow from the directory in which a file is created, not from the user who creates the file
umount	For local filesystems, there is no real equivalent (although there is a freely available **unmount** command). For network filesystems, **net use /delete**.
uptime	**net statistics** (first few lines)
vi	The native text editor is **Wordpad**. A version of **vi** is included among UWin utilities and in the MKS Toolkit, and there are several other ports as well (see Appendix B).
vmstat	**Start➤Administrative Tools (Common)➤Windows NT Diagnostics➤Memory** (**winmsd** command)
wall	**net send /users**
whoami	Resource Kit's **whoami** command
write	net send

Table A-1. Finding the Windows NT Command You Want (continued)

UNIX Command	Similar Windows NT Command or Facility
xargs	The Resource Kit's **forfiles** command provides limited but somewhat similar functionality.
xlock	Ctrl-Alt-Del➤Lock Workstation

Table A-2 lists the Windows NT locations of the equivalents for standard UNIX system directories and important system configuration files. Note that the environment variable *%SystemRoot%* points to the top of the Windows NT installation directory, which is normally *C:\WinNT.*

Table A-2. Corresponding Directory and File Locations

UNIX File or Directory	Corresponding/Similar Windows NT Location
/	Each disk partition and logical drive has its own root directory under Windows NT.
/bin	Some user commands are built into the command processor (*Cmd.Exe*). Others are stored primarily in *%SystemRoot%* and *%SystemRoot%\System32.*
/dev	No exact Windows NT equivalent. Many device drivers are stored in the directory *%SystemRoot%\System32\Drivers.*
/etc	Administrative executables are generally stored in *%SystemRoot%\System32.* Configuration files are located in the same location or one of its subdirectories (especially *Config*).
/etc/exports	Filesystems and subdirectories are made available to other systems by being shared. Sharing data is stored with the item itself, so there is no configuration file. The **net share** command lists exported directories on the local system.
/etc/fstab	No similar configuration file. Local disk partitions are mounted automatically at system startup. The **showdisk** command (in the Resource Kit) gives detailed information about all disk partitions, and the **net use** command lists remote shares that have been assigned drive letters on the local system.
/etc/group	*%SystemRoot%\System32\Config\SAM,* modified with the User Manager and the **net group** and **net localgroup** commands (these commands also list the names of all defined groups).
/etc/hosts	*%SystemRoot%\System32\Drivers\etc\hosts*
/etc/hosts. equiv	Within a domain, network operations assume full trust between all systems. Trust must be explicitly extended beyond the local domain (see Chapter 10).
/etc/inittab	Processes can be started at boot-time in several ways: configuring them as a service and starting them from the Resource Kit's *AutoExNT.Bat* facility are two effective ways. Processes can be started when a user logs in using that user's Startup folder (generally *%SystemRoot%\Profiles* username*Start Menu\Programs\Startup*).

Table A-2. Corresponding Directory and File Locations (continued)

UNIX File or Directory	Corresponding/Similar Windows NT Location
/etc/motd	There is no built-in equivalent, but you can create such a facility in several ways: e.g., via user login scripts or via users' Startup folders.
*/etc/named.**	DNS configuration settings are stored in the system registry and in the configuration files located in *%SystemRoot%\System32\DNS* (see Chapter 8).
/etc/nologin	There is no equivalent facility.
/etc/passwd	*%SystemRoot%\System32\Config\SAM**, a binary file that can be modified with the User Manager and the **net user** command (which can also list the names of all user accounts).
*/etc/rc** */etc/rc*.d/**	The Resource Kit provides the *AutoExNT.Bat* facility for creating a system startup script. The **Services** facility also specifies processes and facilities to be automatically initiated by the operating system.
/etc/ resolv.conf	DNS configuration settings are stored in the system registry and in the configuration files located in *%SystemRoot%\System32\DNS* (see Chapter 8).
/etc/ syslog.conf	System status and error messages are managed by the Event Log facility and may be viewed with the Event Viewer administrative tool (see Chapters 2, 10, and 12). See Appendix B for Windows NT **syslog** servers and a facility for sending event log data to the **syslog** daemon on a UNIX system.
/sbin	Administrative executables are generally stored in *%SystemRoot%\System32*.
/tmp	Usually *C:\Temp*
/usr/bin	Some user commands are built into the command processor (*Cmd.Exe*). Others are stored primarily in *%SystemRoot%* and *%SystemRoot%\System32*.
/usr/lib	System shared libraries (DLLs) are generally stored in *%SystemRoot%\System32* and elsewhere in the *%SystemRoot%* subtree.
/usr/man	Operating system–related help files are generally located in the *Help* and *System32* subdirectories of *%SystemRoot%*.
/usr/sbin	Administrative executables are generally stored in *%SystemRoot%\System32*.
/var/spool	*%SystemRoot%\System32\Spool*

Making Windows NT Feel Like UNIX

In this section, we'll look at some freely available and commercial software packages that can make Windows NT seem more like the familiar UNIX environment. Sources for these freely available and commercial tools are listed in Appendix B.

The Resource Kit's POSIX Utilities

The Resource Kit includes a set of command-line utilities known as the POSIX Utilities. They are located in the *Posix* subdirectory of the Resource Kit installation directory (usually *C:\NTResKit*). The following utilities are included: **cat, chmod, chown, cp, find, grep, ln** (for hard links only), **ls, mkdir, mv, rm, rmdir, sh, touch, vi,** and **wc**. Most of these commands function in the normal UNIX manner, but the **find** command is somewhat eccentric. All of them treat filenames as case sensitive (filenames on FAT filesystems are automatically converted to uppercase). See their accompanying documentation for further information.

GNU Utilities for Win32 Systems

The GNU utilities collection has been ported to the Win32 environment by Cygnus. The following examples will give you a sense of how closely these Windows NT and Windows 95 versions mirror their UNIX counterparts. To begin with, **grep** and **ls** operate normally:

```
C:\> grep "u.* .*see[^ ].* .*p" *.html
TIPS3.html:submit the solution to a problem you've seen occur, please


C:\> ls -l *.html
-rw-r--r--  1 544      everyone     22256 Mar 29 18:54 TIPS.html
-rw-r--r--  1 544      everyone     12843 Mar 29 15:55 TIPS2.html
-rw-r--r--  1 544      everyone      3980 Mar 28 19:05 TIPS3.html
```

The **ps** command is more limited than on UNIX systems:

```
C:\> ps -ef
     PID      PPID      WIN32-PID   UID  COMMAND
    1000      1000            327  500  C:\\ps.exe
```

The **find** command is the normal GNU version of this utility, which differs somewhat from the standard UNIX version. For example, the following command shows one way to locate all of the HTML files in the current directory:

```
C:\> find . -regex .*\.html -print
./TIPS.html
./TIPS2.html
./TIPS3.html
```

You can combine the GNU commands in pipes with Windows NT commands. For example, the following command extracts a **ps**-style process list from the output of the Resource Kit's **pstat** command:

```
C:\> pstat | awk "/Pri/ || /^  0:00/ {print $0}"
  User Time    Kernel Time   Ws Faults Commit Pri Hnd Thd Pid Name
0:00:00.000 20:58:41.945     16       1      0   0   0   1   0 Idle Process
0:00:00.000  0:00:56.240    120    2016     36   8 251  30   2 System
0:00:00.180  0:00:00.220    120    2032    164  11  36   6  23 smss.exe
0:00:03.575  0:00:21.420   1304    1899   1220  13 246   7  31 csrss.exe
0:00:02.012  0:00:08.722    568   15470    668  13  67   2  37 WINLOGON.EXE
  ...
```

Similarly, the following command lists the five current processes with the highest priorities:

```
C:\> pstat | awk "/Pri/ || /^  0:00/ {print $0}" | sort +5 | head -6
   User Time    Kernel Time   Ws Faults Commit Pri Hnd Thd Pid Name
   0:00:00.000  21:00:11.243  16    1       0   0   0   1   0 Idle Process
   0:00:00.000   0:00:00.000  52   10     108   8   5   1 196 sort.exe
   0:00:00.000   0:00:00.010  52   10     104   8   5   1 236 head.exe
   0:00:00.020   0:00:00.010 524  128     280   8   8   1 230 awk.exe
   0:00:00.010   0:00:00.020 892  222     332   8  14   1 237 PSTAT.EXE
```

The Hamilton C Shell

The GNU utilities collection includes the **bash** shell. Users who prefer the C shell may be interested in the excellent Hamilton C Shell package (Hamilton Laboratories). It includes a C shell supporting all of the normal features and will correctly execute most existing C shell scripts.

The package also includes a variety of UNIX-style utilities which may be run either from within the C shell or from the Windows NT command line. Among them are the following utilities, which are missing from the GNU set:

- A **cron**-style facility (named "cron" but implemented somewhat differently). It can be configured as a Windows NT service.

- A **df** command, inexplicably named **du**:

```
C:\> du
c:    612.832 M Total =  561.337 M Used +   51.495 M (08.40%) Free ariadne
d:    511.784 M Total =  469.248 M Used +   42.536 M (08.31%) Free ananke
e:    620.206 M Total =  620.206 M Used +    0.000 M (00.00%) Free ntsrv40a
g:   1044.095 M Total =    4.421 M Used + 1039.674 M (99.58%) Free aporia
h:    522.112 M Total =    4.419 M Used +  517.693 M (99.15%) Free acrasia
i:    700.287 M Total =    4.379 M Used +  695.908 M (99.37%) Free aveya
j:   1189.888 M Total =   91.325 M Used + 1098.563 M (92.32%) Free amelia
k:    308.208 M Total =  286.457 M Used +   21.751 M (07.06%) Free amanda
l:    449.788 M Total =  165.800 M Used +  283.988 M (63.14%) Free anitra
```

- An **mt** command for manipulating tapes.

- **uudecode** and **uuencode** utilities.

- A shell script functioning as a **whereis** command.

The package also includes cool sample scripts and the following useful utilities:

- **des**: a DES encryption utility/filter (United States and Canada only)

- **binedit**: a **sed**-like binary file editor

- **xd**: a hexadecimal dump tool

- An enhanced version of the **pwd** command, which displays the current directory on every disk drive on the system:

```
C:\> pwd
c:\ntreskit\perl
d:\sun_expert\columns
e:\
...
k:\
l:\hamilton\bin
```

Demonstration versions of the Hamilton C shell are available from the Hamilton Laboratories web site.

The MicroImages X Server

The freely available MIX X server software from MicroImages will allow you to display X-based processes on an Intel-based Windows NT system. Once you have installed the package, the most straightforward way to get started is to initiate a **telnet** session from the Windows NT system to the desired UNIX system and start the X Server executable (**xs**). Then run the following commands on the UNIX system:[*]

```
unix-102>> setenv TERM xterm
unix-103>> setenv DISPLAY nt_host:0
unix-104>> xterm &
```

where *nt_host* is the name of the Windows NT system. These example C shell commands cause an **xterm** window to appear within the X Server application window (after which the **telnet** session may optionally be terminated).

Figure A-1 illustrates the X Server environment with several X-based applications running: **xclock**, **xbiff**, **xtetris**, **xterm**, and the separate-windows version of the **emacs** editor. Note that all of these X-based windows appear inside the single Windows NT windows maintained by the X server.

The package includes the **twm** window manager, which is fully customizable in the normal manner, so you can create a startup file to automatically initiate X applications when the X Server is started.

The OpenNT UNIX Environment

The OpenNT package from Softway Systems provides an impressively complete UNIX-style working environment for Windows NT systems. Architecturally, the OpenNT package is structured as an enhanced POSIX subsystem. Accordingly, it can provide a full POSIX-compatible programming environment (designed to making porting UNIX applications to Windows NT simpler) in addition to user-level commands and utilities. From an administrative point of view, OpenNT's

---

[*] You may substitute the equivalent Bourne shell commands if desired.

Figure A-1. The MicroImages X server

strategy is to interface standard UNIX functionality to the native Windows NT facilities as completely and transparently as possible. Thus, its **umask**, **chmod**, and **chown** commands provide an alternative interface for the standard ACL file protection mechanisms.

OpenNT includes four shells, including full job control: **sh**, **csh**, **ksh**, and **tcsh**. It also includes a variety of UNIX commands, including some that are usually missing from the free software collections (e.g., **strings** and **umask**).

The following examples illustrate some features of the OpenNT environment. To begin with, here is a **find** command that conforms completely to the standard syntax:

```
open_nt> find . -mtime -1 -name \*z\* -print
/OpenNT/usr/lib/perl5/auto/DynaLoader
/OpenNT/usr/lib/perl5/opennt/5.00305/DynaLoader
/OpenNT/usr/lib/perl5/Sys
```

Of course, you will find a few minor glitches. For example, the **ps** command's output may surprise you:

```
open_nt> ps -ef
    USER      PID     PPID  ELAPSED TTY     TIME CMD
  197108  1638400        1  0:54.95 n00  0:00.45 tcsh
  197108  6422529  1638400  0:00.03 n00  0:00.02 ps -ef
```

This is not a bug, but simply a limitation of using a POSIX subsystem as the product's base: only those processes running under the subsystem appear in the list.

Mixing Windows NT commands and OpenNT is sometimes a bit tedious; consider this command to define the C shell prompt:

```
open_nt> set prompt = "`HOSTNAME.EXE`-\!>> "
vala^M-58>> _
```

The **hostname** command is a Windows NT command (located in *C:\WinNT\System32*). In order for it to be found, its location must be in the search path, and its full name (including extension) must be entered in the correct case (uppercase). The newline character produced by the command is also placed literally into the resulting prompt.

In general, extensions are not applied by default to command names, and all pathnames are truly case sensitive. Both of these restrictions are completely in line with standard UNIX practice, but they are inconvenient after you have gotten used to Windows NT's normal functioning.

The OpenNT product also includes many X programs, and the server version includes an X server as well (it may also be purchased separately). Figure A-2 illustrates a Windows NT desktop when the X server is running: there is an **xterm** window onto a remote UNIX host, a Windows NT file browsing window, a Microsoft Word session, two other X-based utilities (one of which is running from the remote UNIX system), as well as the usual Windows NT icons on the desktop. Each process runs in its own window, and multiple processes of any type are supported.

The UWin Facility

David Korn (author of the Korn shell) and others at AT&T Labs have also developed a UNIX-style environment for Windows NT, named UWin. It is available free of charge to educational institutions, and sells for a modest price to commercial sites. The software may be downloaded from its web site (see Appendix B) by educational institutions and for evaluation purposes by commercial entities.

UWin is based around a Korn shell, and the package includes a variety of UNIX utilities. For example, here is its **df** command (run from the Korn shell):

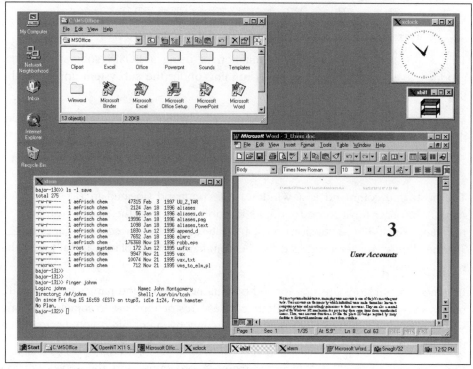

Figure A-2. OpenNT windows on the Windows NT desktop

```
$ df
```

Filesystem	Type	Mbytes	Used	Avail	Cap	Mounted on
Ariadne	NTFS	598	524	74	88%	/C
ANANKE	FAT	499	490	9.2	98%	/D
Janus	NTFS	1342	157	1185	12%	/E
Aporia	NTFS	1019	4.3	1015	0%	/G
Acrasia	NTFS	509	4.3	505	1%	/H
Aveya	NTFS	683	4.3	679	1%	/I
Amelia	NTFS	1161	229	932	20%	/J
Amanda	NTFS	300	285	15	95%	/K
Anitra	NTFS	439	171	267	39%	/L

The package includes the most important UNIX user utilities (**cp**, **mv**, **rm**, **mkdir**, **rmdir**, **find**, **grep**, **diff**, **vi**, **du**, **df**, **more**, **sort**, **uniq**, **compress**, **file**, **strings**, **xargs**, **uuencode** and **uudecode**, and so on), as well as versions of **tar**, **pax**, **awk**, **sed**, **yacc**, and a **cron** facility. UWin also includes a UNIX-compatible development environment, structured as an interface to the Microsoft Visual C/C++ compiler. Future developments include X11 and networking support facilities.

The MKS Toolkit

The MKS Toolkit from Mortice Kern Systems also provides a UNIX-compatible environment under Windows NT. It too is based around a Korn shell, and it includes a large set of UNIX commands, a **vi** editor, and Perl. Many of them have graphical user interfaces.

The Toolkit also includes additional commands designed to make performing Windows NT tasks easier in the UNIX-compatible environment and from within Korn shell scripts, including the following:

- Utilities to view and manipulate ACLs (**lsacl** and **chacl**).

- The **dlg** utility to manage Windows NT dialog boxes.

- Utilities for displaying information about the domain, user accounts, and groups. The latter two programs can also modify user accounts and groups from the command line.

- The **db** utility for sending SQL queries directly to an ODBC-compliant database.

- The **registry** utility for accessing and modifying the registry.

- The **service** command for managing Windows NT services.

Miscellaneous Items

It is not much of an exaggeration to state that virtually any UNIX facility you might want to put on a Windows NT system is available somewhere (although not always for free). Consult Appendix B for the locations of major Windows NT software archives. The following items are requested frequently enough that they deserve special mention here:

- Perl for Win32 systems can be obtained at *www.perl.com/perl/info/software.html.*

- Various TCP/IP daemons and WWW-related facilities can be obtained at Jim Buyens' amazing software site, *www.primenet.com/~buyensj/ntwebsrv.html.*

B

Useful Windows NT Resources

Books

- Albitz, Paul, and Cricket Liu. *DNS and BIND, Second Edition.* (Sebastopol, CA: O'Reilly & Associates, 1996).

- *Computer Security Products Buyer's Guide.* Published annually by the Computer Security Institute (CSI), San Francisco, CA; (415) 905-2626.

- Custer, Helen. *Inside Windows NT.* (Redmond, WA: Microsoft Press, 1993).

- Custer, Helen. *Inside the Windows NT File System.* (Redmond, WA: Microsoft Press, 1994).

- Garfinkel, Simson. *PGP: Pretty Good Privacy.* (Sebastopol, CA: O'Reilly & Associates, 1994).

- Garfinkel, Simson, and Gene Spafford. *Practical UNIX & Internet Security* (Sebastopol, CA: O'Reilly & Associates, 1996).

- Garfinkel, Simson, Daniel Weise, and Steven Strassmann. *The UNIX-HATERS Handbook.* (Programmer's Press/IPG Books, 1994) [One of the funniest books I've read in years.]

- Hunt, Craig. *TCP/IP Network Administration, Second Edition.* (Sebastopol, CA: O'Reilly & Associates, 1997).

- Hunt, Craig. *Networking Personal Computers with TCP/IP.* (Sebastopol, CA: O'Reilly & Associates, 1995).

- *Microsoft Windows NT Resource Kit.* (Redmond, WA: Microsoft Press, 1996).

- Moeller, Robert T. *Computer Audit, Control and Security.* (New York: Wiley, 1989).

- Nagar, Rajeev. *Windows NT File System Internals.* (Sebastopol, CA: O'Reilly & Associates, 1997).

- Pearce, Eric. *Windows NT in a Nutshell.* (Sebastopol, CA: O'Reilly & Associates, 1997).

- Schwartz, Randal L., Erik Olson, and Tom Christiansen. *Learning Perl on Win32 Systems.* (Sebastopol, CA: O'Reilly & Associates, 1997).

- Srinivasan, Sriram. *Advanced Perl Programming.* (Sebastopol, CA: O'Reilly & Associates, 1997).

- Sutton, Stephen A. *Windows NT Security Guide.* (Reading, MA: Addison-Wesley, 1997).

- Thompson, Robert. *Windows NT 4 for NetWare Administrators.* (Sebastopol, CA: O'Reilly & Associates, 1997).

- Tidrow, Rob. *Windows NT Registry Troubleshooting.* (Indianapolis, IN: New Riders, 1996).

- Vallabhaneni, S. Rao. *Auditing Computer Security.* (New York: Wiley, 1989).

- Wall, Larry, Tom Christiansen, and Randal Schwartz. *Programming Perl, Second Edition.* (Sebastopol, CA: O'Reilly & Associates, 1996).

- Zimmermann, Phil. *The Official PGP User's Guide.* (Cambridge, MA: MIT Press, 1995).

Articles

- Farmer, Dan and Wietse Venema. "Improving the Security of Your Site by Breaking into It." 1993. Available from *ftp://ftp.porcupine.org/pub/security/admin-guide-to-cracking.101.Z.* See also the author's discussion of transitive trust in the documentation to their *Satan* package (the file *satan_doc_tar.Z* in the same location). Although these works focus on UNIX systems, much of what they discuss applies to any system on a TCP/IP network.

- Russinovich, Mark. "Inside the Difference Between Windows NT Workstation and Windows NT Server" *Windows NT Magazine* (November 1996); also available at *http://www.winntmag.com/Magazine/Article.cfm?IssueID=14&ArticleID=2816.*

- Schulman, Andrew. "Differences Between NT Server and Workstation Are Minimal." Available from *ftp://ftp.ora.com/pub/examples/windows/win95.update/ntnodiff.html.*

- Schulman, Andrew. "Microsoft Deliberately Limiting NT Workstation 4.0 as a Web Server." Available from *ftp://ftp.ora.com/pub/examples/windows/win95.update/ntwk4.html.*

Periodicals

"NTegration" column
SunExpert
Computer Publishing Group, Inc.
320 Washington Street
Brookline Village
Brookline, MA 02146
617-739-7001
circulation@cpg.com
www.cpg.com/se/subscribe.html

SysAdmin
P.O. Box 59170
Boulder, CO 80322-9170
800-365-2210
303-678-0439
samag@neodata.com
www.samag.com/sub

Windows NT Magazine
P.O. Box 447
Loveland, CO 80539-0447
800-621-1544
970-663-4700
subs@winntmag.com
www.winntmag.com

Windows NT Systems
411 Borel Avenue, Suite 100
San Mateo, CA 94402
415-358-9500
ntsys@halldata.com
www.ntsystems.com
www.synasoft.com/hallmark/nt/ntnew.html

Internet Mailing Lists

- The Windows NT Tip of the Day: subscribe at *www.tipworld.com*

- Windows NT Magazine Update: subscribe at: *www.winntmag.com/update*

- NT Security Digest: for a sample issue, send an email message to *ntsd-sample@ntsecurity.net*; subscribe at *www.ntsecurity.net/security/subscribe-ntsd.htm*

Web Sites

Site Lists

- Main Yahoo Windows NT site: *www.yahoo.com/Computers_and_Internet/ Operating_Systems/Microsoft_Windows/Windows_NT*

- An amazing alphabetical list of Windows NT-related sites: *www.indirect.com/ www/ceridgac/ntsite.html*

- *www.netmation.com/listnt.htm*

Windows NT Information

The best of the best

- *NT Internals: www.sysinternals.com* (Mark Russinovich and Bryce Cogswell). Although its scope is limited, this is the single best Windows NT site anywhere!

- *NT Security: www.ntsecurity.net* (note: *www.ntsecurity.com* is a different site)

- Information on available hot fixes: *www.winntmag.com* (also the latest Windows NT–related news)

- Integrating Windows NT and UNIX: *www.performancecomputing.com/unixintegration*

Microsoft Windows NT sites

- *www.microsoft.com/ntserver* and *www.microsoft.com/ntworkstation*

- Microsoft knowledge base: *www.microsoft.com/kb*

  You may also go directly to the article Q*nmopqr* via the path *www.microsoft.com/kb/articles/qnmo/p/qr.htm* (*n* may be blank).

- Latest hardware compatibility list: *www.microsoft.com/hwtest/hcl*

- Hardware vendor locator: *notes.msoft.it/hw/default.cfm*

- Service packs and hot fixes: *ftp.microsoft.com/bussys/winnt/winnt-public/fixes* (one subdirectory tree per language version)

Digital's Windows NT site

- *www.windowsnt.digital.com*

Windows NT training courses

- *www.cctglobal.com/nt4-i.html*

- *www.cit.az.nz/smac/winnt/default.htm*

Software Archives

- Aaron's Alpha NT Applications Archive: *dutlbcz.lr.tudelft.nl/alphant/archive.html*

- Beverly Hills Software: *www.bhs.com/download/default.asp*

- The Coast-to-Coast Software Repository: *www.coast.net/SimTel/nt.html*

- Windows NT-Plus: *www.windowsnt-plus.com/shareware*

- WinSite Windows Archive: *www.winsite.com/winnt*

- Nomad Mobile Research Centre: *www.nmrc.org/files/nt* and */snt* (security/hacker-related items)

- Windows NT Web Server Tools: *www.primenet.com/~buyensj/ntwebsrv.html* and *sysadmin.html* (Jim Buyens)

- Windows NT Internals Utilities: *www.ntinternals.com/ntutil.htm*

- Service Packs and hot fixes: *ftp.microsoft.com/bussys/winnt/winnt-public/fixes* (one subdirectory tree per language version)

Sources for the Software Packages Mentioned in This Book

Many of the software packages we've discussed in this book are available in both Intel and Alpha versions. However, some packages are available only for the Intel platform. These can still be run on Alpha systems via the FX!32 emulation facility (listed below).

Freely Available Software

One major site for each package has been listed. However, most of these items are widely available on the Web. See the preceding section for the locations of major Windows NT software archives.

- **AdminMisc** Perl module for Win32 (Dave Roth): *www.roth.net/perl/admin-misc.htm*

- **AutoLog** (Mark Russinovich): *www.ntinternals.com/misc.htm*

- **CacheMan** (Mark Russinovich and Bryce Cogswell): *www.ntinternals.com/cacheman.htm*

- **Crack**: *www.nmrc.org/files/nt*

- **DFS**: *www.microsoft.com/ntserver/dfsdl.htm*

- **Digital FX!32**: *www.digital.com/semiconductor/amt/fx32/fx-download.html*

- **EffEvent** and **Dump1Evt** utilities (Isabelle Vollant): *www.geocities.com/Silicon-Valley/Heights/3465*

- emacs: *ftp://ftp.agt.net/pub/coast/vendors/gnu/nt*

- **ESentry** Perl script (Richard Stoddart): *www.bhs.com/download/default.asp*

- **GNU software**: *ftp://ftp.cygnus.com/pub/gnu-win32/latest*

- **grant** utility [to assign user rights] (Andreas Hansson): *www.franzo.co.nz/hansson/grant.htm*

- **Iomega tools**: *www.iomega.com/support/software/winnt.html*

- ntape: *www.bhs.com/download/default.asp*

- **NTDure** (Michael G. Martin): *www.bhs.com/download/default.asp*

- **NTFSDOS** (Mark Russinovich and Bryce Cogswell): *www.ntinternals.com/ntfs13.htm*

- **NTFS for Linux** (Martin von Loewis): *sunsite.unc.edu//pub/Linux/system/filesystems*

- **NTHandle** (Mark Russinovich): *www.ntinternals.com/nthandle.htm*

- **NTSync** (Mark Russinovich): *www.ntinternals.com/misc.htm*

- **Perl**: *www.perl.com/perl/info/software.html*

- **PGP**: *web.mit.edu/network/pgp-form.html* (U.S. and Canadian users); *www. funet.fi/pub/crypt/cryptography/pgp/unix/README.html* (users outside North America)

- **PQCount** (Scott Lemieux): *www.coast.net/SimTel/nt/printer.html*

- **SAMBA** (Andrew Tridgell, Jeremy Allison, and many others): *lake.canberra. edu.au/pub/samba;* **libdes** package at *ftp://samba.anu.edu.au/pub/libdes*

- **Security Manager, secmgr** (Martin Weindel): *www.bhs.com/download/default.asp*

- **smbmount for Linux** (Tor Lillqvist): *sunsite.unc.edu//pub/Linux/system/filesystems/smbfs*

- susrv (Steffen Krause): *www.primenet.com/~buyensj/sysadmin.html*

- sysinfo (Mika Malo): *www.winsite.com/winnt/sysutil/page2.html*

- **TreeSize** (Joachim Marder): *www.bhs.com/download/default.asp*

- **unmount** (Christoph H. Hochstaetter): *www.bhs.com/download/default.asp*

- **UWin** (David Korn): *www.research.att.com/sw/tools/uwin* [for noncommercial sites and commercial evaluation purposes only; see the Commercial Software section for commercial ordering contact information]

- vi-style editors [**lemmy**, **vim**, and **xvip**]: *www.coast.net/SimTel/nt/editor.html*

- **wmem** (Steven Chervets): *www.bhs.com/download/default.asp*
- **X server**: *www.microimages.com/freestuf/mix.htm*

Shareware

Demonstration versions of many software packages are available at major Windows NT software archives (listed earlier in this appendix).

EvNTSLog and **NTSLog**
[send event log data to UNIX **syslog** facility; native *syslog* daemon for Windows NT]
Adiscon GmbH
Paul-Klee-Str. 7
50374 Erftstadt, Germany
info@adiscon.com
www.adiscon.com

NT Security Utilities (**NTSec** package)
[ACL manipulation and other security utilities]
Keith Woodard
NT Security Utilities Registration
10 Arnold Road #14
North Quincy, MA 02171
woodardk@netcom.com
www.netcom.com/~trias
ftp://ftp.netcom.com/pub/wo/woodardk

SnagIT
[screen capture utility]
TechSmith Corp.
P.O. Box 4758
East Lansing, MI 48826-4758
517-333-2100
sales@techsmith.com
www.techsmith.com

Syslog for NT
[Franz Krainer's version of a native Windows NT **syslog** server]
www.primenet.com/~buyensj
sysadmin.html#Event
Register via the utility included in the package

SyslogD for NT
[native **syslog** server for Windows NT]
West Georgia Web Service
P.O. Box 1514
Newnan, GA 30264-1514
info@wgws.com
www.wgws.com

WinZip
[compression/decompression/ archiving utility]
Nico Mak Computing
P. O. Box 919
Bristol, CT 06011
support@winzip.com
www.winzip.com

Commercial Software

Demonstration versions of many software packages are available at major Windows NT software archives (listed earlier).

AccessNFS
[NFS software]
Intergraph Corp.
Huntsville, Alabama 35894-0001
800-345-4856
info@intergraph.com
www.intergraph.com

ArcServe; InocuLAN
[backup software; anti-virus software]
Cheyenne
A Division of Computer Associates
3 Expressway Plaza
Roslyn Heights, NY 11577
516-465-5000
800-243-9462
sales@cheyenne.com
www.cheyenne.com

BackupExec
[backup software]
Seagate Software
920 Disc Drive
Scotts Valley, CA 95066
800-327-2232
407-531-7500
sales@smg.seagatesoftware.com
www.seagate.com

Batch Job Server (BJS)
[batch queuing system]
Camellia Software Corp.
7807 126th Street SE
Tenino, WA 98589
camellia@halcyon.com
www.halcyon.com/camellia/

Computer cables
[SCSI and other cables]
CTG (Cables To Go)
1501 Webster Street
Dayton, OH 45404
800-506-9605
www.cablestogo.com

DumpACL and **DumpEvt**
Somarsoft, Inc.
[ACL and event log utilities]
P.O. Box 642278
San Francisco, CA 94164-2278
415-776-7315
info@somarsoft.com
www.somarsoft.com

EZ drives
[removable storage devices]
SyQuest Technology, Inc.
47071 Bayside Parkway
Fremont, CA 94538-6517
510-226-4000
sales@syquest.com
www.syquest.com

Hamilton C Shell
[C shell for Windows NT, Windows 95]
Hamilton Laboratories
21 Shadow Oak Drive
Sudbury, MA 01776-3165
508-440-8307
hamilton@hamiltonlabs.com
www.hamiltonlabs.com

MKS Toolkit
[UNIX utilities for Windows NT]
Mortice Kern Systems, Inc. (MKS)
185 Columbia Street West
Waterloo, Ontario, Canada N2L 5Z5
800-265-2797
519-884-2251
sales@mks.com
www.mks.com

McAfee Anti-Virus
[virus checking package]
McAfee Associates, Inc.
2805 Bowers Avenue
Santa Clara, CA 95051
408-988-3832
mcafeemall@cc.mcafee.com
www.mcafee.com

NFS Maestro
[NFS software]
Hummingbird Communications
1 Sparks Avenue
North York, Ontario
Canada, M2H 2W1
416-496-2200
sales@hummingbird.com
www.hummingbird.com

Networker
[backup software]
Legato Systems
3210 Porter Drive
Palo Alto, CA 94304
415-812-6000
www@legato.com
www.legato.com

NetXRay
[network monitor and packet capture]
Cinco Networks, Inc.
6601 Koll Center Parkway, Suite 140
Pleasanton, CA 94566
510-426-1770
800-671-9272
sales@cinco.com
www.cinco.com

Norton NT Tools
[antivirus and other utilities]
Symantec
10201 Torre Avenue
Cupertino, CA 95014
800-441-7234
541-334-6054
www.symantec.com

NTAV
[antivirus package]
Carmel Software Engineering
Israel
carmel@actcom.co.il

NTRIGUE
[multiuser version of Windows NT]
Insignia Solutions
2200 Lawson Lane
Santa Clara, CA 95054
408-327-6000
ntrigue@isinc.insignia.com
www.insignia.com

NTerprise
[multiuser support]
Exodus Technologies
11130 NE 33rd Place, Suite 260
Bellevue, WA 98004-1448
800-756-7065
425-803-5780
info@exodustech.com
www.exodustech.com

OpenNT
[UNIX environment for Windows NT]
Softway Systems, Inc.
185 Berry Street, Suite 5514
San Francisco, CA 94107
800-438-8649
415-896-0708
sales@opennt.com
www.opennt.com

PartitionMagic
[disk partitioning utility]
PowerQuest Corp.
1083 N. State Street
Orem, UT 84057
800-379-2566
magic@powerquest.com
www.powerquest.com

Ready-to-Run Software
[ready-to-use versions of GNU and other freely available software]
4 Pleasant Street,
P.O. Box 2038,
Forge Village, MA 01886
800-743-1723
978-692-9922
info@rtr.com
www.rtr.com

ScanNT, FileAdmin, RegAdmin, AuditSet, and **EventAdmin**
components of the **Administrator Assistant Tool Kit**
[security- and event log-related utilities]
Midwestern Commerce, Inc. (MWC)
1601 West Fifth Avenue, Suite 207
Columbus, OH 43212
800-263-0036
614-761-9620
support@box.omna.com
www.ntsecurity.com

Solstice products
[NFS software]
Sun Microsystems
2550 Garcia Avenue
Mountain View, CA 94043
888-786-3463
www.sun.com

System Commander
[multiple OS booting]
V Communications, Inc.
4320 Steven's Creek Boulevard., Suite 120
San Jose, CA 95129
408-296-4224
sales@v-com.com
www.v-com.com

UWin
[David Korn's UNIX environment for Windows]
Global Technologies Ltd., Inc.
5 West Avenue
Old Bridge, NJ 08857
908-251-2840
sales@gtlinc.com
www.gtlinc.com/Products/Uwin/uwin.html

WinFrame
[multiuser support]
Citrix Systems
6400 NW 6th Way
Fort Lauderdale, FL 33309
954-267-3000
www.citrix.com

Zip and *Jaz* drives
[removable storage devices]
Iomega Corp.
1821 West Iomega Way
Roy, UT 84067
801-778-1000
www.iomega.com

Contents of the Windows NT Resource Kit

Table B-1 lists the software contents of the Windows NT Resource Kit. The tools are arranged by category and are placed in alphabetical order within each category. Each entry includes the program name (those included only in the server version of the Resource Kit are marked with a dagger), a description of it, its type ([C] for a command line utility and [G] for a GUI tool), the topic category where it is described in the Resource Kit help file (*RKTools.Hlp*), and the subdirectory where it is located on the Resource Kit CD. When only a subdirectory name is given for the latter, the file is located in that subdirectory of the architecture-specific top-level directory: for example, an entry of "Config" means that the file is located in *\I386\Config* and *\Alpha\Config*. The few CD locations which are not relative to these top-level directories are specified by their full path (beginning with an initial backslash). A *b* in the CD Directory column indicates that the program is not included on the CD, but is available at *ftp.microsoft.com/bussys/winnt/winnt-public/reskit/nt40/filewise*; *c* indicates that the program was mistakenly omitted from the CD, but is available for Intel systems at *ftp.microsoft.com/bussys/winnt/winnt-public/reskit/nt40/i386*.

Table B-1. Contents of the Windows NT Resource Kit

Program	Description [Type]	RK Help Topic	CD Directory
Booting-Related Programs			
AutoExNT.Exe	Boot initialization file facility [C]	Batch Tools	*Config*
AutoLog.Exe	Specify an automatic login at system startup [G]	User Account Admin Tools	*Config*
Shutdown.Exe	Shut down local or remote system [C]	Network/Server Admin Tools	*Netadmin*
ShutGUI.Exe	Shut down local or remote system [G]	Network/Server Admin Tools	*Netadmin*
System Configuration Utilities			
DelSrv.Exe	Unregister a service [C]	Registry Tools	*Registry*
Drivers.Exe	Display loaded device drivers [C]	Computer and Net Setup Tools	*Compdiag*

ᵃ Included only in the server version of the Resource Kit.

Table B-1. Contents of the Windows NT Resource Kit (continued)

Program	Description [Type]	RK Help Topic	CD Directory
System Configuration Utilities			
InstallD.Cmd	Install/uninstall the debug version of **NTDetect.Com** [C]	Computer and Net Setup Tools	*Setup*
InstSrv.Exe	Install a service [C]	Computer Admin/ Config Tools	*Config*
SetupMgr.Exe	Enable Windows NT to be installed or upgraded remotely [G]	Computer and Net Setup Tools	*Setup*
SrvAny.Exe	Configure applications as Windows NT services [C]	Computer Admin/ Config Tools	*Config*
SrvInstW.Exe	Service installation wizard [G]	Computer Admin/ Config Tools	*Config*
SysDiff.Exe	Unattended installation support for applications [C]	Computer and Net Setup Tools	*Setup*
TimeServ.Exe[a]	Synchronize system clocks [C]	Computer Admin/ Config Tools	*Config*
TimeZone.Exe	Update time zone information [C]	Computer Admin/ Config Tools	*Config*
TZEdit.Exe	Time zone editor [G]	Computer Admin/ Config Tools	*Config*
UPtoMP.Exe	Convert operating system to multiprocessor version [G]	Computer Admin/ Config Tools	*Config*
File and Disk Utilities			
Associate.Exe	Register/unregister file types (backward compatibility) [C]	Batch Tools	*Filebat*
BreakFTM.Exe[a]	Break or restore disk mirrors [C]	Disk/FT Tools	*Faulttol*
Compress.Exe	Compress files [C]	File Tools	*Filebat*
DirUse.Exe	Display disk space used by directory [C]	File Tools	*Filebat*
DiskMap.Exe	Show disk hardware configuration information [C]	Disk/FT Tools	*Faulttol*
DiskSave.Exe	Save MBR and boot sector to floppy disk [C]	Disk/FT Tools	*Faulttol*
DskProbe.Exe	Disk sector editor [G]	Disk/FT Tools	*Faulttol*
ExeType.Exe	Determine executable's hardware platform [C]	File Tools	*Filebat*
ExpndW32.Exe	Expand files from distribution CD [G]	File Tools	*Filebat*
FTEdit.Exe	Edit fault tolerance disk configuration [G]	Disk/FT Tools	*Faulttol*

[a] Included only in the server version of the Resource Kit.

Table B-1. Contents of the Windows NT Resource Kit (continued)

Program	Description [Type]	RK Help Topic	CD Directory
File and Disk Utilities			
POSIX Utilities	UNIX-style File Tools utilities [C]	Tools for Developers	*Filebat*
RmtShare.Exe	Administer shares on remote systems [C]	Network/Server Admin Tools	*Netadmin*
RoboCopy.Exe	Enhanced copy utility [C]	File Tools	*Filebat*
SCopy.Exe	Copy files, including security (ACL and ownership) data [C]	File Tools	*Filebat*
ShareUI.Exe	Manage shares [G]	Network/Server Admin Tools	*Netadmin*
ShowDisk.Exe	Display disk and partition information [C]	Disk/FT Tools	*Faulttol*
SrvCheck.Exe	List shares and their access permissions [C]	User Account Admin Tools	*Netadmin*
TextView.Exe	Excellent multiple File Tools viewer [G]	File Tools	*Filebat*
WinDiff.Exe	Compare files or directories [G]	File Tools	*Filebat*
System Monitoring Utilities			
ClearMem.Exe	Clear memory for performance testing [C]	Performance Tools	*Compdiag*
Crystal Reports[a]	Report writer and services [G]	Computer Diag Tools	*\Apps\ Crystal*
DumpEL.Exe	Write event log entries to File Tools [G]	Computer Diag Tools	*Compdiag*
ExCtrLst.Exe	Extensible performance counter DLL list [G]	Computer Diag Tools	*Compdiag*
LogEvent.Exe	Add entries to the event log [C]	Computer Diag Tools	*Compdiag*
Monitor.Exe	Automate collection of system performance data [C]	Computer Diag Tools	*Compdiag*
NetWatch.Exe	Show current users of shared directories [G]	Network Diag Tools	*Netdiag*
PerfLog Service	Log performance counters to File Tools [G]	Computer Diag Tools	*Compdiag*
PerfMtr.Exe	Display system performance statistics [C]	Computer Diag Tools	*Compdiag*
Performance Tools	Miscellaneous performance monitoring tools [varies]	Computer Diag Tools	*PerfTools*
PMon.Exe	View continuous process performance data [C]	Computer Diag Tools	*Compdiag*

[a] Included only in the server version of the Resource Kit.

Table B-1. Contents of the Windows NT Resource Kit (continued)

Program	Description [Type]	RK Help Topic	CD Directory
System Monitoring Utilities			
QSlice.Exe	Show CPU use by process [G]	Computer Diag Tools	*Compdiag*
Network Administration Tools			
ATAnlyzr.Exe	AppleTalk network analyzer [G]	Network Diag Tools	*Netdiag*
BrowMon.Exe[a]	Show network browsing service status [G]	Network Diag Tools	*Netdiag*
DHCPCmd.Exe[a]	Administer DHCP services [C]	Internet and TCP/IP Services/Tools	*Inet*
DHCPLoc.Exe[a]	Locate DHCP servers on a subnet [C]	Internet and TCP/IP Services/Tools	*Inet*
DNSStat.Exe	Show DNS server statistics [C]	Internet and TCP/IP Services/Tools	*Netadmin*
DomMon.Exe[a]	Monitor domains and trust relationships [G]	Computer Diag Tools	*Netdiag*
FTPConf.Exe	Configure FTP service [G]	Internet and TCP/IP Services/Tools	*Inet*
GetMAC.Exe	Display MAC address [C]	Computer Diag Tools	*Compdiag*
Inet.Exe	**net**-style command for DNS names [C]	Internet and TCP/IP Services/Tools	*Inet*
Mail Server[a]	SMTP and POP2/POP3 servers and sendmail daemon [C]	Internet and TCP/IP Services/Tools	*Inet\Mailsrv*
MIBCC.Exe	Compiler for SNMP Management Information Base (MIB) files [C]	Computer Diag Tools	*Netdiag*
NetSvc.Exe[a]	Monitor/control services on remote systems [C]	Network/Server Admin Tools	*Netadmin*
NLMon.Exe	List domain controllers and trust relationships [C]	Network/Server Admin Tools	*Netadmin*
NLTest.Exe	Misc. domain administration utility [C]	Network/Server Admin Tools	*Netadmin*
NTuucode.Exe	UNIX-style **uuencode/uudecode** facility [G]	Internet and TCP/IP Services/Tools	*Inet*
RASList.Exe[a]	List RAS server announces [C]	Network/Server Admin Tools	*Netadmin*
RASUsers.Exe[a]	List users connected via RAS [C]	Network/Server Admin Tools	*Netadmin*
RCmd.Exe[a]	Execute a command on a remote system [C]	Network/Server Admin Tools	*Netadmin*

[a] Included only in the server version of the Resource Kit.

Table B-1. Contents of the Windows NT Resource Kit (continued)

Program	Description [Type]	RK Help Topic	CD Directory
Network Administration Tools			
Remote Access Manager	Administer RAS [G]	Network/Server Admin Tools	*Netadmin*
Remote Control Console[a]	Remote command service [C]	Network/Server Admin Tools	*Netadmin\ Rconsole*
Remote.Exe	Run a command on a remote system [C]	Network/Server Admin Tools	*Netadmin*
RshSvc.Exe[a]	Incoming remote shell service (beta version) [C]	Internet and TCP/IP Services/Tools	*Inet*
SNMPMon.Exe[a]	SNMP monitor [C]	Network Diag Tools	*Netdiag*
SNMPUtil.Exe	SNMP browser [C]	Network Diag Tools	*Netdiag*
SrvInfo.Exe[a]	Display information about a remote server [C]	Network Diag Tools	*Netdiag*
TDIShow.Exe	Trace TDI packets [C]	Network Diag Tools	*Netdiag\ TCITrace*
TelnetD.Exe	Incoming telnet server (beta) [C]	Internet and TCP/IP Services/Tools	*Inet\Telnet*
TLocMgr.Exe	Telephony location manager [G]	Computer Admin/ Config Tools	*Setup*
WINSMsdp.Exe	List information in WINS database [C]	Network Diag Tools	*Netdiag*
WINSChk.Exe	Check consistency of WINS database [C]	Internet and TCP/IP Services/Tools	*Inet*
WINSCL.Exe[a]	Administration tool for WINS [C]	Internet and TCP/IP Services/Tools	*Inet*
WINSDmp.Exe[a]	Dump WINS database in CSV format [C]	Internet and TCP/IP Services/Tools	*Inet*
WNTIPCfg.Exe	View IP configuration and renew/release leases [G]	Computer and Net Setup Tools	*Setup*
Printing Utilities			
EnumPrn.Exe	List installed printer drivers [G]	Computer Diag Tools	*Compdiag*
Process Manipulation Utilities			
Kill.Exe	Kill processes [C]	Computer Diag Tools	*Compdiag*
PStat.Exe	Display process list [C]	Computer Diag Tools	*Compdiag*
PUList.Exe	List user's processes [C]	Tools for Developers	*Compdiag*
PView.Exe	Monitor in detail and control process [G]	Performance Tools	*Compdiag*

[a] Included only in the server version of the Resource Kit.

Table B-1. Contents of the Windows NT Resource Kit (continued)

Program	Description [Type]	RK Help Topic	CD Directory
Process Manipulation Utilities			
PViewer.Exe	Monitor and control process [G]	Computer Diag Tools	*Compdiag*
RKill.Exe RKillSrv.Exe	Utility and service to terminate processes on a remote host [C]	Computer Diag Tools	*Compdiag*
SCList.Exe	List services on local or remote host [C]	Network/Server Admin Tools	*Netadmin*
SU.Exe	Run a process as a specified user [C]	Computer Admin/ Config Tools	*Netadmin*
TList.Exe	List process tree [C]	Computer Diag Tools	*Compdiag*
WinAT.Exe	GUI for the AT subsystem [G]	Computer Admin/ Config Tools	*Config*
Programming-Related Utilities			
APIMon.Exe	Track program performance by API call [C]	Tools for Developers	*Compdiag*
DH.Exe	Lock heaps, stacks, tags, and objects [C]	Network/Server Admin Tools	*Compdiag*
HeapMon.Exe	View system heap information [C]	Tools for Developers	*Perftool\ MeasTool*
KernProf.Exe	Kernel profiler [C]	Network/Server Admin Tools	*Compdiag*
Munge.Exe	Change strings (e.g., variable names) in multiple files [C]	Batch Tools	*Filebat*
OLEView.Exe	OLE/COM object viewer [G]	Tools for Developers	*Compdiag*
Perf2MIB.Exe	MIB builder tool (enable performance counters) [C]	Network Diag Tools	*Netdiag*
PFMon.Exe	Page fault monitor for an application [C]	Computer Diag Tools	*Compdiag*
TimeThis.Exe	Computer CPU usage for a process [C]	Computer Diag Tools	*Config*
Registry-Related Utilities			
CompReg.Exe	Compare local and remote registry keys [C]	Registry Tools	*Registry*
RegBack.Exe	Back up registry hives to a disk File Tools [C]	Registry Tools	*Registry*
RegChg.Exe	Edit registry value settings [C]	Registry Tools	*Registry*
RegDel.Exe	Delete registry keys [C]	Registry Tools	*Registry*

a Included only in the server version of the Resource Kit.

Table B-1. Contents of the Windows NT Resource Kit (continued)

Program	Description [Type]	RK Help Topic	CD Directory
Registry-Related Utilities			
RegIni.Exe	Add registry entries (designed for application installations) [C]	Registry Tools	*Registry*
RegKey.Exe	GUI to access some popular registry keys [G]	Registry Tools	*Registry*
RegRead.Exe	Display registry entries (parsed) [C]	Registry Tools	*Registry*
RegRest.Exe	Restore saved registry hives [C]	Registry Tools	*Registry*
RestKey.Exe	Restore saved registry key [C]	Registry Tools	*Registry*
RRegChg.Exe	Edit registry entries on remote host from command line [C]	Registry Tools	*Registry*
SaveKey.Exe	Save registry key to disk File Tools [C]	Registry Tools	*Registry*
ScanReg.Exe	Search registry keys, values, and/or data for a string [C]	Registry Tools	*Registry*
SetX.Exe	Set values in the current environment (including registry settings) [C]	Batch Tools	*Filebat*
Commands Useful in Scripts			
Choice.Exe	Prompt user for a selection [C]	Batch Tools	*Filebat*
Clip.Exe	Send its input to the system clipboard (STDIN) [C]	Batch Tools	*Filebat*
ForFiles.Exe	Run a command on each of a list of files [C]	Batch Tools	*Filebat*
FreeDisk.Exe	Determine if a specified amount of disk space is available [C]	File Tools	*Filebat*
IfMember.Exe	Determine if a user is a member of a specified group [C]	User Account Admin Tools	*Netadmin*
Kix32.Exe[a]	KIXtart 95 scripting language [G]	Batch Tools	*Filebat\ Kix95*
LogTime.Exe	Display current time and a specified string (*Now.Exe* is better—see below) [C]	Batch Tools	*Filebat*
Now.Exe	Display current time and a specified string [C]	Batch Tools	*Filebat*
Perl	Perl 5 scripting language [C]	Batch Tools	*Filebat\Perl*

[a] Included only in the server version of the Resource Kit.

Table B-1. Contents of the Windows NT Resource Kit (continued)

Program	Description [Type]	RK Help Topic	CD Directory
Commands Useful in Scripts			
REXX	Regina REXX scripting language [C]	Batch Tools	*GNU\REXX*
SC.Exe	Interact with services controller process [C]	Computer Admin/ Config Tools	*Config*
Sleep.Exe	Wait for a specified interval of time [C]	Batch Tools	*Filebat*
Soon.Exe	Schedule a command for the near future with the AT facility [C]	Computer Admin/ Config Tools	*Config*
TimeOut.Exe	Sleep until a key is pressed or a timeout period expires [C]	Batch Tools	*Filebat*
Security-Related Utilities			
C2Config.Exe	Check compliance with C2 security [G]	Computer Admin/ Config Tools	*Config*
FileWise.Exe	Compute CRC checksums for files [G]	None	*b*
FixACLs.Exe	Reset ACLs of system files to their default values [G]	None	*c*
FlopLock.Exe	Limit access to floppy drive [C]	Computer Admin/ Config Tools	*Config*
GetSID.Exe[a]	Compare user security IDs [C]	User Account Admin Tools	*Netadmin*
PermCopy.Exe	Copy ACLs between shares [C]	File Tools	*Netadmin*
Perms.Exe	Display File Tools access permissions for a specified user [C]	Computer Admin/ Config Tools	*Netadmin*
RegSec.Exe	Remove *Everyone* from specified registry key permissions [C]	Registry Tools	*Registry*
SecAdd.Exe	Add user permissions to a registry key [C]	Registry Tools	*Registry*
SecEdit.Exe	Modify security context of a running process [G]	Tools for Developers	*Config*
ShowACLs.Exe	Display access control lists [C]	Computer Diag Tools	*Compdiag*
WinExit.Exe	Screen saver with automatic logoff (designed for administrators) [G]	Desktop Tools	*Desktop*

[a] Included only in the server version of the Resource Kit.

Table B-1. Contents of the Windows NT Resource Kit (continued)

Program	Description [Type]	RK Help Topic	CD Directory
Toys and Fun Utilities			
3DPaint.Exe	3D painting program [G]	Desktop Tools	*Desktop*
ANIEdit.Exe	Create and edit animated cursors [G]	Desktop Tools	*Desktop*
Desktops.Exe	Desktop switching application [G]	Desktop Tools	*Desktop*
ImageEdit.Exe	Create/edit icons and cursors [G]	Desktop Tools	*Desktop*
Layout.DLL	Save/restore icon positions on the desktop [G]	Desktop Tools	*Desktop*
NetClip.Exe	Remote clipboard viewer [G]	Network/Server Admin Tools	*Netadmin*
QuickRes.Exe	Change screen resolution [G]	Desktop Tools	*Desktop*
TopDesk.Exe	Manage multiple desktops (bird's eye view) [G]	Desktop Tools	*Desktop*
VDesk.Exe	Maintain multiple desktops [G]	Desktop Tools	*Desktop*
User Account Tools			
AddUsers.Exe	Create and delete user accounts as specified in a file [C]	User Account Admin Tools	*Netadmin*
DelProf.Exe	Delete user profiles [C]	User Account Admin Tools	*Netadmin*
FindGrp.Exe[a]	List group memberships for a specified user [C]	Computer Diag Tools	*Compdiag*
Global.Exe	List the members of a global group [C]	User Account Admin Tools	*c*
GrpCpy.Exe[a]	Copy members between groups [G]	User Account Admin Tools	*c*
Local.Exe	List the members of a local group [C]	User Account Admin Tools	*c*
PassProp.Exe	Enable/disable password complexity testing [C]	Network/Server Admin Tools	*Netadmin*
PathMan.Exe	Edit systemwide PATH definitions [C]	Computer Admin/ Config Tools	*Config*
PolEdit.Exe	System policy editor [G]	Computer Admin/ Config Tools	*\Apps\ Clients\arch*
ShowGrps.Exe	Show a user's group memberships [C]	User Account Admin Tools	*Netadmin*
ShowMbrs.Exe	Display the members of a group [C]	User Account Admin Tools	*c*

[a] Included only in the server version of the Resource Kit.

Table B-1. Contents of the Windows NT Resource Kit (continued)

Program	Description [Type]	RK Help Topic	CD Directory
User Account Tools			
UseStat.Exe[a]	Show last login time of users in domain [C]	User Account Admin Tools	*Netadmin*
UsrToGrp.Exe	Add users to a group [C]	User Account Admin Tools	*Netadmin*
WhoAmI.Exe	Display current user information [C]	Batch Tools	*Filebat*
World Wide Web–Related Utilities			
DBWeb Service[a]	Communication between IIS and ODBC databases [G]	Internet and TCP/IP Services/Tools	*\Apps\ DBWeb*
DFLayout.Exe [contained in the archive file *DFLYDist.Exe]*	Reorganize File Tools layout for optimal browsing [G]	File Tools	*Filebat*
EM2MS.Exe	EMWAC to Microsoft gopher services translation [C]	Internet and TCP/IP Services/Tools	*Inet*
EMWAC CGI Scripts[a]	Scripts for web services [C]	Internet and TCP/IP Services/Tools	*\Common\ Inet\EMWAC*
IndexServer	Index/searching service for web sites [G]	Internet and TCP/IP Services/Tools	*\Appls\ Index\arch*

[a] Included only in the server version of the Resource Kit.

C

Windows NT Scripting Language Summary

This appendix reviews the features of the Windows NT built-in command language so you can understand any scripts written with it. We assume command extensions are enabled (as is the default).[*]

Constructing Commands

The caret character (^) is the command continuation character. It may be used within scripts to extend a command beyond a single line:

```
copy a_very_long_file_name_indeed.rtf ^
   C:\Temp\quite_a_long_directory_name\a_different_file_name.doc
```

The following constructs can be used to create more complex commands from multiple simple commands:

& Joins multiple commands, as in this example, which copies and then deletes a file:

```
copy a.txt \\pele\homes\chavez.txt & del a.txt
```

&& Conditional command execution: the second command is executed only if the first command completes successfully. In this example, the file *A.Txt* is deleted only if the **Copy** command succeeds:

```
copy a.txt \\pele\homes\chavez.txt && del a.txt
```

|| Conditional command execution: the second command is executed only if the first command fails. In this example, the **Echo** command runs only if the **Copy** command fails:

```
copy *.* \\pele\homes\chavez.txt || echo "Copy operation failed."
```

---

[*] Command extensions are controlled by the HKEY_CURRENT_USER\Software\Microsoft\Command Processor\EnableExtensions registry value (set it to 0 to disable them).

Comments

Comments can be included in scripts by beginning a line with **Rem** (for "remark").[*]

I/O Redirection

The Windows NT scripting language supports the usual I/O redirection constructs:

> *file*
> Send standard output to a file, overwriting any current contents.

>> *file*
> Append standard output to a file.

< *file*
> Get standard input from the specified file.

cmd1* | *cmd2
> Pipe fitting: attach the standard output of *cmd1* to the standard input of *cmd2*.

cmd1* 0> *cmd2
> Alternate format for the pipe character (|).

1> *file*
1>> *file*
> Alternate formats for redirecting standard output.

2> *file*
2>> *file*
> Redirect standard error to the specified file, overwriting it and appending to it, respectively.

NOTE   The form "2>&1" used by the UNIX Bourne shell to combine standard output and standard error is supported only if it follows the initial I/O redirection construct. In other words, "> *file* >2&1" but "> 2&1 > *file*" doesn't.

Accessing Script Arguments

Arguments specified on the command line can be accessed within a script via the notation %*n*, referring to the *n*th argument (numbering begins at 1). The first nine arguments can be referenced in this way. If your script needs to use more than that, the **shift** command may be used to rearrange the argument order. Without any options, the command slides each argument one position to the left—down

---

[*] Commands disabled by adding **Rem** to the beginning of their line are said to be "remmed out."

in argument order—making the second command-line argument correspond to %1, the third command-line argument correspond to %2, and so on. If **shift** is given a numeric option, only those argument positions equal to or above that position are shifted. Thus, **shift /3** begins shifting arguments at %3, leaving %1 and %2 unchanged.

Here is a simple script that illustrates these points:

```
C:\> type shift_em.bat
echo off
echo line 1: %1 %2 %3 %4 %5
shift
echo line 2: %1 %2 %3 %4 %5
shift /3
echo line 3: %1 %2 %3 %4 %5
echo all args: %*
echo command name: %0

C:\> shift_em a b c d e f g h
echo off
line 1: a b c d e
line 2: b c d e f
line 3: b c e f g
all args: a b c d e f g h
command name: shift_em
```

As the final line of the script illustrates, the form %0 holds the command argument (the first item on the command line). The %* refers to the original set of command line arguments (unaltered by any **shift** operations).

Arguments may be modified before use by placing a modification specification between the percent sign and the argument number. For example, the form %~d3 refers to the drive letter portion of the third argument. Modifications are always specified with a tilde, followed by a modification code of one or more letters.

These are the available modification specifiers:

%~f*n*

   Full pathname.

%~d*n*

   Drive letter only.

%~p*n*

   Directory portion only.

%~n*n*

   Filename portion only.

%~x*n*

   File extension only.

%~s*n*

Use 8.3-style names rather than long pathnames (use with **n** and/or **x**).

%~$PATH:*n*

Examines the search path in the **PATH** environment variable and returns the fully qualified pathname for the first match for the command specified as argument *n*, returning an empty string if the item is not found.

Here is a script that includes some examples of these constructs:

```
C:\> type args.bat
echo off
echo whole thing: %1
echo drive: %~d1
echo directory: %~p1
echo filename: %~n1
echo extension: %~x1
echo full pathname: %~f2
echo directory and filename: %~pnx2

C:\> args C:\Temp\My_New_Document.Doc Sample.Junk
echo off
whole thing: C:\Temp\My_New_Document.Doc
drive: C:
directory: \TEMP\
filename: My_New_Document
extension: .Doc
full pathname: C:\Work\Sample.Junk
directory and filename: \Work\Sample.Junk
```

As the final two commands indicate, these constructs may be used to determine drive and directory information about a file specified via a partial pathname. More than one code letter may follow the tilde (as illustrated in the final command). Argument modifiers are discussed in the documentation for the **Call** command (**Call /?**).

Variables

Script variables may be defined using the **set** command, which has the following syntax:

```
set name=value
```

For example, the following commands set the variables *file* and *x* to "a string" and 5, respectively:

```
C:\> set file="a string"
C:\> set x=5
```

Variables are dereferenced by surrounding their names with percent signs.

The **set** command's **/A** option may be used to set a variable to the result of an arithmetic expression:

```
C:\> set /A x=%x%+1          Increments x by 1.
C:\> set y=%x%+1 & echo y is %y%    y holds a string value.
y is 5+1
```

The **setlocal** and **endlocal** commands may be used to delimit a region of a script where changes to environment variables are local: variables revert back to their previous values upon leaving such a section.

Built-In Environment Variables

There are several useful built-in environment variables:

%username%

Contains the username of the current user (in lowercase).

%homedrive%

Expands to the drive letter where the current user's home directory is located.

%homepath%

Expands to the directory path for the current user's home directory.

%homeshare%

Expands to the share containing the current user's home directory.

%processor_architecture%

Expands to a keyword indicating the CPU processor manufacturer for the current system (*x86* or *alpha*).

%processor_level%

Expands to a number indicating the CPU processor model within its processor family.

%errorlevel%

Holds the exit status from the most recent command. A value of 0 generally indicates a successful command, and a value of 1 generally indicates a failed command. Some commands use this variable to specify a return value whose interpretation is command specific.

Here are some examples:

```
C:\> echo %username%
administrator

C:\> echo %homedrive%
C:

C:\> echo %homepath% & echo %homedrive%%homepath%
\
C:\
```

```
C:\> echo %processor_architecture%
x86

C:\> echo %processor_level%
5                                Indicates a Pentium processor.
```

Jumps

The Windows NT command language contains several constructs for moving immediately to a different part of the script and otherwise transferring control to some statement other than the next one in the file.

goto label

Jump to the statement with the specified label.

goto :EOF

Exit from the script immediately. This is often preferable to the **exit** command which also terminates the current command processor.

:label

Define a statement label.

call

Run another script.

Here is a simple example:

```
C:\> type jump.bat
echo off
echo 1
goto frog
echo 2
:frog
echo 3
call lily
echo 4

C:\> type lily.bat
echo lily 1
goto :EOF
echo lily 2

C:\> jump
echo off
1
3
lily 1
4
```

Loops

The Windows NT command language has two loop constructs:

for %%*n* **in** (*list*) **do** *cmd*	*Loop over items in a list.*
for /**L** %%*n* **in** (*start*,*incr*,*end*) **do** *cmd*	*Traditional indexed loop.*

In the first form, the specified script parameter is assigned each of the items in *list* in turn. In the second form, the specified script parameter is initialized to the value in *start*, incremented by *incr* each time the loop completes, and the loop exits when its value goes beyond the limit set by *end* (i.e., is less than or greater than *end*, depending on the direction that counting is progressing).

Here is a simple script illustrating these constructs:

```
C:\> type loop.bat
echo off
for %%1 in (a b c) do echo %%1
rem Traditional DOS way to get a "blank" output line
echo                                    .
for /L %%1 in (0,5,15) do echo %%1

C:\> loop
echo off
a
b
c

0
5
10
15
```

There are additional, less-used forms for the **for** command. See the output of **for** /? for information about them.

Conditional Commands

The **if** command can construct conditional statements. It has the following forms:

if [**not**] **errorlevel** *n* *cmd*	*Test the value of the errorlevel variable.*
if [**not**] **exist** *file* *cmd*	*Test for file existence.*
if [**not**] [/**I**] *str1 op str2* *cmd*	*Compare character strings.*
If [**not**] **defined** *var* *cmd*	*Test whether a variable has been defined.*

In their nonnegated forms, the first type executes the specified command when the value of the *errorlevel* variable is greater than or equal to *n*, the second form executes the specified command if the specified file exists, and the third type executes the specified command if the indicated string comparison is **True** (the /**I** option performs a case-insensitive comparison operation). Finally, the fourth type executes the specified command, if the indicated variable has been defined.

The following string comparison operators are available (they are case-sensitive):

EQU

> == (double equals sign); the two strings are equal.

NEQ

> The two strings are different.

LSS

> The first string is lexically less than the second string.

LEQ

> The first string is lexically less than or equal to the second string.

GTR

> The first string is lexically greater than the second string.

GEQ

> The first string is lexically greater than or equal to the second string.

Here are some simple examples:

```
C:\> type maybe.bat
echo off

silly 2> junk.junk
if errorlevel 1 echo Command failed.

if not exist c:\boot.ini echo Missing BOOT.INI file.

if not defined PATH echo No PATH variable defined.

set a="apple"
set b="pear"
if /I %a% == "APPLE" echo crunch
if not %a% EQU %b% echo apples aren%'t pears
if %a% LSS %b% echo munch

C:\> maybe
Command failed.
crunch
apples aren't pears
munch
```

Accepting User Input

The following commands are used to accept user input within a script:

pause

> Pause script execution until the user presses a key.

choice *[/C:choices] [/S] [/T:c,n] prompt*

Present a user with a prompt string and accept a response. This command sets the *errorlevel* variable to the number of the selected choice (numbering starts at 1). The valid one-letter responses are specified as a string to the /C option (the default is **YN**). The /S option makes the choice letters case-sensitive (they are not by default), and the /T option says that choice letter *c* is selected by default after a timeout period of *n* seconds.

Here is a simple example:

```
C:\> type pick.bat
echo off
choice /C:abcde /T:b,4 "Pick a letter between A and E: "
echo You chose number %errorlevel%.

C:\> pick
Pick a letter between A and E: [A,B,C,D,E]? D
You chose number 4.

C:\> pick
Pick a letter between A and E: [A,B,C,D,E]?        Times out.
You chose number 2.
```

This command is found in the Resource Kit.

Glossary

A

ACE
Access Control Entry, a single component of an access control list (ACL).

ACK
Acknowledgment, sent in response to a received TCP/IP transmission.

ACL
Access Control List, specifies allowed and denied access to objects like files and directories.

API
Application Programming Interface, standard library routines that applications use to carry out common tasks (via services provided by the operating system).

ARC
Advanced RISC Computer. ARC addresses are used to specify disk partition locations in the *Boot.Ini* file.

B

BDC
Backup Domain Controller, an NT server that holds backup copies of the domain account databases and can become the primary domain controller (PDC), if necessary.

bindings
The linkages between network adapters, network protocols, and network services.

BIOS
Basic Input/Output System, underlying all I/O operations on DOS-based systems.

C

CDFS
CD-ROM File System.

CIFS
Common Internet File System, a synonym for filesystem resource sharing via the SMB protocol.

cooperative multitasking
Operating system scheduling strategy in which a running process has complete control of the system until it voluntarily gives it up.

CSN
Client Services for NetWare, a facility designed to allow NT systems to participate in NetWare networks as clients.

D

DAC
Discretionary Access Control, the sort of access control provided by ACLs.

DCOM
Distributed Component Object Model, OLE extended to networks.

Dfs
Distributed File System, a directory tree composed of items from various network loca-

tions that looks like a single filesystem to an end user.

DHCP
Dynamic Host Configuration Protocol, a TCP/IP facility for dynamic assignment of IP addresses to network hosts.

DLL
Dynamic Link Library, a shared library of routines that can be used by multiple simultaneous applications/processes.

DNS
Domain Name Service, the TCP/IP service responsible for translating hostnames to Internet addresses.

domain
A Windows NT domain is a collection of computers sharing common configuration data. DNS uses the term in a different way: to designate a subtree of the overall DNS hierarchical structure (a domain usually corresponds to an organization).

DVD
Digital Video/Versatile Disk (follow-on to CD-ROM).

E

EIDE
Enhanced IDE, a common PC I/O interface.

ERD
Emergency Repair Diskette, used to access an unbootable Windows NT system.

F

FAT
File Allocation Table, and also the DOS file system type.

fault tolerance
The ability for a computer to continue operating despite the failure of one or more of its components. Windows NT offers fault tolerant filesystem facilities.

FQDN
Fully qualified domain name, consisting of the hostname plus the domain name (for example, *vala.aurora.com*).

FTP
File Transfer Protocol.

G

GUI
Graphical user interface.

H

HAL
Hardware Abstraction Layer, a part of the NT kernel responsible for most interfacing to hardware devices.

hardware profile
A defined set of system configuration and service startup settings, which may be selected at boot-time.

hive
A subtree of registry keys and values that are stored together in a single file.

hostname resolution
The process of translating a hostname into an IP address.

HPFS
High Performance File System, the OS/2 file system type (discontinued in NT 4).

HTTP
Hypertext Transfer Protocol, the primary protocol used by the World Wide Web.

I

IDE
Integrated Drive Electronics, generally superseded by EIDE.

IP
Internet Protocol.

IRQ
Interrupt Request level, a signal used for device communication with the kernel.

ISA
Industry Standard Architecture, a common PC bus architecture.

K

kernel mode
Privileged execution mode allowing complete access to every system resource and all of memory.

L

LAN
Local Area Network.

M

MAC
Media Access Control, an address uniquely identifying a network adapter (for example, an Ethernet address).

MBR
Master Boot Record, located at the beginning of a bootable disk on Intel-based systems, containing the boot loader, which loads the boot program from the active partition.

MFT
Master File Table, a filesystem data structure holding file structure data and some file contents.

microkernel
The program that serves as the central core of the operating system, designed to be as small and efficient as possible.

mirroring
A fault-tolerating disk strategy in which two identical copies of the entire contents of a disk partition are maintained.

N

NetBEUI
NetBIOS Extended User Interface, transport protocol for NetBIOS designed for LANs.

NetBIOS
Network BIOS, BIOS I/O interface extended to I/O via the network.

NOS
Network Operating System, an operating system with integrated networking support.

NTFS
NT File System, the native file system type.

NTVDM
NT Virtual DOS Machine, the emulated DOS environment in which DOS-based programs run.

O

OLE
Object Linking and Embedding, a data sharing facility between distinct applications.

orphaned partition
A healthy partition that is part of a mirror set, stripe set, or volume set, in which one or more other components has failed.

P

packet
A generic term for a network transmission.

PCI
Peripheral Computer Interface, a 32- or 64-bit bus architecture.

PDC
Primary Domain Controller, the master NT server in an NT domain holding authoritative configuration information for a Windows NT domain.

POST
Power-On Self Test, simple functionality tests performed by the computer hardware when it is first powered on.

PPP
Point-to-Point Protocol, a protocol for networking over serial lines.

PPTP
Point-to-Point Tunneling Protocol, a facility for connecting two private networks via an encrypted link over the public Internet.

preemptive multitasking
Operating system scheduling strategy in which the scheduler facility decides which process will run at any given time, and when one process must pause in order to let a different one run.

printer pool
A single print queue that sends print jobs to more than one physical printer.

process
Windows NT execution construct, consisting of one or more threads.

R

RAID
Redundant Array of Independent Disks (used for performance or fault tolerance).

RAS
Remote Access Service, the facility for dial-up network connections under NT (runs on top of PPP or SLIP).

registry
The central database of system configuration settings on a Windows NT or Windows 95 system.

resolver
A system that relies on the DNS service for host name resolution (operates as a DNS client).

RISC
Reduced Instruction Set Computer, a processor that supports a small number of fast, simple instructions.

RPC
Remote Procedure Call, interprocess communication over a network via message passing, allowing applications to use hosts' services without regard to their network location.

S

SAM
Security Accounts Manager, an NT subsystem that maintains the database of user account information.

SAT
Security Access Token, used by the NT Security Manager to determine access to objects.

SCSI
Small Computer Systems Interface.

service
Server process started and maintained automatically by the Windows NT operating system (and the facility that the server provides).

share
A disk partition or directory tree made available to network users via a textual label.

shortcut
A file that serves as a pointer to another file (in UNIX terms, a symbolic link).

shortcut menu
Context-specific menu of operations for an object, including its **Properties**, produced by right-clicking on it.

SLIP
Serial Line Internet Protocol, a protocol for TCP/IP networking over serial lines.

SMB
Server Message Block, application layer communication protocol used on Microsoft LANs.

SMP
Symmetric Multiprocessing, multiprocessor architecture in which all processors are equal and the operating system runs on each one.

SNMP
Simple Network Monitoring Protocol, a facility used by TCP/IP network monitoring tools and packages.

spooling
The process of sending a print job to a print queue and then to an actual printer.

SRM
Security Reference Manager, part of the NT kernel responsible for granting and denying access to objects associated with system resources.

striping
The process of splitting disk I/O operations into multiple parts which are written to separate disk partitions in parallel. Parity data may be included for fault tolerance.

SYN
Synchronize, a TCP flag used to initiate a connection.

system services
System-level routines and facilities available to ordinary processes to carry out common tasks.

T

TCP/IP
Transmission Control Protocol/Internet Protocol.

thread
The fundamental executable object. One or more threads constitute a process.

thunking
The process of translating 16-bit Windows API calls to/from Win32 API calls (in the WOW).

U

UI
User interface.

UNC
Uniform Naming Convention, which begins with two backslashes and prepends the hostname to the share name and pathname (e.g., *vala**ntreskit**perl**sample.pl*).

Unicode
16-bit internationalized character set.

UPS
Uninterruptible Power Supply, a battery backup device that supplies power to a computer in the event of a power failure on the usual supply line.

user mode
Unprivileged execution mode in which processes can obtain access to system resources only by making requests to the operating system.

V

volume set
A set of two or more disk partitions, which are treated by the operating system as a single logical volume (transparently to users).

VPN
Virtual Private Network, networks linked via PPTP, or some other tunneling protocol.

W

WfW
Windows for Workgroups.

WINS
Windows Internet Naming Service, the service responsible for translating NetBIOS names to computer addressees.

working set
In Windows NT parlance, the minimum memory space required by a process to execute (sometimes referred to as the minimum working set). In normal use, the amount of physical memory currently in use by a process.

WOW
Windows on Win32, the environment in which 16-bit Windows applications execute (within an NTVDM).

WWW
World Wide Web, a series of sites on the Internet accessible via the HTTP protocol.

Z

zone
A subtree of a DNS domain.

Numerals

10Base2
Thin coaxial (Ethernet) cable.

10Base5
Thick coaxial (Ethernet) cable.

10BaseT
Unshielded twisted-pair cable.

Index

About the Author

Æleen Frisch has been a system administrator for over 15 years, tending a plethora of VMS, UNIX, and Windows NT systems. Currently, she looks after a very heterogeneous network of UNIX and Windows NT systems. Her other books include *Essential System Administration* (O'Reilly & Associates) and *Exploring Chemistry with Electronic Structure Methods* (Gaussian, Inc.). She also writes the "NTegration" column for *SunExpert* magazine (discussing Windows NT from a UNIX perspective). She has degrees from Caltech and Pitt.

Æleen is a third generation native Californian, living in exile in Connecticut with her partner Mike and her cats Daphne, Lyta, Talia, and Susan. When she is not writing technical books and articles or computer programs, she divides her spare time between writing a novel, painting, and creating murder mystery games.

Æleen can be reached via email at *aefrisch@lorentzian.com*.

Colophon

The animal featured on the cover of *Essential Windows NT System Administration* is a mandrill. Mandrills live in the rain forests of equatorial West Africa. These gentle baboons are one of the largest species of all the monkeys, and certainly one of the most colorful. Male mandrills, who weigh as much as 75 pounds, have bright red noses surrounded by blue ridges and purple grooves, and greenish-yellow fur. Female mandrills are much smaller, weighing up to 35 pounds, and lack the bright red nose and purple grooves of the male. Both male and female mandrills have bluish-lilac buttocks. The colors on the face and the buttocks deepen when the mandrill is excited or threatened.

Mandrills travel in large groups, led by one dominant adult male. The male often travels at a distance from the group, but returns as soon as a danger to the group appears. He then threatens the enemy by lowering his impressive head, spreading his arms, and baring his teeth.

Fruit, nuts, plants, and small animals are the preferred diet of mandrills. In their pouched cheeks they can store the equivalent of a stomach's worth of food. As a result of hunting and the destruction of their natural habitat, mandrills are endangered.

Edie Freedman designed the cover of this book, using a 19th-century engraving from the Dover Pictorial Archive. The cover layout was produced with Quark XPress 3.3 using the ITC Garamond font.

The inside layout was designed by Nancy Priest and implemented in FrameMaker 5.0 by Mike Sierra. The illustrations that appear in the book were created in Macromedia Freehand 7.0 and Adobe Photoshop 4.0 by Robert Romano. This colophon was written by Clairemarie Fisher O'Leary.

Whenever possible, our books use RepKover™, a durable and flexible lay-flat binding. If the page count exceeds RepKover's limit, perfect binding is used.

How to stay in touch with O'Reilly

1. Visit Our Award-Winning Web Site

http://www.oreilly.com/

★"Top 100 Sites on the Web" —*PC Magazine*
★"Top 5% Web sites" —*Point Communications*
★"3-Star site" —*The McKinley Group*

Our web site contains a library of comprehensive product information (including book excerpts and tables of contents), downloadable software, background articles, interviews with technology leaders, links to relevant sites, book cover art, and more. File us in your Bookmarks or Hotlist!

2. Join Our Email Mailing Lists

New Product Releases
To receive automatic email with brief descriptions of all new O'Reilly products as they are released, send email to:
ora-news-subscribe@lists.oreilly.com
Put the following information in the first line of your message (*not* in the Subject field):
subscribe ora-news

O'Reilly Events
If you'd also like us to send information about trade show events, special promotions, and other O'Reilly events, send email to:
ora-news-subscribe@lists.oreilly.com
Put the following information in the first line of your message (*not* in the Subject field):
subscribe ora-events

3. Get Examples from Our Books via FTP

There are two ways to access an archive of example files from our books:

Regular FTP
- ftp to:
  ftp.oreilly.com
  (login: anonymous
  password: your email address)
- Point your web browser to:
  ftp://ftp.oreilly.com/

FTPMAIL
- Send an email message to:
  ftpmail@online.oreilly.com
  (Write "help" in the message body)

4. Contact Us via Email

order@oreilly.com
To place a book or software order online. Good for North American and international customers.

subscriptions@oreilly.com
To place an order for any of our newsletters or periodicals.

books@oreilly.com
General questions about any of our books.

software@oreilly.com
For general questions and product information about our software. Check out O'Reilly Software Online at **http://software.oreilly.com/** for software and technical support information. Registered O'Reilly software users send your questions to: **website-support@oreilly.com**

cs@oreilly.com
For answers to problems regarding your order or our products.

booktech@oreilly.com
For book content technical questions or corrections.

proposals@oreilly.com
To submit new book or software proposals to our editors and product managers.

international@oreilly.com
For information about our international distributors or translation queries. For a list of our distributors outside of North America check out:
http://www.oreilly.com/distributors.html

5. Work with Us

Check out our website for current employment opportunites:
http://jobs.oreilly.com/

O'Reilly & Associates, Inc.
101 Morris Street, Sebastopol, CA 95472 USA
TEL   707-829-0515 or 800-998-9938
         (6am to 5pm PST)
FAX   707-829-0104

O'REILLY®

International Distributors

UK, EUROPE, MIDDLE EAST AND AFRICA (EXCEPT FRANCE, GERMANY, AUSTRIA, SWITZERLAND, LUXEMBOURG, AND LIECHTENSTEIN)

INQUIRIES
O'Reilly UK Limited
4 Castle Street
Farnham
Surrey, GU9 7HS
United Kingdom
Telephone: 44-1252-711776
Fax: 44-1252-734211
Email: information@oreilly.co.uk

ORDERS
Wiley Distribution Services Ltd.
1 Oldlands Way
Bognor Regis
West Sussex PO22 9SA
United Kingdom
Telephone: 44-1243-843294
UK Freephone: 0800-243207
Fax: 44-1243-843302 (Europe/EU orders)
or 44-1243-843274 (Middle East/Africa)
Email: cs-books@wiley.co.uk

FRANCE

INQUIRIES & ORDERS
Éditions O'Reilly
18 rue Séguier
75006 Paris, France
Tel: 1-40-51-71-89
Fax: 1-40-51-72-26
Email: france@oreilly.fr

GERMANY, SWITZERLAND, AUSTRIA, LUXEMBOURG, AND LIECHTENSTEIN

INQUIRIES & ORDERS
O'Reilly Verlag
Balthasarstr. 81
D-50670 Köln, Germany
Telephone: 49-221-973160-91
Fax: 49-221-973160-8
Email: anfragen@oreilly.de (inquiries)
Email: order@oreilly.de (orders)

CANADA (FRENCH LANGUAGE BOOKS)

Les Éditions Flammarion ltée
375, Avenue Laurier Ouest
Montréal (Québec) H2V 2K3
Tel: 00-1-514-277-8807
Fax: 00-1-514-278-2085
Email: info@flammarion.qc.ca

HONG KONG

City Discount Subscription Service, Ltd.
Unit A, 6th Floor, Yan's Tower
27 Wong Chuk Hang Road
Aberdeen, Hong Kong
Tel: 852-2580-3539
Fax: 852-2580-6463
Email: citydis@ppn.com.hk

KOREA

Hanbit Media, Inc.
Chungmu Bldg. 210
Yonnam-dong 568-33
Mapo-gu
Seoul, Korea
Tel: 822-325-0397
Fax: 822-325-9697
Email: hant93@chollian.dacom.co.kr

PHILIPPINES

Global Publishing
G/F Benavides Garden
1186 Benavides Street
Manila, Philippines
Tel: 632-254-8949/632-252-2582
Fax: 632-734-5060/632-252-2733
Email: globalp@pacific.net.ph

TAIWAN

O'Reilly Taiwan
1st Floor, No. 21, Lane 295
Section 1, Fu-Shing South Road
Taipei, 106 Taiwan
Tel: 886-2-27099669
Fax: 886-2-27038802
Email: mori@oreilly.com

INDIA

Shroff Publishers & Distributors Pvt. Ltd.
12, "Roseland", 2nd Floor
180, Waterfield Road, Bandra (West)
Mumbai 400 050
Tel: 91-22-641-1800/643-9910
Fax: 91-22-643-2422
Email: spd@vsnl.com

CHINA

O'Reilly Beijing
SIGMA Building, Suite B809
No. 49 Zhichun Road
Haidian District
Beijing, China PR 100080
Tel: 86-10-8809-7475
Fax: 86-10-8809-7463
Email: beijing@oreilly.com

JAPAN

O'Reilly Japan, Inc.
Yotsuya Y's Building
7 Banch 6, Honshio-cho
Shinjuku-ku
Tokyo 160-0003 Japan
Tel: 81-3-3356-5227
Fax: 81-3-3356-5261
Email: japan@oreilly.com

SINGAPORE, INDONESIA, MALAYSIA AND THAILAND

TransQuest Publishers Pte Ltd
30 Old Toh Tuck Road #05-02
Sembawang Kimtrans Logistics Centre
Singapore 597654
Tel: 65-4623112
Fax: 65-4625761
Email: wendiw@transquest.com.sg

ALL OTHER ASIAN COUNTRIES

O'Reilly & Associates, Inc.
101 Morris Street
Sebastopol, CA 95472 USA
Tel: 707-829-0515
Fax: 707-829-0104
Email: order@oreilly.com

AUSTRALIA

Woodslane Pty., Ltd.
7/5 Vuko Place
Warriewood NSW 2102
Australia
Tel: 61-2-9970-5111
Fax: 61-2-9970-5002
Email: info@woodslane.com.au

NEW ZEALAND

Woodslane New Zealand, Ltd.
21 Cooks Street (P.O. Box 575)
Waganui, New Zealand
Tel: 64-6-347-6543
Fax: 64-6-345-4840
Email: info@woodslane.com.au

ARGENTINA

Distribuidora Cuspide
Suipacha 764
1008 Buenos Aires
Argentina
Phone: 5411-4322-8868
Fax: 5411-4322-3456
Email: libros@cuspide.com

O'REILLY®

Nineteenth century wood engraving
of a bear from the O'Reilly &
Associates Nutshell Handbook®
Using & Managing UUCP.

BUSINESS REPLY MAIL
FIRST CLASS MAIL   PERMIT NO. 80   SEBASTOPOL, CA

Postage will be paid by addressee

O'Reilly & Associates, Inc.
101 Morris Street
Sebastopol, CA 95472-9902